HOW TO ENJOY THE
BIBLE

Books by E. W. Bullinger

Commentary on Revelation

Companion Bible (notes by E. W. Bullinger)

*A Critical Lexicon and Concordance to the
English and Greek New Testament*

Great Cloud of Witnesses

How to Enjoy the Bible

Number in Scripture

Ten Sermons on the Second Advent

The Witness of the Stars

Word Studies on the Holy Spirit

HOW TO ENJOY THE
BIBLE

12 Basic
Principles for
Understanding
God's Word

E. W. Bullinger

Kregel
Classics

How to Enjoy the Bible
by E. W. Bullinger

Published in 1990 by Kregel Classics, a division of Kregel, Inc.,
2450 Oak Industrial Dr. NE, Grand Rapids, MI 49505.

Library of Congress Cataloging-in-Publication Data
Bullinger, E. W. (Ethelbert William), 1837-1913.
  How to enjoy the Bible: a guide to better understanding and
enjoyment of God's Word / by E. W. Bullinger
        p.   cm.
  Reprint. Originally published: 4th ed. London: Eyre and Spot-
tiswoode, 1916.
  Includes indexes.
  1. Bible—Study. 2. Bible—Hermeneutics. 3. Bible—Lan-
guage, style. I. Title.
BS600.B855   1990   220.6'1—dc20   89-77694
                                                CIP

ISBN 978-0-8254-2027-6

Printed in the United States of America

5 6 7 8 9 / 18 17 16 15 14

CONTENTS

Part II: THE WORDS

The Twelve Canons or Rules of Interpretation

NOTE TO THE READER

Because of the unfamiliarity of most of us today with the Roman numeral system used throughout this book, the following conversion table may offer welcome assistance to many readers:

i	1	xxii	22
ii	2	xxiii	23
iii	3	xxiv	24
iv	4	xxv	25
v	5	xxvi	26
vi	6	xxvii	27
vii	7	xxviii	28
viii	8	xxix	29
ix	9	xxx	30
x	10	xl	40
xi	11	l	50
xii	12	lx	60
xiii	13	lxx	70
xiv	14	lxxx	80
xv	15	xc	90
xvi	16	c	100
xvii	17	cx	110
xviii	18	cxx	120
xvix	19	cxxx	130
xx	20	cxl	140
xxi	21	cl	150

PREFACE

IT will add greatly to the interest of this work if I briefly describe the circumstances to which, under God, it owes its origin. Nothing will so clearly show its aim and object, or so well explain its one great design as embodied in its title: *How to Enjoy the Bible*.

In the autumn of 1905 I found myself in one of the most important of the European Capitals. I had preached in the morning in the Embassy Chapel, and at the close of the service, my friend, His Britannic Majesty's Chaplain, expressed his deep regret at the absence of two members of his congregation, whose disappointment, he said, would be very great when they discovered they were away on the very Sunday that I was there.

As it was a matter which I could not possibly alter I was compelled, perforce, to dismiss it from my mind with much regret, and returned to my hotel.

In the afternoon a visiting card was brought to my room, announcing a gentleman holding a high Government position.

In explaining the object of his visit he began by saying that he had been brought up as a Roman Catholic; and that, a few years ago, there came into the office of his department a copy of *The Illustrated London News*. As he was learning English at the time, he was naturally interested in reading it. The number contained an account of the funeral of the late Charles Haddon

Spurgeon, the illustrations of which attracted his attention. The letterpress made some reference to Mr. Spurgeon's sermons and the world-wide fame which they had
obtained. This led him to procure some copies of the
sermons, and these, by God's grace and blessing, were
used for his conversion.

He was at the time thinking of marriage, and felt the
importance now of finding a Christian lady for his wife.
At the same time he began to attend my friend's English
Services, and before long he found an English lady,
residing at that time in ——, and in due course the
engagement ended in marriage.

The lady, however, was, she told him, an "Anglican";
and saw no necessity for her future husband to make any
formal recantation, but for private and public reasons
advised him to make no change in his religion.

But grace had changed him so completely, that it was
not a case, merely, of his holding the truth, but of the
truth holding him: consequently he could not rest until
he had renounced not only his former Roman Catholic
religion, but all religion that had anything to do with
the flesh; for he had found his all in Christ, and was
satisfied with the completeness which God had given
to him in HIM.

After their marriage they began to read together the
sermons which had proved, under God, so great a blessing
to himself; and, before long, the same happy result took
place in his wife's case, and they rejoiced together in the
Lord.

They soon however began to find that they had much
to learn. Reading the sermons and the Word of God
they felt that there were many subjects in the Bible which
they found little of in the sermons. True, they found the
same sound doctrines and useful teaching, and spiritual
food; but, they found also the absence of other truths
which they longed to know.

They spoke to my friend their minister, and told him
of their trouble. He lent them my book on *The Church
Epistles*. This book they began to study together, and
as the husband told me, " we went over it, three times,
word by word." This they did to their great edification.
" But," he said, " we soon discovered that *you* did not
" tell us everything, and there were many things which
" you assumed that we knew; and these we naturally
" wished to learn more about. So, a few weeks ago,
" we resolved to take our holiday in London ; find you
" out; and talk over with you the things which filled our
" hearts.

" In due course we went to London ; ascertained your
" address on enquiry at the office of *The Christian*, and
" made our call. We found, to our disappointment, that
" you were here, in the very place from which we had
" set out to seek you.

" So we returned here at once, and arrived only last
" night, but were too tired to get from our suburb to the
" service this morning."

Not till that moment did I discover that these were
the same two persons to whom my friend the chaplain had
referred when he spoke of his regret at their absence
from the service that morning, and of the disappointment
which he was sure they would experience.

"I have lost no time in searching you out (he said),
" and am delighted to find you. You must come out to
" us and see us in our home to-morrow."

"To-morrow (I replied) I am going to P——."

"Oh, you cannot go," he said ; and in such a tone of
voice and manner as made me really feel I could not.

I said, "I am not travelling alone, but my friend is
standing near in conversation ; I will go and speak to
him on the subject."

We soon concluded that as our proposed journey was only for pleasure, it was clearly my duty to remain for a day, so we postponed our projected journey to another season. I returned to my new friend, and said we would gladly go out to him on the morrow.

At this he was very pleased; and spoke, now, freely, of the great desire of himself and his wife to know more of God's Word.

"We want (he said) to study it together, and to be as " independent as possible of the teachings and traditions " of men. In fact,

" WE WANT TO ENJOY THE BIBLE.

" We want to read it, and study it, and understand it " and enjoy it for ourselves!"

This, of course, sounded very sweetly in my ears; and it was arranged that he should come into the city, the next morning early, and fetch us out to his home in the suburbs.

He arrived soon after 8 o'clock, and by 9 o'clock we were sitting down together over the Word of God. There we sat till noon! In our preliminary conversation reference had been made to some work the lady had undertaken in the village. So we opened our Bibles at Matt. x. 5, 6, where I read the following words :—

> "Go not into the way of the Gentiles . . . but go rather to the lost sheep of the house of Israel."

I did not know until a year afterwards that my friend naturally held the usual anti-Semite views of the governing party, or this would probably have been the last Scripture I should have quoted. But though, at the time, I little thought of what I was doing, God was over-ruling all to the accomplishment of His own purposes.

The lady, at once, very honestly exclaimed, "Oh, but I do go to the Gentiles."

I replied, "But you see what this Scripture says."

She said, "Is there not another passage which tells us to go into all the world?"

"Yes" (I replied); and, finding that passage, I asked, "What are we to do with the other?"

She confessed her perplexity and asked me to answer my own question.

I replied, "Both are the words of God, and both must be absolutely true. We cannot cut one passage out of the Bible and leave the other in. Both are equally true, and we may not use one truth to upset another truth."

I proceeded to explain, alluding to the universally acknowledged fact—that "circumstances alter cases."

The circumstances connected with the former passage showed that the Lord was sending forth the twelve to *proclaim the King, and the Kingdom at hand :* while those of the latter showed that the Proclamation had been unheeded; the Kingdom rejected, and the King crucified. And I asked "Were not the circumstances so different in " character and time as to fully account for the fact that " the former command was no longer appropriate to the " changed conditions?"

I pointed out that there was a precept which specially set forth our responsibility to the Bible as being "the Word of Truth" (2 Tim. ii. 15), and that was that it must be *rightly divided.* This command to rightly divide, being given us in connection with this special title "the Word of truth," spoke to us, if we had ears to hear, and told us that unless we rightly divided the Word of Truth we should not only not get the truth; but, as God's workmen we should indeed have need to be "ashamed."

I showed that, if we would indeed *enjoy the Bible* it was absolutely necessary that we should rightly divide all that it contained, in connection with its subject-matter, as well as in connection with its times and dispensations.

In illustration of this important duty I pointed to such

passages as Luke ix. 2, 3, compared with chap. xxii. 36,
where the words "BUT NOW" gave the Lord's own
example; showing how He distinguished the difference
between the two occasions.

I also referred to Rom. xi. and showed how, by
"rightly dividing" the subject-matter, the great difficulty
was avoided of supposing that those who were assured in
Rom. viii. 39 as to the impossibility of their separation
from the love of God, could ever be addressed in
chap. xi. 21, 22 in words of threatening and warning lest
they "be cut off." The key to the solution of the difficulty
was in chap. xi. 13, where the Apostle distinctly states
that he was addressing "Gentiles," as such, and of course
as distinct from the Jews, and, the Church of God :

"I SPEAK TO YOU GENTILES."

I also illustrated the subject by a reference to
Heb. vi. 4—6; and x. 26—30. But, as these and other
passages are all dealt with at length in the following
pages I need not do more now than refer my readers to
them.

Our conversation continued (as I have said) till noon ;
and, as it proceeded, my friends could hardly contain
themselves for joy. As for myself I began to see in
what form I should respond to my friends' desire to
"enjoy the Bible."

On my journey home to England I thought much, and
long, and often, of my pleasant intercourse with my new
friends : and I was impressed by the thought that *what
they needed, thousands needed ;* and that the vast
majority of Bible readers who were filled with the same
deep desire to "enjoy the Bible" were beset by the same
difficulties in attaining that desire.

Shortly after my return to England my thoughts
began to take shape, and finally resolved themselves into
what now appears in the "Table of Contents," and which

in the following September I had the great joy of going over with my new friends.

I visited them again in their home this September (1907), and had the pleasure of reading over with them the proof of this "Preface," so that it might faithfully record all that had so happily taken place.

This explanation of the origin of this work will show that no better title could be chosen, or would so well describe its object, and explain its end. My prayer is that, the same Spirit who inspired the words in the Scriptures of Truth, may also inspire them in the hearts of my readers and may cause each to say (with David), "I rejoice in Thy words as one that findeth great spoils" (Ps. cxix. 162): and to exclaim (with Jeremiah), "Thy words were found and I did eat them, and Thy Word was unto me the joy and rejoicing of my heart" (Jer. xv. 16.)

It was this combination of the "WORD" and the "WORDS," both here and in John xvii. 8, 17, that suggested the sub-title: *"The Word and the words; how to study them."*

Part I. deals with the "Word" as a whole. Part II. deals with the "words"; and, under twelve Canons, gives the important methods which must be observed and followed if we would understand, and enjoy them. A varying number of illustrations is given under each division; these are by no means exhaustive; and are intended only as a guide to further study.

This work should be gone carefully through, with Bible in hand, in order to verify the statements put forward, and to enter on the margins of the Bible notes for future use.

This may be done individually; but, better still, in small classes meeting for the purpose, when each point could be made clearer and more profitable by mutual study and conversation.

With the hope that this course will be adopted by its many readers in many countries and climes, this work is at length sent forth.

My thanks are due to all those who, on hearing of its projection, volunteered their financial help to ensure its publication : and, above all, to "the God of all grace," and "the spirit of wisdom and understanding" for bringing it to a happy issue.

ETHELBERT W. BULLINGER.

INTRODUCTION

"Man doth not live by bread only, but by every word that proceedeth out of the mouth of Jehovah doth man live."—Deut. viii. 3.

THUS is it asserted that the WORD and the WORDS of Jehovah constitute the food of the New nature.

As in the natural sphere so in the spiritual, the desire (or appetite) for the food which is the proper support of each respectively, is the sign of natural and spiritual health.

Attention to *diet* is becoming more and more recognized as essential to nutrition and growth.

A low condition of bodily health is produced by inattention to the laws of nature as to suitable diet. As this leads to the "drug habit," or to the immoderate use of stimulants in the natural sphere, so it is in the spiritual sphere. A low condition of spiritual health is produced by improper feeding or the neglect of necessary food, which is the Word of God; and the end is a resort to all the many modern fashions and novel methods and widely advertised nostrums in the Religious world in the attempt to remedy the inevitable results.

The Root of all the evils which abound in the spiritual sphere at the present day lies in the fact that the Word and the words of God are not fed upon, digested, and assimilated, as they ought to be.

If we ask the question, Why is this the case? the answer is, The Bible is not enjoyed *because the Bible is not understood.* The methods and rules by which alone such an understanding may be gained are not known or followed; hence the Bible is a neglected book.

The question Philip addressed to the Eunuch (Acts viii. 30, 31) is still greatly needed :

Understandest thou what thou readest ?

And the Eunuch's answer is only too true to-day:

How can I, except some man should guide me ?

The following pages are written with the object of furnishing this " guide." Certain canons or principles are laid down, and each is illustrated by applying them to certain passages by way of examples. These are intended to be taken only as examples; and the principles involved are intended to be used for the elucidation of other passages in the course of Bible study.

The Word of God is inexhaustible. It is, therefore, neither useful, nor indeed practicable to extend these examples beyond certain limits.

By the aid of these twelve simple canons or rules, other passages and subjects may be taken up and pursued both with pleasure and profit—subjects which are even yet matters of controversy and of conflict.

We have to remember that the Bible is not a book of pure Science on the one hand, nor is it a book of Theology on the other. Yet all its science is not only true, but its statements are the foundation of all true science.

And, it is Theology itself; for it contains all that we can ever know about God.

The cloud that now rests over its intelligent study arises from the fact that it is with us to-day as with the Jews of old—"The Word of God has been made of none effect by the traditions of men " (Matt. xv. 1—9).

Hence it is that on some of the most important questions, especially such as Biblical Psychology, we are, still, in what the great Lord Bacon calls "a desert." He alludes to those " deserts " in history, where discovery or research comes to a stand-still, and we get schoolmen instead of philosophers; and clerics instead of discoverers.

The Reformation came as an oasis after one of these deserts. Men were sent from the stagnant pools of tradition to the fountain-head of truth. But within two or three generations the Church entered the desert again; Creeds, Confessions, and Catechisms took the place of the open Bible; the inductive method of Bible study was abandoned, and to day it is scarcely understood.

One party abides by "Catholic consent" or the "Voice of the Church." Other parties in the same way abide by the dicta of some who had stronger minds. Augustine, Luther, Calvin, Darby, and Newton would be surprised to-day to find that those who question what they believed are treated as guilty of presumption, and of a sin to be visited with excommunication!

These good men little thought that the inferences which they drew from the Bible would be raised to a position of almost equality with the Bible itself.

The result of all this is too painfully evident. Controversies, bitterness, strifes have been engendered. These have taken the place of simple Bible study. If studied at all it has been too much with the view of finding support for one or other of the two sides of these controversies, instead of with the object of discovering what God has really revealed and written for our learning.

Failing to understand the Scriptures we cease to feed on them; then as a natural consequence, and in inverse proportion, we lean on and submit to "the doctrines of men," and finally reach a theological desert.

Bishop Butler has pointed out the way back to the land of plenty and of delight. He has shown that the only way to study the Word of God is the way in which physical science is studied. He says:[1] "As it is owned, the whole scheme of Scripture is not yet understood, so if it ever comes to be understood before the restitution

---

[1] *Analogy*, Part II., ch. 3.

of all things, and without miraculous interpositions, *it must be in the same way* as natural knowledge is come at, by the continuance and progress of learning and liberty, and by particular persons attending to, comparing, and pursuing intimations scattered up and down it, and which are overlooked and disregarded by the generality of the world."

On this another writer [1] has remarked, "Thus, the way of discovery still lies open to us in Divine things if we have only the moral courage to go to the fountain-head of truth, instead of filling our vessel out of this or that doctor's compendium of truth . . . Were Bishop Butler's method of inductive research into Scripture more common than it is we should not have stood still so long, as if spell-bound by the shadow of a few great names. 'It is not at all incredible,' Bishop Butler adds, 'that a book which has been so long in the possession of mankind should contain many truths as yet undiscovered.' Such a saying is worthy of Butler. It is only a philosopher who can allow for time and prescription. The majority of mankind think that they think; they acquiesce, and suppose that they argue; they flatter themselves that they are holding their own, when they have actually grown up to manhood, with scarcely a conviction that they can call their own. So it always was, and so it will ever be. The Divine things of the Word are no exception, but rather an instance. The more difficult the subject, and the more serious the consequences of error, the more averse the majority are to what is called 'unsettling men's minds'; as if truth could be held on any other tenure than the knight's fee of holding its own against all comers. Protestantism has brought us no relief against this torpid state of mind, for, as the error is as deep as the nature of man, we cannot expect any deliverance from it so long as the nature of man continues the same,

---

[1] Rev. J. B. Heard, M.A., *Tripartite Nature of Man*, p. 358.

and his natural love of truth almost as depraved as his natural love of holiness."

But the way of discovery, as Bishop Butler has pointed out, still lies open before us; and it is our object in this work to enter on that way, and study the Bible *from within* and not merely from without.

We believe that only thus we shall be furnishing just that help which Bible students need.

It may be the work of others to explore Geography, History, Natural History, Chronology ; the antiquities of Assyria, Palestine, Egypt, and Babylon ; all these are legitimate subjects of systematic research, which cannot but help us in understanding more of the Word of God.

But our object is to " Open the book " ; to let it speak; to hear its voice ; to study it *from within itself ;* and have regard to other objects and subjects, only from what it teaches about them.

The method of the " Higher " criticism is to discredit a Book, or a passage on *internal evidence.* Our method is to establish and accredit Holy Scripture on internal evidence also, and thus to derive and provide, from its own pharmacopœia, an antidote to that subtle and malignant poison.

This method of study will reveal more convincing and "infallible proof" of inspiration than can be adduced from all the reasonings and arguments of men.

Like Ezra of old, our desire is to

"OPEN THE BOOK"

and let it speak for itself, with the full conviction that if this can be done it can speak more loudly, and more effectively for itself, than any man can speak on its behalf

May the Lord deign to use these pages, and make them to be that "guide" to a better understanding and a greater enjoyment of His own Word.

E. W. B.

HOW TO ENJOY THE BIBLE:
A Guide to Better Understanding and Greater Enjoyment of God's Word

PRELIMINARY REMARKS

A REVELATION in writing must necessarily be given in "words." The separate words, therefore, in which it is given must have the same importance and authority as the revelation as a whole. If we accept the Bible as a revelation from God, and receive it as inspired by God, we cannot separate the words of which that inspired revelation is made up, or admit the assertion "that the Bible *contains* the Word of God, but *is not* the Word of God." The position conveyed by such an expression is both illogical and impossible.

As we design this work for those who accept the Scriptures as the Word of God, we do not propose to offer any arguments in proof of its inspiration.

The Bible is its own best proof of its inspiration. It claims to be "the Word of God;" and if it be not what it claims to be, then it is not only not a "good book," but is unworthy of our further attention.

We cannot understand the position of those who assert and believe that many of its parts are myths and forgeries, while at the same time they continue to write commentaries upon it, and accept their emoluments and dignities for preaching or lecturing about it.

If we were told and believed that a bank-note in our possession is a forgery, we certainly should take no further interest in it, beyond mourning the loss which we had sustained: Our action would thus be consistent with our belief.

We write, therefore, for those who, receiving the claims of the Scriptures as being the Word of God, desire to study it so as to understand it and enjoy it.

When this claim is admitted, and a course of study is undertaken in this spirit, we shall be at once overwhelmed with proofs as to its truth; and on almost every page find abundant confirmation of our faith.

The Bible simply claims to be the Word of God. It does not attempt to establish its claim, or seek to prove it. It merely assumes it and asserts it. It is for us to believe it or to leave it.

Hence we do not now attempt to prove or establish that claim; but, believing it, our aim is to seek to understand what God has thus written for our learning.

Nor do we attempt to explain the phenomena connected with Inspiration. We have no theories to offer, or suggestions to make, respecting it.

We have the Divine explanation in Acts iii. 18, where we read:

> "Those things which God before had showed by the mouth of all his prophets . . . he hath so fulfilled."

The particular "things" referred to here are "that Christ should suffer;" but the assertion is comprehensive and includes all other things "showed" by God.

Note, that it was God who, before, had showed them. It was the same God who had fulfilled them. The "mouth" was the mouth of "all His prophets," but they were not the prophets' words. They were the words of God.

Hence, concerning other words, it is written:

> "This Scripture must needs have been fulfilled, which the Holy Ghost, by the mouth of David, spake before concerning Judas" (Acts i. 16).

It was David's "mouth," and David's pen, David's vocal organs, and David's hand; but they were *not David's words*. They were the words "which the Holy Ghost spake before concerning Judas." David knew nothing about Judas, David could not possibly have spoken anything about Judas. David's "mouth" spake concerning Ahithophel; but they were the words "which the Holy Ghost spake concerning Judas."

David was "a prophet": and, being a prophet, he "spake as he was moved by the Holy Ghost" (2 Pet. i. 21). Hence, in Psalm xvi., he spake concerning the resurrection of the Lord Jesus (Acts ii. 30, 31). In the same way he "spake before concerning Judas."

In like manner, in the Book of Exodus Moses wrote about the Tabernacle, but he himself did not and could not know what "the Holy Ghost signified" (Heb. ix. 8).

Here, then, we have all that God condescends to tell us about the phenomena of inspiration.

This is the Divine explanation of it; and this is all that can be known about it.

It is not for us to explain this explanation, but to receive it and believe it; and there leave it. It is enough for us that God speaks to us; and that He says "Thus saith Jehovah." We do not question the fact; we believe it; and only seek to understand it.

We desire to be in the position of those Thessalonian saints who, in this, "were ensamples to all that believe," and to whom it was written: "For this cause thank we God without ceasing, because, when ye received the word of God which ye heard of us, ye received it not as the word of men, but as it is in truth, the Word of God, which effectually worketh in you that believe" (1 Thess. ii. 13).

The Word of God is thus for those "that believe." The "*Word*" as a whole; and the "*words*" of which it is made up. They cannot be separated.

It is Jeremiah who says (Jer. xv. 16):

> "THY WORDS were found,[1] and I did eat them;
> And THY WORD was unto me the joy and rejoicing of my heart:
> For I am called by Thy name, O Jehovah Elohim of hosts."

Here again, it is those who are called by Jehovah's name who feed upon His "words," and rejoice in His "Word."

---

[1] מָצָא (*mātza'*), *to discover.* Gen. ii. 20. Here referring to the historic fact (2 Kings xxii. 8. 2 Chron. xxxiv, 14, 15) of the finding the book of the Law by Hilkiah in the reign of Josiah.

The same distinction is made in the New Testament by the Lord Jesus in John xvii. :

> "I have given unto them the WORDS which thou gavest me" (*v.* 8).
> "I have given them thy WORD" (*v.* 14).

Those who are referred to in the word "them" are described seven times over, as having been "*given*" to Christ by the Father.[1]

These had "received" the words; these had "known surely"; these had "believed" (*v.* 8).

It is for such as these we now write, who receive, believe, read, and desire to feed upon the "*words*" of God; that the "word" of God may become "a joy, and the rejoicing" of the heart (Jer. xv. 16, R.V.).

True, this joy within will be tempered by trouble without. Jeremiah prefaces the statement, quoted above, with the words immediately preceding it in verse 15 :

> "For Thy sake I have suffered rebuke."[2]

And the Lord Jesus after saying (John xvii. 14):

> "I have given them Thy WORD"

immediately adds,

> "And the world hath hated them."

Those who thus feed upon and rejoice in God's Word will soon realize their isolated position; but, in spite of the "reproach" and "hatred" of the world, there will always be the "joy and rejoicing" of the heart.

It was so on another occasion when the neglected Word of God was brought forth,

"AND EZRA OPENED THE BOOK,"

the people were assured that "the joy of the LORD was their strength" (Neh. viii. 5, 10, 12, 17). And we are told:

> "So they read in the book in the law of God distinctly, and gave the sense, and caused them to understand the reading" (*v.* 8).

---

[1] See verses 2, 6, 6, 9, 11, 12, 24.

[2] חֶרְפָּה (*cherpāh*), *reproach;* and so nearly always rendered.

It must be the same with us if that "Word" and those "words" are to be the cause of our joy and rejoicing. And this is our object in writing now. We do not write for casual readers, or for those who read a daily portion of the Word merely as the performance of a duty and as a matter of form, but for those who "search the Scriptures," and who seek, in them, for Him of whom the Scriptures testify (John v. 39).

Such a one was the eunuch who went up to Jerusalem from Ethiopia in Acts viii. He sought the Saviour, but he did not find Him in Jerusalem. He found "religion" there, and plenty of it; but he did not find that Blessed One; for He had been rejected, "crucified, and slain." So the eunuch was returning, and was still seeking for the *Living* Word in the *Written* Word; "and, sitting in his chariot, read Isaiah the prophet."

Being directed by the Divine Angel-messenger, Philip "ran thither to him and heard him reading the prophet Isaiah, and said

UNDERSTANDEST THOU WHAT THOU READEST?

And he said:

"How can I except some man should guide me?
"And he desired Philip that he would come up and sit with him" (Acts viii. 27-31).

Philip's question (*v.* 30) implies (in the Greek) a doubt on Philip's part as to whether the eunuch did really understand. And the eunuch's reply (*v.* 31) implies a negative answer. It begins with the word "for," which is not translated either in the A.V. or R.V. If we supply the ellipsis of the negative which is so clearly implied we can then translate the word $\gamma \acute{\alpha} \rho$ (*gar*), *for;* thus;

"[No]: for how should I be able unless some one should guide me."

Of course, the Holy Spirit Himself is THE guide and teacher of His own Word. But sometimes, as in this case, He sends a messenger, and uses human instruments and agencies.

The word *to guide* is ὁδηγέω (*hodēgeō*), *to lead* or *guide
in the way*.[1] It is this guidance which the ordinary
reader stands in need of to-day; and never more than
to-day, when so many would-be guides are "blind leaders
of the blind." On all hands there are so many attractions
to draw readers out of "the way" altogether; and so
many "good" books and "helps" to lead them astray.

We cannot pretend to be a Philip, or to have his
special commission. But, without assuming to teach
others on such an important subject we may at least tell
them what lines of study we have ourselves found help-
ful; and what principles we have found useful in our own
searchings of God's Word.

But these will be useless unless we are first prepared
to *unlearn*.

If any think they know all, or that they have exhausted the Divine Word; or that what they set out to
learn is only to be in *addition* to what they already
know, instead of sometimes in substitution for it, then
we shall be of little service to them: and they need not
follow us any further.

When we come to ask ourselves, and say, "Where did
I learn this?" "How did I get this?" "Who taught me
this?" it is astonishing to find how much we have imbibed
from man, and from tradition; and not *directly* and for
ourselves, from the Word of God.

All that we have learned from our youth up must be
tested and proved by the Word of God. Where we find
it is true we must *learn it over again, from God.* And
where it will not stand the test of His Word we must
be not only content, but *thankful to give it up;* and receive Divine revelation in the place of man's imagination.

With these introductory remarks we shall proceed to
divide what we may call our essential and fundamental
principles of Bible study into two parts:

> *First,* those connected with THE "WORD" as a
> whole; and
>
> *Second:* those connected with THE "WORDS" of
> which the Word is composed.

---

[1] From ὁδός (*hodos*), *a way*; and ἡγέομαι (*hegeomai*), *to lead.* It occurs only in
Matt. xv. 14. Luke vi. 39. John xvi. 13. Acts viii. 31. and Rev. vii. 17. It is
used both in its literal or proper sense (Exod. xiii. 17; xxxii. 34. Num. xxiv. 8;
Deut. i. 33); and in a Tropical sense (Ps. v. 8; xxiii. 3; xxv. 5, 9; lxxvii. 20, etc.).

Part I: THE WORD

I. THE ONE GREAT OBJECT OF THE WORD

The first great and essential principle which must be ever present with us, when we study the Word of God, as a whole, is not to treat it as something which we have to interpret, but as being *that which God has given in order to interpret Himself and H s will to us.*

i. This applies to Christ ; as the Living Word.

When we speak of the "Word" we can never separate the *Living* Word, the Lord Jesus Christ; and the *written* word, the Scriptures of Truth.

Each of these is called the "Word," because the Greek word *Logos* is used of both.

Logos means the spoken or written word, because it makes manifest, and reveals to us the invisible thoughts.

It is used of Christ, the Living Word, because He reveals the invisible God. "No man hath seen God at any time ; the only begotten Son, He being in the bosom of the Father, This one [hath] declared [Him]" (John i. 18).

It is not that we have to explain Christ, but that His mission is to explain God to us. He interprets the Father. And we have to believe Him.

The word "declare" in John i. 18 is important in this connection, and deeply interesting. It is from *ἐκ (ek), out of,* or *forth,* and *ἡγέομαι (hēgeomai), to lead.* Hence the whole compound verb means *to lead forth, to make known, to guide, interpret, unfold, reveal,* and *expound* (Luke xxiv. 35).[1] It is from this verb that we have the cognate noun *Exegesis* which means *Exposition.* Wycliffe renders it "He hath told out." The best meaning is *to make known.*

---

[1] The word occurs only in Luke xxiv. 35. John i. 18. Acts x. 8; xv. 12, 14; xxi. 19.

This is why Christ is called "The Word of God," because He makes known, reveals, and explains the Father.

This is why the Scriptures are called "the Word of God," because they make known the Father and the Son, by the Holy Spirit, the author of the Word.

Christ is "the Way" to the Father (John xiv.). He makes God known to us in all His attributes, will, and words. "I have given them Thy Word." It is always "THY Word" (John xvii. 8, 14, 17).

ii. In like manner the Written Word, the Scripture, is given in order to interpret, and to testify of Christ; and this is why (as we shall see as our next essential principle) Christ is the one great subject of the Word.

This is why the Holy Spirit is the interpreter of both. His mission is to glorify Christ (John xvi. 14). He receives and shows the "things of Christ" (John xiv. 26). But He shows them in the Written Word (1 Cor. ii. 9—14). And this is why it must be He and He alone who enables us to preach that Word.

Thus we have the Word in three manifestations:—

> The Incarnate Word,
> The Written Word,
> The Preached Word.

There is no other. Christ reveals the Father. The Scripture reveals Christ. The Spirit reveals both in the written and in the preached Word (1 Cor. xii. 7, 8).

How wonderfully does this magnify the preached Word; and show the solemnity of the charge in 2 Tim. iv. 2, "Preach the Word."

It shows how small and worthless are all the schemes, tricks and contrivances of present-day evangelists and mission preachers with their ever-new fashions and modern methods, when we see what a high and dignified place God has given to the Preached Word.

How careful should we be that nothing in our manner or matter should lower that dignity, or imply in the slightest degree that the Written Word has lost any of its power; or needs any handmaids or helpmeets.

"I HAVE GIVEN THEM THY WORD"

is the all-sufficient assurance of the Lord Jesus Christ, speaking to the Father. He did not say I have given them Aids to devotion. He did not say I have given them a Hymn-book, or I have given them thy Word AND something else.

He did not give anything instead of, or in addition to, that Word.

And that being so, we are assured that the Word which He gave is all-sufficient, in itself, to accomplish all the purposes of God.

The Word that is preached makes known the Written Word; the Word that is written makes known Christ the Living Word; and Christ makes known God our Father.

iii. Hence it is, that the same things are stated of both the Living and the Written Word, as it is well put by Joseph Hart :—

> The Scriptures and the Word
> Bear one tremendous name,
> The Living and the Written Word
> In all things are the same.

This may be seen by noting carefully, in our reading, how precisely the same things are predicated of both one and the other.

We give a few by way of example :—

SIMILAR PREDICATES OF "CHRIST" AND "THE SCRIPTURES."

" His name is called THE WORD OF GOD " . . . Rev. xix. 13.
They " pressed upon Him to hear THE WORD OF GOD " Luke v. 1.

The *Prince* of PEACE . . . . Isa. ix. 6.
The *Gospel* of PEACE . . . . Rom. x. 15.

Jesus said, . . . " No man cometh unto the Father, but
  BY ME " . . . . John xiv. 6.
" Make me to go in the PATH of Thy *Commandments* ". Ps. cxix. 35.

" *Jesus* saith unto him, I am THE WAY " . . . John xiv. 6.
" Teach me, O Lord, THE WAY of *Thy Statutes* " . . Ps. cxix. 33.

" I am . . . THE TRUTH " . . . . . . John xiv. 6.
" Thy Word is TRUTH " . . . . . John xvii. 17.

Christ—" Full of grace and TRUTH " . . . . John i. 14.
" All *Thy Commandments* are TRUTH ". . . . Ps. cxix. 151.

" These things saith He . . . that is TRUE "   .   .   Rev. iii. **7.**
" The *Judgments* of the Lord are TRUE "   .   .   Ps. xix. 9.

" *Jesus Christ.* This is the true God, and eternal LIFE "   1 John v. **20.**
" Holding forth the *Word* of LIFE "   .   .   .   Phil. ii. 16.

" A bone of Him shall not be broken " .   .   .   John xix. 36.
" The scripture cannot be broken "   .   .   .   John x. 35.

" I am the Living Bread . . . if any man eat of *this*
     Bread he shall LIVE for ever "   .   .   .   John vi. 51.
" Man shall not LIVE by bread alone, but by *every*
     Word of God "   .   .   .   .   .   .   Luke iv. 4.

" With *Thee* is the FOUNTAIN OF LIFE "   .   .   Ps. xxxvi. 9.
" Thy *Law* . . . is a FOUNTAIN OF LIFE "   .   .   Prov. xiii. 14.

Jesus said, " I am the LIGHT of the World "   .   John viii. 12.
David said, " Thy *Word* is a LIGHT unto my path "   .   Ps. cxix. 105.

" The *Life* was the LIGHT "   .   .   .   .   John i. 4.
" The *Law* is LIGHT "   .   .   .   .   .   Prov. vi. 23.

" *Thou* art my LAMP, O Lord "   .   .   .   2 Sa. xxii. 29.
" Thy *Word* is a Lamp unto my feet " .   .   .   Ps. cxix. 105.

" I, saith the Lord, will be unto her a wall of FIRE "   .   Zech. ii. 5.
" Is not My *Word* like as a FIRE ? saith the Lord "   .   Jer. xxiii. 29.

" The *Light of Israel* shall be for a FIRE "   .   .   Isa. x. 17.
" I will make *My Words* in thy mouth FIRE "   .   Jer. v. 14.

" To you which believe, *He* is PRECIOUS "   .   .   1 Peter ii. 7.
" Exceeding great and PRECIOUS *Promises* " .   .   2 Peter i. 4.

" *My beloved* is . . . chiefest among ten THOUSAND "   .   Song v. 10.
" The *Law of Thy mouth* is better unto me than
     THOUSANDS of gold and silver "   .   .   .   Ps. cxix. 72.

" *His Mouth* is most SWEET " .   .   .   .   .   Song v. 16.
" How SWEET are *Thy Words* unto my taste "   .   Ps. cxix. 103.

" *His Name* shall be called WONDERFUL "   .   .   Isa. ix. 6.
" *Thy Testimonies* are WONDERFUL "   .   .   .   Ps. cxix. 129.

" *Christ*, the POWER OF GOD "   .   .   .   .   1 Cor. i. 24.
" The *Gospel* is the POWER OF GOD "   .   .   .   Rom. i. 16.

Lord, " *Thou* art GOOD, and doest *Good* "   .   .   Ps. cxix. 68.
" GOOD is *the Word of the Lord* "   .   .   .   Isa. xxxix. 8.

" Ye have known *Him* that is FROM THE BEGINNING " .   1 John ii. 13.
" Thy *Word* is true FROM THE BEGINNING " .   .   Ps. cxix. 160.

" From Everlasting to EVERLASTING *Thou* art God "   .   Ps. xc. 2.
" The righteousness of Thy *Testimonies* is EVERLASTING " Ps. cxix. 144.

"Thy throne, O God, is FOR EVER AND EVER".   .   Heb. i. 8.

": Thy *Testimonies*, . . . Thou hast founded them FOR EVER"   .   .   .   .   Ps. cxix. 152.

" The *Lord* shall ENDURE for ever "   .   .   .   Ps. ix. 7.

" The *Word of the Lord* ENDURETH for ever"   .   .   1 Peter i. 25.

" Christ ABIDETH for ever "   .   .   .   .   .   John xii. 34.

" The *Word* of God . . . ABIDETH for ever ".   .   .   1 Peter i. 23.

" Worship *Him* that LIVETH for ever ".   .   .   Rev. iv. 10.

" The *Word of God* LIVETH for ever "   .   .   .   1 Peter i. 23.

Christ's Kingdom " shall STAND FOR EVER "   .   .   Dan. ii. 44.

" The *Word of our God* shall STAND FOR EVER "   .   .   Isa. xl. 8.

The STONE . . . " on whomsoever it shall fall, it will grind him to powder "   .   .   .   .   .   Luke xx. 18.

" Is not *my Word* . . . saith the Lord, like a HAMMER that breaketh the rock in pieces ? ".   .   .   Jer. xxiii. 29.

Christ, " A STUMBLING Stone "   .   .   .   .   Rom. ix. 33.

They " STUMBLE at the *Word* "   .   .   .   .   1 Peter ii. 8.

" Lo, *I am* with you ALWAY, even unto the end of the world "   .   .   .   .   Matt. xxviii. 20.

" Thy *commandments* . . . are EVER WITH ME "   .   .   Ps. cxix. 98.

" *Christ* may DWELL in your hearts by faith "   .   .   Eph. iii. 17.

" Let the *Word* of Christ DWELL in you richly "   .   .   Col. iii. 16.

Christ said, " ABIDE in me, and I IN YOU "   .   .   John xv. 4.

" If . . . . my *Words* ABIDE in you "   .   .   .   John xv. 7.

" Hereby we know that *He* ABIDETH in us "   .   .   1 John iii. 24.

" The *Word* of God ABIDETH in you "   .   .   .   1 John ii. 14.

Christ called, " FAITHFUL and true "   .   .   .   Rev. xix, 11.

" Thy *Testimonies* . . . . are very FAITHFUL "   .   .   Ps. cxix. 138.

" Out of *His* mouth goeth a sharp SWORD " .   .   .   Rev. xix. 15.

" *The Word of God* . . . . is sharper than any two-edged SWORD "   .   .   .   .   .   .   Heb. iv. 12.[1]

" The *Lord* TRIETH the Righteous "   .   .   .   Ps. xi. 5.

" The *Word* of the Lord TRIED him "   .   .   .   Ps. cv. 19.

Christ a " TRIED Stone "   .   .   .   .   .   Isa. xxviii. 16.

" The *Word* of the Lord is TRIED "   .   .   .   Ps. xviii. 30.

SIMILAR EFFECTS ATTRIBUTED TO "CHRIST" AND "THE SCRIPTURES."

We are " BORN OF *God* "   .   .   .   .   .   1 John v. 18.

" BORN . . . . by the *Word* of God "   .   .   .   1 Peter i. 23.

---

[1] Heb. iv. 12 probably refers to *both* the *Living* Word and the *written* Word also.

" Begotten . . . . by . . . . *Jesus Christ* " .	1 Peter i. 3.
" Begotten . . . . through *The Gospel* "	1 Cor. iv. 15.
" The *Son* Quickeneth whom He will "	John v. 21.
" *Thy Word* hath Quickened me "	Ps. cxix. 50.
" You hath He Quickened who were dead," &c. .	Eph. ii. 1.
" *Thy Precepts* . . . with them thou hast Quickened me "	Ps. cxix. 93.
" He that *eateth* me, even he shall Live by me " .	John vi. 57.
" Desire the sincere milk of *The Word,* that ye may grow thereby "	1 Peter ii. 2.
" Christ hath made us Free "	Gal. v. 1.
" The *Truth* shall make you Free "	John viii. 32.
" The *Blood* of Jesus Christ . . . . Cleanseth us from all sin "	1 John i. 7.
" Ye are Clean through the *Word* which I have spoken "	John xv. 3.
Christ " is able also to save them to the uttermost that come unto God by Him "	Heb. vii. 25.
" Receive . . . . the engrafted *Word,* which is able to save your souls "	James i. 21.
" Sanctified in *Christ Jesus* "	1 Cor. i. 2.
" Sanctified by the *Word of God* and prayer "	1 Tim. iv. 5.
" Sanctified through the offering of the body of Jesus Christ once for all "	Heb. x. 10.
" Sanctify them through Thy Truth. Thy Word is truth "	John xvii. 17.
" *Christ Jesus,* who of God is made unto us Wisdom " .	1 Cor. i. 30.
" The *Holy Scriptures* . . . able to make thee Wise unto salvation "	2 Tim. iii. 15.
Christ " Healed them "	Matt. iv. 24.
" He sent His *Word* and Healed them "	Ps. cvii. 20.
" Striving according to *His Working* which Worketh in me mightily "	Col. i. 29.
" The *Word of God* which effectually Worketh also in you that believe "	1 Thess. ii. 13.
" The *Lord Jesus Christ* . . . shall Judge the quick and the dead "	2 Tim. iv. 1.
" *The Word* that I have spoken . . shall Judge him ".	John xii. 48.
" I will go unto *God,* my exceeding Joy "	Ps. xliii. 4.
" *Thy Word* was unto me the Joy and rejoicing of my heart "	Jer. xv. 16.

Thus we see that the Living Word and the Written Word cannot be separated. And we can understand also why they cannot be separated in the preaching of the Word.

To preach the Written Word without preaching Christ is not preaching at all. Neither is it done in the power of the Spirit.

When Paul went to Thessalonica, he ("as his manner was") "reasoned with them out of the SCRIPTURES" (not as is done to-day, out of the newspapers, or out of the preacher's own head or experience); but he did not end there. We are immediately told that this preaching consisted in "opening and setting forth that CHRIST (the Living Word) must needs have suffered, and risen again from the dead, and that this Jesus, whom I preach unto you, is Christ (the Messiah)" (Acts xvii. 1—3).

If the Living Word and the Written Word cannot be separated, we learn that in sitting down to the study of the Word and Words of God it is to hear His voice, to choose that "better part"; to sit at Jesus's feet, and hear HIS word (Luke x. 39).

And it is only a "part." The best is to come; when we shall "behold His glory" (John xvii. 24), the glory of our Ascended Lord; as the glory of our Incarnate Lord was beheld when on Earth (John i. 14). Then, in the future, as in the past (as now by the Holy Spirit), the wonderful "Word"—our Glorified Lord—will continue the blessed work which He began as our Risen Lord, "expounding in all the Scriptures the things concerning Himself"; and will declare and make known the Father to the Saints, who shall then have been gathered together unto Him (2 Thess. i. 10; ii. 1).

II. THE ONE GREAT SUBJECT OF THE WORD

i. CHRIST IN THE WORD AS A WHOLE.

The one great subject which runs through the whole Word of God is Christ: the promised seed of the woman in Gen. iii. 15.

This verse marks the depth of the ruin into which man had descended in the Fall; and it becomes the foundation of the rest of the Bible.

All hope of restoration for man and for creation is centred in Christ; who in due time should be born into the world, should suffer and die; and, in resurrection, should become the Head of a new creation, and should finally crush the head of the Old Serpent, who had brought in all the ruin. Christ, therefore, the King, and the Kingdom which He should eventually set up, become the one great subject which occupies the whole of the Word of God.

Hence, He is the key to the Divine revelation in the Word; and apart from Him it cannot be understood.

The contents of the Bible must therefore be seen and arranged with reference to Him. The counsels and purposes of God are all centred in Christ.

1. *In the Old Testament* we have the King and the Kingdom in Promise and Prophecy, Illustration and Type.

2. *In the Four Gospels* we have the King and the Kingdom presented and proclaimed by John the Baptiser, and by Christ Himself. And we see the Kingdom rejected, and the King crucified.

3. *In the Acts of the Apostles* we have the Transition from the Kingdom to the Church. The Kingdom is once again offered to Israel by Peter; again it is rejected, Stephen is stoned, and Peter imprisoned (ch. xii.).

Then Paul, who had been already chosen and called (ch. ix.), is commissioned for His Ministry (ch. xiii.), and on the final rejection of his testimony concerning the Kingdom, he pronounces for the third and last time the sentence of judicial blindness in Isaiah vi.,[1] and declares that "the salvation of God is sent to the Gentiles" (Acts xxviii. 25—28).

In his final communication to Hebrew believers it is written that while in God's counsels all things had been put under Christ's feet, "we see NOT YET all things put under Him" (Heb. ii. 7—9).

The Kingdom thenceforth is in abeyance.

4. *In the Epistles* we have the King exalted, and (while the Kingdom is in abeyance) made the Head over all things to the Church, during this present Interval; the Dispensation of the grace of God.

5. *In the Apocalypse* we have the Revelation of the King in judgment; and we see the Kingdom set up, the King enthroned in power and glory, the promise fulfilled, and prophecy ended.

We may exhibit the above to the eye in the following Structure :—[2]

The one Subject of the Word as a Whole.

A | The King and the Kingdom in Promise and Pro-
  | phecy. (*The Old Testament.*)

   B | The King presented, proclaimed, and re-
     | jected. The Mysteries (or Secrets) of the
     | Kingdom revealed. Matt. xiii. 11, 34, 35.
     | (*The Four Gospels.*)

      C | Transitional (*The Acts*). The King-
        | dom again offered and rejected (*The
        | earlier Pauline Epistles*).

   B | The King exalted and made Head over
     | all things to the Church, "which is His
     | body, the fulness of Him that filleth all in
     | all" (Eph. i. 22, 23). The Great Mystery
     | revealed (*The later Pauline Epistles*). The
     | Kingdom in abeyance (Heb. ii. 8).

A | The King and the Kingdom unveiled. The King
  | enthroned, and the Kingdom set up with Divine
  | judgment, power, and glory (Rev. xix., xx.). Pro-
  | mise and prophecy fulfilled (*The Apocalypse*).

---

[1] The other two citations of Isa. vi. were by our Lord, in Matt. xiii. 14, 15, and John xii. 40.

[2] See Part II., Canon II.

Here the correspondence is seen between these five members.

In A and *A* we have the King and the Kingdom.

In B and *B* we have the King and the mysteries (or secrets) of the Kingdom (Matt. xiii.).

In C, the central member, we have the present Interval, while the King is absent, the Holy Spirit present, and the Kingdom in abeyance, and the mystery of the Church revealed (Eph. iii).

It may be illustrated also by the diagram on the opposite page.

From the Structure, and from this illustration, it will be seen that the great subject of the whole Book is one. From Gen. iii. 15 to Rev. xxii. "THE COMING ONE" fills our vision.

This teaches us that the Coming of Christ is no newly-invented subject of some modern faddists or fanatics, or cranks ; but that Christ's coming *has always been the Hope of His people.*

In "the fulness of time" He came : but having been rejected and slain He rose from the dead, and ascended to Heaven. There He is "seated" and "henceforth expecting until His enemies shall be placed as a footstool for His feet" (Heb. x. 13).

Hence, Christ, "the Coming One," is the one all-pervading subject of the Word of God as a whole.

He is the *pneuma* or life-giving spirit of the written Word, without which the latter is dead. "As the body without the *pneuma* is dead" (Jas. ii. 26), so the written Word without the *pneuma* is dead also. Christ is that *pneuma* or spirit. This is the whole argument of 2 Cor. iii.[1]

This is why the Lord Jesus could say of the Scriptures : "They testify of ME" (John i. 45; v. 39. Luke xxiv. 44, 45).

Their one great design is to tell of the Coming One. All else is subordinated to this. This is why we see the ordinary events in a household combining with the grandest visions of a prophet to testify of Him who fills all Scripture. It may be said of the written Word, as it is of the New Jerusalem, "The Lamb is the light thereof" (Rev. xxi. 23).

---

[1] See *The Giver and His Gifts*, republished as *Word Studies on the Holy Spirit*, by Kregel Publications, pp. 135-141.

THE
BIBLE

OLD TESTAMENT: *The King and the Kingdom in Prophecy and Promise.*

GOSPELS: *The King and the Kingdom proclaimed and rejected.*

THE ACTS: *Transitional. King & Kingdom re-offered, rejected: withdrawn*

THE EPISTLES: *King exalted as HEAD of the Body Kingdom in abeyance.'Not yet.' Heb II, q.*

APOCALYPSE: *The Kingdom set up in Judgment & Glory. King enthroned.*

Apart from Him, the natural eye of man sees only outward historical details and circumstances; some in themselves appearing to him trifling, others offensive, and pursued at a length which seems disproportionate to the whole; while things which "angels desire to look into" are passed over in a few words, or in silence.

But once let "the spiritual mind" see Christ testified of "in Moses and all the prophets," then all assumes a new aspect: trifles that seem hardly worth recording fill the whole vision and light up the written Word and make it to shine with the glory of the Divine presence.

Then we see why the Inspired writer dwells on a matter which to the outward eye seems trivial compared with other things which we may deem to be of world-wide importance.

Then we observe in an event, seemingly casual and unimportant, something which tells forth the plans and counsels of God, by which He is shaping everything to His own ends. Nothing appears to us then either great or small. All is seen to be Divine when the Coming One is recognized as the one subject of the Word of God.

This is the master-key of the Scriptures of truth.

"These are they that testify of ME." Bearing this key in our hand we can unlock the precious treasures of the Word; and understand words, and hints; apparently casual expressions, circumstances, and events, which in themselves, and apart from Him, are meaningless.

It is the use of this master-key and this first great foundation principle which is to be observed in the study of the "Word" and "words" of God. It is when we, in every part, have found "HIM of whom Moses in the law, and the prophets, did write" (John i. 45), that we can understand those parts of Scripture which are "a stone of stumbling and a rock of offence" to many; that we can explain much that is otherwise difficult; see clearly much that before was obscure; answer objections that are brought against the Word; and "put to silence the ignorance of foolish men."

The moment this master-key is used types will be seen foreshadowing the Coming King, and showing forth His sufferings and His Glory. Events and circumstances will show forth His wondrous deeds and tell of the coming glory of His kingdom.

ii. CHRIST IN THE SEPARATE BOOKS OF THE WORD.

In GENESIS we shall understand the record of Creation (ch. i.), for we shall see in it the counterpart of our
new creation in Christ Jesus (2 Cor. v. 17).

In the light which shined out of darkness (Gen. i. 2, 3)
we shall see the light which has shone "in our hearts to
give the knowledge of the glory of God in the face (or
person) of Jesus Christ" (2 Cor. iv. 6). No wonder that
those who know nothing of this spiritual light of the New
Creation know nothing of the light that was created on
the first day as revealed in the record of the old creation.[1]
The natural man sees only a myth and an old wives' fable
in the Creation record, and seems actually to prefer the
Babylonian corruption of primitive truth. These "other
Gentiles walk in the vanity of their mind, having the
understanding darkened, being alienated from the life of
God through the ignorance that is in them, because of the
blindness of their heart" (Eph. iv. 17, 18). Woe be to those
who follow these blind leaders, for "they shall both fall
into the ditch" they have prepared for themselves by
their fleshly knowledge and worldly wisdom.

In the Creator we shall see Christ (John i. 3. Col. i. 16).

In the first Adam we shall see the last Adam (1 Cor.
xv. 45. Rom. v. 14). In the first man we shall see "the
second man, the Lord, from heaven" (1 Cor. xv. 47).

In the "seed of the woman" (Gen. iii. 15) we shall see
the coming son of Abraham, the son of David, the Son of
man, the Son of God; while those who are in the black
darkness of Rome see either a helpless Infant, or a dead
man, and a living woman—the Virgin Mary; having
corrupted their Authorized Vulgate Version (in Gen. iii,
15),[2] to make it the foundation of this blasphemy.

In Abraham's shield we shall see the Living Word,
coming, speaking, and revealing Himself to him (ch.
xv. i. John viii. 56).

---

[1] Though the recent discovery of *Radium* is beginning to open our eyes
and show how light can exist without the sun.

[2] Where the Hebrew masculine is misrepresented as feminine, and is thus
made, as Dr. Pusey has said, the foundation of Mariolatry, and the basis of the
Immaculate Conception.

In Isaac we shall see Christ the true seed of Abraham
(Rom. ix. 7. Gal. iii. 16). In the Annunciation to the
Mother (Gen. xviii. 10. Luke i. 30—33), the miraculous conception (Gen. xviii. 14. Luke i. 35) and the pre-natal
naming (Gen. xvii. 19. Matt. i. 21. Luke i. 31; ii. 21). In
the projected death of the one we see the foreshadowing
of the other, two thousand years before, and on the same
mountain, Moriah; and this Mount, selected not by
chance, or for convenience (for it was three days' journey),
but appointed in the Divine counsels as the site of the
future altar of burnt offering (Gen. xxii. 2. 1 Chron. xxi.
28—xxii. 1. 2 Chron. iii. 1). In the *wood* laid upon Isaac
(Gen. xxii. 6), and not carried by the servants or on the
ass, we shall see Him who was led forth bearing His
Cross (John xix. 17).

In Joseph, of whom the question was asked, "Shalt
thou indeed reign over us?" we see Him of whom His
brethren afterwards said, "We will not have this man to
reign over us" (Luke xix. 14). But we see the sufferings
of the one followed by the glory, as we shall surely see
the glory of the true Joseph following His sufferings in
the fulness of time (1 Pet. i. 11), of which glory we shall
be the witnesses, and partakers (1 Pet. iv. 13; v. 1).

We must not pursue this great subject or principle in
its further details, though we have but touched the fringe
of it, even in the book of Genesis. As the Lord Jesus
began at Moses so have we only made a beginning, and
must leave our readers to follow where we have pointed
out the way.

It may be well, however, for us to indicate one or
two of the leading points of the other books of the Old
Testament.

EXODUS tells of the sufferings and the glory of Moses,
as Genesis does of Joseph, and in both we see a type of the
sufferings and glory of Christ.

Joseph's sufferings began with his rejection, his own
brethren asking, "Shalt thou indeed reign over us? Or
shalt thou indeed have dominion over us?" (Gen. xxxvii. 8).
Moses's sufferings began with his rejection and the question of "two men of the Hebrews,"—"Who made thee a
ruler and a judge over us?" (Exod. ii. 14). In all this
we see the rejection of Christ by a similar question, the

thought of their hearts being put into their lips, in the parable, where "his citizens hated Him and sent a message after Him saying, 'We will not have this man to reign over us'" (Luke xix. 14).

But the issue in all three cases is the same. Of each it is true, as it is said of Moses, "This Moses whom they refused, saying, 'Who made thee a ruler and a deliverer?' The same did God send to be a ruler and a judge by the hand of the angel which appeared to him in the bush" (Acts vii. 35).

Even so will God surely "send Jesus Christ . . . whom the heavens must receive until the times of restitution of all things which God hath spoken by the mouth of all His holy prophets since the world began" (Acts iii. 20, 21).

Thus early, in Genesis and Exodus, we have the great subject of the sufferings and the glory of Christ more than foreshadowed (1 Pet. i. 11; iv. 13; v. 1. Luke xxiv. 26).

Exodus tells us also of Christ as the true Paschal Lamb (1 Cor. v. 7, 8); as the true Priest (Exod. xxx. 10. Heb. v. 4, 5); and the true Tabernacle which the Lord pitched and not men (Heb. ix).

LEVITICUS gives us, in the offerings, a fourfold view of the Death of Christ (the Sin and Trespass Offerings being reckoned as one), as the Gospels give us a fourfold view of His life.

NUMBERS foreshadows the Son of Man come to be "lifted up" (ch. xxi. 9. John iii. 14, 15); the Rock (ch. xx. 11. 1 Cor. x. 4); the Manna that fed them (ch. xi. 7—9. Deut. viii. 2, 3. John vi. 57, 58); and the future Star that should arise "out of Jacob" (ch. xxiv. 17. Luke i. 78. 2 Pet. i. 19. Rev. ii. 28; xxii. 16).

DEUTERONOMY reveals the coming Prophet "like unto Moses" (ch. xviii. 15. Acts vii. 23—26); the Rock and Refuge of His people (chs. xxxii. 4; xxxiii. 27).

JOSHUA tells of "the Captain of the Lord's host" (ch. v. 13—15. Heb. ii. 10; xii. 2) who shall triumph over all His foes; while Rahab's scarlet cord (ch. ii. 12—20) tells of His sufferings and precious blood which will shelter and preserve His people in the coming day of His war.

JUDGES tells of the Covenant Angel whose name is "Secret," *i.e.* "Wonderful" (ch. xiii. 18, margin; compare Isa. ix. 6, where the word is the same).

RUTH reveals the type of our Kinsman-Redeemer, the true Boaz; and the question of ch. ii. 10 is answered in Prov. xi. 15.

SAMUEL reveals the "sufferings" and rejection of David, who became a "Saviour" and a "Captain" of his followers (1 Sam. xxii. 1, 2), foreshadowing David's Son and David's Lord, "the Root and the Offspring of David" (Rev. xxii. 16).

KINGS shows us the "glory which should follow," and the "greater than Solomon" (Matt. xii. 42); the "greater than the Temple" (Matt. xii. 6), where everything speaks of His glory (Ps. xxix. 9 and margin).

CHRONICLES reveals Christ as "the King's Son," rescued "from among the dead," hidden in the House of God, to be manifested in due time, "as Jehovah hath said" (2 Chron. xxii. 10—xxiii. 3).

EZRA speaks of "a nail in a sure place" (ch. ix. 8), which according to Isa. xxii. 23 is used of Eliakim, who typifies Christ.

NEHEMIAH tells of the "bread from Heaven" and "water out of the Rock" (ch. ix. 15, 20), which are elsewhere used as typical of Christ (John vi. 57, 58. 1 Cor. x. 4).

ESTHER sees the seed preserved which should in the fulness of time be born into the world. His name is there, though concealed,[1] but His will and power is manifested in defeating all enemies in spite of the unalterable law of the Medes and Persians.

JOB reveals Him as his "Daysman" or "Mediator" (ch. ix. 33); and as his "Redeemer" coming again to the earth (ch. xix. 25—27).

THE PSALMS are full of Christ. We see His humiliation and sufferings and death (Ps. xxii.), His Resurrection (Ps. xvi.), His anointing as Prophet with grace-filled lips (Ps. xlv. Luke iv. 22); as Priest after the order of Melchisedec (Ps. cx. Heb. v. 6; vi. 20; vii. 17, 21); as King enthroned over all (Ps. ii.), and His kingdom established in the earth (Ps. ciii.; cxlv., &c.).

PROVERBS reveals Christ as the "Wisdom of God" (ch. viii. 1 Cor. i. 24); the "Path" and "Light" of His

---

[1] See *The Name of Jehovah in the Book of Esther*, in Four Acrostics, by the same author.

People (ch. iv. 18); the "Surety" who smarted for His people while strangers (ch. xi. 15. Rom. v. 8—10. Eph. ii. 12. 1 Pet. ii. 11); the "strong tower" into which the righteous run and are safe (ch. xviii. 10); the friend who loveth at all times, and the brother born for adversity (ch. xvii. 17).

ECCLESIASTES tells of the "one among a thousand" in the midst of all that is vanity and vexation of spirit (ch. vii. 28).

THE SONG OF SONGS reveals Him as the true and faithful Shepherd, Lover, and Bridegroom of the Bride, who remained constant to Him in spite of all the royal grandeur and coarser blandishments of Solomon.

ISAIAH is full of the sufferings and glories of Christ. He is the "despised and rejected of men, a man of sorrows, and acquainted with grief" (ch. liii. 5); wounded for our transgressions, oppressed, afflicted, and brought as a lamb to the slaughter; cut off out of the land of the living (ch. liii. 2—9). Yet the glory shall follow. "He shall see of the travail of His soul and be satisfied" (ch. liii. 11). He will be His people's "Light" (ch. lx. 1, 2. Matt. iv. 16); "The Mighty God" (ch. ix. 6. Matt. xxviii. 18); Salvation's Well (ch. xii. 3); the King who shall "reign in righteousness" (ch. xxxii. 1, 2); Jehovah's Branch, beautiful and glorious (ch. iv. 2).

JEREMIAH tells of "the Righteous Branch," and "Jehovah our Righteousness" (ch. xxiii. 5, 6); of the "Righteous Branch" and King who shall reign and prosper (ch. xxxiii. 15).

EZEKIEL reveals Him as the true Shepherd (ch. xxxiv. 23), and as "the Prince" (ch. xxxvii. 25); the "Plant of Renown" (ch. xxxiv. 29), and "Jehovah Shammah" (ch. xlviii. 35).

DANIEL reveals Him as the "Stone" become the Head of the corner (ch. ii. 34. Ps. cxviii. 22. Isa. viii. 14. xxviii. 16. Matt. xxi. 42, 44. Acts iv. 11. 1 Pet. ii. 4, 6). Also as the Son of Man (ch. vii. 13, 16); and "Messiah the Prince" (ch. ix. 24).

He is HOSEA'S true David (iii. 5), the Son out of Egypt (xi. 1);

JOEL'S "God dwelling in Zion" (ch. iii. 17);

AMOS'S Raiser of David's Tabernacle (ch. ix. 11; Acts xv. 16. 17);

OBADIAH'S "Deliverer on Mount Zion" (v. 17);

JONAH'S "Salvation" (ch. ii. 9); the "Sign" of Christ's resurrection (Matt. xii. 39—41);

MICAH'S "Breaker," "King" and "Lord" (ch. ii. 13; v. 2, 5);

NAHUM'S "Stronghold in Trouble" (ch. i. 7);

HABAKKUK'S "Joy" and "Confidence" (ch. iii. 17, 18);

ZEPHANIAH'S "Mighty God in the midst of Zion" (ch. iii. 17);

HAGGAI'S "Desire of all nations" (ch. ii. 7);

ZECHARIAH'S Smitten Shepherd; The Man, Jehovah's Fellow (ch. xiii. 7); Jehovah's "Servant—the Branch" (ch. iii. 8); "the Man whose name is the Branch" (ch. vi. 12);

MALACHI'S "Messenger of the Covenant" (ch. iii. 1); the Refiner of the Sons of Levi (ch. iii. 3); "The Sun of Righteousness" (ch. iv. 2).

Thus, the "Word" of God has one great subject.

That one great all-pervading subject is Christ; and all else stands in relation to Him. He is "the beginning and the ending" of Scripture, as of all beside.

Hence, the Word of God, at its ending, shows how the beginning all works out; and how, that to which we are introduced in Genesis is completed in Revelation.

Satan's first rebellion is implied between the first and second verses of the first chapter of Genesis, and his final rebellion is seen in Rev. xx. 7—9. His doom is pronounced in Gen. iii. 15, and is accomplished in Rev. xx. 10.

We have the primal Creation, "the world that then was," in Gen. i. 1 (2 Pet. iii. 6). "The Heavens and the Earth which are now" in Gen. i. 2, etc. (2 Pet. iii. 7). And "The New Heavens and the New Earth" in Rev. xxi. 1 (2 Pet. iii. 13).

We have "night" in Gen. i. 1; and see "no night there" in Rev. xxii. 5.

We have the "sea" in Gen. i. 10; and "no more sea" in Rev. xxi. 1.

We have the "sun and moon" in Gen. i. 16, 17; and "no need of the sun or the moon" in Rev. xxi. 23; xxii. 5.

We have the entrance of sorrow and suffering and death in Gen. iii. 16, 17; and "no more death, neither sorrow nor crying" in Rev. xxi. 4.

We have the "curse" pronounced in Gen. iii. 17; and "no more curse" in Rev. xxii. 3.

We have banishment from Paradise and the Tree of Life in Gen. iii. 22—24; and the welcome back and "right to it" in Rev. xxii. 2.

This will be sufficient[1] to show the unity of the "Word" as a whole; and to stimulate Bible students to a further study of it on the line of this great fundamental principle.

---

[1] More instances will be found in *The Apocalypse; or, the Day of the Lord*, republished as *Commentary on Revelation*, by Kregel Publications, pp. 58, 59.

III. THE ONE GREAT REQUIREMENT OF THE WORD: "RIGHTLY DIVIDING" IT

The one great requirement of the Word is grounded on the fact that it is "the Word of truth." And this fact is so stated as to imply that, unless the Word is thus rightly divided we shall not get "truth"; and that we shall get its truth only in proportion to the measure in which we divide it rightly.

The Requirement is thus stated in 2 Tim. ii. 15: "*Give diligence to present thyself approved to God, a workman having no cause to be ashamed rightly dividing the word of truth.*"

The word in question here is ὀρθοτομοῦντα (*orthotomounta*).[1]

As this word occurs in no Greek writer, or even elsewhere in the New Testament, we can get little or no help from outside, and are confined to Biblical usage.

It is used twice in the Septuagint for the Hebrew יָשַׁר (*yāshar*), *to be right*, or *straight*. In Prov. iii. 6; xi. 5, the Hebrew is *Piel* (or *causative*), *to make right* (as in 2 Chron. xxxii. 30. Prov. xv. 21. Isa. xl. 3; xlv. 2, 13).

But it is the Greek word that we have to do with here, in 2 Tim. ii. 15; and we cannot get away from the fact that τέμνω (*temnō*) means *to cut*; or, from the fact that we cannot cut without *dividing*. *To divide* belongs to the very nature of the act of *cutting*. Even as applied to *directing one's way*, it implies that we divide off one way from others—because we desire to follow the right way and avoid the wrong.

The only Biblical guide we have to the *usage* of the word is in Prov. iii. 6:

> "In all thy ways acknowledge him
> And he shall direct thy paths."

In the margin the R.V. gives, "*make straight* or *plain*" as an alternative rendering for "*direct.*" But *our* ways can only be *made straight* or *plain* by God's causing

---

[1] From ὀρθός (*orthos*), *right*, and τέμνω (*temno*), *to cut.*

us to proceed on our way aright—*i.e.*, by avoiding all
the ways that are wrong, and going in the one way that
is right; in other words, the right way is divided off from
all the wrong ways.

What else can the word mean in 2 Tim. ii. 15?

It matters little what others have thought or said.
We could fill a page with their names and their views,
but we should learn but little and only become confused.
The duties of Priests, Furriers, and Ploughmen have been
referred to as indicating the correct meaning. But we
need not leave the Biblical usage, which associates the
word with *guidance in the right way*.

The scope of the verse plainly teaches that:

   (1) Our one great study is to seek GOD'S approval,
       and not man's.
   (2) We are to show all diligence in pursuing this
       study.
   (3) As workmen, our aim is to have no cause to
       be ashamed of our work.
   (4) In order to gain God's approval and avert our
       own shame we must rightly divide the word of
       truth.
   (5) To do this we must *direct our studies in the
       right way*.
   (6) This great requirement is associated with the
       Word in its special character as being the
       Word of truth; *i.e.*, "the TRUE Word."

All this tells us that we shall not get the truth if we
do not thus rightly divide it; and that we shall get the
truth only in proportion to our "rightly dividing" it.

Other titles of the Word have their own special re-
quirements. As "the engrafted Word" it must be *received with meekness* (Jas. i. 21). As "the Faithful Word"
we must *hold it fast* (Tit. i. 9). As "the Word of life" we
must *hold it forth* (Phil. ii. 16).

But, because this is "the Word of truth," its paths
must be well noted, the sign-posts must be observed, the
directions and guides which are in the Word itself must
be followed.

We are to "give diligence" to this great Requirement
of the Word just because it is "the Word of truth."

It is true that there are many who altogether ignore this precept; and have no thought as to obeying this command in their study of the Word.

There are many who make light of our insistence on obedience to this precept.

On what ground, we ask, are we to treat such an important command as though it had never been given?

Why is not this command as binding on Bible students as any other command in the Word of God?

What motive can such have to blunt the point and dull the edge of this "Sword of the Spirit" in this matter?

Strange to say, those who would be-little our efforts in rendering due obedience to this command, are themselves obliged not only to accept its division into chapters, and verses, and punctuated sentences; but they go further, and adopt the division of its subject-matter which is made by the insertion of chapter-headings and running page-headings according to man's own ideas.

The only question is, Do they divide it rightly, or wrongly?

For example, in the English Bibles which our readers use, over Isaiah xxix. we notice the running page-heading "*Judgment upon Jerusalem*"; and on the opposite page, over ch. xxx. we notice the page-heading "*God's mercies to His church.*"

Again, over Isaiah lix. we note the chapter-heading "*The sins of the Jews*"; in the chapter-heading of ch. lx. we note "*The glory of the church.*" And this in spite of the declared fact that this book contains "the Vision of Isaiah the son of Amoz, which he saw *concerning Judah and Jerusalem*" (ch. i. 1).[1]

Surely, this is dividing the Word. But the only question for us to ask is, whether it is divided "rightly" or wrongly.

In the consideration of this great and important requirement there are *four principal spheres* in which we

---

[1] If these headings are not found in some of the current editions of our English Bibles, it is only a proof that still greater liberties are taken in changes of these headings.

are to give diligence so that we may follow the right ways which are so clearly cut and marked out for our studies.

We must rightly divide the Word of Truth:

    i. As to its Literary Form.
    ii. As to its Subject-matter.
    iii. As to its Times and Dispensations.
    iv. As to its Dispensational Truth and Teaching.

We will consider these in their order.

i. RIGHTLY DIVIDING THE WORD AS TO ITS LITERARY FORM.

The "Word" comes to us in our English Translation. But it comes with much that is human in its Literary Divisions; and it is far from being rightly divided.

1. *The Two Testaments.*

"THE WORD OF GOD" as a whole comes to us in two separate parts: one written, originally, in Hebrew; the other in Greek. Only in the Versions are these two combined, and bound together in one Book.

These divisions, of course, are not human, though the names are by which they are commonly known.

Up to the second century the term "Old Covenant" was used by the Greeks to describe the Hebrew Bible. This passed into the Latin Vulgate as "*Vetus Testamentum*," from which our English term "Old Testament" was taken.

By way of distinction, the Greek portion was naturally spoken of as the "New Testament." But neither of these names is Divine in its origin.

2. *The Separate Books of the Bible.*

When, however, we come to the Separate Books, though their origin is Divine, the human element is at once apparent.

(*a*) *The Books of the Old Testament.* — The Books as we have them to-day are not the same as in the

Hebrew Canon, either as to their number, names, or order.[1]

The change first came about when the first Translation of the Hebrew Bible was made into Greek in the Version known as the Septuagint.

It was made in the latter part of the third century B.C. The exact date is not known, but the consensus of opinion leans to about 286—285 B.C.

It is the oldest of all the translations of the Hebrew Text, and its Divisions and arrangement of the Books have been followed in every translation since made.

Man has divided them into four classes: (1) The Law, (2) The Historical Books, (3) The Poetical Books, and (4) The Prophetical Books.

The Lord Jesus divides them into *Three* classes: (1) The Law, (2) The Prophets, and (3) The Psalms. And who will say that HE did not rightly divide them! But His Division was made according to the Hebrew Bible extant in His day, and not according to man's Greek Translation of it—*which was extant* also at that time.

In the Hebrew Canon these three Divisions contain twenty-four Books, in the following *order:—*

(i) "The Law" (*Torah*).

1. Genesis
2. Exodus
3. Leviticus
4. Numbers
5. Deuteronomy

These *five* books form the *Pentateuch.*

(ii) "The Prophets" (*Nevîim*).

6. Joshua
7. Judges
8. Samuel
9. Kings

"*The Former Prophets*" (Zech. vii.).

10. Isaiah
11. Jeremiah
12. Ezekiel
13. The Minor Prophets

The Latter Prophets.

[1] See a pamphlet on this subject, by the same author, entitled *The Names and Order of the Books of the Old Testament.*

(iii) "The Psalms" (*K'thuvim*) or the [other] writings.

14. Psalms
15. Proverbs
16. Job
17. Song of Songs
18. Ruth
19. Lamentations
20. Ecclesiastes
21. Esther
22. Daniel
23. Ezra–Nehemiah
24. Chronicles

The Five "*Megilloth*" (or scrolls).

This is how the Books are *rightly divided* in the Hebrew Bible. And it is sad to find so many good men exercising their ingenuity in order to find some Divine spiritual teaching in the utterly human and different order of the Books given in the Translations. One actually manufactures "five Pentateuch's," quite dislocating the Books of the Bible ; and he arbitrarily re-arranges them to suit his theory. Another divides them by re-arranging them in what he conceives to be the *chronological* order, which results, among other calamities, in the Psalms being dispersed among the Historical Books.

The "Higher" Critics would have us make a Hexateuch instead of a Pentateuch.

We fear it is hopeless ever to look for the books to be rightly divided and arranged in the order of the Hebrew Canon ; so we shall have to make the best of man's having wrongly divided the Word of truth from the very outset.

The number of Concordances and Commentaries and general works where reference is made to the present chapters and verses would be sufficient to make such a change impossible, however desirable it might be on other grounds.

Nevertheless, it is well for those who would study the Word of truth to have this information, and to be in possession of the facts of the case, even if the result is only to prevent them from attaching any importance to the present order of the books, and keep them from elaborating some scheme of doctrine or theology based on what is only human in its origin.[1]

(*b*) *The Books of the New Testament.*—As to the Books of the New Testament the problem presented is somewhat different. We find them in the Manuscripts generally in *five* groups: (1) the Gospels, (2) the Acts, (3) the General Epistles, (4) Paul's Epistles, and (5) the Apocalypse.

The order of these groups varies in certain MSS.; and the order of the books also in the different groups varies. There is, however, one exception which we have elsewhere pointed out:[2] the Epistles of Paul which are addressed to Churches are always in the same order as we have them in our English Bible to-day. Out of the hundreds of Greek MSS. not one has ever yet been seen where the Canonical order of these Epistles is different from that in which they have come down to us.[3]

We can therefore build our teaching on a sure foundation, though we cannot do so on the order of the other New Testament books.

3. *The Divisions of the Hebrew Text*

The Hebrew Text is divided (in the MSS.) into five different forms:—

(*a*) Into open and closed Sections, answering somewhat to our paragraphs. These were to promote facility in reading.

(*b*) Into *Sedarīm* or the Triennial *Pericopes;*[4] *i.e.*, Portions marked off: so that the Pentateuch is divided into 167 Pericopes or "Lessons," which are completed in a course of three years' reading. There are 452 of these *Seders*[5] in the Hebrew Bible, indicated by ‫ס‬, in the margin.

---

[1] *The Cambridge Companion* (p. 7) suggests another classification, based on the subject-matter (as is that of the Septuagint): (1) Historical, (2) Prophetical, (3) Poetical, (4) Didactic, (5) Sapiential, (6) Apocalyptic. It is not necessary to indicate the Books under these heads, as the Divisions are so intensely human as to be unworthy of our notice.
[2] *The Church Epistles*, p. 13, by the same author. Also Part I., ch. iii., § 6, *f.* below.
[3] *The Twentieth Century New Testament* has the impertinence to change this into a chronological order!
[4] Greek, from *peri* (around) and *koptō* (cut); a portion or extract. Pronounced Pe-ric′-o-pe.
[5] From ‫סָדַר‬ (*sadar*), *to arrange in order.*

(*c*) Beside these the Pentateuch was divided into 54 *Par'shioth*[1] or Annual Pericopes, by which the Law was read through once a year.

(*d*) The division into *verses.* The verses in the Hebrew Bible are of ancient origin, and were noted by a stroke (⊤) called *Silluk* under the last word of each verse.

These words were carefully counted for each book. Hence the Scribes were so called not because of their *writing* (from the Latin word *Scribo*), but they were called *Sopherim* or *Counters* (from the Hebrew, *Sopher, to count*). The Massorah gives the number of verses as 23,203.[2]

4. *The Divisions of the Greek Text.*

In the Greek MSS. of the New Testament there is an indication of sections in the margin, dividing the text according to the sense.

There is also a division of the Gospels ascribed to Tatian (Cent. II.) called *Kephalaia, i.e. heads* or summaries: these are known also as *Titloi* or titles. Ammonius, in the third century, divided the Text according to sections, known by his name: "The Ammonian Sections." In the fifth century Euthalius, a deacon of Alexandria, divided Paul's Epistles, the Acts, and the General Epistles into *Kephalaia;* and Andreas (Archbishop of Cæsarea in Cappadocia) completed the work by dividing the Apocalypse into 24 *Logoi* or paragraphs, each being again divided into three *Kephalaia.*

These dividings of the New Testament can be traced back to individual men, and are all essentially human.

5. *The Divisions of the Versions.*

(*a*) *The Chapters.*—There are other more modern divisions into CHAPTERS. These are quite foreign to the Original Texts of the Old and New Testaments. For a long time they were attributed to Hughes de St. Cher (Hugo de Sancto Caro). He was Provincial to the Dominicans in France, and afterwards a Cardinal in

---

[1] From פָּרַשׁ (*pārash*), *to divide.*

[2] See Ginsburg's *Introduction to the Hebrew Bible*, Trinitarian Bible Society, 7, Bury Street, Bloomsbury, London.

Spain: he died A.D. 1263. But it is now generally believed that they were made by STEPHEN LANGTON, Archbishop of Canterbury, who died in 1227.

(*b*) *The Verses.*—Hugo made use of Langton's chapters
and added subdivisions which he indicated by letters.
This was in 1248. ROBERT STEPHENS, finding these letters
inadequate, introduced numbers in their place in his
Greek Testament of 1551. This was the origin of our
verse-divisions, which were first introduced into the
English Version known as the Geneva Bible (1560), and
from that into our Authorized Version in 1611. These
verses do not correspond always with those of the Hebrew
Bible.

(*c*) *The Chapter Breaks.*—As to these chapter divisions,
they were not of Jewish origin; and were never associated
with the Hebrew Bible until A.D. 1330, when RABBI
SALOMON· BEN ISMAEL adopted the Christian chapters by
placing the numerals in the margin, to facilitate reference
for purposes of controversy.[1]

In many cases they agree with the Massoretic divisions
of the Hebrew Bible, though there are glaring instances
of divergence.[2]

It will thus be seen how very modern, and human,
and how devoid of all authority are the chapter and
verse divisions which obtain in the versions of the Bible
generally, and in our English Bible in particular. Though

---

[1] This appears from a note appended to MS. No. 15, in the Cambridge University Library. See Dr. Ginsburg's *Introduction*, etc., p. 25.

[2] Up to A.D. 1517 the Editors of the Printed Text of the Hebrew Bible closely
adhered to the MSS. and ignored the Christian or Gentile chapters.

The first to reverse this practice were the Editors of the Complutensian
Polyglot of CARDINAL XIMENES (1514-1517); but still confining the indications to
the margin, in Roman Numerals.

FELIX PRATENSIS was the first to substitute Hebrew Letters for the Roman
Numerals in his Edition printed by Bomberg, Venice, in A.D. 1517; though he
retained the Massoretic divisions.

JACOB BEN CHAYIM adopted the same practice in his standard Edition
(A.D. 1524-5); and it was continued down to 1571, when

ARIAS MONTANUS actually went so far as to break up the Hebrew Text, and
insert the Hebrew Letters (or Numerals) into the body of the Text, in his Edition
printed at Antwerp in 1571.

From this, the "pernicious practice," as Dr. Ginsburg well calls it, has
continued in the Editions of the Hebrew Text since printed, though it is discarded in his own Massoretico-Critical Edition, printed in Vienna in 1894, and
published by the Trinitarian Bible Society of 7, Bury Street, Bloomsbury,
London.

they are most useful for purposes of *reference*, we must be careful never to use them for *interpretation*, or for doctrinal teaching. They seldom accord with the breaks required by the Structure.[1] Sometimes they break the *connection* altogether; at other times they materially affect the *sense*.

As examples, where the chapter-breaks interfere with the *Connection* and the *Sense*, we may notice Gen. i. and ii., where the Introduction (ch. i. 1—ii. 4) is broken up, and the commencement of the first of the Eleven Divisions (or, "Generations") is hidden. This wrong break has led to serious confusion. Instead of seeing in ch. i. 1—ii. 3 a separate Summary of Creation in the form of an Introduction, many think they see two distinct creations, while others see a discrepancy between two accounts of the same creation.

The break between 2 Kings vi. and vii. should come after ch. vii. 2; that is to say, ch. vii. 1, 2, should be ch. vi. 34, 35.

The break between Isa. viii. and ix. is, to say the least, most unfortunate, dislocating, as it does, the whole sense of the passage.

Isa. liii. should commence at ch. lii. 13. This agrees with its Structure:

> A lii. 13—15. The foretold exaltation of Jehovah's Servant, the Messiah.
>
> B | liii. 1—6. His rejection by others.
>
> *B* | 7—10-. His own sufferings.
>
> *A* | -10—12. The foretold exaltation of Messiah.

Isa. lii. 1—12 should have been the concluding portion of ch. li.

Jer. iii. 6 begins a new prophecy which goes down to the end of ch. vi.

Matt. ix. 35—38 should belong to ch. x.

John iii. should commence with ch. ii. 23, thus connecting the remarks about "men" with the "man of the Pharisees."

John viii. 1 should be the last verse of ch. vii., setting in contrast the destination of the people and that of the Lord.

---

[1] See Part II., Canon II.

In Acts iv. the last two verses should have been the first two verses of ch. v.

We can quite see that Acts vii. is already a long chapter; still, the break between it and ch. vi. is unfortunate, because the connection between "these things" in ch. vii. 1 is quite severed from the "things" referred to in ch. vi.

The same is the case in Acts viii. 1. Also in xxii. 1.

Romans iv. ought to have run on to v. 11, as is clear from the argument, as shown by the Structure.[1]

In the same way Rom. vi. ought to run on, and end with ch. vii. 6, which concludes the subject. The commencement of ch. vii. 7, "What shall we say then?" would thus correspond with ch. vi. 1.

Rom. xv. 1—7 really belongs to ch. xiv.[2]

1 Cor. xi. 1 should be the last verse of ch. x.

2 Cor. vi. should end with vii. 1; for ch. vii. 2 commences a new subject, and leaves the "promises" of vii. 1 to be connected with the rehearsal of them in ch. vi.

In the same way Phil. iii. ought to end with ch. iv. 1 to complete the sense.

Col. iii. should end with iv. 1. Thus "masters" would follow, and stand in connection with, the exhortation to "servants"; and ch. iv. 2 would commence the new subject.

In 1 Pet. ii. 1 the word "wherefore" points to the fact that this verse is closely connected with ch. i.

2 Pet. ii. 1, in the same way, concludes ch. i., and the "false prophets" are contrasted with the Divinely inspired prophets.

In 2 Tim. iv. 1 the force of the word "therefore" is quite lost by being cut off from the conclusion of ch. iii.

Rev. iii., as a break, ought to be ignored, as it quite dislocates the seven letters to the Assemblies.

Rev. xiii. 1 belongs to, and is the conclusion of, ch. xii. The break is thus actually made in the R.V., and the correct reading of the Greek MSS. followed shows the close connection of the words "and he (i.e. Satan) stood upon the sand of the sea," with ch. xii. 17, and also with ch. xiii. as containing the result of Satan's thus standing.

[1] See *The Church Epistles*, by the same author.
[2] See Part II., Canon VII, below.

In the same way the break between Rev. xxi. and xxii. is unfortunate, as the real chapter-break should correspond with the Structure and should come between verses 5 and 6 of ch. xxii.

Other examples may easily be found, but these will be sufficient to show the importance of "rightly dividing the Word of Truth," even as to the Chapter Divisions.

(*d*) *The Chapter, and Running Page-Headings.*—When these chapter divisions are combined with (1) the *chapter headings*, and (2) the *running page-headings*, they become positively mischievous, partaking of the nature of *interpretation* instead of translation. It is needless to say that we may absolutely disregard them, as always aggravating the chapter-break, and often misleading the reader.

The *running page-headings* are a fruitful source of mischief. Over Isa. xxix. (as we have said above) in an ordinary Bible we read "*God's judgments upon Jerusalem.*" On the opposite page we read over Isa. xxx. "*God's mercies to his church.*" The same may be seen in the concluding chapters of Isaiah, both in the running page-headings and in the chapter-headings. But there is no break or change in the subject-matter. It consists of all "the vision which Isaiah saw concerning Judah and Jerusalem" (ch. i. 1). Here is a "dividing" of the Word. But, the question is, can it be called "rightly dividing" when God's "mercies" are claimed for the Church, and His "judgments" generously given over to the Jews? Such "dividing" of the Word can hardly be said to be "without partiality."

(*e*) *Punctuation.*—One other mode of dividing the Word as to its Literary Form is by Punctuation; which is a still more important manner of dividing the Word, as it seriously affects the Text by dividing its sentences, and thus fixing its sense.

The importance of this will be seen when we note that its effect is to fasten the *interpretation* of the translator on to the Word of God by making his *translation* part of that Word. It thus comes to the ordinary reader as part and parcel of the Truth of God, whereas it is absolutely arbitrary, and is wholly destitute of either Divine or human authority.[1]

The Greek Manuscripts have, practically, no system of punctuation: the most ancient, none at all; and the later MSS. nothing more than an occasional single point even with the middle, or in line with the top of the letters. Where there is anything more than this it is generally agreed that it is the work of a later hand.

So that in the Original Manuscripts we have no guide whatever to any dividing of the Text, whether rightly or wrongly. Indeed, in the most ancient MSS. there is not only no division at all, but there is not even any break between the words! So that we can find no help from the MSS.

When they came to be collated, edited, and printed, a system of punctuation was introduced by the respective Editors. Each one followed his own plan, and exercised his own human judgment. No two editors have punctuated the text in the same way; so that we have no help from them.

When we come to the English Authorized Version we are still left without guidance or help.

The Authorized Version of 1611 is destitute of any authority; for the Translators punctuated only according to their best judgment. But even here, few readers are aware of the many departures which have been made from the original Edition of 1611; and how many changes have been made in subsequent Editions.[2]

Some of these differences arise doubtless from oversight, but other changes have been made undoubtedly with deliberate intent. Who made them, or when they were introduced, no one can tell. A few, however, can be traced.[3]

---

[1] Sometimes a change of punctuation may be made through inadvertence or through ignorance. We have heard of 1 Cor. ix. 24 being read aloud thus: "They that run in a race, run. All but one receiveth the prize." The ignorance that perpetrated this failed to see the bad grammar which resulted in the last clause.

[2] These changes affect not merely punctuation, but the marginal notes and references, the uses of capital letters and italic type, orthography, grammatical peculiarities, etc.

[3] A full account of these may be seen in the Report of the Select Committee of the House of Commons on the Queen's Printers' Patent, 1859, a Blue Book full of interesting information; also in Dr. SCRIVENER's Preface to *The Cambridge Paragraph Bible* of 1873.

The Edition of 1616 was the first edition of the A.V. which shows any considerable revision. The first Cambridge Editions of 1638 and 1639 appear to have been a complete revision, though done without any authority.

The Edition of 1660 added many marginal notes. That of 1701 was the first to introduce the marginal dates, tables of Scripture measures and weights, &c.

The Edition of 1762 contained serious attempts at improvements made by Dr. Paris. He was the first to substitute a full stop for the colon of 1611 in Zech. xi. 7, after "staves." This edition considerably extended the use of Italic type ; and incorporated Bishop Lloyd's chronological notes.

Dr. Blayney's Edition of 1769 introduced many changes and many glaring errors which, unfortunately, have been followed without enquiry and without suspicion. These imperfections led to a great controversy, and a Public Enquiry, which included the policy of the Royal Patent and the working of the University Presses.

A Revision of the American Bible Society (1847—1851) prepared the way for our English Revised Version (1881—1885).

The "Advertisement" to the Universities' Edition, called "The Parallel Bible" (of the R.V. and A.V.), fully endorses all we have said :—

"The left hand column contains the text of the Autho-"rized Version *as usually printed*, with the marginal "notes and references of the Edition of 1611, the spelling "of these being conformed to modern usage. In the left "hand margin are also placed, in square brackets, *the* "*more important differences* between the edition of "1611 and the text *now in use,* whether these differences "are *due to corrections* of the edition of 1611 or to errors " which have subsequently crept in."

In spite of all these facts many ill-informed readers of the English Bible take the punctuation as "Gospel truth;" and not only build their own theories, and bolster up their traditions upon it, but treat as heretics, and cast out almost as apostates any one who dares to question the authority of this human interference with the Word of truth, if it should run counter to their Traditions, which are generally based on such human foundations.

In view of this indefensible attitude we shall have to show its utter groundlessness.

It is beside our present object to enumerate all the cases where the punctuation has been changed, though all are of interest, and many are of importance.

These changes may be classed under three heads.

(1) Where the Edition of 1611 is to be preferred to the later Editions.

(2) Where the changes in the later Editions are improvements; and

(3) Where there are other proposed changes which we suggest as being most desirable.

We shall proceed to give a few examples under each of these three heads.

(1) Changes in punctuation where the Edition of 1611 is certainly to be preferred to the later Editions.

1 Kings xix. 5, "And as he (Elijah) lay and slept under a juniper tree, behold then, an angel touched him." In 1769 this was altered to "behold, then." This comma after "behold" has continued to the present day.

Neh. ix. 4, "Then stood up upon the stairs of the Levites, Joshua, &c." In the Edition of 1769 this was changed to "Then stood up upon the stairs, of the Levites, Joshua."

Ps. lxxix. 11, "come before thee, according to the greatness of thy power: Preserve thou, etc.": instead of "come before thee; according to the greatness of thy power preserve thou." This change was made in 1769.

Ps. lxxxix. 46, "How long, LORD, wilt thou hide thyself, for ever?" instead of "How long, LORD? wilt thou hide thyself for ever?" The third comma of 1611 was removed in 1629,[1] 1638, 1744, 1769, and in the current editions.

In Prov. i. 27, the final colon of 1611—1630 after "cometh upon you:" is preferable to the present full-stop, introduced in 1629, and retained in the current editions.

---

[1] Not 1630. In 1762 this comma was replaced by a semicolon.

In Prov. xix. 2, the comma before "sinneth" should be restored, which was discarded in 1762.

In Prov. xxi, 28, the comma before "speaketh" should be restored, which was removed in 1769.

Hos. vii. 11, "a silly dove, without heart" instead of "silly dove without heart," since 1629; as though the last two words related to the dove, instead of to Ephraim.

John ii. 15, "and the sheep and the oxen." In 1630,[1] 1762, and current editions, a comma was introduced after "sheep."

John xviii. 3, "a band of men, and officers." In 1769 the comma after "men" was dropped; hence, the Roman cohort is not distinguished from the Jewish officers.

Acts xi. 26, "taught much people, and the disciples were called." This was so from 1611 to 1630, both clauses being dependent on the verb "it came to pass." Two things came to pass, (1) that the people were taught, and (2) that the disciples were first called Christians. But in 1638—1743 the comma was replaced by a semicolon, and in 1762 by a full stop: the latter being quite against the Greek.[2]

2 Cor. xiii. 2, "as if I were present the second time." This was so pointed from 1611—1762. But since 1769 a comma is inserted after "present," connecting "the second time" with the foretelling, instead of with the being present.

Col. ii. 11. The comma was removed after "flesh," in 1762, thus making one statement instead of two. The two clauses beginning with $\dot{\epsilon}\nu$ $\tau\tilde{\eta}$ (en tē)—"by the putting off," and "by the circumcision of Christ." That is to say: "In whom [Christ] ye are circumcised with a circumcision not done by hand, by the stripping off of the[3] body (*i.e.*, the flesh),[4] by the circumcision of Christ." Thus, this comma after "flesh" makes the last clause explanatory of the one preceding it: and shows that in Christ there is something more than the stripping off the old nature which is *sinner ruin;* even the flesh itself which is involved in *creature ruin.*

---

[1] Not 1638 and 1743.
[2] The R.V. goes back to the semicolon, but not to the comma of 1611.
[3] All the textual critics with R.V. omit "of the sins."
[4] Genitive of apposition.

2 Thess. i. 8, "in flaming fire, taking vengeance." By removing this comma in 1769 the "fire" is wrongly connected with the "vengeance," instead of with the being "revealed" in *v.* 7.

Heb. ii. 9. The comma was removed in 1769 after the word "angels," compelling us to connect "for the suffering of death" with Christ's humiliation, instead of with His crowning. If we rightly divide these words, the suffering will be practically put in a parenthesis by the two commas, thus : "We see Jesus who was made a little lower than the angels, (for the suffering of death crowned with glory and honour), that he by the grace of God, should taste death for every[1] man." This comma is wrongly replaced in the R.V.

Jude 7, "the cities about them, in like manner." The comma after "them" was removed in 1638 and 1699;[2] while in 1762 it was placed after "in like manner," thus increasing the error.

(2) *Changes in punctuation where the later editions of the A.V. are improvements.*

These hardly need enumeration, seeing that they are not likely to be missed. We may, however, note a few :—

Matt. xix. 4, 5. In 1611 the mark of interrogation was placed at the end of verse 4, but for many years it has been removed to the end of verse 5.

John xii. 20, "And there were certain Greeks among them, that came up to worship at the Feast." This needless comma after "them" was not removed till 1769.

Titus ii. 13, "The appearing of the great God, and our Saviour Jesus Christ." This misleading comma, after "God," lingered till 1769; thus hiding the fact that only one Being is spoken of, viz., "God even our Saviour:" *i.e.* our great Saviour-God, Jesus Christ.

Luke xxiii. 32, "And there were also two other malefactors, led with him to be put to death." This of course

---

[1] *I.e*, every, *without distinction,* not without exception.
[2] Not 1743.

practically classed the Lord Jesus as being one of three malefactors. But since 1817 a comma has been placed after the word "other," to avoid this implication.[1]

Acts xxvii. 27, "as we were driven up and down in Adria about midnight, the shipmen deemed that they drew near to some country." Not until after 1638 was the comma removed from after "midnight," and placed after "Adria"—"driven up and down in Adria, about midnight the shipmen deemed," &c.

(3) *Changes of punctuation which are now proposed as being most desirable.*

These proposed changes we consider to be improvements not only in the punctuation of the Edition of 1611 but of the subsequent editions. These suggestions are made from a better understanding, closer study of, and respect for the Context, as modifying or correcting traditional interpretations.

That we are more than warranted in such an attempt is shown by the Revisers in a note they affix to Rom. ix. 5. In this passage, in all the editions, the full stop is placed after the word "ever," thus: "Of whom as concerning the flesh Christ came, who is over all, God blessed for ever. Amen."

This text, being so weighty in witnessing to the Godhead of the Lord Jesus, was evidently distasteful to the Socinian member of the Company of Revisers: and, judging from the note placed in the margin, one can imagine what line the discussion had taken. All other marginal notes in the R.V. refer either to alternative *renderings* which affect the Translation, or to ancient manuscript "Authorities" which affect the Text. There is no example, so far as we have seen, where *interpretation* has been introduced; or where there is any reference to the interpretations of commentators. But here, there is the following lengthy marginal note, which exhibits the compromise reached by the Revisers and the Unitarian. They evidently declined to touch the Text; and

---

[1] This is far better than changing "other" to "others," as is done in the American Bible, 1867. This antiquated plural is continued in the American Edition of the R.V. of 1898.

consented to put this note in the margin. Its intention will be at once seen:

> "Some modern interpreters place a full stop
> "after *flesh*, and Translate, *He who is over all be*
> "*(is)* blessed for ever:[1] or *He who is over all is*
> "*God blessed for ever.* Others punctuate, *flesh*,
> "*who is over all*, God *be blessed for ever.*"

The object of this note is too painfully apparent; but it shows how important is the subject of *punctuation*. Moreover, it justifies us in not only calling attention to faulty punctuation, but in suggesting changes where improvements may be made, which do not touch vital truth, except to strengthen and enforce it. Whereas, sad to say, some of the changes made by the Revisers are, unfortunately, those which interfere either with the Deity of Christ, the Inspiration of the Scriptures, or the freeness of God's grace.

In 2 Sam. xxiii. 5, if we make the last clause a question instead of a statement, we get the clue to a better rendering of the verse.

As it stands in the A.V. and the R.V. it is difficult to make any sense of the verse, at all. Not seeing the Structure or the true punctuation, the Translators were obliged to translate the Hebrew word כִּי (*kî*), *for*, in four different ways: not that one way is necessary, for its usage is somewhat elastic. It may often connect the hypothesis or condition with the result, either as a reason or conclusion.

If we ask what the word "so" (in verse 5) means in the first line, we have the answer in verse 4, where we have a description of God's King; and David immediately adds that it will be even so with himself as God's King and with his house in virtue of God's covenant (in 2 Sam. vii.) with him and of the sure mercies of (or mercies made sure to) David.

In verse 4 we have an alternation, the first and third lines speaking of the shining forth of God's light from heaven; and in the second and fourth lines, its effect on the earth.

---

[1] What is to be done with the "Amen," in this case, is not stated.

2 Sam. xxiii. 4.

A | And He shall be as the light of the morning,
    B | When the sun ariseth,
A | Even a morning without clouds;
       B | When, from brightness and from rain,[1]
         | the tender grass shooteth forth out of
         | the earth.

Then David goes on to say that, as that is a picture of what it will be, when He that ruleth shall rule righteously among men, ruling in the fear of God; even so will it be with his house and kingdom in virtue of the Covenant of God.

In verse 5 the A.V. renders the word יִּכ ($k\bar{\imath}$) in these four ways:—

     "Although," "yet," "for" "although."

The R.V. renders them

     "Verily," "yet," "for," "although."

The Structure of the verse shows that the four lines are arranged as an *Introversion*, in which the first and fourth lines concern *David's house;* while the second and third lines are about *God's covenant.*

Now, if we punctuate the first and fourth lines *as questions* we may have this rendering, which certainly has the merit of consistency and clearness.

2 Sam. xxiii. 5.

C | "Verily, is not my house even so with God?
    D | For He hath made with me an everlasting
      | covenant, ordered in all things, and
      | sure:
    D | Now, this Covenant is all my salvation and
       | all my desire,
C | For, Shall He not make it (my house) to
   | prosper?"[2]

---

[1] So some Codices, with four early-printed editions, and the Sept., Syr., and Vulg. Versions. See Ginsburg's Heb. Text and note.

[2] Heb., *to shoot forth,* as the tender grass, as in line *B* above.

We may take other examples where improvements can be suggested :—

Isa. lxiv. 5, "Behold thou wast wroth, and we sinned: in them have we been a long time, and, Shall we be saved?" In this case the R.V. thus revises the punctuation of the A.V. to its great improvement.

Jer. iii. 1. The last clause is evidently another question, repeating a similar question earlier in the verse : "And yet shalt thou return unto me saith the LORD?"

Matt. xix. 28, "Ye that have followed me, in the regeneration when the Son of man shall sit on the throne of his glory, ye also shall sit upon twelve thrones, judging the twelve tribes of Israel." This was the punctuation of 1611, which was continued till 1629. But in 1630 a comma was introduced after "regeneration," which entirely alters the sense. It has, happily, since been removed from our modern editions. This improvement should be noted, and retained.

Luke xvi. 9, "And I; say I unto you ' Make to yourselves friends by means of the unrighteous mammon; that, when ye fail,[1] they may receive YOU into the everlasting habitations?' [No![2]] He that is faithful in that which is least is faithful also in much; and he that is unjust in the least, is unjust in much also. If therefore YE have not been faithful," etc.

The context clearly shows that Christ is *contrasting*, and not identifying, human and Divine modes of judgment. This context (*vv.* 10—12), and the logical conclusion of the parable, have no meaning whatever unless the commendation of the unjust steward's lord is set in contrast with the condemnation of Christ. These verses (10—12) are no mere independent irrelevant statement, but are the logical conclusion to the whole argument.

The reception into the "everlasting habitations" of verse 9 is set in contrast with the unjust steward's being received "into their houses" (verse 4); the principles

---

1 "*When it shall fail*," according to Lachmann, Tischendorf, Tregelles, Alford.

2 Beza's Latin and Grashop's English Version both put a full stop after "you." Beza begins the next sentence "Certe" (surely); Grashop begins it "Wherefore." We begin it "No!"

which govern admission there, are the opposite of those that obtain admission here.

Hence our Lord follows this up by adding the great lesson in *v.* 10: "He that is faithful in that which is least is faithful also in much! and he that is unjust in the least is unjust also in much. If therefore ye have not been faithful in the unrighteous mammon, who will commit to you the true riches? And if ye have not been faithful in that which is another man's, who will give you that which is our own."[1]

Luke xvi. 22, 23. As at present translated and punctuated, the words read: "The rich man also died, and was buried; and in hell he lift up his eyes." But if we substitute *Sheol* or *Hades* for "hell," then we have (as in Isa. xiv. 9—20) a representation of dead people talking; as we have of the trees talking in Jotham's parable, (Judges ix. 8—15). If we further observe the Tenses and Moods of the verbs, and repunctuate the passage, we have the result, as follows:

"The rich man also died, and was buried also in *Hades.* Having lifted up his eyes, being in torments, he seeth."[2] There is no "and" before "seeth." It is not an additional statement, "and he seeth"; but it is a second verb, depending on the participle "having lifted up his eyes."

This change in translation is necessitated by the Greek; and the change in punctuation is not suggested as a modern invention to support any particular interpretation: for it is that adopted in the ancient Vulgate translation,[3] which, though not the original text, and of no authority as a text, is yet evidence of a fact. It is punctuated in the same way by Tatian, *Diatessarōn* (A.D. 170) and Marcion (A.D. 145); as well as in the ancient Jerusalem Syriac Version. And the fact is that the first three words of verse 23 form, instead, the last three words of verse 22; a full stop being placed after the word *Hadēs:* while the word "and" is treated by this as meaning "also." So that the whole sentence would read thus: "But the rich man also died, and was buried also in *Hadēs.*"

---

[1] See R.V. margin.

[2] For the further interpretation of the parable as a whole, see *The Rich Man and Lazarus*, by the same author.

[3] "Sepultus est in Inferno," *was buried in Hadēs.*

"Buried also," implies what is only *inferred* as to Lazarus, meaning that the one was buried as well as the other. Whether the punctuation be allowed, or not, it does not affect the matter in the slightest degree. For that is where *he was buried* in any case. It affects only the place where he is said to lift up his eyes.

This is further shown by the fact that the three verbs "died," "buried," and "he lift up," are not all in the same Tense as they appear to be from the English. The first two are in the past tense, while the third is the present participle, ἐπάρας (*eparas*), *lifting up*, thus commencing the 23rd verse with a new thought.

Those who interpret this passage as though *Hadēs* were a place of *life* instead of *death*, make it "repugnant" to every other place where the word occurs, and to many other scriptures which are *perfectly plain, e.g.*, Ps. vi. 5; xxxi. 17; cxv. 17; cxlvi. 4. Eccles. ix. 6, 10. (See Canon VII., Part II. below).

Luke xxiii. 43, "Verily, I say unto thee, to-day shalt thou be with me in paradise."

This is the common punctuation, but, Is it correct? We have already seen enough to show us that we are dependent only and entirely on the context and on the analogy of truth.

The word "verily" points us to the solemnity of the occasion, and to the importance of what is about to be said. The solemn circumstance under which the words were uttered marked the wonderful faith of the dying malefactor; and the Lord referred to this by connecting the word "to-day" with "I say." "Verily, I say unto thee this day." This day, when all seems lost, and there is no hope; this day, when instead of reigning I am about to die. This day, I say to thee, "Thou shalt be with me in paradise."

"I say unto thee this day" was the common Hebrew idiom for emphazising the occasion of making a solemn statement (see Deut. iv. 26, 39, 40; v. 1; vi. 6; vii. 11; viii. 1, 11, 19; ix. 3; x. 13; xi. 2, 8, 13, 26, 27, 28, 32; xiii. 18; xv. 5; xix. 9; xxvi. 3, 16, 18; xxvii. 1, 4, 10; xxviii. 1, 13, 14, 15; xxix. 12; xxx. 2, 8, 11, 15, 16, 18, 19; xxxii. 46).[1]

---

[1] See *Things to Come*, Vol. VIII., pp. 44, 128; also *The Rich Man and Lazarus*, pp. 27—29, by the same author.

"Paradise" was the condition of the earth before the entrance of Satan and the pronouncing of the curse; so it will be the condition of the earth again when Satan shall be bound, and the Lord shall come and reign in His kingdom. It is called in Hebrew "Eden" sixteen times, and "The Garden" nineteen times. The Greek for these is *Paradisos* (which we have Englished "Paradise"). It is never used in any other sense than of a place of beauty and delight *on the earth.* Never of any place *above* or *under* the earth. "The Tree of Life" and "the river of the water of life" are its two earthly characteristics. The traditional idea of any other place is unknown and foreign to Scripture; and is the pure invention of fallen man. It comes down to us from Babylon through Judaism and Romanism.

We see it described in Gen. ii.; lost in Gen. iii.; its restoration pronounced in Rev. ii. 7; and regained and enjoyed in the New Earth (Rev. xxii. 1.—5, 14, 17).

The Lord answered the request of the dying believer, not by promising something for which he did not ask; but by granting him his heart's desire and giving him the request of his lips.

We therefore suggest the following translation and punctuation: "And he said to Jesus, Remember me, O Lord, when thou shalt have come in thy kingdom. And Jesus answered him, Verily I say to thee this day, with me thou shalt be, in Paradise."

But there is more to be noted in the word "to-day" than this. Mrs. A. S. Lewis, of Cambridge, has lately called attention to the reading of the ancient Palimpsest Syriac Gospels at Mount Sinai, in which verse 39 reads, "Art thou not the Saviour? Save thyself alive to-day, and also us."

This was the taunt of the other maléfactor who thus seems to have used the word "to-day." The faith of the other showed that he looked for something more than *present deliverance:* he believed in *future glory* in the coming of the kingdom.

Hence, in the Lord's reply to him, He takes up this word "to-day" to show that "to-day" was not to be the day of deliverance for either himself or others, but the day of death. But though He spoke on that day of death,

He gave the promise of future glory, in which the other malefactor had so blessedly confessed his belief.

In this case there was a special reason for the Lord's use of the word "to-day." It was to correct a mistake; and it was, in spite of *present* circumstances, to give the assurance of the coming *future* glory of the kingdom.

John vii. 37—39. As it stands in the A.V. and R.V. this passage is punctuated as follows:—

"In the last day, that great day of the feast, Jesus stood, and cried, saying, If any man thirst, let him come unto me, and drink. 38 He that believeth on me, as the Scripture hath said, out of his belly shall flow rivers of living water. 39 (But this spake he of the Spirit, which they that believe on him should receive. For the Holy Ghost *(pneuma hagion)* was not yet given, because that Jesus was not yet glorified)."

We have to notice first that there is no article with the second *pneuma* (or Spirit) in verse 39, which shows that what is "*given*" is the subject of the context, *(pneuma hagion)* and not the Spirit Himself, the giver.[1]

Then, we further notice, that the word "should" in the same verse (*v.* 39) is not the sign of any tense, but is a separate verb, ἔμελλον *(emellon), to be about to be.* Lit., "*were about* to receive"; (the latter verb "receive" being in the Infinitive Mood). As to the word "belly" it is put, by the figure of speech called *Synecdoche,* for *the whole person,*[2] which is much stronger than using the mere personal pronoun "him." It is a very emphatic "him."

In this case the "his" is generally taken as referring to the believer, for with our usual selfishness we take every good thing as applying to ourselves. But we submit that it is to be understood of Christ, who is the great fountain from whom the rivers of *pneuma* and grace and blessing flow; and not of the believer, who is only the receiver; and from whom a few drops may go

---

[1] Lachmann, Tischendorf, Westcott and Hort, and R.V. omit ἅγιον *(hagion), holy.* Tregelles and Alford put it within brackets.

[2] See Rom. xvi. 18: "For they that are such serve not our Lord Jesus Christ, but their own belly" (i.e. *their own selves*). Phil. iii. 19: "Whose god is their belly" (i.e. *themselves,* and what they can get). Tit. i. 12: "Slow-bellies" (i.e. slow persons, who by reason of large eating have grown stout, and therefore move slowly).

forth, but certainly not "rivers." With these preliminary observations we would punctuate it as suggested by Stier,[1] as follows:—

"If any man thirst, let him come unto Me; and let him drink, who believeth in Me! Even as the Scripture [concerning Me] hath said 'Rivers out of HIM shall flow, of living water.'"

It is not the one who drinks of Him who becomes the fountain; he is the *receiver* and not the *giver*. The Fountain is the one whom Scripture had already designated as the source of *pneuma*, and the channel whereby the rivers of spiritual grace and blessing should flow. It is not the individual believer who is the subject of the Old Testament prophecies; he, at the best, could only send forth one tiny stream of what he had himself first received; but it is Christ in whom are all our springs, who alone can say, "I will give unto him that is athirst, of the fountain of water of life, freely" (Rev. xxi. 6). The River proceeds "out of the throne of God and of the Lamb" (Rev. xxii. 1). In Christ are the hidden reservoirs of blessing, out of whose abundant flow believers receive their graces and gifts.

Not until Christ had risen from the dead, and ascended into glory, could these gifts be given. Hence, the explanation which is added in verse 39.

The Scriptures are many which speak of Messiah as the giver of these spiritual blessings. (Compare Isa. xii. 3; lv. 1. Ezek. xlvii. 1. Joel iii. 18. Zech. xiii. 1; xiv. 8.) These "rivers" of blessing flow not from the believer, but from the throne of God, from Zion, and from Him who there will sit as king.

The *pneuma*, or water, of which Christ is the giver, will be "in HIM" a well of springing water springing up, and flowing out as a supply for others (John iv. 14). The individual believer receives only enough for his own needs. He has no reservoirs from which rivers can flow forth for the supply of others.

John xii. 27, "Now is my soul troubled; and what shall I say? Father, save me from this hour, but for this cause came I unto this hour."

---

[1] *Words of the Lord Jesus*, in loco.

We would translate and punctuate this as follows: "Now am I[1] troubled; and why[2] should I say, 'Father, save me from this hour?' But for this cause came I unto this hour."

John xiv. 2, "In my Father's house are many mansions: if it were not so, I would have told you.[3] I go to prepare a place for you."

But why would He have told them about it if it were not so. The whole statement seems so inconsequent. But, if we punctuate it as a question, and take out the full stop after "you," we get a beautiful confirmation of what He had said and a further assurance of its truth: "In my Father's house are many mansions: if it were not so, Would I have told you I go to prepare a place for you?"

John xvii. 24. Is it clear as to which was "before the foundation of the world"? Was it the gift, or the love? Punctuated as in the A.V. it is the latter. But may it not well be rendered? "I will that they also whom Thou hast given me may be with me where I am: that they may behold my glory which thou hast given me, because thou lovedst me, before the foundation of the world." The sentence "because thou lovedst me" thus becomes the basis of the whole petition; and ὅτι (*hoti*) gets its usual consequential meaning, *because.*

Acts xv. 17, 18, should be punctuated, and translated as follows, according to all the critical Greek texts, with which the R.V., J. N. Darby, Rotherham, and other translators agree:

"That the residue of men may seek after the Lord.
And all the Gentiles, upon whom my name is called,
Saith the Lord who maketh these things known[4]
from the beginning of the world."

From this punctuation we learn that the mystery is not the subject here; for it was *not* "made known from

---

[1] The Perfect Tense: "I have been and am."

[2] So τί (*ti*) is rendered 66 times in N.T.

[3] So the current editions. The 1611 edition has a colon after "you."

[4] Margin: "or, *who doeth these things* which were *known*." The words "unto God are all his works" are omitted by all the critical Greek texts.

the beginning of the world"; but was the secret "hid in God," until specially revealed to the Apostle Paul.[1]

Acts xxiii. 8, "The Sadducees say that there is no resurrection, neither angel, nor spirit." The comma after "angel" in the editions from 1611 to 1630, having been removed in editions from 1629 to 1743, was restored in 1762; and should be retained.

Rom. viii. 32, 33, "Who shall lay anything to the charge of God's elect? Shall God that justifieth? Who is he that condemneth? Shall Christ Jesus that died?"

Here again the R.V. thus amends the punctuation of the A.V. and sets an example which we follow in

1 Cor. xv. 29. Our revised punctuation will enable the translation to be made more literal and more in agreement with the sense. A wrong punctuation often leads to wrong translation and necessitates liberties which have to be taken in order to make sense.

"Else what are they doing who are being baptized? [It is] for dead [bodies, or corpses[2]], if the dead rise not at all. Why are they then being baptized for dead [bodies]?"

The argument is here continued and taken up from verse 19, after the digression about resurrection, *viz.*, that if there be no resurrection baptism is worse than meaningless. It was merely baptizing dying bodies instead of believers who were going to live again in resurrection: it was only incurring trouble and suffering and persecution and risk of this life for nothing, if there be no resurrection. This illustration, therefore, takes its place with the other illustrations by which the argument is enforced in the following verses:—the "jeopardy" of verse 30 and the "fighting with beasts at Ephesus" of verse 32, connecting these three illustrations of the "misery" of verse 19.

There are other improvements which might be suggested, of less importance perhaps, but still serving to show the wide range which our subject covers.

Eph. iv. 12 has been punctuated in all the editions, "For the perfecting of the saints, for the work of the ministry, for the edifying of the body of Christ."

---

[1] See *The Mystery*, by the same author and publisher.

[2] οἱ νεκροί (*hoi nekroi*) with the article, as here, denotes *dead bodies;* without the article it means *dead people.* See *The Rich Man and Lazarus*, pp. 34, 35, by the same author.

This would be quite correct if the word "for" represented the same Greek word in each of the three clauses.
But the first is πρός (*pros*), *for*, marking the *subjective* purpose originating the gifts; the second and third are εἰς (*eis*),
for, marking the *objective* end for which the gifts were
designed.

The commas after the words "saints" and "ministry"
hide this beautiful distinction, and make three objects
instead of one (which is twofold). The punctuation should
be as follows: "For the perfecting of the saints, with a
view to the work of the ministry, with a [further] view
to the building up of the body of Christ."

So that, instead of three separate propositions, we have
only one—"The perfecting of the saints." And this one
is with a twofold end, *viz.*, the work of the ministry; and
this work has, for its ultimate end, the building up of
"God's building," which is the spiritual body of Christ.
(Compare ch. ii. 21, 22 with ch. iv. 2, 3.)

Hebrews x. 12 presents a peculiarly difficult example.
In the A.V. from 1611—1630 it read, "But this man after
he had offered one sacrifice for sins for ever, sat down on
the right hand of God." But in 1638 the comma was
removed, and placed after the word "sins," and it read
"for ever sat down," thus going back to the punctuation
of the Bishops' Bible of 1568. This is the punctuation
in the Book of Common Prayer to this day,[1] though
the Cambridge Bible of 1858 restored the punctuation of
1611 ("for ever, sat down").

There is something to be said for the older punctuation: "after he had offered one sacrifice of sins, for ever
sat down." This expression, translated "for ever," is not
the usual εἰς τὸν αἰῶνα (*eis ton aiōna*), *for the age*, or *for
ever*, but it is εἰς τὸ διηνεκές (*eis to diēnekes*), *for a continuance*, in distinction from *interruptedly*.[2] It is connected
not with the offering of "*sacrifice*," but with "*sat down*."

It asserts the fact that Christ's work as a Priest is
finished. He has not to stand up again to carry it on

---

[1] The Epistle for Good Friday is so punctuated in the original MS. attached
to the Act of Uniformity of 1662, and now preserved in the House of Lords.

[2] The expression occurs only in Heb. vii. 3, "abideth a priest *continually*";
ch. x. 1, "offered year by year *continually*"; ch. x. 12, *for ever* sat down" (where
it should clearly be *continually*); and verse 14, "hath perfected *for ever*" (where
it should be *continually*).

and continue it. Earthly priests "stood daily" and all day long, for there were *no seats* in the Tabernacle or Temple for the priests; but Christ has "sat down" not to rise up again for the purpose of sacrifice, for, having borne the sins of many, He will appear the second time without any reference to sin, but for the complete salvation of His people. Heb. x. 12 does not contradict Heb. ix. 28. The scope of Heb. x. 12 is not the coming of Christ, but the sacrifice of Christ; and this leads us to the conclusion that the older punctuation is right, which was, as we have said : "But this man, having offered one sacrifice for sins, sat down for a continuance on the right hand of God" (*i.e.*, "took His seat once for all" in contrast with the standing of *v.* 11).

This agrees with the scope[1] of the passage, which is the contrast between the ineffectual sacrifices of the Law and the effectual Sacrifice of Christ; between the "daily standing" of the priests with the continual session of Christ. This may be seen from

The Structure[2] of Heb. ix. 25—x. 18.

A[1] | ix. 25. Yearly sacrifices ineffectual, because "offered often " (πολλάκις, *pollakis*).

    B[1] ix. 26—28. Christ's sacrifice effectual, because offered "once for all" (ἅπαξ, *hapax*).

A[2] x. 1—4. Yearly sacrifices ineffectual, because offered "continually" (εἰς τὸ διηνέκες, *eis to diēnekes*), *for a continuance.*

    B[2] x. 5—10. Christ's sacrifice effectual, because offered "once for all" (ἐφάπαξ, *ephapax*), *v.* 10.

A[3] x. 11. Daily sacrifices ineffectual, because the priest "standeth daily" (καθ' ἡμέραν, *kath hēmeran*), "offering oftentimes" (πολλάκις, *pollakis*).

    B[3] x. 12—18. Christ's sacrifice effectual, because having offered "one" (μίαν, *mian*), He sat down "continually" (εἰς τὸ διηνέκες, *eis to diēnekes*), *for a continuance.*

---

[1] See below, Part II., Canon I.   [2] See below, Part II., Canon II.

Thus, in the members marked A we have what is in-effectual because temporary, set in contrast with the members marked B, in which we have what is effectual because permanent.

In the A members we have the priests, their sacrifices, and standing

> "often'
> "continually"
> "daily"

In the B members we have Christ, His sacrifice, and session

> "once"
> "once for all"
> "continually."

Indeed, the offering of sacrifices *eis to diēnekes* (ch. x. 1) is put in direct contrast with Christ's having sat down *eis to diēnekes,* in verse 12.

2 Pet. ii. 22. It makes all the difference whether we put a comma after the word "and." If we omit it we make one proverb; if we insert it we get two proverbs. "It is happened unto them according to the true proverb, The dog is turned to his own vomit again; and, The sow that was washed to her wallowing in the mire." The A.V. and R.V. and all the editions have no comma after the word "and"; and thus make only one proverb.

In any case, the contrast is between the *washed sow* at the end of 2 Pet. ii. and the *stray sheep* at the end of 1 Pet. ii. Both "return"; but the sheep, however dirty it has become, returns to its shepherd; while the sow, however clean it is washed, returns to her mire.

(*f*) *Parentheses.*—The Edition of 1611 abounded in parentheses. In the subsequent editions there has been an increasing tendency to discard them; and to supply their place by commas; or to ignore them alto-gether.

But parentheses are a means of increasing the empha-sis of ordinary punctuation; and, on that account, they require more careful consideration, rather than less; as the meaning can be either destroyed, changed, or made more clear by their use.

We shall class all under one head, without regard to the changes in the various editions; though we will note the changes where we can discover when they were made.

Many are already so marked, so that there is no need for us to notice them. (See Deut. i. 2. Matt. ix. 6. John ii. 9; iv. 8. Acts i. 15. Rom. iii. 8; v. 13—17[1]; x. 6, 7. Eph. ii. 5. Phil. iii. 18, 19. Col. ii. 21, 22.)

The true Parenthesis is an addition by way of *explanation*, and is complete in itself.

When it is not by way of explanation, but is an independent *additional statement*, complete in itself, the Greeks called it *Parembole* or Insertion; because it is more in the nature of a digression.

When it was by way of *feeling* they called it *Interjection*. (Ps. xlii. 2. Ezek. xvi. 23, 24.)

When it was by way of a *wish* or *prayer*, they called it *Ejaculation*. (Hos. ix. 14.)

When it was by way of *apology* or *excuse* they called it *Hypotimesis*, or under-estimating. (Rom. iii. 5. 2 Cor. xi. 23.)

When it was by way of *detraction* they called it *Anæresis*.

When it was by way of *sudden exclamation* they called it *Cataploce*. (Ezek. xvi. 23, 24. Rom. ix. 3.)

All these parenthetical additions are complete in themselves.

But when the addition is *thrown in*, as it were, casually, and is not complete in itself, the Greeks called it *Epitrechon*, or *Running along*.[2]

In many instances the Structures of Scripture practically place the member in a parenthesis between the two corresponding members; and this, whether it be a large complex member, or whether it be a single sentence.

---

[1] This was first so marked in the edition of 1769, and is continued in all the subsequent editions, though both the English and American Revised Versions reject it.

[2] See *Figures of Speech*, p. 470, etc., by the same author.

For example :—

In Gen. xv. 13, the words "(and shall serve them ; and they shall afflict them)" should be in a parenthesis, as is clear from the Structure.

> a | "Know of a surety that thy seed shall be a
> | stranger in a land that is not their's ;
>   b | and shall serve them ;
>   *b* | and they shall afflict them ;
> *a* | four hundred years."

Here, in the extremes, "a" and "*a*" we have the sojourn and strangership as a whole, while in "*b*" and "*b*" we have the servitude in Egypt. It is this servitude which is thrown in parenthetically ("*Epitrechon*"; *i.e., running along*); so that the sense reads on from "a" to "*a*"; and the *time* is not affected by the addition of what will happen to them in any part of that time.

Gen. xlvi. 26, "All the souls that came with Jacob into Egypt (which came out of his loins) besides Jacob's sons' wives, all the souls were threescore and six." This *Epitrechon* is thrown in to explain the difference between this number (66) and the number 75 in Acts vii. 14, which included "all his kindred," and was necessarily a larger number than that of Jacob's direct descendants.

Exod. xii. 40, "Now the sojourning of the children of Israel (who dwelt in Egypt) was four hundred and thirty years." This is an *Epitrechon* or remark thrown in as an additional fact to explain exactly who these people were. It thus saves us from making the mistake of thinking that they were in Egypt during all those 430 years.

Josh. vi. 1 is a true parenthesis or an independent statement complete in itself, conveying an additional fact ; but inserted in order to explain and introduce the words of the Captain of Jehovah's host, which are continued in verse 2.

1 Kings vii. 19 is a parenthesis and helps us to connect verses 18 and 20.

In 1 Kings viii. 39 and 42 we have two complete and separate parentheses.

In 1 Kings xii. 32 the words "so did he in Bethel" should be marked as a parenthesis, as they were down to 1769. It is the Figure *Epitrechon.*

1 Kings xxi. 25, 26, is a true *Parembole*, as is
Job xxxi. 30, which was rightly marked as such from
1611 to 1744. The brackets were removed in 1762.

In Ps. lxviii. 18 we have an *Epitrechon*—" yea, for
the rebellious also"—which marks and magnifies the free
grace of God, bestowed not merely on the unworthy, but
on those who were rebellious.

In Ps. cix., verses 6 to 19 are to be included in a
parenthesis as being the utterances of "the mouth of
the wicked," and the words spoken with a lying tongue ;
and "the words of hatred" (*vv.* 2, 3).

Then, verse 20 takes up verse 5 and says of all this :—

"This is the work[1] of mine adversaries (from the
LORD)
And of them that speak evil against me (Heb. my
soul)."

In Isa. xxii., verses 21—24 are to be included within a
parenthesis ; carrying on the thought to Him of whom
Eliakim is only a type ; and returning to the type and
the history in verse 25.

The Structure of Isaiah shows that chapters xxxvi.—
xxxix. are a parenthetical parenthesis, being the history
of HEZEKIAH'S siege and sickness ; corresponding with
chapters vii.—xii., which are also a parenthesis, being historic events and prophecies connected with AHAZ.[2]

Matt. ix. 20—22 is more an Episode than a *Parembole*.
But it was marked as a parenthesis down to 1762. The
Edition of 1762 rejected it.

Luke i., verses 55 and 70 should each be placed in a
parenthesis.

Rom. viii. 20. The words "not willingly, but by reason
of him who hath subjected the same" are an *Epitrechon*.

The *Ellipsis* must be supplied by the repetition of the
verb "waiteth," in verse 20 from verse 19.

---

[1] The Hebrew is פְּעֻלָּה (*p'ullah*), *work, labour, acts, deeds.* Not seeing the
parenthesis of verses 6—19, both the A.V. and R.V. are driven to render it
"reward." The fact that it is rendered "reward" in no other place shows that
our contention is correct. (See all the other occurrences of the word :—Lev.
xix. 13. 2 Chron. xv. 7. Ps. xvii. 4 ; xxviii. 5. Prov. x. 16 ; xi. 18. Isa. xl. 10 ; xlix. 4 ;
lxi. 8 ; lxii. 11 ; lxv. 7. Jer. xxxi. 16. Ezek. xxix. 20.)

[2] See *The Vision of Isaiah*, by the same author.

This is shown by

The Structure of Rom. viii. 19—21.

a | 19. Expectation.
 b | 20-. The reason : Creation made subject.
a | -20. Expectation.
 b | 21. Reason : Creation delivered.

This will be seen more clearly if it is set out in full, as follows :—

Rom. viii. 19-21.

a | "19. For the earnest expectation
of the creature waiteth for the } Expectation.
manifestation of the sons of God.

 b 20-. For the creature was
made subject to vanity, not
willingly, but by reason of } Reason.
him who hath subjected the
same ;

a | -20. [*waiteth, I say*] in hope, } Expectation.

 b 21. Because the creature itself shall be delivered from
the bondage of corruption } Reason.
into the glorious liberty of
the children of God."

Rom. ix. 2, 3. *The Epitrechon* should be punctuated as follows ; noting that ηὐχόμεν (*ēuchomen*) is put, by the Figure *Hyperbaton*, out of its place, in order to attract and call our attention to the fact that it is in the Imperfect Tense, which is generally well Englished by our word "used," *i.e.*, "used to wish" (*Lit.*, "was wishing"):

"I have great heaviness and continual sorrow in my heart (for I used to wish, even I myself,[1] to be accursed from Christ) for my brethren, my kinsmen according to the flesh." This shows us that Paul's sorrow was on account of his brethren ; and the *Epitrechon* is thrown in to explain why he had this great heaviness and continual sorrow. As much as to say, it was because he knew

---

[1] The Pronoun, here, is very emphatic.

from his own experience their terrible position; for when he was in their condition he knew what he "used to wish."

In 1 Cor. x. 3—5 there is a true parenthesis; an explanation of what precedes, and it is complete in itself.

"And all ate the same spiritual meat, and all drank the same spiritual drink. (For they drank of that spiritual rock following [*it*]; but the rock was Christ). Nevertheless, with most of them God was not well-pleased."

Here, there is nothing about following "them," as in the A.V. and R.V. and most translations (some putting it in brackets).

Two miracles are referred to: (1) The giving of the manna (related in Exod. xvi. 14); and (2) the gift of the water in the FOLLOWING event, or chapter (Exod. xvii. 5, 6).

This is clearly the obvious meaning of the Greek, both logically, grammatically, and historically. There is no occasion to go back to the Ancient Jewish but childish tradition; nor to charge the Apostle with so doing, as though he were not inspired.[1]

In a succession of miracles, one is mentioned, and then that which followed it.

The verb ἀκολουθέω (*akoloutheō*) is used of any kind of following; and of every mode of sequence. It is used of *logical sequence;* Aristotle says "If there are two, it follows (ἀκολουθεῖ, *akolouthei*) that there must be *one.*"

Longinus,[2] speaking of the Figure *Hyperbaton*, says, "It is a removal of words or thoughts out of their *consecutive* (ἀκολουθία) order."

Thus, it is the miracle and drinking of the water, which *followed* the miracle and eating of the manna; and not the water following the people of Israel throughout their journey. That would be no point in the Apostle's argument which called for the parenthetical explanation which he gives. His point was that both miracles taught *spiritual* truths, which their fathers did not see, either then, or in the days of John (John vi. 47—59).

---

[1] As Alford does, but not Ellicott.
[2] *De Subl.* s. xxii., p. 55, Toup. See also Plato, *Rep.* 332. II.

1 Cor. xv. 20—28 is a true *Parembole*, almost amounting to a digression. It must be carefully noted in order that we may closely connect verses 19 and 29, further consequences being stated if there be no resurrection. (See above, page 53).

2 Cor. iii. 7—16 is a *Parembole* or Digression, concerning the Old and New Covenants, in which the subject is broken off from verse 6 and continued in verse 17. This subject was the fact that "as the body without the *pneuma* (or spirit) is dead" (Jas. ii. 26), so the "letter" (or old Covenant) is dead without Christ; for "the Lord (Christ) is its *pneuma*."[1]

Eph. ii. 1 takes up the words in the middle of ch. i. 19, which does away with the necessity of all the italics in ch. ii. 1. If we observe this parenthesis concerning the fact and results of Christ's resurrection (in ch. i. 19—23) we connect ch. ii. 1 with i. 19-, and preserve the truth and teaching of the whole passage, thus:—

i. 19-, "That ye may know . . . what is the exceeding greatness of his power to usward who believe (. . .)," ii. 1, "even you who were dead in trespasses and sins."

Eph. iii. The whole of this chapter is parenthetical; and is a true *Parembole*, being complete in itself. This should be carefully noted, so that we may connect the "Therefore" of ch. iv. 1 with ch. ii. 22.

There is a smaller parenthesis within the third chapter, *viz.* from verses 1—13, verse 14 taking up the subject (which was broken off in *v.* 1) and repeating the words "For this cause."

Eph. iv. 9, 10 are also two parenthetical verses.

Phil. i. 23 is a true parenthesis, which is an addition by way of *explanation* to show why the Apostle did not know which to choose, "living" or "dying." The reason was that there was a third alternative, better than either, *viz.*, "the Return" of Christ (τὸ ἀναλῦσαι) (*to analusai*), when he would be with Christ. But, as to the other two (which he returns to in verse 24), he concludes that it would be better for him to remain in the flesh than to die; but not better than Christ's Return.

---

[1] See *The Giver and His Gifts*, republished as *Word Studies on the Holy Spirit*, by Kregel Publications, pp. 138-141.

We must put verse 23 in a parenthesis, and render it, "For I am being pressed out of (ἐκ, *ek*) the two, having an earnest desire for the Return (see Luke xii. 36[1]) and to be with Christ, for it is far, far better [than either]," and read on from verse 22 to 24.

Phil. ii. should commence with verse 27 of ch. i.; ch. i. 27—29 being a parenthesis.

Phil. iii. 2—14 is also a parenthesis, the fifteenth verse taking up the subject of the first verse.

Phil. iii. 8—10 is a *Parembole* within the parenthesis, and commences with the words "for whom I have suffered the loss of all things," etc., down to the end of verse 10. All this is a digression to show what he had gained in Christ Jesus his Lord as compared with what he had lost in giving up the Jews' Religion. Verse 11 would then read on from the middle of verse 8, thus:

"8 Yea doubtless, and I count all things but loss for the excellency of the knowledge of Christ Jesus my Lord: (. . . . .) 11 If by any means I might become partaker[2] of the out-resurrection from among the dead."

From what we have said under Division iv., Section 6, below, the Apostle may be referring to a fresh revelation of truth, which he received while in prison in Rome, concerning the prize of our "calling on high," and our removal thither; and this may be either explanatory of 1 Thess. iv. 13—18 or an additional and subsequent revelation pointing to a prior *removal* (as implied in the word *ex-anastasis*).

In any case, it shows that Paul was not desiring to obtain this, or any other advantage, by holiness of life, but by *believing God* concerning this *calling on high* (not "upward calling").

Col. ii. 21 and part of 22 are already rightly printed within a parenthesis, which should be carefully noted.

1 Tim. iii. parts of verses 14 and 15 should be read, "These things write I unto thee (. . .) that thou mayest know," etc.

---

[1] These are the only two occurrences of the verb ἀναλύω (*analuo*), *to return*. The noun ἀνάλυσις (*analusis*) occurs in 2 Tim. iv. 6, and is rendered *departure;* but the sense is the same, *return*, viz., the return of the body to dust and of the spirit to God; as in Gen. iii. 19. Eccles. xii. 7. See *The Rich Man and Lazarus,* pp. 30—33; *The Church Epistles,* p. 157, 158.

[2] See note on Phil. i. 21, Canon IV. Div. 2, below.

Hebrews i., ii., presents us with a beautiful example of the manner in which the Structure of a passage puts its various members into their respective parentheses, showing the true connections and logical continuations.

a | i. 1, 2-. God speaking.
> b | i.-2—14. The Son: God.   "better than angels."
a | ii. 1—4. God speaking.
> *b* | ii. 5-18. The Son: Man.   "lower than angels."

It will be seen from this that the member "b" (*vv.* 2—14) is practically a digression, concerning the Son of whom God had spoken in *v.* 1.

Similarly, the member "*a*" (ch. ii. 1—4) is a parenthesis standing between ch. i. 14 and ch. ii. 5. So that ch. ii. 1 (the word "therefore") reads on from the word "Son" in ch. i. 2. And ch. ii. 5 (the word "for") reads on from the word "salvation" in ch. i. 14.[1]

The study of the Structure of God's Word is therefore necessary, if we would discover its logical divisions, as well as the perfection of its literary divisions.

Heb. ii. 9, "But we see Jesus who was made a little lower than the angels (for the suffering of death crowned with glory and honour) that he by the grace of God should taste death for every[2] man."

This parenthesis teaches us that the Lord Jesus was crowned with glory and honour for the suffering of death. At His Transfiguration we see Him so crowned (2 Pet. i. 17).[3]

We have already included this passage under the former division on Punctuation (see page 42, above).

1 Pet. i. 3—5. These verses are parenthetical, verse 6 being the continuation of verse 2.

In 2 Pet. i. 19 the *Epitrechon* should be thus carefully marked: "Whereunto (*i.e.*, to the prophetic Word) ye do well that ye take heed (as unto a light that shineth in a dark place, until the Day dawn and the Day-star arise) in your hearts."

---

[1] See Part II., Canon II., below.

[2] *Without distinction*, not without exception : this epistle being written to *Hebrew* believers.

[3] See separate pamphlet on *The Transfiguration*, by the same author.

The words "in your hearts" must be connected with the words "ye do well to take heed," and not with the dawning of the coming Day or with the rising of the Morning Star. That rising will not be in our hearts, but it will be Christ's glorious manifestation to Israel and to the world (Luke i. 78. Rev. xxii. 16).

This world is a dark place, and the prophetic word is the only light in it to which we do well to "take heed in our hearts."

Tradition says that Prophecy is a dark place, and that we do well to avoid it. But this only proves the truth of the Scripture in which Jehovah declares, "My thoughts are not your thoughts, neither are your ways my ways, saith the LORD" (Isa. lv. 8).

These examples will be sufficient to show the importance of this branch of "rightly dividing the Word of truth," as to its Literary Form.

ii. RIGHTLY DIVIDING THE WORD AS TO ITS SUBJECT-MATTER.

It is the common belief that every part of the Bible is to be interpreted directly as referring to the Church of God; or as pertaining to every person, at every stage of the world's history.

This neglect of the precept to rightly divide it is an effectual bar to the right understanding of it, and to our enjoyment in its study.

This non-understanding of the Word is the explanation of its neglect, and this neglect is the reason why so many who should be feeding on the spiritual food of the Word are so ill-fed in themselves; and so ill-furnished for every good work (2 Tim. iii. 17).

While the Word of God is written FOR all persons, and FOR all time, yet it is as true that not every part of it is addressed TO all persons or ABOUT all persons IN all time.

1. *The Jews, the Gentiles, and the Church of God.*— Every word is "written FOR our learning," and contains what all ought to know: yet, its subject-matter is written according to the principle involved in 1 Cor. x. 32,

and is written concerning one or other of three distinct classes of persons, separately or combined:—

> "The Jews,
> The Gentiles, and
> The Church of God."

According to the general belief, everything that goes to make up the subject-matter of the Word of God is about only one of these three: and, whatever may be said about the other two (the Jews and the Gentiles), all is to be interpreted of only the one, *viz.*, the Church of God.

This comes of that inbred selfishness which pertains to human nature: which, doing with this as with all beside, is ever ready to appropriate that which belongs to others.

But no greater impediment to a right understanding of the Word could possibly be devised.

We are quite aware that, in saying this, we lay ourselves open to the charge which has been made by some, that we are "robbing them of their Bible."

But the charge is groundless; and it arises from a total misapprehension of what we mean, or from a perversion of what we have said.

It is necessary, therefore, for us to repeat, and to state categorically our belief that every word from Genesis to Revelation is written FOR the Church of God. There is not one word that we can do without: not one word that we can dispense with, without loss.

We deprive no one of any portion of the Word of Truth.

We protest against robbery in this sphere, as in all others.

It is not we who rob the Church of God; but it is they who rob the Jews and the Gentiles. We would fain restore stolen property to the rightful owners; property which has been stolen by the very persons who charge us with robbery!

We may indeed retort in the words of Rom. ii. 21: "Thou that preachest a man should not steal, Dost thou steal?"

We are prepared to make this counter-charge, **and to** sustain it.

The charge against us we disclaim; while those who make it are themselves guilty of the very offence for which they condemn us.

We hold that what is written to and about the Jew, belongs to and must be interpreted of the Jew.

We hold that what is written of and about the Gentile, belongs to and must be interpreted of the Gentile.

We hold that what is written to and about the Church of God, belongs to and must be interpreted of the Church of God.

Is this robbery? or, Is it justice?

Is it stealing? or, Is it restitution?

Evidence of the misappropriation (to use a milder term) is furnished by the Bible which lies open before us, to which we have already referred in speaking of the page-headings of Isa. xxix. and xxx, in our current editions of the English Bibles, in which the former is declared to be "*Judgment upon Jerusalem*"; and the latter, "*God's mercies to his church.*" (See page 28.)

What is this but not only wrongly dividing the Word of truth, but the introduction of error, by robbing Jerusalem of her promised "mercies" and appropriating these stolen mercies to the Church? while the "judgments" are left for Jerusalem, just as burglars take away what is portable, and leave behind what they do not want or cannot carry away.

We believe God when He says that the Visions shown to Isaiah were "CONCERNING Judah and Jerusalem" (Isa. i. 1).

True, they were written FOR us; and "for our learning" (Rom. xv. 4); but they are not addressed TO us, or written CONCERNING us, but "concerning Judah and Jerusalem."

It would be an act of dishonesty, therefore, for us thus to appropriate, by interpreting of ourselves, that which was spoken of Israel.

In like manner, if we take, as some do, the words of the Epistle to the Ephesians as though they were written to or concerning the Gentiles (or the unconverted world), then we not only rob the Church of God of its most precious heritage, but we teach the "universal Fatherhood of God" instead of His Fatherhood of only those who are His children in Christ Jesus.

It will thus be seen that unless we rightly divide the subject-matter of the Word of truth we shall not get the truth, but shall get error instead.

Every part of the Bible is written "concerning" one or other of these three divisions, or classes of persons.

Sometimes in the same passage or book there may be that which is concerning all three.

Sometimes a whole book may be concerning only **one** of these three, and the other two be altogether excluded. We may all three *learn* much from what is written of only the one; for the inspired, God-breathed Word is "profitable for doctrine, for reproof, for correction, for instruction," FOR all who shall read it (2 Tim. iii. 16). That which happened to Israel happened unto THEM for ensamples; "and they are written for OUR admonition" (1 Cor. x. 11). "Whatsoever was written aforetime was written FOR our learning" (Rom. xv. 4).

But while this is so, and remains true ; what we mean is that every Scripture is written CONCERNING one or other of these three classes; and is specially addressed TO that particular class. This class has therefore the prior claim to that Scripture. The *interpretation* of it belongs to that class; while the other two may apply it to themselves, and are to learn from it. But, inasmuch as it is only an *application* and not THE *interpretation*, such application must be made only so far as it agrees with the interpretation of those Scriptures which are specially addressed to and relate to such class. Otherwise we shall find ourselves using one truth to upset another truth ; we shall be setting what is true of one class in opposition to what is true of another class.[1]

All that we are concerned with now is the right dividing of the *subject-matter* of the Bible, which is three-fold. And the great requirement of the Word as to this is, that we should, and must, whenever we study any portion of the Word of God, ask the question,

CONCERNING WHOM IS THIS WRITTEN?

Whichever of the three it may be, we must be careful to confine and limit the *interpretation* of that passage to the class whom it concerns; while we may make any

---
[1] See further on this subject in Part II., Canon **X.**

application of it to ourselves so long as it does not conflict with what is written elsewhere concerning "the church of God."

We must not take that which concerns the Jew and interpret it of the Church. We must not take that which concerns the Church and interpret it of the world. We must not take what is said concerning the Gentile and interpret it of the Church.

If we do, we shall get darkness instead of light, confusion instead of instruction, trouble instead of peace, and error instead of truth.

To see this, we have only to notice the effect on such a Scripture as Rom. xi.

2. *The Gentiles.*—What child of God who has "access by faith into this GRACE wherein we stand" has not rejoiced "in hope of the GLORY of God" (Rom. v. 2), as he went on to learn, in chapter viii. 1, that there is "no condemnation to them which are in Christ Jesus"; and that "neither death, nor life, nor angels, nor principalities, nor powers, nor things present, nor things to come; nor height, nor depth, nor any other creature shall be able to separate us from the love of God, which is in Christ Jesus our Lord" (Rom. viii. 38, 39).

But when we turn over one leaf (or two, perhaps in some Bibles), we read, in chapter xi. of the "Olive tree," and of the solemn threats, and warnings to the branches (that had been grafted into it in place of the natural branches): "If God spared not the natural branches, take heed lest he also spare not thee" (*v.* 21): and "behold, therefore the goodness and severity of God : on them which fell, severity ; but toward thee goodness, if thou continue in his goodness ; otherwise thou also shalt be cut off" (*v.* 22).

Having read these words in the eleventh chapter of Romans, the reader remembers what he had read in the eighth chapter, and is perplexed. He imagines that they are both written "concerning" him, and the result is he cannot understand either passage. God says in chapter viii. that "nothing can separate" the child of God from His love, and in chapter xi. God tells him that if he does not take heed he will be "cut off."

How is the reader to solve the difficulty?

Only by "rightly dividing" this chapter according to the subject-matter; then, and only then, will he not only remove that which is the cause of the trouble, but at the same time he will produce new beauty, light, and instruction, out of the darkness and confusion.

He must ask what the subject-matter is about. Then he will look at the context[1] to see if he can discover it. He will go back to chapter viii., which he remembers was all about the Church of God; and, on looking at the next chapter (ch. ix.) he finds that the subject-matter is no longer about the Church, but about "the Jews"; the Apostle's "brethren according to the flesh" (ch. ix. 3). He finds it is the same with chapters x. and xi., and notices that in chapter xi. 11, the "Gentiles" are introduced. Indeed, in verse 13 the Apostle distinctly says,

"I SPEAK TO YOU GENTILES."

Thus he learns that those warnings and threats of chapter xi. 21, 22, are "for his learning"; but that they are neither addressed *to* him, nor are they written *concerning* him as a member of "the Church of God."

On following up this clue he begins to notice the figure of the Olive tree, and remembers that it is one of three trees to which Israel is compared in the Old Testament, the Fig tree being the symbol of Israel's national privileges; the Olive tree, of Israel's religious privileges; and the Vine, of Israel's spiritual privileges.

Here he learns that the natural branches are broken off for a season, and the branches of the wild Olive (as the Gentiles are called) are grafted in, also for a season.

Israel is shown to have lost their religious privileges, which have passed over to the Gentiles as such. Israel once had their own land, their own metropolitan city, their own government, their own religious privileges, which are summed up in this context (ch. ix. 4, 5), and in chapter iii. 1, 2, where the question is asked, "What advantage then hath the Jew?" and the answer is, "Much every way, but chiefly that unto them were committed the Oracles of God."

---

[1] So that this passage would serve equally well for an illustration of Canon I., Part II.

Up to the rejection (Acts xxviii. 25, 26) of Peter's offer (Acts iii. 19, 20) no Gentile could get a blessing except in connection with Israel. In Acts viii., ix., and x. we have three typical examples grouped together, as though to emphasise the fact by giving one from each of the three great branches of the human family : The Ethiopian (from Ham), Saul (from Shem), and Cornelius (from Japhet).

In the present dispensation no Jew can come into blessing except in Christ, in connection with Gentiles.

But in the New Dispensation of the Acts of the Apostles the Israelite branches were already being " broken off," and Gentile branches were already being grafted in. These latter had no greater privileges as Gentiles as to standing than Israelites (as Israelites). Hence the words of Rom. xi. 18-21 applied to all such; for though the doctrinal foundation of the Mystery had been laid in Rom. i.—viii., the Mystery itself was not revealed until it was committed to writing in the Prison Epistles (Ephesians, Philippians, and Colossians). The Epistle itself was not written until nearly the end of the Acts, and only a short time before Ephesians.

Now we can see the cause of all the confusion. The olive tree is almost universally taken as symbolizing the Church. We know of no commentary where this is not done. The Word of truth is not rightly divided as to its subject-matter; and, though the Apostle says, " I speak to you Gentiles," yet what he says is interpreted as addressed to the Church of God. Hence, the immutable truth concerning the standing of the Church of God in Christ Jesus is overthrown by what is equally true concerning the Gentile; and all this evil comes from not heeding the Divine precept of 2 Tim. ii. 15.

True, it is all written *for* us, *for* the Church, "for our learning." There may be a kind of *general application* for us as to our use of *any* privileges which God may have given us as individuals; but, the true interpretation as it concerns the Gentiles, as such, will alone give us the "truth" of this portion of the Word.

Oh, what confusion is brought into the Word, and what trouble is brought into our minds by not rightly dividing the subject-matter of this Scripture.

We have only to take up almost any commentary on this chapter, and we see at once the struggles that have to be made to bring Rom. xi. into harmony with Rom. viii. It cannot be done; hence it is that the effort is so painfully obvious.

Look, for example, at one of the best commentaries on Romans, by one of the best commentators (the present Bishop of Durham, Dr. Handley Moule). He sees the difficulty, and he grapples with it. He dare not ignore the truth of chapter viii., and yet he treats chapter xi. in a way that practically upsets it. His words are:—

"Here . . . we have man thrown back on the thought of his responsibility, of the contingency, in a certain sense, of his safety on his fidelity, 'If you are true to mercy, mercy will be true to you; otherwise you too will be broken off,' . . . Let him put no pillow of theory between the sharpness of that warning and his soul. Penitent, self-despairing, resting on Christ alone, let him 'abide by the goodness of God.'"

These words would be true if slightly modified and spoken of the Gentile, as such. But they are not true as addressed to "man," as such; still less as a warning to the individual child of God, who can never be separated from that goodness and love of God by all the powers of earth and hell combined (Rom. viii. 38, 39).

We could hardly have a more suitable and powerful example of the importance of attending to the one great requirement of "the Word of Truth"; as to rightly dividing its subject matter.

In the matter of letters, or epistles, it is very important in our social life to carefully observe the *address* written on the envelope. It makes for peace and harmony, and prevents awkward mistakes and misunderstandings.

It is a mistake that is sometimes made, and it may be that when we have opened a letter that is not addressed to us we commence to read it; and as we read on we find things said that are exceedingly interesting and most instructive; but we come upon other things which we cannot make out, and we find references to matters which we do not understand, and to circumstances with which we are unacquainted, because we are not the persons directly written to.

Then, if we are wise, we turn to the address, and there we discover the mistake we have made, and the cause of all our confusion. It is exactly so with

3. *The Epistles to the Dispersion.*—No Epistle has been the source of such confusion, and none has received such treatment as that written by James.

(*a*) *The Epistle of James* is addressed :—

> *To the Twelve Tribes*
> *which are scattered abroad.*

Doubtless they were believers, up to a certain point; but exactly what they believed, or how far they believed we are not told.

They evidently, as Jews, believed that Christ was the Messiah, and had a certain amount of light : but the question is, Did they, *as sinners*, believe in Christ *as their Saviour*; or know that "Christ is the end of the law for righteousness to every one that believeth"? It is clear from the surface of the Epistle that they did not have the standing of those who were "called to be saints": or of members of the spiritual Body of Christ, as set forth in the Epistles addressed to the churches of Ephesus, Philippi, and Colosse.

They were "Christians" as distinguished from Jews and Gentiles, but were they members of "the Church of God?" Who are the "ye" in chapter iv? Who are the "rich men" in chapter v. 1? The stand-point of the epistle is wholly Jewish. They were monotheists as appears from chapter ii. 19. Their place of worship was the "Synagogue" (ch. ii. 2, margin).

In chapter v. 12 the prohibition of swearing is according to the Jewish formula; and, in verse 14 the anointing with oil is in accordance with Jewish practice at that time.

Spiritual and vital Christianity is nowhere seen. Only twice is "Christ" named at all (ch. i. 1; ch. ii. 1). The word "Gospel" is not used, and the "Mystery" is unknown. The fundamental doctrines of the Gospel are not even alluded to: such as Incarnation, Atonement, Redemption, Resurrection, or Ascension.

The Morality of the Law is there (ii. 8, 13).   The coming
of the Lord as the Judge is there (ch. v. 8, 9).   Justification
by works is there (ch. ii. 20—26).

All the errors combated refer to Judaism.   Religion
(*thrēskeia*) is there, but it is shown that the works of mercy
and charity are better than all the outward forms of
religious worship.   Fatalism, formalism and hypocrisy,
arrogance and oppression, are specially dealt with; but
surely these are not the sins which distinguish and characterize the Church of God.

All the phenomena are Palestinian or Eastern, as we
may gather from the references to the early and latter
rain (ch. v. 7); to the fig, oil, and wine (ch. iii. 12); to
drought (ch. v. 17, 18); to salt and bitter springs
(ch. iii. 11, 12); and to the hot wind (ch. i. 11).

The Epistle is full of references to the Sermon on the
Mount, which (as we shall see below) has reference to the
past Dispensation, not to the present.[1]   We may compare

James i, 2 ; v. 10, 11 with Matt. v. 10–12.

„	i. 4	„	v. 48.
„	i. 5, 17 : v. 15	„	vii. 7. 11.
„	i. 9 ; ii. 5	„	v. 3.
„	i. 22–25 ; ii. 10, 11	„	v. 19.
„	i. 20	„	v. 22.
„	i. 22 ; ii. 14 ; v. 7–9.	„	vii. 21–26.
„	ii. 1–3	„	vi. 2, 5.
„	ii. 8	„	vii. 12.
„	ii. 10, 11	„	vii. 12.
„	ii. 13	„	vi. 14, 15 ; **vii. 2.**
„	ii. 14	„	vii. 21.
„	iii. 1 ; iv. 11	„	vii. 1.
„	iii. 12	„	vii. 16.
„	iii. 17, 18	„	v. 9.
„	iv. 3.	„	vii. 8.
„	iv. 4	„	vi. 24.
„	iv. 8	„	v. 8.
„	iv. 9	„	v. 4.
„	iv. 10	„	v. 3, 4.
„	iv. 11	„	vii. 1.
„	iv. 13–16	„	vi. 25.
„	v. 2	„	vi. 19.
„	v. 10	„	v. 12.
„	v. 12	„	v. 34.

_____
[1] See below, No. iv. of these sections.   .s.

From other parts of the Lord's teaching in connection with the Kingdom we may compare

James i. 14 with Matt. xv. 19.
„ iv. 12 „   „ x. 28.
„ v. 1   „   Luke vi. 24.

These phenomena in the subject-matter, when interpreted of the Church of God, and appropriated by those who are "in Christ," and "complete in Him," led to such confusion that, though the Epistle was in the primitive Syriac version from the first (cent. ii.), and was quoted as Canonical by the great Greek Fathers of cent. iv., yet there were always great doubts about its canonicity, and delays in receiving it.

These doubts were revived when translations of the Bible began to be made at the Reformation. Erasmus, Luther, and others questioned the canonicity of the Epistle; and it is well known that Luther went so far as to call it "a veritable Epistle of straw."[1]

The same difficulties and doubts are felt to-day. But they are all caused by interpreting of the Church of God that which is written to quite a different class of people belonging to "the Twelve Tribes."

The question is, Do we belong to "the Twelve Tribes"? Do we worship in a Synagogue? Is it our custom, as a People, to anoint with oil? Is not the "Assembly" of James v. 14[2] identical with the "Synagogue" of ch. ii. 2?[3]

The answers to these questions will show that the Epistle is not addressed *to* us, *i.e.*, *to* those who are "in Christ," and who are "the Church of God."

The moment we discern this, and rightly divide off, the class of persons addressed, there will be an end of all the laboured arguments to bring the Epistle of James into harmony with the Epistle to the Romans; and of all attempts to reconcile its teaching with that of Ephesians or Colossians. There will be nothing either to harmonize or to reconcile. James will be seen to be true in what he wrote to those whom he addressed, and Paul will be seen to be true in what he wrote. Both will be

---

[1] "*Eine rechte stroherne Epistel* " (Ed. of Germ. N.T., 1522).

[2] Which is translated "church" in A.V. and R.V.

[3] Which is translated "Assembly" in A.V. and "Synagogue" in R.V.

seen to be true in what they said to those to whom they were respectively inspired to write, if we rightly divide those portions of the Word of truth.

(b) *The Epistle to the Hebrews.*—We have another example, very similar to this, in the Epistle addressed to other Hebrew believers.

These were evidently more advanced than those who were addressed by James, and less, perhaps, than those who were addressed by Peter. All these three belonged to the same class; the *Diaspora*,[1] or Dispersion, of Israel.

The epistle of James was addressed to the *Diaspora.* Two were written by Peter (compare 1 Pet. i. 1 with 2 Pet. iii. 1): and another was written to them by Paul. This is distinctly so stated in 2 Pet. iii. 15, where Peter says "our beloved brother Paul also according to the wisdom given unto him hath written UNTO YOU:" *i.e.*, you believers among the *Diaspora.*

Paul was thus the writer of the Epistle to Hebrew believers among the Dispersion; for no other such Epistle of Paul has ever been heard of. Who these Hebrews were, or what they believed, or what their earlier standing was, may be gathered from Acts xxi. 20, where James says to Paul on the arrival of the latter at Jerusalem: "Thou seest, brother, how many thousands of Jews there are which believe; and *they are all zealous of the law.*" If they were "all zealous of the law," and continued to offer sacrifices for sins (as it is clear they did from *v.* 26), they could not have believed that Christ was "the end of the law for righteousness to every one that believeth" (Rom. x. 4); and they could not have known their standing in Christ. In Acts xxi. they are not distinguished from those who beat Paul (*v.* 32), and cried "Away with him" (*v.* 36): and their zeal for the law was so great, that, they not only observed it themselves, but would persecute and destroy those who forsook it (Acts xxi. 21—24; compare 1 Thess. ii. 14—16).

---

[1] The word διασπορά (*diaspora*), *a scattering* or *dispersion*. In the Septuagint it was used of Israelites dispersed among foreign nations (Deut. xxviii. 25; xxx. 4. Isa. xlix. 6, Heb. "preserved." Ps. cxlvii. 2). In the N.T. *Diaspora* becomes a proper title, *the Dispersion.* See John vii. 35 (*dispersed*), 1 Pet. i. 1 (*scattered*), Jas. 1. 1 (*scattered*).

It was to such Hebrews as these, who believed so little, and worked so much, that Paul was afterward inspired to write an Epistle.

It was written to those who had "a zeal for God, but not according to knowledge. For they, being ignorant of God's righteousness, and going about to establish their own righteousness, had not submitted themselves to the righteousness of God. For Christ is the end of the law, for righteousness, to every one that believeth" (Rom. x. 2—4).

To make this known to them the Epistle to the Hebrews was written. For Paul's name to have been prefixed to it, as it was to all his other Epistles, would have been (humanly speaking) fatal to its acceptance or usefulness, after the events recorded in Acts xxi. 17—40: events which ended his public ministry.

The Holy Spirit therefore suppressed Paul's name, and put the name of "God" at the beginning of the Epistle. Thus, "God," who had given the law, was the God who showed how it had been fulfilled and ended in Christ.

In spite of all this, Christians, to-day, take the Epistle as addressed directly *to* themselves; and, when they come to passages like Heb. vi. 6, and read about "falling away," or to ch. x. 26, and read how "there remaineth no more sacrifice for sins" for those who "sin wilfully," they are naturally greatly perplexed and perturbed : for all this is in direct contradiction to what is written and specially addressed to them concerning their own standing in Christ, in Rom. viii. and the other Church Epistles.

All this confusion comes from not "rightly-dividing" the class of persons *to* whom, and concerning whom, the Epistle to the Hebrews is addressed.

It may be applied by any and all believers who are still "zealous of the law"; and therefore it concerns such, and only such, to-day, whether Romanists, Romanizers, or Sacramentarians.

Of course it is written "for" us, yea, "for our learning."

In the Epistle to the Romans we learn the *fact*, that "Christ IS the end of the law for every one that believeth," but in Hebrews we learn *how* Christ BECAME the end of the law, and the end of Priests and Sacrifices. We learn the true meaning of the types of Exodus and Leviticus; which we could never otherwise have known.

But to interpret the Epistle to the Hebrews now of, or as addressed to, those who are "complete in Christ," "found in Him, not having their own righteousness, which is of the law, but that which is through the faith of Christ, the righteousness which is of God by faith" (Phil. iii. 9), is to produce only confusion and trouble. And, to take what was perfectly true of such Hebrew believers who were still "zealous of the law," and to understand it of those who have died to the law in Christ, is not only to disobey the precept as to "rightly dividing" the Word of truth, but it is to pervert that very Word and make it teach error in the place of truth.

Many other examples might be given; but several others will come better under our fourth division of this ONE GREAT REQUIREMENT.

In 2 Tim. ii. 15 God's children are compared to workmen, whose chief Work lies in connection with His "Word of truth." He who gave that Word has directed them how to work, so as to excel as His workmen; and that they may not be ashamed of their work at His coming. He has sent them a special message showing how they are to work in order to secure this happy result. He has sent them an inspired instruction so that they may find the "truth" they seek; and at the same time have the blessed assurance of showing themselves and their work, alike, "approved unto God."

iii. RIGHTLY DIVIDING THE WORD AS TO ITS TIMES AND DISPENSATIONS.

"Hear, O heavens, and give ear, O earth; For
Jehovah hath spoken" (Isa. i. 2).

1. *The Word "Dispensation."*

God hath spoken, "at sundry times," as well as "in divers manners" (Heb. i. 1).

And, if we are to understand what He has spoken, we must learn to distinguish, not only the various peoples to whom He has spoken, but the "sundry times" at which He has spoken to them, and also the "divers manners."

It is true that the word πολυμέρως (*polumerōs*) means strictly, *in many parts*, or *portions*. But it is equally true that these parts were spoken at different, or "sundry times"; so that the rendering of the A.V. is literal as to the fact, and to the sense—though not literal to the ·*Words*.

The "time" when God spoke "to the fathers" is manifestly set in contrast with the time in which He hath "spoken unto us." The "time" in which "He spake by the prophets" stands in contrast with the time in which "He spake by His Son." And the "time past" is obviously distinguished from "these last days " (Heb. i. 1).

So that Times and Dispensations are inseparable from the Divine Word; not only the Times in which the Words were spoken, but the Times of which they were spoken, and to which they refer.

These different times are called Dispensations.

The Greek word rendered Dispensation is οἰκονομία (*oikonomia*), and refers to *the act of administering*. By the Figure *Metonymy*, the *act of administering* is transferred to *the time during which that administering* is carried on.

The word itself is from οἶκος (*oikos*), *house*, and νέμω (*nemō*), *to dispense, to weigh* or *deal out*, as a steward or housekeeper. Hence the word was used of the management or administration of a household.

Our English word "Dispensation" comes from the Latin: *dis* (apart), and *pendere* (to weigh): *a weighing out*. We still use the word in this particular sense in connection with medicine which is *dispensed*, *i.e.*, weighed or measured out: the place where it is done being called "a Dispensary." [1]

The Greek word *Oikonomia* is transliterated in our English word *Economy;* and we still preserve its original meaning when we speak of Political, Domestic or Social

---

[1] The Church of Rome uses it of the giving out of privileges called "indulgencies"; but as these are generally privileges to *do without* certain things, or to do certain things without incurring the penalties or penances, the word comes to have the sense of "doing without" or "dispensing with."

Economy, etc. This was its meaning at the date of our
A.V. 1611, and it was used in the sense of *administration.*
But, like many other words it degenerated by its usage;[1]
and, as such administration was carried out rather
with the view to *saving* than spending, so *Economy*
came to mean frugality or thrift.

But the meaning of the Greek in the New Testament
is not affected by these modern changes.

It is always *Administration.*

In Isa. xxii. 21 it is rendered "government," and in
verse 19 it is rendered "station" (R.V. "office").

In the New Testament it is a question whether the
word is used in any other sense than that of *administration.* It is either the ACT of administering or of the
TIME during which such act of administration is carried
out.

The word occurs in Luke xvi. 2, 3, 4, where it is
rendered "stewardship."

In four other places it is rendered "dispensation."

In 1 Cor. ix. 17, Paul says that "an *administration*
is committed unto me."

In Eph. i. 10 we learn that God's secret purpose[2]
which He hath purposed in Himself is with a view to
(not "in") the Administration of the fulness of times
(R.V. the times, marg. *seasons*); when He will head up
(R.V. *sum up*) "all things in Christ."

In Eph. iii. 2 we learn that the "administration of
the grace of God" was committed specially to Paul, that
he might be the means of first making known the
Mystery (or Secret).

This is further shown in verse 9, where the rendering
"fellowship" should be *administration:*—"to bring to
light, or enlighten all [as to] what [is] the administration of the Mystery (or Secret)."

In Col. i. 25 we read "I am made a minister, according
to the administration of God which is given to me for
you, to fully preach the word of God."

In 1 Tim. i. 4, "neither give heed to fables and end-
less genealogies, which bring (R.V. minister) questionings,

---

[1] See below, Part II, Canon III., under the Biblical usage of words.
[2] This is the meaning of the words rendered, "mystery of His will.

rather than an administration[1] of God which is in faith."

These are all the places where the word *Oikonomia* occurs, and, in each, the idea is the same.

Our use of the term, now, in these pages, agrees with this usage; *i.e.* either *the act of administration;* or, by an easy transition (*Metonymy*), *the time* or *period* during which any special form of administration is carried on. This transference, however, is not necessary; for we may still think of Dispensational truth as being the same thing as *Administrational Truth.*

It is manifestly clear that God's principles of administration must always have been perfectly adapted to the "times and seasons" during which they have been respectively carried out.

God's principles of administration with Adam, before the Fall, must have been quite different from those with his immediate posterity after the Fall.

His administration with Israel "under the Law" was carried out on different principles from those which obtain now, during this present administration of grace.

These again are obviously quite different from those which will characterize God's coming administration in Judgment.

And these, again, will be necessarily quite different from those which will belong to the administration of glory in "the fulness of times" when all things shall be gathered together in one under the Headship of Christ (Eph. i. 10).

The present administration of God is in Grace; not in Law, Judgment, or Glory. It belongs to the time which is called "the Administration of the Mystery" (or Secret): that Secret (as the word Mystery means in the Greek) "which in other ages was not made known to the sons of men," (Eph. iii. 5). It was "hid in God from the beginning of the world" (Eph. iii. 9). It "was kept secret since the world began" (Rom. xvi. 25). But Paul was made the special administrator of all the truth

---

[1] It is *oikonomia* in the Received Text (1550), though the Translators of 1611 must have read it οἰκοδομία (*oikodomia*), for they translated it "edifying." It is *oikodomia* in Beza's Text (1565) and Elzevirs (1624).

connected with it. It was committed to him by God: and the Word of God could not be "*fully preached*" without it (Col. i. 25, margin). The Word of truth can be preached to-day, but it cannot be "fully preached" without the truth connected with this Mystery.

Here then, at the outset, we have various administra- tions suited to the various and corresponding Times and Dispensations, during which they were carried out, and in force. In "other ages" certain truths were hidden, which are contrasted with the truths which are "now revealed."

In the same way the Lord Jesus said, "I have yet many things to say unto you, but ye cannot bear them now" (John xvi. 12).

It is clear therefore that, while "God hath spoken," everything which He has said belongs to its own proper Time and Dispensation. These times in which, or con- cerning which, He spoke, must therefore be carefully distinguished. "The Word of truth" must be rightly divided in this important matter, or, clearly, we shall *not get the truth.*

If we read into one Time or Dispensation that which belongs to another, we must necessarily have only con- fusion; and, confusion so great, that it will be absolutely impossible for us to have any idea of the purpose or meaning of what "God hath spoken."

We are specially enjoined by the Lord not to separate what God hath joined together; and it is equally true that *we must not join together what He has separated.*

If we take what God said and did in one Dispensation, and carry it forward to another in which His Adminis- tration was on quite a different principle; or, if we take a truth subsequently revealed, and read it backward into the Time when it was hidden from the sons of men, it is impossible for us to understand what we read: we shall find ourselves taking what is quite true of one Time, and using it to contradict what is also true of another Time.

God deals not only with the three distinct classes of persons (the Jew, the Gentile, and the Church of God), but He deals with them in distinct ages and epochs;

and on different principles of Administration. If therefore we mix them all up together, and indiscriminately take what was said of one time and interpret it of another, we only create insuperable difficulties, and make it impossible for us to arrive at the truth of the revealed Word.

When the Lord Jesus in Luke xxi. 24 speaks of "the times of the Gentiles," He necessarily, by implication, contrasts these "times" with other times which are, obviously, "times of the Jews." He thus divides off, in a very marked manner, two of these "times," and sets one in contrast with the other.

Leaving these to be considered in their proper place and order, we must note that the right division of the subject-matter of "the Word of truth" will thus necessarily lead us in the second place to a right division of

2. *The Seven Times or Dispensations.*

We shall find that there are at least seven distinct Administrations each having its own beginning and ending clearly revealed and marked off.

These seven are, in turn, characterized by the principles of God's Administration, which mark all that He said and did during each special and distinct period.

We have for instance, the Theocratic Administration suited to the time of Innocence before the Fall (Gen. i. ii.).

We have the Patriarchal Administration suited to mankind after the Fall, but before the Law was given (Gen. iv.—Exod. xx.).

We have the Legal Administration suited only to Israel under the Law.

We have the present Administration of Grace which is for Jew and Gentile alike, *i.e.*, for individuals out of both, without the distinction previously made.

After this will come the Judicial Administration preparatory to the restoration of all things which were spoken before by the prophets.

Then will follow the Millennial Dispensation: ending with the Administration of Glory in the Eternal State.

These may be thus exhibited to the eye:

A | The Edenic State (Innocence)
  B | Mankind as a whole (Patriarchal)
    C | Israel (under Law)
      D | The Church of God. The Secret.
        | The Dispensation of Grace.
    C | Israel (Judicial)
  B | Mankind as a whole (Millennial)
A | The Eternal State (Glory)

We thus see that these times and periods of different Administrations have their correspondence: in which
  The *first* corresponds with the *seventh;*
  The *second* with the *sixth;*
  The *third* with the *fifth;*
  The *fourth*, occupying the central position, stands out alone by itself, and has no correspondence with any of the others.

The *first* and *seventh* correspond, each being characterized as Divine, in its origin and principles, God being in direct communion and intercourse with man; the one before the entrance of *sin*, and the other after the ending of sin.

The *second* and *sixth* are each occupied with mankind as a whole, the former being Patriarchal and the latter Millennial.

The *third* and *fifth* are occupied with Israel; in the former being governed under Law, in the latter judged "by the law."

The *fourth*, the Church of God, stands alone and by itself, as occupying the great central position, showing the "purpose of God"—round which all His counsels circle, and with reference to which they all exist according to His eternal purpose.

Let us look at them in order:—

(a) *The Edenic Dispensation.*—It is clear that the period beginning with Gen. i. 26 and going down to the end of Gen. ii. is perfectly unique. There is nothing like it until we come to the last, or seventh, Dispensation, which is the Eternal state. In these two there is only the innocence of man; and both are characterized by the absence of sin and the presence of God. God came down and communed with Adam, revealing Himself to him: and the mark of the Eternal state is given in the words, "The Tabernacle of God is with men, and He will dwell with them" (Rev. xxi. 3).

Adam was directly under the Divine *administration* and tuition of God Himself. God was his Teacher, revealing Himself and His wonderful works to Adam. He visited Adam at certain definite times, with audible sounds by which His coming was known (Gen. iii. 8[1]). He came for the definite purpose of teaching man. He brought the animals to Adam to instruct him (Gen. ii. 19, 20); He gave him a companion (Gen. ii. 21, 22); and we know not what else He did, and would have done, had not all this Divine communion been suddenly snapped and suspended by the Fall. Such direct communion of man with God has, since that moment, been in abeyance, and will continue to be so until the curse shall have been removed, and the Edenic state of Bliss find more than its counterpart in the Eternal state of Glory.

In this first Administration Adam was dealt with as innocent; and man can never be dealt with in a corresponding manner during all the succeeding Dispensations, until the curse and all its effects shall have been done away.

Man was then what is called "under probation." This marks off that Administration sharply and absolutely; for *man is not now under probation.* To suppose that he is so, is a popular fallacy which strikes at the root of the doctrines of Grace. Man has been tried and tested, and has been proved to be a ruin. Ever since that moment man has been dealt with as lost, guilty, ruined, helpless, unclean, and undone; and all this because of what he *is*, and not merely from what he has *done*. That is to say, he is not only a ruined *sinner*, but a ruined *creature*.

Man failed, just as Satan and Angels before him had failed under their trial. Man showed the same result,

---

[1] The Heb. כֹּל (*chōl*), rendered *voice*, means any *sound* or *noise* in an extensive sense ; e.g. *crackling*, Eccles. vii. 6 ; *trumpet*, Exod. xix. 16 ; *thunder*, Exod. xx. 18 ; *noise*, 1 Kings i. 45 ; *sound*, 2 Kings vi. 32 ; *proclamation*, 2 Chron. xxiv. 9.

and proved that, apart from the Creator, no created being could stand. By Christ, the Creator, all things not only *exist ;* but in Him only can they *consist* (Col. i. 16, 17).

The one test was THE WORD OF GOD. God had spoken; and the question was; Will man believe God or Satan ?

This was the one simple test. It was not what man whittles down by his tradition to the "eating of an apple;" but in Gen. iii. the first crucial words are, "Hath God said ?" (*v.* 1).

Satan is introduced to us as using these words, and as substituting *two lies* for what God had said :—

(1) "Ye shall be as God";
(2) "Ye shall not surely die."

These two lies are the foundation of Satan's old religion and man's "New Theology," and are the hall-marks of the coming Apostasy, under the Beast of Rev. xiii.

Our first parents believed Satan's lies, and their descendants have followed in their steps. Part of them believe neither God nor the Old Serpent; the bulk of them believe only Satan.

The teaching of demons is to-day embraced by the strictest of Evangelicals and Protestants, as well as by the Heathen, by Romanists, and by Spiritists: and they all unite in endorsing these two great lies of the Old Serpent. They all believe and hold (1) That man has within him the Divine ("Ye shall be as God"); (2) that "There is no death" ("Ye shall not surely die").

Man *was* under probation, and he failed in the proving.

Never again in any succeeding Dispensation has he been, or can he be thus tried.

Popular theology still teaches that "man is under probation." It is false! Man has been tried, and declared to be, in consequence, utterly ruined, and "at enmity with God;" he is not "subject to the law of God, neither indeed can be," and has "no good thing" in him.

Man needs no further probation to verify this solemn fact.

But we must return to our special point, which is this: All that was said and done by God in that first Administration, the Edenic State, was peculiar to, and appropriate only to that state, and to no other. It can never be characteristic of any other Dispensation.

God was man's teacher—God was His own Revealer. He gave man his trial and his test, and after these had done their work God pronounced His sentence on man, and his doom on the Old Serpent.

(b) *The Patriarchal Dispensation.*—In the second Administration, the one great principle on which mankind was treated was as a whole, and as having completely failed under the probation in which man had been placed. Having lost the Divine teaching, the Dispensation is characterized as the "Times of Ignorance" (Acts xvii. 30).

Mankind fails collectively, as man had failed individually; and furnishes another example of the fact that, no created being or beings can stand, apart from the upholding power of the Creator (Col. i. 16, 17).

All the words and actions of Jehovah were appropriate to this second Administration.

The "times of ignorance" are contrasted in Acts xvii. 30 with later times, which are distinguished by the words, "But now."

In those times God "overlooked" that which He could not overlook after He had given the Law; those things which, before the Law, were "sins," became afterward "transgressions."

The principles which governed God's Administration in those "times of ignorance," could not be appropriate for the times when He revealed His Law by Moses, and made known His will to the sons of men.

It is clear, therefore, that these Dispensations must be rightly divided; for even the future judgment of mankind is based on the distinction which we must make between these two periods, *viz.*, "without law" and "under law." See Rom. ii. 12.

> "As many as have sinned WITHOUT LAW
>> shall PERISH also without law;
> And as many as have sinned IN THE LAW
>> shall be JUDGED by the law."

It is evident that these two principles belong to the two different Dispensations (before and after the Law) respectively. They teach us that the same principles must prevail when the final judgment of those who have lived in both Dispensations shall come.

We may well believe also that the same *principle* will be acted on in the future judgment of those who are living in this present Dispensation; for there are, to-day, those who sin without having heard the Gospel, and there are those who have heard it and have not obeyed it (2 Thess. i. 8).

If we rightly divide these, and their judgments also, as announced in Rom. ii. 10, 12, we shall have the key to a problem which has perplexed many a child of God.

These then are the great principles which govern God's dealings with mankind; those that were "without law," and those who were "under law": those that are without the Gospel, and those who are under the Gospel.

It was not merely, or only, that one dispensation was "without law" and another "under law," but that there were those in each who knew the law and those who did not; those who obeyed and those who obeyed not.

And God dealt with mankind on this principle of judgment in all subsequent dispensations: for all were under His administration as to government.

The second Dispensation, that which succeeded the Fall, was governed by Patriarchal Law, as the following one was governed by Mosaic Law.

Both laws were given by God.

It is often supposed that before the Mosaic Law mankind were left to themselves.

But such was not the case. Mankind as a whole was in a sense "under law," but it was "unwritten law"; while Israel was under written law, "written by the finger of God" (Exod. xxxi. 18).

No sooner had our first parents been driven out from their first abode and passed from God's administration which corresponded with and marked their state of innocence, than the different character of His new administration was seen.

His first act was to point out THE WAY BACK to Himself and to peace with God.

Immediately after the Fall, and the loss of God's presence and teaching, the way back to His favour was opened by Himself.

(1) It is evident that *the way back* was declared to be *by sacrifice*, by substitution, and by blood.

Those who believed God obeyed the commands which He must have given and made known.

It was "by faith" that Abel brought his substitute—the Sacrificial Lamb—to suffer in his stead. But "Faith cometh by hearing, and hearing by the Word of God" (Rom. x. 17). Abel, therefore, with the rest of mankind, must have heard and known God's command. Abel obeyed it. It was "by faith": otherwise it would have been by fancy. Hence, Abel "obtained witness that he was righteous, God testifying of His gifts" (Heb. xi. 4).

God testified of Abel's offering by consuming it with "fire from heaven."

For only by such fire God "accepted" sacrifice (Ps. xx. 3, margin, and compare Lev. ix. 24. Judg. vi. 21. 1 Kings xviii. 38. 1 Chron. xxi. 26. 2 Chron. vii. 1): not by any fire emanating from or kindled on this earth. Only by such formal acceptance with "fire from heaven," did God "testify" of and have respect to Abel's gifts. Only by such acceptance did Abel "obtain witness that he was righteous." Only by such witness did God show, and Cain know, that He "had not respect" to the offering that Cain brought unto the Lord.

The fire fell upon Abel's lamb, instead of upon Abel; upon the substitute, instead of upon the sinner.

But it fell not on Cain's offering—for God did not accept it. It was the "fruit of the ground" (Gen. iv. 2, 3), the fruit of that which God had only just declared, "Cursed be the ground" (Gen. iii. 17).

Thus was the way back to God opened and made clear; and thus was man's disobedience manifested.

There was God's way, which Abel took; and there was man's way, which Cain invented. There have been but those two ways back to God from that day to this.

One was God's, and the other was man's.

One was by faith, the other by works.

One was Christ, the other was Religion.

One was by God's grace, the other was by human merit.

There never have been but these two ways.

This is God's way now, by faith through Grace—faith in Christ—the Saviour whom God has provided, which is summed up in the words,

"NOTHING in my hand I bring."

All other ways are one; for however they may differ, they are all alike in saying,

"SOMETHING" in my hand I bring.

They differ only in what that "something" is to be; and those who differ from them, as Abel did, are ever in great danger of getting killed, as Abel was. For nothing is so cruel as "Religion."

Thus the first act in God's changed administration after the Fall was to open the way back to Himself; and it is placed unmistakably on the forefront of revelation.

But there are many other marks as to the character of God's administration.

If we will search for its principles we shall find various words, expressions, and hints, casually dropped, which give us some insight into the principles which characterized that administration; for there is no attempt to give a detailed description of them. We are left to note and mark them for ourselves.

(2) It is evident that there was a *Place of worship*, a place set apart where access to the LORD was to be had.

At the moment of the Fall, when man was driven out, the LORD God "placed [as in a tabernacle], at the east of the Garden of Eden, Cherubim" (Gen. iii. 24). The word "placed" is שָׁכַן (*shākan*), *to place, station* or *dwell in a tabernacle.* Hence it is used of God's dwelling-place among His people.[1]

Hither Abel and Cain brought their offerings (Gen. iv. 3, 4; compare Lev. i. 3). Thither Cain "went out from the presence of the LORD" (*v.* 16). At its "door" lay the sin-offering which Cain might have brought as well as Abel (Gen. iv. 7).

---

[1] Exod. xxv. 8; xxix. 45, 46. Josh. xviii. 1; xxii. 19. 1 Kings vi. 13; viii. 12. 2 Chron. vi. 1. Ps. lxviii. 18. It is from this word that we have the word *shekinah,* that glorious light which was the symbol of God's presence in that tabernacle.

Thither Rebekah went to "inquire of the LORD" (Gen. xxv. 22).

Hence, the statement that certain things were done "before the LORD" expressed a great reality (Gen. xiii. 13; xviii. 22; xix. 27; xxvii. 7. Compare Exod. xvi. 9, 33; xxiii. 17; xxxiii. 7, etc.).

(3) *Certain persons* evidently had official positions. Shem was one who probably had charge of this tent or tents (Gen. ix. 26, 27).

Melchisedek was "a priest of the Most High God" (Gen. xiv. 18). Heads of families so acted (Gen. viii. 20; xii. 8; xxxv. 7).

Tithes were already paid (Heb. vii. 9).

The first-born evidently had certain privileges, among them the duty of offering sacrifices. Who else can "the young men" be whom we find so acting in Exod. xxiv. 5, before the consecration of Aaron and his sons under the Law, as priests of the nation as such?

If there were priests, so were there preachers also (2 Pet. ii. 5), and prophets (Gen. xx. 7. Jude 14, 15).

(4) *Certain official garments* appear to have been worn by those who thus officiated. What was the "goodly raiment of her eldest son Esau," which Rebekah stored so carefully, but clothes or garments afterward used by the priests under the Law? (compare Lev. xxi. 10. Exod. xxxv. 19. Lev. x. 6[1]). The word "goodly" is also used (though not exclusively) of *sacred* things in connection with the Temple (2 Chron. xxxvi. 10. Isa. lxiv. 11. Lam. i. 10[2]).

If this be so, we can understand why Esau was "profane" when he despised his birthright (Heb. xii. 16).

Joseph's "coat of many colours," instead of being (according to some) a peculiar coat of "gaudy patchwork," or, according to others, an ordinary "long tunic" in general wear, seems to have been a special garment by which Jacob designated him for one, at least, of the three parts of the birthright which Reuben had

---

[1] In all these passages the Hebrew word בְּגָדִים (*begādim*) is the same; but *not* so in Deut. xxix. 5, where Moses says that the ordinary clothes of the people, "your clothes waxed not old." Here it is, שַׂלְמָה (*salmāh*).

[2] Rendered "pleasant" in the latter passages.

forfeited.[1]   At any rate, the word rendered colours
(פַּסִּים, *passīm*) is always used of *colours*[2] and never
of *pieces;* and though Aaron's coat is not actually so
called, it was so in fact, as we see from Exod. xxxix. 1
and Exod. xxviii. 4, 39, where it is said to be *embroi-
dered.* The word rendered "coat" (כְּתֹנֶת, *k'thoneth*) is
also associated with the coats of the priests,[3] or with
those of royalty (2 Sam. xiii. 18, 19).

(5) Again, *certain forms and ceremonies* are also incidentally mentioned, which give us a still further insight
into the nature of the administration of that dispensation.
Thus we have anointing or consecration with oil (Gen.
xxviii. 18; xxxi. 13); building of altars (Gen. viii. 20; xii. 7;
xxxv. 1, 3, etc.); pouring out drink offerings (Gen. xxxv.
14); the making of a covenant by sacrifice (Gen. xv. 9—18);
the keeping of the Sabbath, before the actual proclamation of the Law (Exod. xvi. 23; compare Exod. xv. 25,
and Deut. v. 12); the offering of "seven ewe lambs" (Gen.
xxi. 31); the distinction between "clean" and "unclean"
(Gen. vii. 2; viii. 20); the prohibition of blood as food (Gen.
ix. 4); the execution of the murderer (Gen. ix. 6; xlii. 22);
the prohibition of adultery (Gen. xii. 18; xxvi. 10; xxxix. 9;
xlix. 4); the binding nature of oaths (Gen. xxvi. 28); the
obligation of vows (Gen. xxviii. 20—22; xxxi. 13); the sin of
fornication (Gen. xxxiv. 7); marriage with the uncircumcised
(Gen. xxxiv. 14; compare Exod. xxxiv. 16); honouring of
parents (Gen. ix. 25, 26); purification, or ceremonial cleans-
ing for worship (Gen. xxxv. 2); the birthright of the
firstborn (Gen. xxv. 31; compare Exod. xxii. 29 and Deut.
xxi. 17); and the marrying of the brother's widow (Gen.
xxxviii. 8).

What are all these but so many hints and glimpses
which reveal the existence of an orderly administration, which must have been Divinely promulgated,
and exactly suited for that dispensation? All was not

---

[1] According to 1 Chron. **v.** 1, 2, Reuben forfeited his birthright (Gen. xxxv. 22.
Compare xlix. 3, 4). This birth-right consisted of three parts. Levi obtained
the *priestly* office; as Judah had the part connected with *rule*, indicated by
the possession of the tribal "staff" or "sceptre," and as Joseph had the first-
born's *double portion*, in Ephraim and Manasseh, according to Deut. xxxiii. 17.

[2] Gen. xxxvii. 3, 23, 32. 2 Sam. xiii. 18, 19.

[3] See Ezra ii. 69. Neh. **vii.** 70, 72.

confusion as the unobservant reader might suppose. Men were not left to themselves during that Patriarchal Dispensation.

But to bring the laws of that administration into another dispensation, either for the purpose of limitation or supplement, is to mix up together things which are perfectly distinct, and to introduce confusion where all is otherwise in perfect order.

(c) *The Israelite Dispensation "under Law."*—In the *third* Administration we have a totally different principle involved. All is changed by the giving of the Law. This *third* Dispensation stands out in contrast with the previous one, which was "without Law"; as it does from this present Dispensation, which is characterized by Grace.

The communications of God, and His dealings with Israel, were appropriate to, and in harmony with, the principles of His administration "under law."

If we read all that into this present Dispensation, and interpret it of ourselves, we at once place ourselves under a covenant of works, and practically deny our standing in grace.

Unless we rightly divide the Word of truth in this matter we shall be filled with confusion.

It was true, in that Dispensation of Works, to say: "When the wicked man turneth away from his wickedness and doeth that which is lawful and right, he shall save himself [Heb., *his soul*] alive" (Ezek. xviii. 27). But to *interpret* that of ourselves, now, is contrary to fact: and to do so is to flatly deny our true church-standing which declares, that we are not saved by works,[1] but by grace (Tit. iii. 5. Rom. xi. 6).

The Ceremonial Law was given to Israel; not to Assyria or Egypt, or any other nation. Any precepts, of course, that may be of universal application will be wisely applied. The commands as to the food to be used or avoided were neither meaningless nor arbitrary, but were given according to the infinite knowledge of God. It will be our wisdom, therefore, if we are guided by them

---

[1] If any think of Jas. ii. as contradicting this, let them turn to Jas. i. 1, and they will see that the Epistle is addressed "To the Twelve Tribes," and is therefore quite in harmony with that Epistle (see above, p. 73).

for our health's sake; but in no sense as being "under law."

The Ceremonial Law continued down to the destruction of Jerusalem, and the burning of the Temple, when it ceased absolutely, as it had already ceased relatively, by the death and sacrifice of Christ, which fulfilled the law (Col. ii. 14, etc.).

The four Gospels and the Acts of the Apostles do not belong to this present Gospel Dispensation of Grace, but they rather close up the Dispensation of the Law (the Acts being transitional).

Christ did not come "to found a church" as those assert who do not heed the difference between the various Dispensations. That is man's, and Rome's, constant assertion. But God's revelation tells us that "Jesus Christ was a MINISTER OF THE CIRCUMCISION, for the truth of God, to confirm the promises made unto the Fathers, and that the Gentiles (after Israel's salvation) might glorify God for His mercy" (Rom. xv. 8, 9).

Christ's coming had reference to the Jew and Gentile, not to the founding of a church.

The Jews rejected the Kingdom and crucified their king. And the Gentiles (as such) have not yet glorified God for His mercy.

A subsequent offer was afterward made by Peter, to whom "the keys of the kingdom" were given (not of the Church, but of the Kingdom). The Kingdom was again proclaimed in the Acts, and the promise of Christ's return on their national repentance was repeated (Acts iii. 19—21, R.V.).

But the command to repent was unheeded by the nation and its rulers; and so, in the Acts of the Apostles, we see the gradual transition taking place, until the final pronouncement of God's rejection of the nation is formally made by Paul in Acts xxviii. 24—28.

(*a*) *The Ecclesia: the Dispensation of Grace.*—In this the *fourth* Dispensation neither Jews nor Gentiles are dealt with *as such:* but, individuals, both "transgressors" of the Jews and "sinners of the Gentiles," are called out, and made into a new body, a third People, called "the Church of God," in which now "there is neither Jew nor Gentile

. . . but all are one in Christ Jesus"; being baptized into the Body of Christ, not with the old *material* element of water, but with the new spiritual medium or element of *pneuma hagion* (Gal. iii. 27, 28).

All this had been kept secret until it was revealed to Paul and made known by the prophets and apostles in "prophetic writings" (Rom. xvi. 25, 26).

Had it been made the subject of prophecy the Jew, to-day, could reply against God and say that he was obliged to fulfil prophecy. It was therefore "hid in God" (Eph. iii. 9). God kept the secret to Himself. What He would have done had the nation of Israel obeyed the command to repent, in Acts iii. 19, 20, none can tell. God is sovereign, and we may be perfectly sure that the Scripture would have been fulfilled. Nothing was un-foreknown, or unforeseen; for the members of the Church of God were "chosen in Christ BEFORE the foundation of the world" (Eph. i. 4). All we can say is that "the secret things belong unto God." Those that are revealed alone concern us.

One of these secrets, the "Great" one (1 Tim. iii. 16. Eph. v. 32), has been revealed; and we now rejoice in its revelation.

This Dispensation of "the Church of God," of "the grace of God," and of the "Spirit of God" commenced outwardly by the ministry of Paul, in the Dispensation or administration committed formally to him; and inwardly by the revelation of the mystery as further set forth in its fulness in those epistles which he wrote from his prison in Rome: Ephesians, Philippians, and Colossians.

This Dispensation will end by the members of Christ's body, the Church of the living God, being "received up in glory" (1 Tim. iii. 16); "caught up to meet the Lord in the air, so to be ever with the Lord" (1 Thess. iv. 17. Phil. iii. 20, 21). This is called in 2 Thess. ii. 1, "our gathering together unto Him"; and this glorious rapture will close this fourth Dispensation.[1] The one object, therefore, of this Dispensation is not, as is popularly

---

[1] See *The Pauline Epistles* and *The Good Deposit*, by the same author.

supposed, the conversion of the world; still less its social improvement: but the formation of the one spiritual Body of Christ by calling out those who were chosen in Him "before the foundation of the world."

To that end, and that alone, is this good news made known to-day in all the world. In no former Dispensation was such a Gospel ever preached; and in no subsequent one will the good news of such free grace be proclaimed.

Before this Dispensation, and after it, all is connected with man, and what he is, and what he is to do. But in this Dispensation it is a question of what Christ is, and of what He has done.

This Dispensation of grace will be followed by:

(e) *The Dispensation of Judgment.*—In the *fifth* Dispensation, which is characterized by judgment, Israel becomes once again the central object.

When the Church, the mystical body of Christ, has been "received up in glory" the day of grace will be over. And Israel will once more be dealt with, not again under law, but under judgment.

The present Dispensation is (apart from God's purpose in the election of grace) called "Man's Day" (1 Cor. iv. 3, marg.), because it is during this present period that man is judging. But, the next Dispensation is called "the Lord's Day"[1] (Rev. i. 10), because that will be the time when He will judge. Man's day of judging will be closed and the Lord's day of judging will begin.

Hence "the day of the Lord" is the day of the Lord's judging and ruling; and the first occurrence of the expression gives us its essential meaning; and the object and aim of that judgment.[2] It will be the day when

"The lofty looks of man shall be humbled,
  And the haughtiness of men shall be bowed down:
  And the LORD alone shall be exalted in that day."
    (Isa. ii. 11, 12, 17).

Whatever may be the dealings of God with men,

---

[1] See two separate pamphlets on *The Lord's Day* and *Four Prophetic Periods*, by the same author.

[2] See below, under Canon I. 5 and Canon V. ii.

and whatever may be His judgments, this is the end and aim and object of them all:

The abasement of Man

and

The exaltation of Jehovah.

The whole of that dispensation is called "the Day of the Lord." It is the day which has to do with "times and seasons"; with Israel and the Gentiles. But which has nothing to do with "the Church of God."

This is clear from 1 Thess. v. 1—5. That day cannot overtake the Church of God "as a thief," because the Church has nothing to do with "times and seasons." That day has to do with those whom it will thus "overtake."

All that is said and done in that coming dispensation is appropriate to, and in harmony with, the great principle which will characterize God's administration in that day.

It will then be right for Israel to rejoice over the judgments inflicted on all their enemies.

Then, the "Imprecatory Psalms" will be in their appropriate place.

That dispensation of judgment will have its own peculiar characteristics; and language is therefore used of it which could never have been used in any former dispensation.

Israel will not again be under law; but it will be under a "new covenant," when the stony or hard heart of flesh will be taken away, and a new heart implanted within them, and a new spirit imparted to them (Jer. xxxi. 31—34. Ezek. xxxvi. 24—38), making Israel, then, the only indefectible nation that the world has ever seen.

This belongs, with the Dispensation which follows it, to "the times of the restitution of all things which God hath spoken by the mouth of all his holy prophets since the world began" (Acts iii. 21).

So that, here again, we have certain definite times spoken of.

These "times of restitution" include the succeeding, or

(*f*) *The Millennial or Theocratic Dispensation.* — The *Sixth* Dispensation, in which mankind will again be dealt with as a whole. It will begin with the binding of Satan

(Rev. xx. 1, 2) and will end with the great white throne
and the lake of fire (Rev. xx. 15). A thousand years will
be the period of its duration.

The principle of God's dealings with men during these
Millennial days will be neither Law, nor Grace, nor Judgment; but Righteousness, Power, and Glory. It will be
the administration of Righteousness in all its purity. The
prayer for the coming kingdom will then, at length, find
its abundant answer; the kingdom of God will have come
at last; and His will will then be done on earth as it is
done in heaven.

That dispensation is characterized by the binding of
Satan. It is clear, therefore, that language peculiar to
that time would not be appropriate to any other preceding dispensation, in which Satan is not bound.

It stands alone, unique; and it issues in the last or
seventh Dispensation, which corresponds with the first
Edenic state, and may be called

(*g*) *The Eternal State.*—Very little is said about this
last. In this respect it is like the first. It begins at
Rev. xxi. 1, with "the new Heavens and the new Earth,"
and nothing is said about its end.

Beyond this, therefore, we cannot go. In these last
two chapters of Revelation we have all that can be known.

These, then, are the seven Times or Dispensations;
each of which has its own defined beginning and ending;
and its own special characteristics. It is necessary for
us to rightly divide them, and rightly to divide the Word
of truth which tells us of them.

3. *The Special Characteristics of the Dispensations.*

It may help us if we summarize these, by connecting
each with a definite characteristic word or thought.

(*a*) As to *man's condition* in each, it is, in the

> 1st. Innocence.
> 2nd. Without Law.
> 3rd. Under Law.
> 4th. Under Grace.
> 5th. Under Judgment.
> 6th. Millennial.
> 7th. Glory.

(*b*) As to the *Crisis,* or Judgment, in which each ends:

    1st. The Edenic state ended in the expulsion from Eden.

    2nd. The Period without Law ended with the Flood and the Judgment on Babel.

    3rd. The Period under Law ended in the Rejection of Israel.

    4th. The Dispensation of Grace will end in the Rapture of the Church, and "the Day of the Lord."

    5th. The Dispensation of Judgment will end in the Destruction of Anti-Christ.

    6th. The Millennium will end in the Destruction of Satan, and the Judgment of the Great White Throne.

    7th. Will have "no end."

It must be evident that, in all these seven Dispensations, we have a variety of different characteristics which demand the utmost care and attention which we are able to give them.

There are, however, two further matters on which to speak; for beside these distinct landmarks by which these dispensations are known, there are larger "times" which embrace or overlap more than one of these divisions.

4. "*The Times of the Gentiles.*"

We have "the times of the Gentiles," which not only embrace this present Church Dispensation, but stand specially in contrast with the Jews. They commence with Jerusalem falling under the power of Babylon; they continue during the whole period while Jerusalem is "trodden down of the Gentiles" (Luke xxi. 24); and they will end only when the Gentiles shall cease thus to tread down Jerusalem, and its streets shall be again trodden by its rightful owners, the People of Israel. Then those "times of the Gentiles" will be changed for *the times of the Jews.*

Those times therefore are not co-terminous with any of the seven dispensations mentioned above, but overlap.

They begin before the present Church period, and do not close until after it has ended.

These same times are referred to in Rom. xi. 25: "Blindness in part is happened to Israel until the fulness of the Gentiles be come in." This is usually spoken of as pertaining to the completion of the Church. But the Church is not in question here at all. It is the relation between the Jews and the Gentiles; and the Church is not composed of Gentiles as distinct from Jews, or of Jews as distinct from Gentiles. For it is made up both of Jews and Gentiles, who, on becoming members of "the Church of God," lose this distinction altogether, being made members of a Body in which now there is neither Jew nor Gentile. This is expressly stated in Gal. iii. 28. Col. iii. 11. (Compare Rom. x. 12. 1 Cor. xii. 13. Gal. v. 6. Eph. ii. 15.) This must therefore refer to the fulness or filling up of the *times* of the Gentiles; and the word "Gentiles" must be understood as being put for the "times" which they fill up.

Moreover, Israel will not be saved by the Rapture of the Church, but by the coming of "the Deliverer out of Zion, turning away ungodliness from Jacob." It is Isaiah lix. 20 that is being quoted in Rom. xi. 26, and not 1 Thess. iv. 16; and there is nothing about the "fulness" or completion of the Church in Isaiah.

Before the Deliverer comes there must be that from which Israel is to be delivered; and that will be the great Tribulation, "when the enemy shall come in like a flood." (See Isa. lix. 19—21).

It is clear, therefore, that Rom. xi. 25 refers to the same "times of the Gentiles" of which the Lord speaks in Luke xxi. 24.

5. *The Parenthesis of the Present Dispensation.*

There is another matter connected with these Times and Dispensations. This is revealed by our Lord's own action in the synagogue at Nazareth. (Luke iv. 16—20.) He stood up and read Isaiah lxi. 1, 2. He read the first verse; but, after He had read the first sentence in the second verse, "HE CLOSED THE BOOK, and he gave it again to the minister, and sat down." (Luke iv. 20.)

Why did the Lord close the book at that point? The answer to this question is the revelation to us of the great principle which we are now, and here, insisting upon. The next sentence belonged, and still belongs, to a yet future dispensation. "The acceptable year of the Lord" had come. But "the day of vengeance of our God" had not (and has not even yet) come. The Lord divided these two Dispensations off *by closing the book*, and that is what we must do if we are not to join together, and thus confuse and confound, to our own great hindrance and loss, that which God has separated and distinguished. But alas! most Christians insist on keeping that book open, and refuse to learn the lesson here emphatically taught and enforced by the Lord.

There is no mark in the Hebrew text to indicate such a break, which involves an interval of nearly 2,000 years: and yet the break is surely there.

As to "the acceptable year of the Lord," Christ could and did say: "This day is this Scripture fulfilled in your ears" (Luke iv. 21). But He could not have said it if He had read the next sentence, "and the day of vengeance of our God." And yet the whole of this present Church Dispensation, the present interval of the Dispensation of Grace, comes between those two sentences. Only a comma divides them in our English Translation.

This is because the Mystery (or Secret) of the Church was "hid in God," and had not yet been revealed to the sons of men. How then could mention be made of it? It was necessarily passed over. Hence the Lord "closed the book" and "sat down."

This was why the prophets who spoke and wrote "as they were moved by the Holy Ghost" (2 Pet. i. 21) "enquired and searched diligently what, or WHAT MANNER OF TIME (concerning Christ) the Spirit which was in them could signify, when it testified beforehand of the SUFFERINGS of Christ, and the GLORY which should follow" (1 Pet. i. 10, 11). There was nothing to tell them what length of "time" should elapse between "the sufferings and the glory"; whether the glory should follow immediately on the sufferings; or whether there should be any interval of time at all between them. Hence, their enquiry, and their search. The prophets themselves revealed the sufferings; they saw them, and, just as it is when one views the outline of a nearer range of mountains, they saw the outline of another range beyond them as they testified of the "glory": but what distance separated those two mountain ranges, or what valleys and hills, and cities and lakes, lay between them they could not see. In like manner the events which lay between the "sufferings" and the glory that should follow was not revealed either to them, or by them. *We* know, now, that nearly 1,900 years have passed since the first coming and the "sufferings" of Christ; but the "glory" has not yet been revealed. Notwithstanding this, many treat these times and dispensations as of no account, and of no importance in their study of the Scriptures. The majority of Bible Students do not "enquire" at all; they neither search, nor "search diligently," as to these times; nay, they even reproach those who would thus search. Those who, like ourselves, would thus humbly search are derided; and this special time between the present and the coming Dispensation has been nick-named by them "the Gap theory." But it is no theory at all. The action of our adorable Lord in the Synagogue at Nazareth when He "closed the book" was no "theory." He showed that there was a gap, and that gap was a *fact* and not a fiction.

We are content to follow His example and share His rejection when at Nazareth. We would learn the lesson that He there taught. We would "open the book," the Bible, like Ezra, and search, and try and find out why the Lord "closed the book" of Isaiah; and, like the prophets of old, would search diligently as to "what manner of time" is taught by the Holy Spirit of God in these Scriptures of truth.

In the English Bible there is only a comma between the "sufferings and the glory" in 1 Pet. i. 11. See also 1 Pet. iv. 13; v. 1; and Luke xxiv. 26, where we have the same two "times" spoken of, with the "gap" of our present Dispensation passed over, as silently as though to the inspired speakers and writers this Dispensation of the Church of God were non-existent.

This is why the closing words of the Four Gospels do not lead us on *into* this present Dispensation, but *leap over it.* Having been occupied with the proclamation of the Kingdom they "close the book," and when it is opened again, it is opened at the Apocalypse, where we see the Kingdom set up with Divine power and glory.[1]

The period during which the rejected kingdom is *in abeyance* is not taken account of in the four Gospels, for it had not yet been revealed.

It was one of "the secrets of the kingdom" spoken of by our Lord in Matt. xiii. 11, and then made known by Him.

The seven parables of the Kingdom in Matt. xiii. leap over this present Dispensation, as if it had no existence. They carry over the truths concerning the Kingdom, and continue them as though the Kingdom had never been in abeyance. To understand these seven parables aright we must entirely exclude the Church of God, and the period of its Dispensation, and read them without any reference whatever to it. We can then easily see which part of each parable belongs to the past Dispensation, and which part belongs to the next.

There are many places in Scripture in which this passing over of the present Dispensation is very plainly evident; and where, in our reading, we have, like our Lord, to "close the book." If we fail to do this, and if we refuse to notice these so-called "gaps," we cannot possibly understand the Scriptures which we read.

We give a few by way of example, placing this mark (—) to indicate the parenthesis of this present Dispensation, which comes between the previous Dispensation of Law, and the next Dispensation of Judgment[2] which is to follow this Present Dispensation of Grace.

Ps. cxviii. 22, "The stone which the builders refused (—) is become the head-stone of the corner."

Isa. ix. 6, "For unto us a child is born, unto us a son is given : (—) and the government shall be upon his shoulder : and his name shall be called Wonderful, Counsellor, The mighty God, The everlasting Father, The Prince of Peace." (Compare Luke i. 31, 32.)

---

[1] See further on this point in Section **II.** of Chapter **II.** of Part **I.**, page 16.

[2] *I.e.*, between C and *C*, page 84.

Isa. liii. 10, 11, "It pleased the LORD to bruise him; he hath put him to grief; when thou shalt make his soul an offering for sin (—) he shall see his seed, he shall prolong his days, and the pleasure of the LORD shall prosper in his hands. He shall see of the travail of his soul and be satisfied."

Zech. ix. 9, 10, "Rejoice greatly, O daughter of Zion; shout, O daughter of Jerusalem; behold, thy King cometh unto thee : he is just and having salvation; lowly, and riding upon an ass, and upon a colt the foal of an ass. (—) And I will cut off the chariot from Ephraim, and the horse from Jerusalem, and the battle-bow shall be cut off: and he shall speak peace unto the heathen: and his dominion shall be from sea even to sea, and from the river even to the ends of the earth."

Luke i. 31, 32, "And, behold, thou shalt conceive in thy womb, and bring forth a son, and shalt call his name Jesus. (—) He shall be great, and shall be called the Son of the Highest: and the Lord God shall give unto him the throne of his father David." [1]

All this shows us the far-reaching consequences of the Lord's example in the Synagogue at Nazareth. Far-reaching in the confusion which arises from not heeding it; and far-reaching also in the happy results of applying the same principle that He applied to Isa. lxi. 1, 2, in all the other passages where the present Dispensation is passed over, and indicated only by a comma.

This applies only to Scriptures where the two other Dispensations are actually referred to. But there are many where only one is in question; and more care is then required to detect it, so as not to interpret of one Dispensation that which refers to another.

God's dealings in each period correspond with its distinct character; and if we would understand those dealings we must be able, readily, to classify the truth appropriate to each.

This classification forms a subject quite distinct from the Dispensations themselves, and demands separate treatment, which we propose to give in our next chapter.

---

[1] Others may be seen in Amos ix. 10, 11. Dan. ix. 26, 27. Hab. ii. 13, 14. Zeph. iii. 7, 8. Zech. viii. 2, 3. Luke xxi. 26. See *Things to Come* for Dec. 1904, Vol. X.

iv. RIGHTLY DIVIDING THE WORD AS TO ITS DISPENSA-
TIONAL TRUTH AND TEACHING.

This part of the great Requirement of the Word flows
from, and, at the same time, depends upon a thorough
understanding of the Times and Dispensations themselves.

When these are rightly divided then it will be easy
for us to keep the truth pertaining to each quite distinct.

There are whole departments of Truth which belong
exclusively to one or other of these Dispensations, and
not to the rest.

If we take a truth which belongs to one Dispensation
and interpret it of another it will lead not only to confusion in the mind, to discordance in the Word, and
uncertainty as to the truth; but it will lead to disaster
in the life. For, if the Word be not understood, there
will be no enjoyment in the study of it; consequently,
the reading of it will be neglected, and we shall cease to
feed upon it; our spiritual strength will grow weak and
we shall be unfit for God's service, beside being a misery
to ourselves.

Not only, therefore, must we rightly divide the Word
of truth as to its Times and Dispensations, but as to its
Truth and Teaching also: we must learn to appropriate
each truth to the particular Dispensation to which it
belongs.

Unless we do this we shall not "grow in knowledge":
for we are to increase in knowledge as well as in "grace"
(2 Pet. iii. 18).

To do this we must empty ourselves of all Tradition.
We must question all that we have thus received; and
be prepared to *unlearn* what we have previously been
taught by man if it does not recognize this great requirement of the Word of truth.

If we think we know, it will be impossible for us to
learn. If a vessel be full it is impossible for its contents
to be increased. We must make room for this blessed
increase by continually replacing what we have learnt
from man with what we learn from the Lord. And even
if what we have learned from man does *agree* with the
Word, then we must be prepared to learn it over again,

direct from the Word, so that the Truth may hold us, instead of our holding the Truth.

There are six distinct departments in which the truth of the Word has to be rightly divided in order to obtain its Teaching in connection with the Times and Dispensations.[1]

In order to keep this Dispensational truth and teaching rightly divided—

1. *We must not take Truth belonging to* ONE PART *of a* PAST *Dispensation and read it into* ANOTHER PART *of the* PAST.

The whole of the four Gospels belongs to the Old Dispensation; to the special period of Time during which the Kingdom was proclaimed and afterward rejected.

Truth pertaining to the proclamation period is not truth for the rejection period.

(*a*) For example, in Matt. x. 5, 6, we find the command, "Go not into the way of the Gentiles, and into any city of the Samaritans enter ye not: but go rather to the lost sheep of the house of Israel."

If the Word is not to be divided at all, rightly or wrongly, as some who oppose our teaching assert, then this command must be still binding on all the Lord's servants.

If it belongs to all persons, for all time, and for all times, then it is of universal interpretation. According to this, there ought to be no Missionary Societies for work among the Gentiles; but every Missionary Society should be only for the Jews.

But this is not quite the principle which pertains to and governs modern missionary operations.

Then there must be something wrong somewhere. Either this command remains in force and modern Missions set it at naught, and are carried on in defiance of it;

---

[1] All this refers, of course, only to *Interpretation*, and not to *Application.* This will form a chapter by itself when we come to consider the "Words" (see Canon X., Part II., below). We may *apply* all that is written so long as we do so in harmony with what is addressed especially *TO us* in this Dispensation. All was and is "written for our learning:" all is FOR us. But not all is addressed or applies TO us. We must not apply what was true of one Dispensation to upset what is true of another Dispensation.

or, there must be some explanation which shall exonerate such contumacy.

If it be said, in defence, that there are later commands, such as "Go ye into all the world and preach the Gospel to every creature" (Mark xvi. 15); then this is to argue (1) that the Word of God either flatly contradicts itself as to the fundamental principle of the missionary work; or (2) that *some* division must be made between the two commands.

But this latter is all that we are contending for. Only, the division which we would make does not ignore either command, but gives each its own due and proper place, significance, and importance. It does not exalt one at the expense of the other, but assigns to each its own appropriate sphere.

The former command, "Go not," etc., was given in connection with the proclamation of the King and the kingdom: but, when both had been rejected, and the King was about to be crucified, then this command was no longer appropriate to the changed circumstances.

Another command could then be given, "Go ye," instead of "Go not."

Both were equally true. The one was true as to its special reference to the lost sheep of the house of Israel; the other is true as to its general reference to all. But both commands were given in the past Dispensation.

(*b*) Luke ix. 3. In connection with the above command there were other precepts given. "Provide neither gold, nor silver, nor brass in your purses, nor scrip for your journey, neither two coats, nor yet staves" (Marg. Gr. *a staff*). Matt. x. 9, 10.

But when the kingdom had been rejected, and the King was on the eve of being crucified, *these commands were formally abrogated* by the Lord Himself, as being no longer suitable to the changed circumstances. The Lord repeats them, and asks whether they did not find His promise true: "When I sent you without purse, and scrip, and shoes, lacked ye anything? And they said, Nothing."

"Then said he unto them, BUT NOW, he that hath a purse, let him take it, and likewise his scrip: and he that hath no sword, let him sell his garment and buy one" (Luke xxii. 36).

Those two words "But now" announce the fact that even in that same Dispensation, with only a brief interval of time between them, those two commands are to be rightly divided.

The whole principle for which we contend is wrapped up in those two words "But now." According to this principle, that which belongs to one part of the past Dispensation, must not necessarily be interpreted of another part of that same Dispensation. How much more then must the truth and teaching of the different Dispensations themselves be carefully divided: when not only different circumstances prevail, but where the whole sphere has changed: not only where the people dealt with are different, but where the principle on which they were dealt with by God is changed.

And yet, in spite of these two examples from Matt. x. and Luke ix., the whole Bible is jumbled together, Law, Gospel, Grace, Judgment, Glory, Jew, Gentile, Church of God, Times and Dispensations, all confused in one vast tangle, till it is no wonder that thousands of readers, if they do not give it all up in dismay, neglect it to their own present loss of peace and joy and strength.

2. *We must not take Truth belonging to a PAST Dispensation and interpret it of the PRESENT.*

If we do we at once put ourselves under the Law, to which we died, in Christ, and from which Christ hath therefore made us free; the Law having no power over a man that has died.

(a) *Law and Grace.*—To those who lived under the Law it could rightly and truly be said: "It shall be our righteousness, if we observe to do all these commandments before the LORD our God, as he hath commanded us" (Deut. vi. 25). But to those who live in this present Dispensation of grace, it is as truly declared, "By the deeds of the Law there shall no flesh be justified in his sight" (Rom. iii. 20; see also Gal. ii. 16; iii. 11, &c.). But this is the very opposite of Deut. vi. 25! What then are we to say, or to do ?   Which of these two statements is true ? and which is false ?

The answer is, that neither is false.   But both are true if we rightly divide the Word of truth as to its Dispensational truth and teaching.

Deut. vi. 25 was true, then, "concerning" Israel; and is in harmony with the covenant of works under which Israel had placed itself.   But Rom. iii. 20 and Gal. ii. 16 are true now "concerning" all three, Jew, Gentile, and Church of God.   The statement in these two passages concerning all "flesh" was made after Israel had broken that covenant (Heb. x. 29); and after Christ had introduced the unconditional "everlasting covenant" (Heb. xiii. 20) of grace, into which He entered for His people "before the foundation of the world" (Eph. i. 3, 4).

These are two statements exactly opposite to each other.   Is it then the fact that the one is true and the other false ?   Nay, both are true; absolutely true.   And this will be seen at once if we appropriate each to, and interpret each of, the Dispensation to which it properly belongs.   The former is not true now in this Present Dispensation.   It was true of those under the Law.   The latter is as true now of those who are under Grace.

But we fear that multitudes as they hear the Old Testament read in our churches fail so to divide them rightly, but understand the interpretation of them as belonging to themselves now.   They thus put themselves under law, and deny their standing which God has given them in Christ; hence it is that they fail to enjoy that liberty wherewith Christ hath made His people free (Gal. v. 1).

In the Old Dispensation God dealt with one nation only ; but in the Present Dispensation He no longer deals with any one nation, but with individuals out of all nations.   This is the key to the understanding of those many passages where the words "all" and "every" and "world" are used in the New Testament.   "All" must mean one of two things: either "all" *without exception,* or "all" *without distinction;* and it is in this latter sense it is constantly used in contrast with the one nation of Israel.

"I, if I be lifted up from the earth [1] will draw all men unto me" (John xii. 32). If this means "all" *without exception*, then it is not true, for all men have not been drawn unto Him. But it *is* most blessedly true, if it means "all" *without distinction*, as it surely does.

The expression He tasted death "for every man" (Heb. ii. 9) must be understood in the same sense; *i.e.*, not limited as heretofore to Israel; but extended *without distinction* to all, whether Jews or Gentiles. With this agrees 1 John ii. 1, 2.

In the Old Dispensation God's light shone only in and on Israel; but now, having come into the world, it lighteneth "every man" *without distinction* of nation, race, or creed (John i. 9; compare Titus ii. 11).

In the Old Dispensation God dealt according to man's work: now He deals according to Christ's work.

In the Old Dispensation, Israel was to work *for* life: now we work *from* life.

The Law gave *works* for man to do: Grace brings *words* for man to believe.

Two words distinguish the Two dispensations. "Do" distinguishes the former; "Done" the latter. Then, salvation depended on what man was to *do;* now it depends upon what Christ has *done*.

(b) *The Imprecatory Psalms.*—These have been a trouble to most Christians: who among us has not been disquieted by them? Critics speak of them as "very unfit for the lips of our Lord." [2] There must be very, very few who have not felt the difficulty; and though they have realized it they have not seen the way out of it: neither will they, nor can they do so, until they learn to rightly divide the Word of truth, and interpret these Psalms of the Dispensation to which they belong. They must be appropriated to the Old Dispensation of the Law. There they are in place; as they will be in place again in the coming Dispensation of Judgment.

"The righteous shall rejoice when he seeth the vengeance" (Ps. lviii. 10, 11). So will the great voice of much people in heaven say "Hallelujah . . . for true and

---

[1] *I.e.,* in crucifixion, as the next verse (33) distinctly states.
[2] *How God Inspired the Bible,* Rev. J. Paterson Smyth.

righteous are his judgments" (Rev. xix. 1, 2).[1] This clearly shows that these and all such "Cursing" Scriptures (as they are called) are in perfect keeping with the Dispensation to which they belong.

In all probability Ps. cix. admits of another explanation by putting verses 6—19 within a parenthesis; in which case verse 20 may be rendered as explaining it :—

"This is the work of mine adversaries from the LORD,
And of those that speak evil against my soul (*i.e.* me)."

Verses 6—19 will then be the "evil" which David's enemies spake against him.[2] These will be the words that came from "the mouth of the wicked and deceitful" : and the proceeds of the "lying tongue" (*v.* 4). These will be the "words of hatred" (*v.* 3), and the "evil for good" with which David's enemies rewarded his love (*v.* 5).

But Psalm cxxxvii. 8, 9 does not admit of such an explanation. The spirit is appropriate to the Dispensations of Law and Judgment, but not to the present Dispensation of Grace :—

"Remember, O Jehovah, the children of Edom in the day of Jerusalem :
Who said, Rase it, Rase it even to the foundation thereof.
O daughter of Babylon, who art to be destroyed:
Happy shall he be that rewardeth thee as thou hast served us.
Happy shall he be that taketh and dasheth thy little ones against the stones."

There is a time of judgment coming for which all such language will be appropriate (Isa. xxvi. 9. Rev. ii. 26, 27); but that language is not for this present Dispensation of grace. If we do so interpret it, then there is an end of ever hoping to find the "truth": and all hope of ever understanding the Word of God is destroyed.

(*c*) *As to the Sabbath.*—Obedience to 2 Tim. ii. 15 clears away heaps of confusion, and delivers from the bondage

---

[1] Thus the first "Hallelujah" (praise ye the LORD) in the Old Testament (Ps. civ. 35) agrees with the first in the New Testament in connection with vengeance and judgment.

[2] See above, under Section I. of this Chapter III. of Part I., p. 59.

of law, in which so many, through disobedience to that great precept to "rightly divide the Word of truth," are still bound : some of them "bound hand and foot."

The Ceremonial Laws of the Sabbath were given to Israel, and not to the Gentile nations of the earth, Pagan or otherwise. While the interpretation therefore belongs to Israel, it would be wise for all nations to make an *application* of the *great principle* laid down in the Law, as to resting from servile labour on one day in seven. But the law of the Sabbath is neither abrogated, changed, nor transferred to any other day of the week. And if any believe that the Law is to be obeyed now, they have no liberty to alter that law, or to modify it in any way ; but are bound to "keep holy the seventh day." They have no choice in the matter, and dare not take the liberty of altering the law of God.

But, on the other hand, Christians in this present Dispensation are "not under law, but under grace." We "died to the law," in Christ (Rom. vii. 4), and the law has no power over one who has died. "We are delivered from the law, having died to that wherein we were held" (*v.* 6). We are "under [obedience to the] commandments of Christ" (1 Cor. ix. 21).

To those in Galatia who desired "to be under the law" (Gal. iv. 21) the Apostle wrote, "How turn ye again to the beggarly elements (*i.e.*, religious ordinances) whereunto ye desire again to be in bondage ? Ye observe days, and months, and times, and years. I am afraid of you, lest I have bestowed upon you labour in vain" (Gal. iv. 9—11).

This Scripture is specially addressed to, and is to be interpreted of the Church of God, to-day ; and all who would thus have us return to and put ourselves under law we have great need to be "afraid."[1]

As towards others and himself, the Christian can apply those laws as far as they are compatible with his own Church Epistles. There he is told that, "one man esteemeth one day above another : another [man] esteemeth every day alike. Let every man be fully persuaded in his own mind. He that regardeth the day, regardeth it unto the Lord : and he that regardeth not

---

[1] See *The Church Epistles*, pp. 109, 176, etc., by the same author.

the day, to the Lord he doth not regard it" (Rom. xiv. 5, 6).

It is a matter of being persuaded in one's own mind, and not as being under law; still less as being under the judgment of our fellow believers in this matter. "Let no man therefore judge you in meats or in drink; or in respect of a holy day, or of the new moon, or of the Sabbath" (Col. ii. 16). We do not "let them judge" us, but they do so all the same. We shall be judged, yea, and condemned by many for writing even as much as this: and though we quote the Word of God, we shall be met by arguments of expediency, which are all based on a total disregard to another command, equally binding, belonging as it does to this present Dispensation; and that is the command, as to "rightly dividing the Word of truth" (2 Tim. ii. 15).

The Sabbath laws are either still binding on us, or they are not still binding. If they are, then those who keep "the seventh day" and not "the first," are right. If they are not binding, then we are all "free from the law," and we have our guidance in Rom. xiv. 5, 6. Col. ii. 16 and Gal. iv. 1—11.

But, if we read into the present Dispensation that which pertained only to the former, there can be nothing but confusion in our own minds, and conflict and arguments with our fellow-Christians.

And, beside this conflict with them, we shall be seeking to put not only the Church of God, but all the Gentiles also under the laws which were given by Moses to Israel alone.

It will be seen that thus "rightly dividing the Word of truth" as to Sabbath-keeping is the only effectual answer to the large body called "Seventh Day" Christians; who, not seeing the blessed truth that we are free from the law of Moses, and under the law of Christ, who is the Lord of the Sabbath, are not only observing the seventh-day Sabbath themselves, but are carrying on an active propaganda to induce all Christians to join their ranks.

(d) *As to the Kingdom.*—There are some Past Dispensational truths, like those which *concern the Kingdom,* which leap over the Present, and belong both to the Past and the Future.

They were truth in the Past Dispensation; and they will be truth in the Future: but, they are not truth in or for this Present Dispensation.

This Present Dispensation, so far as regards the truth pertaining to the other two, is not reckoned; and this present interval is passed over as though it did not exist.

The Past and the Coming Dispensations have to do with the Kingdom. This Present Dispensation has to do with the Church of God.

The former had to do with the Law, the next has to do with Judgment: but, the Present Dispensation has to do with Grace.

If therefore we read into the present that which has to do both with the past and the future; and, if we read into the Dispensation of Grace that which has to do with Law and Judgment we at once leave the high ground of Grace on which God has set us; we lose the blessing of that standing which is ours in Christ; and we interpret of ourselves, language, which is appropriate only to a Dispensation of Judgment or of Glory. This means, not only loss of blessing to ourselves, but it means the introduction of confusion into our minds, and contradiction into the Word of God.

This is specially true if we take that which was spoken of the KINGDOM and understand it of the CHURCH of God.

Of course, if anyone holds that the Kingdom IS the Church, it would be consistent so to take it. But those who do so make no attempt to rightly divide the Word of truth: and they treat language as being useless for the purposes of Revelation.

If, when God says one thing He always means another, then the Bible becomes a book of Enigmas instead of Enlightenment; and the door is opened for all those differences of interpretation which are not only a puzzle to the children of God, but are a source of all those divisions among Christians which are a defilement of God's building (1 Cor. iii. 17); and of all those controversies which are a scandal and a stumblingblock to those that are without.

It would be a sufficient answer to those who say that the Kingdom is the Church, to reply, "You say so." Or, to those who say the Church is the Kingdom to answer, "So you say": for no such assertion is made in the Word of truth. It is only an inference; and it is wrong, because it comes of wrongly dividing the Word of truth.

But, as we write, not for confutation, but for instruction, we may mention the following facts for the guidance of those who would, like the Eunuch of Ethiopia, understand what they read.

The Kingdom, as we have said, belongs to the past Dispensation. It was proclaimed by John the Baptist; and afterward as being then "at hand"; it was the first subject of the Lord's own ministry (Matt. iv. 17); but, having been rejected, it is now in abeyance until the time comes to set it up in Divine power and glory.

It is clear, therefore, that truth which is appropriate for that Kingdom, whether past or future, is not truth appropriate for the present Dispensation of the Church. Even the expressions used and the terminology employed are not the same. What is said of the Kingdom is not true when spoken of the Church.[1]

The Kingdom is said to be "set up" (Dan. ii. 44. Acts xv. 16). The Church is "built up" (Eph. ii. 20—22. 1 Cor. iii. 9. Col. ii. 7).

We hear much about the "extension of the Kingdom" and the "advancement of the Kingdom"; but these are non-scriptural expressions when spoken of the Kingdom, and un-scriptural when used of the Church.

We read of those who are "heirs of the Kingdom" (Jas. ii. 5), but not of the Church; of "Children of the Kingdom" (Matt. viii. 12); but not of the Church (except in the Church of Rome).

We read of having "received the Kingdom" (Luke xix. 12, 15); and of "entering" it (Matt. xviii. 3); of "seeing" it (John iii. 3); and of "inheriting" it (Matt. xxv. 34). But never do we once find such expressions used in Scripture of the Church of God! In no sense can any one "*inherit*," or "*see*," or "*receive*" the Church.

---

[1] See a pamphlet, *The Kingdom and the Church*, by the same author.

Among all the Figures used for the Church the *Kingdom* is never so used. We find it compared to a *"house"* (1 Tim. iii. 15); *"a Temple"* (1 Cor. iii. 16, 17); *"a Body"* (1 Cor. xii. 27, &c.), but never to the Kingdom.

The Kingdom, proclaimed in the past, and now in abeyance, is yet to come; and all Christians pray "Thy kingdom come." But the Church is here, now; and is soon *going away:* for it is waiting to be "caught up to meet the Lord in the air, so to be ever with the Lord" (1 Thess. iv. 14—17). If the Church, therefore, is the Kingdom, the prayer ought to be "Thy kingdom go"!

Again, the Church is an *election*, hence its name *Ecclesia*, which means *a calling out*. But the Kingdom, when it is set up, will be universal and all-embracing (Ps. ciii. 19. Rev. xi. 15).

Christ is now the Head over all things to His Body, the Church (Eph. i. 22; iv. 15. Col. i. 18); but He is never called its King. How much error and confusion is created from the use of non-scriptural expressions it is impossible to tell.

We quite understand that, as the word βασιλεία (*basileia*), *kingdom*, means not the material country or the subjects, but the *sovereignty* or *administrative rule* of the King, so, the Church necessarily finds its sphere and place within that rule. But, in this case it is always "the kingdom (*i.e.* the sovereignty) of God" (Rom. xiv. 17. 1 Cor. iv. 20. Col. iv. 11); or "the kingdom (or sovereignty) of the Son of His love" (Col. i. 13). Amid all the realms of this all-embracing Sovereignty of God in heaven and on earth, among angels and men, the Church has its proper, distinctive, and unique place; just as in the sovereignty of a house, there is the place for the Head, the Wife, the Children, the Friends, the Visitors, the Guests, the Officials, and the Servants. This is not to say that any one of these IS the other. Each one has its own peculiar position within this universal sovereignty; and the Church of God its own unique position within it. It is part of the "Body" of which Christ is the "Head"— part therefore of the Head, "one NEW MAN" (Eph. ii. 15), "a PERFECT MAN," even "the measure of the stature of the fulness of the Christ" (Eph. iv. 13). If these scriptural expressions had been heeded we should never hear the Church spoken of as in our Hymns and Sermons as "she" and "her"; as though the Church were "one new woman," or "a perfect woman."

But, while this is so, as to the Church having its own place in the vast and universal sovereignty of God, it is never included in the more limited expression "the kingdom of heaven" as it appears in the Gospel of Matthew, and which belongs peculiarly to Israel. Nor is it included in the wider, but yet limited, Kingdom of Heaven to which the Lord's prayer refers; for the sphere of this is on the earth.

"*The Kingdom (or Sovereignty) of HEAVEN*"

Has the Messiah for its King.

It is from heaven, and under the heavens upon earth.

It is limited in its scope.

It is Political in its sphere.

It is Jewish and Exclusive in its character.

It is National in its aspect.

And is the special subject of Old Testament prophecy.

"*The Kingdom (or Sovereignty) of GOD*"

Has God for its ruler.

It is in Heaven, over the Earth.

It is Unlimited in its Scope.

It is Moral in its sphere.

It is Inclusive in its character (including even the Church).

It is Universal in its aspect.

And in its wider aspect is the subject of New Testament revelation.

All this is true, and yet it is equally true that, if we call the Church the Kingdom, we are not "rightly dividing the Word of truth."

Thus, even though the Church, as such, comes within and under the universal Divine Sovereignty, we may not put one part of that Sovereignty for another part without injuriously affecting the whole.

When the Lord said to Peter "I will give unto thee the keys of the kingdom of Heaven" (Matt. xvi. 19), He did not mean *the keys of the Church*. This, at one stroke, does away with the preposterous claim of the Church of Rome. Keys are used for opening and for admission. Peter used these keys when he again proclaimed the kingdom to Israel (Acts ii.—vii.), and afterward to Gentiles (Acts viii.—xii.).[1]

(e) *The Various Gospels.*—From this confusion between the Kingdom and the Church comes the confusion between the various Gospels of which the Scripture speaks.

There is no dispute as to the meaning of the word. The English word Gospel may mean either *good news*, or *God's News*. But the Greek word means only *good news*. This does not carry us far. It tells us only the fact that the news is good. There is a further question for us to ask; viz., *What is the news that is so good?*

News is of different kinds. In our Newspapers we find Political News, Financial News, Judicial News, Social News, Sporting News, and indeed news of all kinds.

We have therefore to answer our own question as to what this "News" from God is, and what it is that makes it "good."

We read for example of—

> The Gospel of the Kingdom,
> The Gospel of God,
> The Gospel of the grace of God,
> The Gospel of the Glory, and
> The Everlasting Gospel.

The question is, Do all these expressions mean the same thing? Is the "good news" the same in each case? If God has thus put these five Gospels asunder, are we at liberty to join them together? Has God thus distinguished them, and, shall we say that there is no distinction whatever?

It is very general not only for those who read, but for those who teach, to say that there is only one kind of Gospel, and those who say this do not hesitate to use

---

[1] The other part of the Commission (*v.* 19) was likewise confined solely to Peter. To no one else was this commission given, and Peter had neither the power nor authority to transfer that commission to others, still less to give to the others the power of transmitting either the one or the other. This is the explanation also of those other passages as to "binding" and "loosing," "retaining" and "remitting."

harsh language of us, and of those who seek rightly to divide these Gospels and endeavour to apportion them and their peculiar news to the Time or Dispensation to which they respectively belong.

" The Gospel of the Kingdom "

Was the *good news* that, the Kingdom, which had been the subject of Old Testament promise and prophecy, was at length "at hand." That was good news indeed for all those who waited "for the consolation of Israel" (Luke ii. 25); who "looked for redemption in Jerusalem" (*v.* 38); and who "waited for the Kingdom of God" (Mark xv. 43). Many believed this good news concerning Christ the King, and "trusted that it had been he who should have redeemed Israel" (Luke xxiv. 21).

But, after the Kingdom had been rejected, and the King crucified, it was again proclaimed to Israel, and the announcement made that the King was ready to return (Acts ii. 38; iii. 19—21), on the one condition of national repentance. But the making of this proclamation was still opposed by the People through their rulers (Acts iv. 17, 18); and the preachers of this "Gospel of the Kingdom" were "threatened" (*v.* 21).

When Peter's Ministry to the Circumcision ended in his imprisonment (Acts xii.), and Paul was raised up and sent forth, it was with the *added good news* of Grace. This was what is again and again claimed by Paul as "my Gospel." Then after all this : after the rejection and Crucifixion of the King, after the Martyrdom of Stephen, and after the Imprisonment of Peter, the Epistle to the Romans (which stands first of the subsequent Canonical writings) opens with the words, "Paul, a servant of Jesus Christ, called to be (or, by Divine Calling) an Apostle, separated unto

" God's Gospel."

This was good news of a *different* character. This was news of *grace* proclaimed, not to Israel only, or to any one nation, but to individual transgressors of the Jews, and sinners of the Gentiles alike; to all *without distinction*,[1] It was *grace* proclaimed to Jews who deserved wrath, and to Gentiles who deserved nothing. Hence it is called

The Gospel of the Grace of God.

This was further *good news*, as set forth in Romans and the other Church Epistles. It was the good news that those who are in Christ are reckoned by God (and hence are to be reckoned by us) as having died with Christ and having risen with Him; and that when this Gospel shall have accomplished its object and gathered out from Jews and Gentiles all the members of the one Body, these shall be gathered together unto Christ the Glorious Head in glory (2 Thess. ii. 1).

This *good news* is called THE GLORIOUS GOSPEL, or better,

"The Gospel of the Glory

of the blessed God which was (Paul says) committed to my trust" (1 Tim. i. 11). In 2 Cor. iv. 4 it is called "the glorious Gospel of Christ," *i.e.*, the good news of the "glory" which is to follow the "sufferings" of Christ; and which is to be the outcome of those sufferings. This good news is preached now. It is part of the good news of the Grace of God; for grace and glory are inseparably bound together. There is no Gospel of the grace of God, without the Gospel of the glory of God. Grace is the flower, Glory will be the fruit. The Church is not always to be in sorrow and trial; and the good news concerning the glory is "the knowledge of the glory of God in the person of Jesus Christ" (2 Cor. iv. 6).

But when the preaching of this double Gospel of Grace and Glory shall have closed, we read of another Gospel which is to be proclaimed in the midst of the Dispensation of Judgment. It is called

"The Everlasting Gospel."

It is not proclaimed until the very crisis of the apocalyptic judgments; after the Judgments of the Seven Seals, the Judgments of the Seven Trumpets, and the revelation of the Beast in his superhuman stage

---

[1] See above, p. 110.

(Rev. xiii.). Then, before the final judgments of the seven Vials, seven angels make seven proclamations (Rev. xiv. 6—20). The first is the proclamation of "the everlasting Gospel"; of mercy in the midst of judgment. It is the command to mankind simply to "Fear God" as the Creator. Not a word as to the Redeemer, or as to grace or glory, but a simple command to "Fear God." What else will be contained in that Gospel of the coming Day of Judgment we know not now.

It is called "everlasting" because the acknowledgment of God as the Creator was before all other news; and will follow after all news of the kingdom, grace and glory will have passed away. It announces God, only as the Creator; not as Lord, or as Jehovah (the Covenant God), but as "God" (the Creator). It is not "Repent," or "do this" or "do that," but only "Fear God and give glory to Him, for the hour of His judgment is come; and worship Him that made heaven and earth, and the sea, and the fountains of waters." (Compare Exod. ix. 30. Ps. xxxiii. 8.)

Is it not strange that this should ever have been supposed to be the same as the Gospel of the Grace of God? Is it not strange that news of God's present grace should ever be taken as being the same as the news of God's mercy in the midst of judgment?

Nothing can account for such perversity but the fact that it comes only from human selfishness, and the determination to take everything, past, present, and future, as belonging to, or having to do with, the Church of God.

Rightly divide these different Gospels, according to the Dispensations to which they belong, and we have only harmony, consistency, and truth.

(*f*) *The Sermon on the Mount.*—Few portions of God's Word have suffered more from want of compliance with the one great requirement of the Word of truth as given in 2 Tim. ii. 15.

It occupies the greater part of the first of the four periods of the Lord's ministry.[1]

---

[1] For the other three Subjects of His Ministry, see *Christ's Prophetic Teaching*, by the same author.

The first period was occupied with the Proclamation of the King and the Kingdom.

It begins in Matthew at ch. iv. 17, and goes on down to the end of ch. vii., and thus occupies the whole of chs. v., vi., and vii.

This shows us that what we call "the Sermon on the Mount" (which, after all, is only Man's name for it) has to do with the Kingdom. It shows that the laws of that Kingdom which was the sole subject of that first period of Christ's ministry were to be very different from the laws given by God through Moses on Mount Sinai; and very different also from the traditions which had made so many of them of none effect. This teaching follows, naturally, as being in harmony with the truth which pertains to the Kingdom, and not with that which pertains to the Church of God. It is appropriate to a Dispensation of Law and not to a Dispensation of Grace; to a Past or Future Dispensation, but not to the Present Dispensation.

This is, of course, the case so far as *interpretation* is concerned. But, when it comes to *application*, then, if there be truths of eternal application we may, of course, apply them; and if there be truths in harmony with what is addressed specially to the Church of God, and agreeing with the truth addressed directly to it in the Church Epistles, then we may *apply* it, so far, but no further.

"Till heaven and earth pass, one jot or one tittle shall in no wise pass from the law, till all be fulfilled" (Matt. v. 18). This is truth, of eternal application.

"Where your treasure is, there will your heart be also" (Matt. vi. 21) is also truth of eternal application.

But the instruction as to "agreeing with our adversary" (ch. v. 25); instructions as to "fasting" (ch. vi. 16—18), the "danger of the Council" (ch. v. 22); the "Judge," the "Officer," and the Altar (ch. v. 24, 25); the seeking the kingdom (ch. vi. 33), the profession "I never knew you" (ch. vii. 23), the doing, and works (ch. vii. 21, 24); all these are like a foreign language when compared with the language addressed to us in our Church Epistles.

Moreover those who hold that this discourse is to be interpreted of the Church of God make no attempt to obey its precepts. Instead of loving their enemies (ch. v. 44) they do not even love their brethren, if they commit the unpardonable sin of daring to differ from them in opinion.

Instead of trying to agree with their adversary quickly (ch. v. 25) they do not try to agree with their fellow-believers, even slowly.

Instead of not judging others (ch. vii. 1) it is the one thing that they are most addicted to, and well-practised in. If any sue them and would take away their coat (ch. v. 40), then, instead of letting him have their cloak as well, they let him have the law.

They read (ch. v. 42), "Give to him that asketh thee, and from him that would borrow of thee turn not thou away," but, all we say is, "*Try it; go and 'ask*,*'* and see how they carry out this precept which they maintain is written and *addressed to them.*" As for ourselves we feel under no such obligation, either on the one hand to give or to lend *whenever* we may be asked ; or, on the other hand, to *wait till we are asked.*

And then, to what altar do they carry and lay their gift, or offering (ch. v. 23, 24)? unless they count Flowers, and Eggs, and Dolls, as "Sacrifices," and their Communion Tables as Altars.

Who is to compel them to go one mile, and they go two miles?[1] (Matt. v. 41).

Finally we strongly advise our readers, if they smite those who interpret this "Sermon" of the Church on one cheek (ch. v. 39), not to wait and see whether they turn the other, but to get out of the way as quickly as they can.

They will glibly pray "thy kingdom come" (ch. vi. 10), but with the same breath, and the same persistent inconsistency shown throughout, they will pray for the "advancement" and the "extension" of the same kingdom which, according to this, *has come* and is already here.

---

[1] This was perfectly intelligible in that Past Dispensation, though it can have no place in the Present. The verb ἀγγαρεύω (*aggareuō*) is a word brought into the Greek language from Persia, and refers to the practice of commandeering or forcing others into the royal service. The ἄγγαροι (*aggaroi*) are mentioned as royal couriers, in the *papyri*. The verb had come into general use, and was naturalized as early as the third century B.C., and was well understood by the people, though quite technical. It is still found in modern Greek in the sense of *compelling*. (See Deissmann, *Bible Studies*, p. 86.)

They will not think of measuring the forgiveness they ask God for, by the forgiveness which they extend to those who have sinned against them.

As to asking why they behold the mote in their brother's eye (ch. vii. 3), we would ask why they behold so many which are not there at all.

All this confusion comes from interpreting what is said of the *Kingdom,* and was spoken to those who were proclaiming it, of a condition of things wholly different. The kingdom, whose laws the King was there laying down, was, after that, rejected.   And the King having been crucified, the kingdom is therefore now in abeyance.   The precepts pertaining to it are in abeyance also.   His own words "BUT NOW" in Luke xxii. 36 [1] are sufficient not only to warrant us in so treating "the Sermon on the Mount," but sufficient to *compel* us to do so.

If we do not heed the corrective instruction contained in the words "But now," and thus carry out the principle involved in them, then all must be confusion.

The world can plainly see the inconsistency produced by it; and, in consequence, turns it against the Church, and against Christians; and uses that very inconsistency, which is so manifest, as an argument against the truth of Christianity itself.

Those Christians who say that these chapters are addressed to them are charged by the world with direct disobedience to their precepts.   And Christ also is charged with the inconsistency of giving commands which cannot possibly be carried out.

But once we rightly divide the Dispensations, and *the truth pertaining to them,* we see that "the Sermon on the Mount" belonged to a past brief Dispensation, while the kingdom was being proclaimed; and will be appropriate again to a succeeding Dispensation when the kingdom shall have come: but it neither belongs to, nor can be interpreted of, nor even applied to the totally different circumstances of this present Dispensation of Grace.

Those who are imbued with the precepts peculiar to the Church of God, in the Epistles addressed to it, could never for one moment make the grave mistake of putting them-

---

[1] See pages 107, 103, **above.**

selves under these laws of the kingdom which are *infinitely more stringent and spiritual than the laws of Sinai;* nor could they thus mislead the world and give it its strongest argument against the very truth of the Gospel of the Grace of God.

(*g*) *The Lord's Prayer.*—This occurs in the "Sermon on the Mount," and it manifestly forms an integral part of it.

That it pertains wholly to the kingdom is clear. It is a prayer for that kingdom to come, in order that God's will may be done on earth, as it is done in heaven.

Its standard is Law, and not Grace.

Forgiveness is sought not on the ground of grace, but of works; and not on the ground of mercy, but of merit.

The future and approaching Tribulation is contemplated as imminent, if not present.

The Evil One, the Beast, is present in power. None are able to buy or sell except that which has his mark (Rev. xiii. 17). Daily bread must be miraculously "*given*," if those who use this prayer are to be kept alive.

No name of Christ is in it, nor is it offered in His name or merits, as He Himself declared it should be (John xvi. 23, 24).

It is a prayer suitable to the time, while the kingdom was being proclaimed as "at hand." And when the Church shall have been removed it will be seen how appropriate it will be when the kingdom shall be again proclaimed as "at hand"; and the "Gospel of the kingdom" shall be again preached in the coming days of "the Great Tribulation."[1]

(*h*) *As to Priesthood.*—All the false doctrine connected with Priestly assumptions in the present day arises from this same misplacement of truth, which takes that which was true for the Past and Future Dispensations, and mistakenly regards it as being true for the Present Dispensation, which it is not.

Not only does priestcraft and all its attendant evils spring from this misplacement, but the mischief can be

---

[1] See a pamphlet on "The Lord's Prayer," by the same author.

met and remedied only by replacing the truth in the Dispensation to which it belongs.

The difficulty is experienced; and to get over it, truth is taken from the coming Dispensation and put into the present in order to meet the error which comes from first taking truth from the Past and putting it into the Present Dispensation. These are the shifts which have to be resorted to in consequence of disobedience to 2 Tim. ii. 15.

It is urged that in this present Dispensation "all are priests"; but this is just as incorrect as to say that some, or any, are priests.

On earth, God has never recognized a priesthood except that which He ordained Himself and confined to the nation of Israel (Exod. xix. 6), and to the tribe of Levi (Exod. xxix. 9). To those who had put themselves under the Law it was said, "If ye shall obey my voice and keep my covenant then ye shall be a peculiar treasure unto me above all people: for all the earth is mine, and ye shall be unto me a kingdom of priests and an holy nation" (Exod. xix. 5, 6).

That was a true promise and prophecy of and for Israel, in the past Dispensation. But Israel failed to fulfil the condition necessary for national priesthood as announced in Exod. xix. 5. Israel did not keep the covenant. Hence the conditional promise, "Ye shall be unto me a kingdom of priests," was not performed. The tribe of Levi was substituted for the nation, and the national performance of that promise remains still in abeyance until such time as Israel shall turn to the Lord. Hence, the prophecy was repeated at a later period in the prophecy of Isa. lxi. 1, which the Lord read, only in part, in the Synagogue at Nazareth, when He "closed the book," and stopped at the point where the prophecy had been fulfilled (Luke iv. 18—20). After "the day of vengeance" (which the Lord omitted, because it was still future) shall have passed, then it is declared of the nation as a whole: "Ye shall be named the Priests of the LORD; men shall call you the ministers of our God" (Isa. lxi. 6; lxvi. 21).

John sees in proleptic vision, *i.e.*, by anticipation, the yet future fulfilment of this prophecy. In Rev. i. 6 he announces it when he gives glory to God for what He will then have done, even to "Him who hath made us (*i.e.*,

John and his brethren according to the flesh) kings and priests unto God and his Father."

In Rev. v. 9, 10, John hears the four *Zōa* (or Living Creatures), and the Twenty-four Elders sing a new song referring to that yet future day; "Thou hast redeemed [a People] to God by thy blood out of every kindred, and tongue, and people and nation; and hast made them unto our God a kingdom and priests; and they shall reign on the earth."

This is the true reading and rendering[1] of Rev. v. 9, 10; and with this the R.V. practically agrees.

Peter, who wrote specially to believers among the Dispersed (the *Diaspora*) of Israel, could speak of *them* as the spiritual house (of Israel) and call them "a holy Priesthood to offer up spiritual sacrifices."

But in no case could this be said of believing sinners of the Gentiles either then, or now, or in the future.

Is it not strange that those who do this, do not see that they are compelled to take only one of the two classes mentioned? Only the "priests!" We never hear of their claiming to be "kings," now, in this day of grace. Wrongly dividing the word of truth, or not dividing it at all, introduces "priests" into the Church of God, and those who do that are driven into a further and necessary inconsistency, and are, perforce, obliged to leave out the "kings" altogether!

Surely this is sufficient to show us the error of Sacerdotalists and the error also of their opponents. Both are wrong. The one is wrong in making a baseless claim, and the other is wrong for attempting to refute it by a baseless argument. Both the false claim and the false argument proceed alike from the same cause.

The fact is there is no priesthood recognized by God on the earth during this present Dispensation, while Israel as a nation is excluded.

It is said even of the Lord Jesus Himself, that now, "IF HE WERE ON EARTH He would not be a priest" (Heb. viii. 4).

And the reason given is that, on earth, priesthood belongs to the tribe of Levi only; and "our Lord sprang

---

[1] See the author's work: *Commentary on Revelation*, republished by Kregel Publications, p. 242.

out of Judah; of which tribe Moses spake nothing concerning priesthood" (Heb. vii. 12–14).

Christ is a Priest, but HIS priesthood belongs to Heaven, and not to earth; and is "after the order of Melchizedek," and "not after the order of Aaron."

To see the truth as to priesthood, Dispensationally, puts an end to all controversy as to the claims of Sacerdotalists, as well as to all the weak replies of Protestants, which only serve to strengthen those claims instead of meeting them.

To see this Dispensational truth makes a priesthood in the Church of God an impossibility. For *Christ never was a priest on earth;* and He would not be a priest if He were *on earth* to-day.

Once we rightly divide the Word of truth as to Priesthood, away goes all Prelacy and Priestcraft, which have created "Christendom," and turned it into a Babylon; a "hold of every foul spirit, and a cage of every unclean and hateful bird" (Rev. xviii. 2).

True, Peter can write to Believers among "the Dispersion" (1 Pet. i. 1; compare John vii. 35) and *apply* Exod. xix. 6, as the Lord applied Isa. lxi. 1, in the Synagogue at Nazareth, and show how those believing Israelites to whom he wrote fulfilled the past, and anticipated the future in a "spiritual" manner (1 Pet. ii. 4—10). All this could be applied to them, as it could not be even *applied* to us; though, even here, there was one thing that could not be then applied to them. They were priests only in a "spiritual" sense; but they were not "kings" in any sense at all. So the reference to the past Dispensation was rightly divided so far as it could be *applied* to the new (though transitional) condition of things.

Here we have, then, another example of how, and how far, we may *apply* a scripture to that of which it cannot be *interpreted.*

(*i*) *As to Baptism.*—We have the same confusion in Truth and Teaching, and all the controversies as to doctrine and practice.

It is clear, from the Gospels, that it has to do with the kingdom. The very first time it is mentioned is in connection with the kingdom (Matt. iii. 1—6).

It was preached by John who was known as "the Baptiser"; and John was not a minister of the Gospel of the Grace of God, but a prophet under the old covenant appointed to "prepare the way of the Lord," who came "to confirm the promises made unto the fathers" (Rom. xv. 8).

His ministry was unique; and his message was "Repent, for the kingdom of heaven is at hand": and he baptized those who believed his preaching and confessed their sins. The reason why he baptized was in order that Christ should "be made manifest to Israel" (John i. 31).

Moreover he testified of the One who should come after him, and who should baptize also; not with material water, as John did, but with *pneuma hagion* or spiritual water, that is, with "power from on high."[1]

This the Lord Himself confirmed in Acts i. 4, 5.

But, as we have already abundantly shown and seen, the kingdom was rejected, and the King crucified.

John, as we have said, baptized individuals who "believed on Him who should come after him" (see Acts xix. 4).

But, in Matt. xxviii. 19, 20, the Lord speaks of a future baptism, not of individuals, but of all "nations," not in the name of Him as the coming One, for He had already come, and would be with them; but "in the name of the Father, and of the Son, and of the Holy Ghost."

Strange to say, this command was never obeyed on any one of the several occasions recorded in the New Testament, when baptism was "administered." Not once do we find any of the apostles, nor any of the first preachers of the Gospel making any exception to the use of this one particular formula. This practice was *invariable*.

In Acts ii. 38 Peter commands those of the Dispersion who believed: "Repent, and be baptized every one of you *in the name of Jesus Christ*."

In Acts viii. 16 Peter and John "baptized in the *name of the Lord Jesus*."

In Acts x. 48 Peter "commanded them to be baptized *in the name of the Lord*" (R.V. Jesus Christ).

In Acts xix. 5 (whether this refers to those who heard John or those who heard Paul[2]; or whether it refers to

---

[1] See *Word Studies on the Holy Spirit*, republished by Kregel Publications, pp. 26-35.
[2] See *Word Studies on the Holy Spirit*, pp. 104-107.

John's act or Paul's) it is certain that "they were baptized *in the name of the Lord Jesus.*"

In Rom. vi. 3 Paul speaks of "as many of us as were baptized *into Jesus Christ.*"

And in 1 Cor. i. 13, 15, "baptized in the name of Paul," is clearly contrasted with baptism *in the name of Christ.*

There is not one exception to this practice.

It is equally certain that Matt. xxviii. 19, 20 definitely commands the DISCIPLING of "THE NATIONS" by baptizing them in the Triune name of Father, Son, and Holy Ghost.

The full command is as follows:

"Go ye therefore and make all nations disciples, baptizing them into the name of the Father, and of the Son, and of the Holy Spirit, teaching them to observe all things whatsoever I have commanded you: and behold, I (even I) am with you all the days until the end of the age."

This command speaks of "nations" (or Gentiles), and thus excludes the Jews, for it is distinctly declared of them that they should "not be reckoned among the nations" (Num. xxiii. 9). Whereas, the Gospel of the Grace of God is preached to day to Jew and Gentile alike.

The command speaks of "all nations," and it says, "make all nations disciples" or "Disciple all nations" as such; whereas this present Dispensation is eclectic, and it is individual Jews and Gentiles who are taken *out of all nations.*

The word rendered "teach" in verse 19 is not the same as "teaching" in verse 20. The former means to "make disciples"; while the latter means to instruct the individuals who are thus made disciples. But neither of these terms is peculiar to the *present* Dispensation. Ministerial work to-day is, according to the Church Epistles, not to "disciple nations" or Gentiles, but to preach and proclaim the Gospel of the Grace of God to individuals, as lost sinners, that they may be taken out not only from among the Jews, but from AMONG the nations. It is to "preach the Word"; and we are to do this the more earnestly because, as the days get darker, men will be less ready to "endure sound doctrine" (2 Tim. iv. 1—4).

The command in Matt. xxviii. manifestly applies to a very different condition of things from that which is common to our experience.

The only ground for this command is that "all power is given unto me in heaven and in earth." For, while, in the Divine counsels, it can be said, "Thou hast put all things under his feet," yet, it is immediately added (Heb. ii. 8), "we see NOT YET all things put under him." The references given in the margin of Matt. xxviii. 18 fully bear this out. Not until the yet future opening scene in the coming Dispensation of Judgment will the gift of "all power" *on the earth* be formally made and received, and the heavenly song burst forth, "Worthy is the Lamb that was slain, to receive power," etc. (Rev. v. 12, etc.).

But this is the only reason given for obedience to this command : "Go ye THEREFORE."

Moreover, certain definite days seem to be marked off ; and this, at the end of the age, or of that Dispensation of the kingdom, when the proclamation of "the gospel of the kingdom" will again be made [1] and accompanied by its companion ordinance of baptism.

That baptism will not be into the name of the One who was to come (as in the Gospels); not into the name of One who had come and been rejected (as in the Acts of the Apostles); but into the Triune name of "the Father, and of the Son, and of the Holy Ghost." This will indeed be a work which will require "all power" in order to secure the submission of Jews and Mahommedans, as nations, to receive this baptism as the sign and token that they have acknowledged and submitted themselves to Christ, the Messiah, as their Lord and King.

This national work is that referred to in Matt. xxiv. 13, 14, "He that shall endure unto the END shall be saved. And this Gospel of the kingdom shall be proclaimed in the whole world for a witness, and then shall come the END"; *i.e.*, the end of "the days" referred to in Matt. xxviii. 20.

This is the "end" here referred to in Matt. xxviii. 19, 20.

---

[1] Matt. xxiv. 14 (see pp. 113—119, above).

132 RIGHTLY DIVIDING DISPENSATIONAL TRUTH:

The whole of this Dispensation is leaped over, as is done in Isa. lxi. 2, and many other passages, as we have shown above.[1]

This command spoken of the Future, in a past Dispensation, entirely disregards this present interval and contemplates obedience to it as being carried out not in the Present, but in the Future Dispensation.

We have exactly the same phenomenon in Matt. x. There the Lord commissions the Twelve for their immediate proclamation of the kingdom to Israel alone, as distinct from the Gentiles (Matt. x. 1—15). The Lord then passes on, and passes over this present Dispensation; and contemplates the yet future proclamation in which the heralds will be sent forth as "sheep among wolves." This Gospel of the kingdom is to be "for a testimony" to the nations (here rendered Gentiles) as well as to Israel; and we have the same promise made to the preachers in Matt. x. 22 as in ch. xxiv. 13. The words are exactly the same in both passages (in the Greek): "He that endureth to the END the same shall be saved." The command is continued in the next verse (ch. x. 23): "But when they persecute you in this city flee ye into another: for verily I say unto you, Ye shall not have gone over the cities of Israel, till the Son of Man be come."[2]

If this coming be the same as the destruction of Jerusalem (as is generally supposed) then it is perfectly certain that the Twelve could not have gone on proclaiming the kingdom as being "at hand" for nearly forty years after it had been rejected, and the King crucified!

Moreover, in the ministry of the Disciples as recorded in the Gospels, we have not the slightest hint of their going among "wolves," and of their being "persecuted," and "fleeing" from city to city. On the contrary, their ministry seems to have been most peaceful and peaceable; and they had no such report of trial and trouble to give the Master when they returned from their mission. On the contrary it was marked as having had great success (Luke x. 17—19).[3]

---

[1] See pp. 100—104.

[2] Greek, ἔλθῃ (elthē), *shall have come.*

[3] It seems as though, after they had spoken of the Present, that the Lord, in proleptic vision, passes over and sees beyond this Present Dispensation; and, beholding Rev. xii. 9, repeats the promises suited to that time, as given in Matt. x. 16—33; xxviii. 19, 20. Mark xvi. 15—18.

That mission must indeed have been very brief, for we gather from the Gospel record that they were with the Lord the greater part of His ministry.

And where did His promise to be "with" them "all the days" of that proclaiming and baptizing, find its fulfilment, if He were immediately going away, and about to send the Holy Spirit to be with them during His absence. When the promise is so strongly personal and definite it seems very forced to interpret that presence as being spiritual or delegated to the Holy Spirit. The pronoun ἐγώ (*egō*), *I*, is very emphatic: "And, behold, I, even I, am with you all the days, until the completion of the age (*sunteleia*, or Dispensation)." (R.V. margin, *until the consummation of the age.*)

It seems clear, therefore, that the proclamation referred to in Matt. xxviii. 19, 20, is yet future; and that it is closely connected with the then imminent personal appearance and promised presence of the Son of Man.

From all this it is abundantly manifest that, to take a command which belongs to a Past and Future Dispensation and to interpret it as being operative during the whole of this Present Dispensation can lead only to difficulty and contradiction.

Indeed, the bringing of John's baptism, which belonged to the kingdom, into this present Church period has led to confusion and disruption. It has proved a bomb which has rent the visible Church into fragments.

It has led to controversies and divisions, and strifes and contentions, which are to-day carried on with unabated vigour, and with the same bitterness as of old. It has led to the breaking up of the Church instead of its building up. It is the ordinance which has divided the Church instead of uniting it.

Is it not passing strange that, if the command in Matt. xxviii. 19, 20 really belongs to this Dispensation, the Apostles themselves, to whom the command was given, never once so interpreted it; and never once attempted to obey it?

The Lord had continued with them for forty days "speaking of the things pertaining to the kingdom of God" (Acts i. 3). One would have thought (judging from present-day interpretation) that He spoke only of the things pertaining to the Church, which according to the teaching of most Christians was set up, within ten days. But no! not a word was spoken about the Church. It was all about the kingdom. The Church of God was still kept a "great secret." It was "hid in God" (Eph. iii. 9). It was not yet "made known unto the sons of men" (Eph. iii. 5). It had been "kept secret since the world began" (Rom. xvi. 25).

The only question the Apostles asked was about the kingdom, not about the Church. They did not ask *whether* the kingdom was to be restored to Israel or not. They asked only *as to the "time" when* it was to be restored; whether it would be *now*, "at this time," or at some future time. They neither doubted nor questioned the *fact* of its restoration.

It is certainly very strange that Peter, who heard these words, should, *within a few days*, have stood up and said, "Repent and be baptized every one of you IN THE NAME OF JESUS CHRIST" (Acts ii. 38).

It is impossible for us to suppose that Peter, and those who afterward baptized, should be either forgetful of, or disobedient to, the Lord's command, within so *few days* of its having been given.

Having had direct teaching from the Lord Himself on these very subjects, surely we should see, in the immediately subsequent acts of the Apostles, the nature of the instructions they had received.

If we thus rightly divide this portion of the Word of truth, we find that all is truth. There is no confusion. No violence is done to the Word of God. The command of Christ is left untouched. There it stands, through all these centuries, in all its truth and power, waiting for the moment when it will be obeyed (as it has never yet been obeyed), and the promise fulfilled to the very letter.

The action of the disciples is left unimpaired. Their obedience is not called in question. We are not called upon to blame them, or to excuse them; to condemn them, or to defend them. They followed John the Baptiser in their proclamation of the kingdom, and they continued to use the baptism with which he had baptized.

As long as the Divine offer of the kingdom made by Peter in Acts iii. 19—21 (R.V.) was open, baptism with material water was carried on, side by side. with the baptism with spiritual water (*pneuma hagion*), which was administered by the laying on of hands (compare Acts xix. 6[1]); the one *decreasing* and the other *increasing*, on the principle of John iii. 30.

This coming change had been four times foretold (Matt. iii. 11. Mark i. 8. Luke iii. 16 and Acts i. 5), and we see it taking place; but the change is not complete until the offer of the kingdom made in Acts iii. 19, 20 was finally and formally closed and withdrawn in Acts xxviii. 25, 26. Until then baptism with water was continued, though it was *decreasing.* And it is mentioned only in those Pauline Epistles written during that period (1 Cor. and Rom. vi.), but never again afterward. In the Epistles written after that solemn epoch it is never once referred to; but only the "one baptism" with *pneuma hagion.* In Ephesians, Philippians, Colossians, and the Pastoral Epistles there is no mention of any ordinances; except to emphasize the fact that they no longer exist, but are all done away in that completeness which is ours "in Christ."

Ordinances that had to do with the flesh have no place in the Mystery or Secret which was revealed to Paul.[2] There, all is Spiritual.

The Phenomena as to the two Baptisms may be thus presented :—

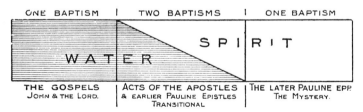

ONE BAPTISM	TWO BAPTISMS	ONE BAPTISM
THE GOSPELS JOHN & THE LORD.	ACTS OF THE APOSTLES & EARLIER PAULINE EPISTLES TRANSITIONAL	THE LATER PAULINE EPP. THE MYSTERY.

When the Mystery was revealed to Paul, and by him was "made known to the sons of men," the Hebrew "doctrine of baptisms" was left behind with many other

---

[1] Verses 4 and 5 were what Paul said, and verse 6 is what Paul did. The "they" in verse 5 were the people who heard John, not they who heard Paul. See *Word Studies on the Holy Spirit*, republished by Kregel Publications, pp. 104-107.

[2] See *The Pauline Epistles*, by the same author, also *Things to Come*, Feb. 1907. *The Acts of the Apostles, Historically and Dispensationally Considered*; and Section No. 6, below, the concluding portion of this Division. Also a series of papers "On Baptist," in *Things to Come*, Vol. XIII.

things, and the new doctrine of the "one baptism" with *pneuma hagion*, or with a spiritual (instead of a material) medium, was brought in.

"Thus, while the Word of truth" is cleared of all confusion the "traditions of men" are torn up by the roots.

The churches to-day profess to take the Acts of the Apostles as their guide to church doctrine and practice (instead of the Epistles that were specially addressed to them as churches); yet they ignore its teaching as to that very ordinance which they all agree in treating as fundamental, though at the same time they differ so widely as to its administration.

They then wrest a command of Christ, given with reference to the totally different and Future Dispensation, and strive to obey it in this present Dispensation in which it has no place.

They thus land themselves in an insurmountable difficulty; and erect barriers which effectually divide up the visible Church into hostile camps.

Failing to divide the Word of truth rightly, they get error instead of truth; and, believing they are obeying the Word of God, they are really only following the tradition of men.

For what is the state of the case historically?

From the Acts of the Apostles we know that they baptized only in the one name.

We know also that for some time this practice must have continued.

We hear nothing of baptism in the *Triune* name till the time of Justin Martyr[1] (A.D. 114—165), and at the London Synod, called by Augustine in 605, any other form of words was pronounced to be invalid. This was confirmed by Pope Zacharius (741—752).

On the other hand, we have evidence of the baptism in the *one* name in the days of Cyprian, for he condemns those who held that it was sufficient to say "in the name of Jesus Christ."[2] But it was declared to be valid by the Council of Frejus, A.D. 792, and also by Pope Nicholas I. as late as (858—867).[3]

---

[1] *Apologia*, lxxix.
[2] Ep. lxxii (Migne), lxxiii. (Oxford).
[3] *Responsa at Bulgaros.*

So that there was evidently confusion of practice as well as of doctrine, down to a very late period.

Various explanations of this diversity are given, but they are all based only on reasoning and probability.

We cannot believe that such a difference between the command in Matt. xxviii. and the practice of the Apostles in the Acts, can be accounted for on the ground that there is no difference between the use of the *three* names and the *one*. For in this case we may ask, What are *words* for? They are useless for the purpose of revelation, if in a simple and yet crucial case like this they do not mean what they say.

We could understand it better if the command had been to baptize in the *one* name, and the practice had been in the *three* names, for then the greater would have included the less. But, How can the less include the greater? How can the *one* include the *three?* and In what respect would this differ from John's baptism? John baptized into the *one* name. Did this include the three? If not, Why not? and Why should Peter's baptism include the three, if John's did not?

The fact is, there is no real explanation of any kind. The actual conflict is between tradition and revelation.

Our choice lies between these two. We may disobey 2 Tim. ii. 15 and follow tradition with all its consequent confusion; or, we may rightly divide the Word of truth, and find clearness of vision and peace of mind.

No question of infant baptism, or of sprinkling, pouring, or immersion, can arise where all is spiritual and Divine.

We must include the closing verses of Mark's Gospel in considering the effect of rightly dividing the Word of truth, as it touches the question of baptism.

Here, again, the difficulties are great indeed, if those verses which refer to the kingdom and its proclamation in the yet Future Dispensation, be taken and read into the Present.

Some of those who do this, logically insist on the point that we ought to see these miraculous signs and gifts in the Church to-day; but, as we do not see them, it is concluded that there must be something wrong in the Christian lives of believers; and. hence it is urged that, an increase of holiness must be acquired by some means or other.

Some, who do not see these wonderful gifts and signs, conclude that the passage refers only to the past, and is now done with.

While others, seeing the difficulty created, treat the whole passage as spurious, and regard it as a corruption of the text which ought to be removed.

These are the difficulties which result from reading the commands that refer to the Past and Future Dispensations into the Present; whereas, if we rightly divide them, all difficulties are at once removed.

(k) *The prophecy of Amos.*—Acts xv. 14—18, in which the prophecy of Amos ix. 11, 12, is quoted, was written in a Past Dispensation, and is to receive its fulfilment in the Future. It must not, therefore, be read into the present Dispensation.

When James quoted it in the Council at Jerusalem, the Mystery had not yet been made known for the obedience of faith, for (as we have seen) it was never the subject of Old Testament prophecy.

The prophecy of Amos refers to what will take place "in that day" (ch. ix. 11). The "day" spoken of is the day when (Jehovah says) "I will bring again the captivity of my people Israel, and they shall build the waste cities and inhabit them" (v. 14). Then:

> "In that day will I raise again the Tabernacle of
>   David that is fallen,
> And close up the breaches thereof;
> And I will raise up his ruins,
> And I will build it as in the days of old;
> That they may possess the remnant of Edom
> And of all the heathen, which are called by my
>   name,
> Saith the LORD, that doeth thus."

This prophecy refers neither to the Church of God nor to the temple of Jerusalem; but to "the Tabernacle of David," which stood on Mount Zion before the Temple was erected on Mount Moriah (2 Sam. vi. 17).

It speaks of the heathen, *i.e.*, the Gentile nations, being called "in that day" by the Name of the LORD.

When Peter declared in the Council how God made choice of him, that the Gentiles by his mouth should hear the word of the Gospel (committed unto him) and believe; and was followed by Paul and Barnabas declaring what signs and wonders God had wrought among the Gentiles by them: then James said that the words of the prophets *agreed with this*, for God had declared by Amos that He would return and build again the Tabernacle of David, and bring the Gentiles into blessing with Israel.

God had just shown this by using Peter to proclaim the good news of the Kingdom, first to Israel (Acts vi., vii.) and afterward to the Gentiles (Acts viii.—xii.).

The moment had come, therefore, for the call to Repentance, which was the one condition of this national blessing of Jews and Gentiles as such.

But we know that the proclamation was unheeded, and Peter's call was not obeyed. All this was followed shortly afterward (Acts xxviii. 25—28) by the solemn and formal proclamation of Isa. vi. 9, and the fulfilment of the threat of judicial blindness which has, from that day, covered Israel's heart (2 Cor. iii. 15. Rom. xi. 25).

Gentile blessing in association with Israel is now in abeyance: and Acts xv. does not refer to the Mystery, or to the Church of God, but to the Gentile nations as such.

The Mystery had not yet been made known, but "these things" had been "made known from the beginning." The following is the correct rendering of what was the Primitive Greek text [1] of Acts xv. 17 and 18, according to the R.V., Rotherham, J. N. Darby, and other translators :—

" That the residue of men may seek after the Lord,
And all the Gentiles, upon whom my name is called,
Saith the Lord, who maketh these things known [2]
from the beginning of the world."

Thus it is quite clear that this Scripture, written in the Past, and referring to the Future, must not be read

---

[1] According to Greek Texts of Griesbach, Scholtz, Tischendorf, Tregelles, Alford, Westcott and Hort, the Revisers' Greek Text. See above, p. 52.

[2] Margin : "Or, *who doeth these things* which were *known*."

into the Present Dispensation of the Mystery, which was "hid in God from the beginning of the world."

(*l*) "*Son of Man.*"—The title of the Lord Jesus Christ as the "Son of Man" is a title that belongs to Him in the Past and Future Dispensations as "the Second Man," "the last Adam," having *dominion in the earth;* and not to the Present Dispensation.

Its first occurrence [1] in Ps. viii., and its first occurrence in the New Testament (Matt. viii. 20), and its last (Rev. xiv. 14—16), all show this connection with the earth.

Out of the eighty-four occurrences of this title in the New Testament, eighty of them are in the four Gospels and *not one in the Church Epistles.* There is only one in the Acts (ch. vii. 56), and after a quotation in Heb. ii. 6, we do not meet with it again until we come to the two places in Revelation (ch. i. 13, and xiv. 14), and these are in connection with His coming to take up His great power and exercise His *dominion in the earth.*

This of itself is sufficient to show us the significance and teaching of this title; and that, quite apart from the principle we are now illustrating, we must not read *past* and *future* Dispensational truths into the *present.*

We have no more to do with the Lord Jesus as "the Son of Man," than the Gentile woman of Canaan had to do with Him as the "Son of David." When she made her plea and based it on that relationship, what could the Lord say but "I am not sent but unto the lost sheep of the house of Israel"? (Matt. xv. 21—24). [1]

The Church of God is brought into union with the risen and exalted Christ as "THE SON OF GOD," and in no sense are we associated with Him in His title "Son of Man."

This at once shuts the Church out of the Gospels, and out of the Tribulation of Matt. xxiv. (of which we have more to say below), and out of all the passages in which we have the title "the Son of Man."

If we were imbued with the words employed in the Church Epistles, and had them ever in our minds, we should instinctively reject any teaching which would

---

[1] See Canon V., below, Part II.

bring us into union with Christ as the "Son of Man," or into Tribulation and Judgment scenes where that title is, and will be, so appropriate.

3. *The PRESENT not to be read into the PAST.*

As we may not read the Past into the Present, so we may not read the Present into the Past.

A few examples will suffice.

(a) *The Mystery, or Secret, concerning "the Church of God."*—This was first "made known to the sons of men" directly, by special revelation from God to the Apostle Paul, and by the "Apostles and prophets" specially raised up for that purpose.

Before that, it had been "kept secret since the world began" (Rom. xvi. 25).

"In other ages it was not made known unto the sons of men" (Eph. iii. 5). "From the beginning of the world it had been hid in God" (*v.* 9).

It had been "hid from ages and from generations" (Col. i. 26).

Surely these statements are perfectly plain, and admit of no dispute.

It has been suggested that this secret refers to the blessing of Gentiles, as such, with Israel; but the simple and conclusive answer to this is, that such blessing was *never a secret*, but was made known at the same moment as the blessing for Israel was made known.

In Gen. xii. 3, it was included in, and was an integral part of, the very first promise ever made to Abraham: "In thee shall all the families of the earth be blessed."

This was repeated at various times. In Gen. xviii. 18, Jehovah said of Abraham, "All the nations of the earth shall be blessed in him." (See also Gen. xxii. 18; xxvi. 4, etc. Deut. xxxii. 43. Ps. xviii. 49; lxvii. 2. Isa. xi. 10; xlix. 6. Luke ii. 32. Rom. xv. 8, etc.)

This was blessing for Gentiles as such, in contrast, and yet in conjunction with Israel. But this is a very different thing from what had been "kept secret." The secret was not concerning Jews and Gentiles as such, but concerning a people taken out from both, and made "fellow-heirs" and members of "the same body"

(Eph. iii. 6), *i.e.*, "the one body," the spiritual body of Christ, which is the one great subject of the Epistle to the Ephesians, and in which there is neither Jew nor Gentile (Rom. x. 12. 1 Cor. xii. 13. Gal. iii. 28. Col. iii. 11).

It seems almost unnecessary to say more, for if these plain Scriptures are not convincing, nothing that we may add of our own is likely to make them so. Language, for the purposes of revelation, is useless if what is said to be "hidden" was made known; or what is called a "secret" had never been kept in silence.

If, however, we accept the statements as to the Mystery having been kept secret until revealed to and by Paul, then we shall look in vain to find it in the Old Testament, or in the Four Gospels, or anywhere before its revelation through the Apostle Paul.

If we think we find it, then we shall at once introduce confusion into the older Scriptures, because we shall arbitrarily, and of our own will, dislocate the Scriptures of truth, and read into the Old Testament what God says He carefully kept out of it.

The Church of God is specially instructed in the Epistles addressed to it.

In these Epistles the Holy Spirit fulfils the Lord's promise made in John xvi. 12—15. There, Christ said, "He shall receive of mine and shall show it unto you." Twice over the Lord repeats these words [1] (*vv*. 14 and 15). These things, which related to Christ, included all that God has made Christ to be unto us who are saved, and all that He has made us to be in Christ. Of this truth the Lord says, "I have many things to say unto you, but ye cannot bear them now. Howbeit, when he, the Spirit of Truth shall have come, he will guide you into all the truth" (John xvi. 12, 13).

If, then, we take the truth which was afterwards revealed, and which could not have been then borne or understood, and put it into the Gospels, from which the Lord designedly and purposely excluded it, we do despite to His purpose; we set at nought His wisdom; we attempt to do what He declares could not be done.

---

[1] In the Greek they are the same, though the A.V. unnecessarily renders them differently in the two verses.

His hearers could not have understood His words had He revealed them then, for the great foundation facts of His death and resurrection on which they were based had not then taken place. But people to-day think they can understand the four Gospels if they read this subsequently-revealed truth into them *now*.

It is just this which brings in all the confusion in our reading of the Gospels; and causes us to use one truth to destroy another truth, and prevents us from understanding either.

It is this that makes many exalt what they irreverently call "the teaching of Jesus" in the Gospels, and set it up in opposition to the teaching of Paul.

Whereas both spake by the Holy Ghost: both uttered the words of God as given to them to speak.

The Lord Jesus said of Himself :—

"He whom God hath sent speaketh the words of God" (John iii. 34).

"My teaching is not mine but his that sent me" (John vii. 16).

"I have given unto them the words which thou gavest me" (John xvii. 8).[1]

But the Apostle Paul also spoke only the words given him to speak, and he declares that they were "the words . . which the Holy Ghost teacheth" (1 Cor. ii. 13).

Paul was commissioned to speak and write the truth which, in John xvi. 12, was designedly kept back. If, therefore, we take what Paul wrote, and put it in where the Lord left it out, what can be the result but confusion in our own minds, and a flouting of the expressed purpose and design of the Holy Spirit, in what He withheld and in what He revealed?

This is why, if the Church is put into the Great Tribulation of Matt. xxiv.,[2] it must be to the destruction of that "blessed hope," which should ever be with us as our present comfort and strength.

This is why John vi. is interpreted of the Lord's Supper, which was the subject of a subsequent revelation, and could therefore have no possible teaching concerning it.

---

[1] See below, page 183.

[2] See under No. 5, below, "The Future not to be read into the Present."

This is why the Church of the Pauline Epistles has been read into the Old Testament prophecies and put in the place of the Bride. (See Ps. xlv. Isa. liv. 5—8; lxii. 4. Jer. iii. 14. Hos. ii. 16, 19, etc.)

This is why the Church of God is spoken of as "she," while in the Epistles its members grow up "unto a perfect MAN"; and are part of Him who is the Bridegroom; and in Him are made "one new man," and not a "new woman."

(*b*) The title "sons of God" is closely associated with the Church of God; for, according to the Pauline usage it is the peculiar title of those who are new creations in Christ Jesus. This we see from all the Church Epistles, especially Rom. viii.

We must not therefore read this usage into the Old Testament, and interpret in the same sense the expression "sons of God" which we meet with there eight times: viz., Gen. vi. 2, 4. Job i. 6; ii. 1; xxxviii. 7. Ps. xxix. 1; lxxxix. 6. Dan. iii. 25.

In all these passages the expression "sons of God" is used of *angels.*[1]

The ground on which the two distinct usages are equally true of the two different classes of beings, respectively, is this: that "a son of God" denotes a being which exists as the direct creative act of God; produced by Him in contrast with being produced by man.

The angels are called "sons of God" because they are a separate creation distinct from all others. The first man, Adam, could be called a "son of God" in the same sense (Luke iii. 38), because God created him. But Adam's descendants were not the special creations of God; for Adam, "created . . . in the likeness of God" (Gen. v. 1), BEGAT a son "*in his own likeness*" (*v.* 3). So that, being the sons of the first Adam, we are "sons of men," and we cannot be called sons of God by natural generation. When, however, we are His workmanship, created in "Christ Jesus" (Eph. ii. 10); "new creations" in Christ

---

[1] See below, p. 188, etc. Also a pamphlet on *The Sons of God*, by the same author and publisher. Job xxxviii. 7 was clearly before the creation of man. And in Dan. iii. 25 there is no article, and it does not denote Christ, but an angelic being.

(2 Cor. v. 17); then, in Him, we can be called "sons of God." We are, then, His sons by the act of spiritual regeneration; for, He has created within us a New nature, and given us a "sonship spirit," whereby we are able to say "Abba," *i.e.*, my Father. (Rom. viii. 15. Gal. iv. 6.)

This Pauline usage of the expression is, therefore, quite distinct from the expression as we find it in the Old Testament. Had this been discerned, and the Present Dispensation not read into the Past, it would never have entered into any one's head to have thought that the expression "the sons of God" in Gen. vi. 2, 4, could have been used of *the sons of Seth!*[1]

(c) The word "Church" may be considered here; for the changes in its meaning, though they might be classed under *usage* (See Canon III., Part II., below), depend rather on the changes of Dispensation than on usage, as such; and on Chronology rather than on Grammar.

In the Pauline Epistles the word acquires a meaning which it never had before. The meaning which is peculiar to this present Dispensation must not, therefore, be read into the Word when it is used in the Past Dispensation.

As to its Etymology *Ecclesia* means *Assembly*, or a Congregation of *called out ones*. But there are various classes of people who are *called out* from others.[2]

Israel was an *Ecclesia*, or an assembly of *People called out* from other Peoples and Nations. See Gen. xxviii. 3 (its first occurrence), where it is rendered *multitude*, and is used of Israel as a whole, as *called out* and distinct from all other nations.

It is used, in Gen. xlix. 6, of a smaller company of Israelites, or assembly of people *called out* from Israel, *viz.*, of the Tribal Council of Simeon and Levi.

Later on, in the same Past Dispensation, we find it used of another kind of assembly, *viz.*, of those who were *called out* of all Israel as worshippers assembling themselves together, as such, before the Tabernacle and

---

[1] For, as a matter of fact, we see good and bad men and women marrying every day without any breed of monstrosities such as were the *Nephilim*, *Rephaim*, etc.

[2] The Greek word ἐκκλησία (*ecclēsia*) is used 70 times in the Septuagint for קָהָל (*cāhāl*), from which we have our English word, with its meaning, *to call*. See further, on pp. 248, 249, below.

the Temple. This is the meaning of the word in Ps. xxii. 22, 25, in the Gospels, Acts vii. 38, etc. A further development of the usage of the word was caused in the closing or transition period of the Past Dispensation, which affected the meaning of the word as used in the Gospels, and in the Acts of the Apostles : at any rate, in the earlier portion of the Acts, which is a transitional book.[1] During that period (covered by the Gospels and Acts) the *called out* ones are the "Sheep-fold" of John x. The assembly was composed of "the lost sheep of the house of Israel." "The Porter" (John the Baptist) *opened* it and admitted the true Shepherd and the sheep whom He gathered; Baptism (the pool by the sheep-gate) being the mode of admission. Christ was the good Shepherd of these "lost sheep of the house of Israel" thus *called out*. Hence He was at once the "door" (*v.* 7), and the "shepherd" (*v.* 14).

Peter *called out* the "other sheep" which the Shepherd had (Acts viii.—xii), and brought them in to the "one flock" (*v.* 16). They were "not of this (Jewish) fold," but Gentiles (as such), with Israelites in the place of their dispersion, who confessed Jesus as the Christ, the Son of God.

These are the *Ecclesia* or "Church" of the Gospels and Acts.

They had been led into this fold, but they were to be led out (John x. 9), and this commission was given to Paul. In Acts xix. 9, he began this work when he "separated the disciples," and the "hardening" of Isa. vi. was approaching its "completion." When that Prophecy was fulfilled in Acts xxviii. the change of Dispensation was completed.

Henceforward the word *Ecclesia* acquires a more restricted meaning, and is used of "the Church of God" eleven times in Paul's Epistles.

We must not, therefore, confuse the truth belonging and peculiar to these Dispensations, which is seen in the various usages of the word *Ecclesia*.

There are thus no less than five distinct usages of the word *Ecclesia*.

(1) It is first used of all Israel as *called out* from the Nations.

---

[1] See *Things to Come,* Nov. 1906.

(2) It is used of those of Israel who feared the Lord and were *called out* as His worshippers (Acts vii. 38).

(3) It is used of this company of called-out ones in the Gospels and earlier chapters of the Acts.

In Matt. xvi. 18 the reference was to a future called-out people. "On this rock I WILL BUILD."

There could have been no reference here to the "*Ecclesia* in the wilderness" (Acts vii. 38); nor to the *Ecclesia* of the Church of God in this Dispensation. Those who heard these words of the Lord's promise could not connect them with the Secret or Mystery which was "hid in God," and had not yet been made known to the sons of men. But they could connect them with Hos. i. 10; and ii. 23. This is the promise which the Lord's hearers would have known. Only with that promise in Hosea could they have associated this promise of the Lord in Matt. xvi. 18.

The revelation here made was an addition to the promise in Hosea. The Son of Man was about to be rejected. The prophecies of Him as "the stone which the builders refused" were about to be fulfilled. Nevertheless, the time was approaching when He would become God's "sure foundation" according to Isa. xxviii. 16: "Thus saith Adonai Jehovah, Behold, I lay[1] in Zion for a foundation, a stone, a tried stone, a precious corner stone, a sure foundation,"etc. That may be either "I have laid" (R.V.), or "I will lay." Both are true. Christ had been laid already then, in the counsels of God, and He would yet be laid in their fulfilment by God.

The Lord here repeats that promise. And the whole point was, Who was this Son of Man? Some said one thing and some another, and the Lord asks: "But YE, whom do ye say that I am? And Simon Peter answered and said, Thou art the Messiah, the Son of the living God. And Jesus, answering, said to him, Blessed art thou, Simon son of Jona, for flesh and blood revealed it not to thee, but my Father who is in the heavens. And I say also to thee, that thou art [called] *Petros* (a stone), and on this *Petra* (a rock) I will build my *Ecclesia*, and [the] gates of *Hades* shall not prevail against it, and I

---

[1] Hebrew, יִסַּד (*yissad*) may be either the Piel preterite or the Kal future.

will give to thee the keys of the kingdom of the heavens " (Matt. xvi. 15—19).

In the words which follow we learn that the builders were about to reject God's foundation; for in the very next verse we read "FROM THAT TIME forth began Jesus to show unto His disciples, how that He must go unto Jerusalem, and SUFFER " (*v.* 21).

Thus, His sufferings are not mentioned until the announcement had been made, that, though the foundation-stone was about to be rejected, it would yet be built upon. This rejected "Son of Man" is indeed the Christ, God's "Anointed," and He will become "the head of the corner."

On Him, the Messiah, His Ecclesia or Assembly, spoken of in the Prophets, would yet be built. "I will build" are His words. "I will call" are Jehovah's words in Hosea: "I will call them my people, which were not my people; and her beloved, which was not beloved. And it shall come to pass, that in the place where it was said unto them, Ye are not my people: there shall they be called the children of the living God. Isaiah also crieth CONCERNING ISRAEL, though the number of the children of Israel be as the sand of the sea, A REMNANT SHALL BE SAVED" (Rom. ix. 25—27).

This Remnant is the Ecclesia mentioned by the Lord in Matt. xvi. 18.

The gates of hell will strive against it, as Rom. ix. 29 testifies, but the remnant shall be saved. This future Ecclesia of Israel is to be built UPON Christ, the Messiah, as the Foundation Stone.

The Church of God, as an Assembly, is also compared to a building; its members are built individually *on* a doctrinal foundation, but the building itself is "a holy temple IN the Lord; IN whom ye also are builded together by [the] Spirit."

The Church of God is now a spiritual building IN Christ: but the Ecclesia of Matt. xvi. 18 is the future, corporate, saved "remnant" of Israel.

The present Church of God is composed of Jews AND Gentiles, but the Ecclesia of Matt. xvi. 18 taken with Hos. ii. 23. Isa. x. 22, 23. and Rom. ix. 27, is a "remnant" OF "the children of Israel."

(4) In Acts xix. 32, 41 it is used of the guild or "company" of the Ephesian craftsmen as distinct from the rest of the population of Ephesus (compare verse 25).

(5) In Acts xix. 39 it is used of what we call a "Town's meeting," *i.e.*, a duly summoned gathering of the citizens in meeting assembled.

In Jas. ii. 2 the word "assembly" is not the rendering of the Greek *Ecclesia*, but it is the word Synagogue. "If there come into your Synagogue" (so margin).

From all this it will be seen how necessary it is to confine the meaning of the word *Ecclesia*, or Church, to the Dispensation in which it is used; and to note whether it is used, in the Past Dispensation, of all Israel; or of Godly Israelites; or of the whole of God's people; or of a portion of them in a certain District, City, or House.[1]

The special usage of this word *Ecclesia*, in this Present Dispensation, by the Holy Spirit was not known until it was revealed to Paul as the Secret (or Mystery) which had been "hid in God" (Eph. iii. 9); "hid from ages and from generations" (Col. i. 26); "kept secret since the world began" (Rom. xvi. 25).

No, the "great mystery," or Secret, is concerning the one spiritual unity of "Christ and His church," and the end of it belongs to this present dispensation, and will close it up when the members of that Body will be

"Received up in glory" (1 Tim. iii. 16).

4. *The FUTURE not to be read into the PRESENT.*

(*a*) The Great Tribulation, all believe to be still future; but yet, many Preachers and Teachers hold and teach that the Church of God, altogether or in part, will pass through it in whole or in part.

Some teach that *all* the Church will pass through *all* the Tribulation; others teach that *only a part* of the Church will so pass through it all; while there are yet others who teach that *all* the Church will pass through

---

[1] The word is never used of a building; nor is the Pauline sense used in the Old Testament, nor in the Gospels, nor in the earlier transitional portion of the Acts. Our English word "church" is said to be derived from a combination and corruption of two Greek words, κύριος (*kyrios*), *Lord*, and οἶκος (*oikos*), *house.* Hence *Kyriake*, the Lord's house, preserved in Scotch *kirk.*

a *part* of the Tribulation. These last hold what is known as "the firstfruits view," which identifies the Church of God with the 144,000 of Rev. xiv., and places the Rapture of the Church in or after the middle of the Great Tribulation, and after the revelation of the Beast in his superhuman form, in ch. xiii.

But here, again, we see the confusion and contradiction of reading what refers to Israel in the Future into the Present Dispensation; and interpreting it of the Church of Goa, to the destruction of its present hope of being alive and remaining at the Lord's *coming forth* into the air to receive them, its members, to Himself, before the Day of the Lord bursts suddenly like a thief upon a world which cries "peace and safety."

The Church of God is assured that that Day shall not overtake it as a thief. (1 Thess. v. 1—4.)

The firstfruits in Rev. xiv. are the firstfruits of those who are redeemed "from the earth" (*v.* 3); redeemed "from among men." They *stand* "before the throne" (*vv.* 1, 3); and they "follow the Lamb whithersoever He goeth" (*v.* 4). But all such language as this is foreign to the Church of God. We who are members of the spiritual Body of Christ are already "seated in the heavenlies in Christ Jesus" (Eph. ii. 6); and we shall not "stand before the throne," but be actually seated with Him when He shall have received us up into glory.

The other view, of part of the Church of God passing through the Tribulation is equally erroneous, and misleading. The Body is "one." There is no amputation of the spiritual body of Christ. There can be no deformity such as would be caused by the absence of any of its members. If the Head "cannot say to the feet I have no need of you," while here on earth, how much less can it be said in the day when "the number of the elect shall be accomplished" and the whole body presented perfect, complete, and "faultless" in glory. It is impossible for any one who is imbued with the language of the Pauline Epistles to imagine any connection between the Church of God and the Great Tribulation.

To say that the Church of God will be divided, and part of it go through the Tribulation, and part not; and that this division is based on the degree of holiness or watchfulness, or light, or doctrinal views, is to destroy the whole foundation of Grace, and put human merit in its place. Membership in the body of Christ is based on *life*, not on *light*. It depends neither on wages nor works; but, on the "gift of God," not on the acquirement of knowledge; on the reception of God's grace, not on the reception of man's tradition.

Still less is there anything to warrant the belief that the Church of God must pass through the whole, or any part, of the Tribulation.

If we fail to rightly divide the Word of truth as to this we shall bring dishonour upon the free grace of God.

Indeed the Spirit of God seems to have taken special care to preserve us from such mistakes.

The Tribulation is everywhere either distinctly stated or specially indicated as being connected with Israel. The words are spoken "concerning Israel and concerning Judah" (Jer. xxx. 4). This fact, of itself, shows that it has no connection with the Church of God.

In Jer. xxx. 7 it is called "the time of Jacob's trouble." And why "Jacob?" Because that name carries us back to that night of Jacob's trouble in Gen. xxxii. 24—30, when, after many years of exile, he was about to return to his own land, and had reached its borders. There he heard of Esau's preparations to come and meet him at the head of 400 armed men. When he heard this, "Jacob was greatly afraid and distressed" (*v.* 7), and he cries to God in his distress, and pleads the "mercies" of God, and deliverance from the hand of Esau lest he come and smite. It was the crisis of Jacob's life; when, had "the mother with the children" been smitten, there would have been an end of the future nation of Israel, whose name was, for the first time, revealed on that eventful night.

Even so the coming Tribulation will be the time of "Jacob's trouble," the crisis of the coming nation. It will not arrive until Israel returns to the land. This is clear from Jer. xxx. 3, which proceeds to describe the "trembling" and "fear," and adds "Alas! for that day is great, so that none is like it: it is even the time of Jacob's trouble; but he shall be saved out of it" (*v.* 7). The whole of this chapter should be carefully studied; and with it, Dan. xii. 1: "At that time (*i.e.*, at the crisis of

Antichrist's power, see the end of ch. xi.) shall Michael stand up, the great prince which standeth for the children of thy (Daniel's) people: and there shall be a time of trouble, such as never was since there was a nation even to that same time: and at that time thy (Daniel's) people shall be delivered."

It is positively certain that that time has not yet arrived; for, at the destruction of Jerusalem (which is supposed by some to be the Tribulation), instead of returning to their land the people were driven out of it; instead of being "gathered," they were "scattered"; instead of being "saved" and "delivered," they fled in their terror.

There are many Scriptures which speak of this time of trouble. Dan.vii.8; viii.9—12,23—26; xi.30—39. Rev.vi.—xix. all refer to those days; but it is in Matt. xxiv. that the Lord Himself gives us its outline, and connects it with the Apocalyptic scenes.

In verses 4—6 its beginnings *in "that generation"* are described; but this introduction is closed with the words "THE END ($\tau\acute{\epsilon}\lambda o\varsigma$, *telos*) IS NOT YET." This is emphatic, and is repeated in Mark xiii. 7, and Luke xxi. 9.[1] This is what is referred to in Matt. xxiv. 34, and Luke xxi. 32, where the word is $\gamma\acute{\epsilon}\nu\eta\tau\alpha\iota$ (*genētai*), *to begin to be, arise.*[2] That generation did actually see the *beginning* of those things which the Lord mentions in Matt. xxiv. 4—6.

Then, in verse 7 (Mark xiii. 8. Luke xxi. 10, 11), the Lord describes *the opening scenes* of the Great Tribulation itself, which correspond exactly with the opening of the seals in Rev. vi.

> The 1st Seal (*vv.* 1, 2) will be a repetition of what took place in that past generation, *viz.*, the coming of *many false Messiahs.*
> The 2nd Seal: *Wars* (*vv.* 3, 4). "Nation shall rise against nation and kingdom against kingdom"

"BUT THE END IS NOT YET" (Matt. xxiv. 4—6).

---

[1] The English "by and by" meant (in 1611) exactly what the Greek means here, *immediately* ($\epsilon\dot{v}\theta\acute{\epsilon}\omega\varsigma$, *eutheōs*). (See below, Part II., Canon III., 2.)

[2] This is not the word used in Luke xxi. 24 for "*fulfilled*," which is quite another word, viz., $\pi\lambda\eta\rho\acute{o}\omega$ (*plēroō*), *to fulfil, or fill full.*

Then:

> The 3rd Seal: *Famines* (*vv.* 5, 6).
> The 4th Seal: *Pestilences* (*vv.* 7, 8).
> The 5th Seal: *Martyrdoms* (*vv.* 9—11).
> The 6th Seal: *Signs in Heaven and Earth* (*vv.* 12—17).

Then it is added in Matt. xxiv. 7, 8, and Mark xiii. 8,

"THESE ARE THE BEGINNING OF SORROWS."[1]

But in Luke xxi. 12 it does not go on to describe these events, which belong to the Great Tribulation, but *it goes back* to what shall be

"BEFORE ALL THESE THINGS,"

and describes the events up to the destruction of Jerusalem in A.D. 70 in verses 12—24. Then the description (having passed over the details of the Tribulation itself given in Matt. xxiv. 9—28 and Mark xiii. 9—23) joins with them in describing the end, and what shall be "immediately after the tribulation of those days," culminating in the coming of the Son of Man, which is the common subject of Matt. xxiv. 29—31. Mark xiii. 24—27. Luke xxi. 25—28.

The very title of Christ as "Son of Man" in this description of the Tribulation shows that the Church of God is not here. That title, as we have seen (page 140), has nothing to do with the Church or with this Dispensation of grace. It has to do with the earth, and with Christ's dominion in the earth. It contemplates the Jews as in their own land, observing their own Sabbath laws (Matt. xxiv. 20). It concerns those who are "in Judea" (*v.* 16). All the expressions used point to a people under the Mosaic law. This cannot therefore refer to the Church of God, which is "not under the law" (Rom. vi. 14. 1 Cor. ix. 21).

True, the Church of God has tribulation NOW, in the world, at least many of its members have, but not the Church, *as such.* But this is a very different thing from the Church, or any part of it, being IN "the tribulation, the great one."

On the other hand, the Scriptures, other than the epistles addressed to the Church of God, constantly refer

---

[1] Greek, ὠδίνοι (*ōdinoi*), *birth-pangs*, or *throes.* Compare Isa. lxvi. 6—11 with Jer. xxx. 5 24.

to that coming time of tribulation (Matt. x. 16—23.[1] Rev. i. 9; ii. 9, 10, 13; iii. 10; vii. 13—17).

Thus, the moment we recognize the great duty of "rightly dividing" the different principles of administration, apportioning each to its own distinct time and Dispensation, we see that the Church of God can have no place in the Great Tribulation; and that, being "not under the law," it must be excluded from all those Scriptures which have the law for its governing principle, and Judæa for the scene of its adminstration.

(b) In the same way, we must not interpret the 144,000 of Rev. vii. or xiv. of the Church of God. We see them involved in the horrors of the Great Tribulation, and in the Dispensation of Judgment; and specially sealed so that they should be preserved through it; whereas the promise to those who belong to the Church of God is very positive that that Day shall not overtake, or come upon it (1 Thess. v. 4).

But beside this, the very enumeration of them excludes all except those who belong to the *tribes of the children of Israel.* Not only are these tribes mentioned thus, collectively, in Rev. vii. 4, but, in verses 5—8, each tribe is afterward mentioned separately by name.

The promise to Daniel was, that when that time of trouble should come, "thy people shall be delivered." Here we see how that deliverance will be secured. This is the deliverance which is referred to in Joel ii. 28—32.

As the Lord had 7,000 who had not bowed the knee to Baal, in the days of Ahab and Jezebel, so He will have 144,000 of those who will refuse to bow the knee to the Beast, or receive his mark in the days of the Great Tribulation.

In Rev. vii. we have two of the three peoples with whom Scripture deals. In verses 1—8 we have the Jews; in verses 9—17 we have the Gentiles. It is clear therefore that we must not put in the Church of God where He has left it out. As for the Jews, we are told that "they shall not be reckoned among the nations" (or Gentiles), Num. xxiii. 9, and as to the Church of God, there is neither

---

[1] See above, page 132.

4. THE FUTURE NOT INTO PRESENT: THE 144,000

Jew nor Gentile (as such) in it (Gal. iii. 28; v. 6; vi. 15. Col. iii. 11).

If we, therefore, join together what God has thus kept distinct, we must get error instead of truth.

Besides, what do we gain by this disobedience to 2 Tim. ii. 15? Where does our advantage come in, by thrusting the Church of God in everywhere, whether the Scripture speaks of Israel or the Gentiles, or the Cherubim, or the Twenty-four Elders, the Bride, Zion, and the New Jerusalem, and everything else? How much must be lost to us of what God would teach us about these various subjects of revelation.

Here, then, we have another example as to our not reading what is still future into this present Dispensation. We need not put the Church of God among those who are numbered of the twelve Tribes of Israel, nor into the innumerable Gentile multitude. A time is coming when the nations will "learn righteousness," not by the grace of God, but by the judgments of God; not by the preaching of the Gospel, but by the proclamations of wrath. "O LORD . . . when thy judgments are in the earth, the inhabitants of the world will learn righteousness" (Isa. xxvi. 9). These are the learners who will make up this "great multitude which no man can number." Many may be of that number who will be left behind when the members of the "One Body" shall have been received up in glory. Many who have been members of churches, but not members of the Church of God. Many who have been labouring at trying to make a unity of the Body, instead of "endeavouring to keep the unity of the Spirit." They will then learn from the judgments of God what they failed to learn from the grace of God; and they will pass through and come out of the Great Tribulation and stand before the throne of God.

Those who believe they will pass through the Great Tribulation must not be surprised if God deals with them "according to their faith"!

(c) Sundry Prophecies relating to the Future Dispensation are interpreted of the Present, to the loss of coherency in the Word, and the gain of perplexity in the mind; to say nothing of the evils produced by perverting, and even "wresting" certain Scriptures from their own specific teaching.

"*The heathen for thine inheritance.*"—How often, for example, have we all heard Ps. ii. 8 quoted on the platforms of missionary meetings:—

> "Ask of me, and I shall give thee the heathen for
>   thine inheritance,
> And the uttermost parts of the earth for thy
>   possession."

This promise to Christ, as Messiah, is quoted, as though it was to be fulfilled by the preaching of the Gospel of the grace of God in this present Dispensation; whereas, the very next verse, if quoted with it, would make such an interpretation, or even application, impossible; for it would show us exactly how that promise is going to be made good; and that it will be by judgment, not by grace.

> "Thou shalt break them with a rod of iron;
> Thou shalt dash them in pieces like a potter's
>   vessel."

When missionaries go forth equipped with a sceptre of iron, instead of the gospel of peace, we may regard such an application as being consistent.

This, really, comes under another head,[1] which we propose to consider below, viz., the Importance of the Context; and the evils which are brought in by wresting any passage from its context. The context of Ps. ii. 8, when read with verse 9, shows decisively what the true interpretation of verse 8 should be; and the scope of the whole Psalm would be seen to confirm it.

"*The mountain of the Lord's house.*"—Isa. ii. is another example. We must all have heard verse 2 quoted again and again of the Church of God:—

> "And it shall come to pass in the last days,
> That the mountain of the LORD's house shall be
>   established in the top of the mountains,
> And shall be exalted above the hills;
> And all nations shall flow unto it," etc.

---

[1] See under Canon IV. in Part II.

This is supposed to teach the future extension of the Church of God, and its universal blessing to the nations; and this, in spite of the many passages in the Epistles which plainly tell us of the dark and terrible character of the last days of the Church on earth : evil men waxing worse and worse, scoffers walking after their own lusts, the departure of many from the faith, turning away their ears from the truth, and the turning them unto fables, and all this culminating in "the apostasy" and the revelation of Antichrist (1 Tim. iv. 2 Tim. iv. 2 Thess. ii. 2 Peter iii., etc.)

But beside all this, the immediate context of Isa. ii. 2 should have made such an interpretation (or even, application) impossible; for the previous verse distinctly states that it was "the word that Isaiah saw concerning Judah and Jerusalem," and not concerning the Church of God.

No application may be made of any Scripture that is not in harmony with what is revealed elsewhere.[1] Such an *application* is forbidden by the subsequent teaching of the Epistles as to the last days of this Dispensation; while such an *interpretation* is forbidden by the context.

"*Thy light is come.*"—Isa. lx. 1, 3, 11, 12 is another portion which is continually applied to the Church, and used to set forth the ultimate triumph of the Gospel, in order to the encouragement of missionary enterprise :

> "Arise, shine for thy light is come,
> And the glory of the Lord is risen upon thee" (Isa. lx. 1).

Whose light? And, Risen upon whom? Not the Church of God, but upon Jacob's seed, and his seed's seed (Isa. lix. 20) when "the Redeemer shall come to Zion."

So far from the Church being in this Scripture, verse 3 distinguishes Jew and Gentile; and Gal. iii. 27, 28 distinguishes the Church from both :

> "And the Gentiles shall come to thy light,
> And kings to the brightness of thy rising."

Here we see that the subject-matter is the Jew and the Gentile; while in the Church of God there is neither

---

[1] See Canon X., below, Part II.

the one nor the other. The prophet is speaking of the Future Dispensation, after the Church shall have been "received up in Glory"; he is speaking of that moment in the Millennial Dispensation, when the Jew shall no longer be the tail, but the head of the nations; and when the Gentiles shall bring their wealth and their glory to Israel. This flowing of the nations for the aggrandizement of Israel is spoken of in other prophecies, and in such terms as to make even an application of them impossible; to say nothing of the interpretation. See Isa. lxi. 3—6, and Zech. xiv. 16—24, where it is distinctly stated that all this shall be when "the LORD shall be king over all the earth" (*v.* 9); when "Jerusalem shall be safely inhabited" (*v.* 11); and all this, not until Messiah's feet shall have stood "upon the Mount of Olives"; even that mount "which is before Jerusalem on the East" (*v.* 4).

(*d*) "The Day of the Lord" is the Day when the Lord shall rule the world in Judgment and Righteousness.

We shall see below, under the section which deals with the importance of first occurrences of words and expressions (Canon v.), that the one great outstanding fact that will characterize that day will be that man will be abased, and Jehovah exalted (Isa. ii. 11, 17). Whatever may be the judgments, or the means employed, the result will be that the day of man's activities will come to an end, and Jehovah will begin to work : and truly, our hearts begin to say even now :

"It is time for Thee, LORD, to work:
For they have made void Thy law" (Ps. cxix. 126).

In this day, and in all previous Dispensations, judgment and rule and power in the earth have been committed unto man. It is called "Man's Day" in 1 Cor. iv. 3, where it is translated "man's judgment" (Margin, "Greek, *day*"). Though the Greek word is "day" it is thus beautifully translated; for, this is the day when man is judging, nationally and individually. Nationally he is a failure; for, the end of nearly six thousand years finds good government to be the great want of the age, and the great problem of the nations. Individually, man is a worker of untold evils, and this in the Church as well as in the world, or even more so. For, the judgment of others instead of himself seems to be his one great object, while the wreckage of broken hearts and ruined lives testifies to the extent of the evils he has wrought.

Yes, this is "man's day." But, "the Lord's Day" is coming,[1] and John sees it laid out in vision before him, when by the Spirit he was shown its course and its end (Rev. i. 10).[2]

This is the day that concerns the world, and it will suddenly overtake it, at the moment when "peace, peace" shall be its cry, and "safety" its creed.

But we must not read that future Day into the present hope of the Church of God, to the destruction of that hope, and the loss of our peace, and the extinction of our joy. For the promise to us is given in no uncertain sound: "that day shall not overtake you as a thief." The reason is, because we are "not in darkness" concerning it; we have the prophetic word which is a light in this darkness (2 Pet. i. 19); and, for that very reason we are called "the children of the light, and the children of the day" (1 Thess. v. 1—5).

By rightly dividing the Word of truth we distinguish between Man's day and the Lord's day; and also between the Lord's day and "the day of Christ" (Phil. i. 6; ii. 16), when He who has begun the good work in us will perfect it; and we shall be with Christ; and rejoice to find that we "have not run in vain, neither laboured in vain."

5. *One Part of* THE FUTURE *not necessarily to be read into another part of the Future.*

There are Advents, and Resurrections, and Judgments which are all still future, and they must be rightly divided the one from the other, respectively, if we would learn, and know the truth respecting them.

(a) *The Advents.*—There is the "Parousia," or Presence of Christ, which is the subject of the earlier Pauline Epistles, involving the Rapture of living saints and the dead in Christ (1 Thess. iv.), and "our gathering

---

[1] *Four Prophetic Periods*, by the same author.
[2] See below, p. 198. Also a pamphlet on *The Lord's Day: Is it a Day of the Week, or the Day of the Lord?* by the same author.

together unto Him" (2 Thess. ii. 1) before His Advent in judgment glory connected with "the Day of the Lord" (Isa. ii. 11, 17. 1 Thess. v. 2).

These two are to be carefully and rightly divided.

The Parousia will be "our gathering unto" Christ, while the Advent will be the gathering of Israel to their Messiah and their Land (Gen. xlix. 10. Isa. xl. 11; xliii. 5; liv. 7. Jer. xxix. 14; xxxi. 10; xxxii. 37. Ezek. xx. 34, 41; xxxiv. 12—14, &c.).

The Church of God has nothing to do with the Day of the Lord. That day will overtake the world as a thief in the night (1 Thess. v. 2).

But the Church of God is distinctly told that "that day shall not overtake you as a thief" (*v.* 4).

The Church is assured that it will be at "rest . . . WHEN the Lord Jesus shall be revealed from heaven with his mighty angels, in flaming fire taking vengeance on them that know not God" (2 Thess. i. 7, 8). These will "be punished with everlasting destruction from the presence of the Lord and from the glory of His power WHEN HE SHALL HAVE COME [1] to be glorified in his saints, and admired in all them that believe" (*vv.* 9, 10). There are two marks of time "WHEN" in 2 Thess. i. 7 and 10; but they are not expressed in the same way in the Greek.[2] The first means "at"; the second means "when."

Verse 7 relates to the Revelation of Christ to His enemies; verse 10 relates to the glorification of Christ with His saints.

The Saints will be *at rest* AT His revelation (verse 7).

And WHEN He is revealed, He will have already come and have been glorified with His saints (*v.* 10).

Scripture can hardly be clearer than this.

In order that there may be no mistake, the same **fact** is put in two ways: *first,* the "rest" which we shall have AT His Advent (His revelation in Judgment); and, *second,* the fact that He shall have already given us this rest, WHEN He is revealed.

---

[1] Greek, ἔλθη (*elthē*), 2nd aorist Tense subjunctive Mood, as in Luke xvii. 10, 1 Cor. xv. 24, where it is so translated. Compare Matt. xxi. 40. Mark viii. 38; x. 23. John iv. 25; xvi. 13. Acts xxiii. 35. Rom. xi. 27.

[2] In verse 7 it is ἐν τῇ ἀποκαλύψει (*en tē apokalupsei*), AT THE APOCALYPSE, or *revelation* (as in the R.V.). In verse 10 it is ὅταν ἔλθη (*hotan elthē*), WHEN HE SHALL HAVE COME to be glorified.

It was this Advent which was the subject of Old Testament prophecy. We read nothing of the Rapture until it was revealed in 1 Thess. iv. 13—v. 11. This revelation was made on purpose that we might not be "ignorant"; as all are, and must be, concerning these things, unless they know what is here made known.

It was revealed for the special purpose, not only of informing the Church of God as to what it was ignorant of, but of comforting it. Twice over we have the exhortation, "Wherefore comfort one another with these words" (1 Thess. iv. 18); and, "Wherefore comfort yourselves together, and edify (or build up) one another" (1 Thess. v. 11). Both exhortations are introduced (in English) with the word "wherefore,"[1] showing the necessary connection between the cause and the effect; and linking them together.

If we read the Scriptures relating to the Rapture, and interpret them of the Advent, what is intended for our "comfort" will be used as an object of fear, and what is given as "blessed hope" (Titus ii. 13) will be taken as our dread.

With many this is the case. And all the mischief is caused by not "rightly dividing" two truths both belonging to the same Dispensation.

At the present moment of writing, both are, of course, future. Hence it is that so many mix them up together. They both concern the Lord's Coming, hence it is they are confused.

It is the same Christ who will gather His saints to Himself at their Rapture; and who will afterwards gather Israel to their Land.

His coming, from Gen. iii. 15, onward, has always been the hope of Creation (Rom. viii. 19 23), and the hope of Israel (Jer. xiv. 8), as it is now the hope of the Church of God (Titus ii. 13). But, as with the Resurrections, each is "in its own order."

In due time He came, but He was rejected and crucified. Israel was "not gathered" at that coming (Isa. xlix. 5);

---

[1] The former is ὥστε (*hōste*), *so that*, marking the exhortation as the logical result of the revelation. The latter is διό (*dio*), *on which account, wherefore,* marking the revelation as being the ground of the exhortation.

therefore that gathering is now in abeyance, until the Lord's Advent, the Day of the Lord.

In that, which we speak of (for the sake of convenience) as the "*first* coming," we have an illustration of what we call the "*second* coming."

There were prophecies even of that *first* coming which had to be rightly divided in order to be understood, even when read by those who lived in the Past Dispensation; and which might have been understood had the words of those prophecies been carefully noted. As these prophecies serve to illustrate the order of events connected with the *second* coming it may be well to look at them more closely:

In Micah v. 2, and Zech. ix. 9, we have two passages which both foretell and relate to that same first coming; and, fortunately, the English Version is as clear as the Hebrew in both cases.

In Micah v. 2 the word is יָצָא (*yātza'*), *to come out.*

In Zech. ix. 9 it is בּוֹא (*bō'*), *to come in.*

In Micah v. 2 the former is rendered "come forth," and in Zech. ix. 9 the latter is rendered "come unto."

Both were then future. The one prophesied of Christ's "coming forth" at Bethlehem, and the other prophesied of Christ's "coming unto" Jerusalem.

Until the time came for their fulfilment, there was nothing in those prophecies to tell the readers what would be the interval between those two comings, or whether there would be any at all. There was nothing to tell them that they were separated, as we now know, by more than thirty years.

Some readers indeed might interpret them of one and the same event, and come to the conclusion that there was "a discrepancy"; or that the text was corrupt, or that there was something wrong with the translation.

These are the conclusions so readily come to by Higher and Lower Critics, who first create the difficulty by not rightly dividing the Word, and then endeavour to explain it by cutting it to pieces with their pens, as Jehoiakim did with his pen-knife.

Both these Scriptures speak of the same coming of the Lord; but they are separated by some thirty-three years. He "*came forth*" from Bethlehem at His Incarnation (Matt. ii. 1). He *"came unto"* Jerusalem six days before His crucifixion (Matt. xxi. 1—10).

Had the Jews carefully read and received these words of God as they were known and understood by many at the time (Matt. ii. 4–6) they would not have stumbled at His birth in humiliation.

All the events connected with those thirty-three years we speak of as having taken place at His first coming.

In like manner, all the events that will take place between Christ's "coming forth" into the air and His "coming unto" Jerusalem in the Day of the Lord go to make up what we speak of as His second coming.

But those events are all perfectly distinct, and are to be rightly divided off the one from the other, and are not to be confused or confounded.

All the events which will occur between the *coming forth* or the Descension of the Lord into the air, for our "gathering together unto Him" there, and His *coming unto* the earth, in power and great glory to execute judgment, must be rightly divided in order to be rightly understood.

We cannot, of course, speak positively as to the exact duration of that interval between the "coming forth" and the "coming unto."

Those who do not divide the Word at all make no interval, but jumble all the Scriptures up in confusion.

Others, who do make some attempt to divide it, make the mistake, we believe, of limiting that interval to "seven years," as being the "last week of Daniel."

True, there is such a period of "seven years" (Dan. ix. 27): but there is no need thus to limit that interval. They may be the last seven of a larger number of years: for many events have to take place and many things have to be done during that interval.

Moreover, there is the συντέλε:α (*sunteleia*), *the consummation of the ages;* and there is the τέλος (*telos*), the *crisis* or *end* of the age.[1]

If the whole *sunteleia* should be forty years, and the *telos* should be the last seven years, then we should

---

[1] For the former see Matt. xiii. 39, 40, 49; xxiv. 3; and for the latter compare Matt. xxiv. 6, 13, 14.

have both periods of the thirty-three years and the seven years.

(b) *The Resurrections.*—Several resurrections are spoken of in the New Testament.

These have all to be rightly divided if we would learn the truth of the Word.

Like the Coming of Christ, Resurrection was always the hope of God's people.[1]

And this Resurrection was twofold, and its hope consisted of a first resurrection as distinct from a second.[2] These were distinguished as that of the "just" and "unjust" (Acts xxiv. 15), "life" and "condemnation" (John v. 29).

And they were distinguished also as to the times at which they shall take place.

Both are connected with the Advent: the one being immediately *before* the thousand years, and the other at the end of the thousand years (Rev. xx. 4—6, 13).

These are referred to by our Lord: and the times and their order are very definitely stated in 1 Cor. xv. 20—28.

Christ the firstfruits already raised.

Then there will be those who will be raised in their own ranks, or order: "they that are Christ's" at "the first resurrection" of Rev. xx. 5, 6.

Then there will come "the end" or last rank, at the end of the thousand years (1 Cor. xv. 23, 24); when, after the judgment of the great white throne, Christ will deliver up the kingdom to the Father.

But in 1 Thess. iv. we have a special revelation as to another resurrection at the time of the Rapture. We must not confuse it with the "first" and "second" Resurrections of Rev. xx. These are both connected with the Advent, the one, as we have seen, immediately *before* the thousand years, and the other immediately *after.* *Both were the subject of Old Testament prophecy;* while the Resurrection of 1 Thess. iv. 16 was a secret, then, for

---

[1] Job xix. 26. Ps. xvi. 10 ; xlix. 15. Isa. xxvi. 19. Dan. xii. 2. Hos. xiii. 14. It was announced at the Bush (Exod. iii. 6), where Christ says God spake "touching the resurrection of the dead" (Matt. xxii. 31, 32), "for God is not the God of the dead but of the living." Therefore (the argument is), Abraham, Isaac, and Jacob must rise again. This was their hope (Heb. xi. 8—16).

[2] See Ps. xlix. 15. Dan. xii. 2.

the first time, made known in a special revelation "by the word of the Lord." This formula always denotes a special and specific prophetic announcement.[1] Moreover, it is not called a "Resurrection." The word is not a Noun, but a Verb. "The dead in Christ shall rise first." This word "first" has nothing to do with the "first resurrection" of Rev. xx. 5, 6; but only with the fact that it would be the former of the two there spoken of; their mention following closely one on the other. But in 1 Thess. iv., two events are spoken of, not two resurrections: *first* "the dead in Christ shall rise": and *second*, the living who remain shall be caught away in clouds together, with them, unto the meeting of the Lord, into the air; "and so (*i.e.*, in this manner) we shall be ever with the Lord."

Thus, the rising revealed in 1 Thess. iv., though it is still future, at the moment of writing, will be the great closing event of this present Dispensation, and will usher in the succeeding Dispensation of Judgment.

There are some who believe that, in Phil. iii. 11—14, we have a later revelation[2] referring either to an earlier removal of the Saints; or to the hope of our "change" without dying; as the special hope of the "prize of our calling on high" (*v.* 14). This would then be either an expansion of, or addition to, what is revealed in 1 Thess. iv. concerning those who shall be alive and remain; or a fresh revelation of another and perhaps earlier "calling on high."

Certainly we do not seem to have grasped or exhausted all that that wonderful chapter (Phil. iii.) reveals. It seems to be connected specially with the glorious revelations made later in Ephesians and Colossians: and therefore with the Mystery of Christ and the Church in Eph. v.

It may be asked whether 1 Thess. iv. and 1 Cor. xv. completed all that God had then yet to reveal of the riches of His glory: and whether the "prize of our calling on high" may not refer to something special which God

---

[1] See Gen. xv. 1. 1 Sam. ix. 27. 2 Sam. vii. 4. 1 Kings xii. 22. 1 Chron. xvii. 3. 2 Chron. xi. 2; xii. 7. Rev. i. 2, 9; vi. 9; xix. 13; xx. 4.

[2] 1 Thessalonians having been written A.D. 52 and Philippians not till ten or more years afterwards.

had held out for Paul's encouragement when in prison in Rome.

The ἐξανάστασις (*exanastasis*) of Phil. iii, 11 certainly seems to be something beyond the *resurrection* revealed in the former and earlier Scriptures. It means, etymologically, *out-resurrection*, and followed as it is by the pronoun ἐκ (*ek*), *out of*, points to something quite different and special.

The word occurs nowhere else in the New Testament. It is used by Polybius[1] in the sense of *removal*, and by Strabo[2] in the sense of *migration*. In any case it was something Paul hoped for and longed to arrive at.[3]

It may point to our *removal* without dying, or to a more special, wondrous, and glorious change, corresponding more with 1 Tim. iii. 16, "received up in glory," referring only to those who shall be alive and remain.

Is not this, our *removal*, something for us to arrive at? Is it not a great and glorious change to hope for?

In any case, if a special word of this kind is used later, in Phil. iii. 11., are we right in jumping to the conclusion that nothing different is meant, and there is no further truth for us to receive or to rightly divide?

We have certainly several resurrections revealed: and these resurrections being all future, and all in their own proper order, it is impossible for us to avoid confusion if we join them all together and make only one "general resurrection" instead of "rightly dividing" them according to the "order" which God has revealed.

(*c*) *The Judgments.*—The creeds of the churches know of but one judgment, which they speak of as the "general judgment," as they know and speak only of one "general resurrection." Yet, more than one is revealed in Scripture; and they are all still future. But, each will be "in its own order," place, and time (Eccles. iii. 1, 17):—

(1) 2 Cor. v. 10.—First, there is the appearance of the risen and changed saints before the *Bema* of Christ.

---

[1] Polybius, ii. 21, 9.   [2] Strabo, 102.

[3] The word is καταντάω (*katantaō*), *to arrive at* (see all the occurrences: Acts xvi. 1; xviii. 19, 24; xx. 15; xxi. 7; xxv. 13; xxvi. 7; xxvii. 12; xxviii. 13. 1 Cor. x. 11; xiv. 36. Eph. iv. 13; and Phil. iii. 11). The word "attained" in verse 12 is λαμβάνω (*lambanō*), *to receive*.

The *time* of this is "the Day of Christ" in the air, while it is the day of Antichrist on the earth.

The *place* is the *Bema* of Christ: that is the daïs from which rewards and prizes are given; not the Bench from which sentences or judgments are pronounced.

The *reason* why "we" appear is to "receive" rewards for "deeds done," service rendered, and works wrought: as well as the "crown of righteousness" which the righteous Judge shall give in that day. We "appear" there not to receive condemnation (Rom. viii. 1); but to "have praise of God" (1 Cor. iv. 5): we shall "not come into judgment" as to our standing or aught else (John v. 24); for the feeblest, and weakest, and poorest of the children of God will "appear" there as having been *already judged* in the person of their Substitute.

The *persons* who will stand there will be there in all the glory and perfection of their resurrection bodies. We are, even here, and now, "in Christ;" and we shall be none the less that when we are changed and made like Christ Himself. True, "we shall all stand before the Bema of Christ" (Rom. xiv. 9—13), but we shall stand there as saved: with and in our resurrection bodies made like Christ's own glorious body (Phil. iii. 20, 21).

(2) Matt. xxv. 31—46.—In this passage we have another judgment spoken of.

The "*time*" for this will be "when the Son of Man shall . . . sit upon the throne of His glory and before him shall be gathered all the Gentiles" $\left(\tau \grave{a} \ \overset{\prime}{\epsilon} \theta \nu \eta, \ ta \ ethn\bar{e}.\right)$

The persons will be the nations. The word $\overset{\prime}{\epsilon} \theta \nu \eta$ (*ethnē*) is rendered *nations* 64 times, and *Gentiles* 93 times; *heathen*, 5 times, and *people*, twice. The Jews therefore will not be there, for they are "not reckoned among the nations" (Num. xxiii. 9); and the Church of God will not be there, because it bears no relation to Christ as "the Son of Man,"[1] and because it shall not come into judgment at all (John v. 24. Rom. viii. 1).

The *place* is "before the throne of his glory." That this throne will be on earth is clear from Isa. xxxiv. 1, 2. Ezek. xxxix. 21. Joel iii. 1, 2, 11, 12.

---

[1] See above, page 140.

The *ground* of the judgment is not even righteousness, much less holiness. It is not the ground either of grace, or of faith. And as to works, it is not even "good works" generally, and as such, but only one specific work, *viz.*, as to how they have *treated* the "brethren" of the Judge, *i.e.*, the Jews. This can only refer to those nations who are alive to stand before that Judge, and which have thus treated or maltreated His "brethren." For there is not a word about resurrection, and we dare not put into the passage so important a matter when the Holy Spirit has so scrupulously left it out. But there are many who do this, and yet with a strange perversity would leave it out of Rev. xx. 4—6, where God has put it in with all the emphasis of reiteration.

The *reward* is peculiar. It is entrance into "the Kingdom prepared FROM the foundation of the world."

How the Church, which is "in Christ" BEFORE the foundation of the world (Eph. i. 4),[1] can "enter the King-dom," is a problem, which those who make it must solve as best they can.

This kingdom is "under the whole heaven" (Ps. cxv. 16), upon the earth, and before the Millennium when He shall appear with His holy angels "to execute judgment" (Zech. xiv. 5. 2 Thess. ii. 8. Jude 14).[2]

But even this judgment is neither total, nor final, for after the thousand years, Satan "must be loosed for a little season," in order to show that man remains the same in spite of all the evidences of the Glory of the Millennial reign.

The nations of the Gentiles immediately range them-selves under Satan's banner of revolt; and are at once destroyed without parley, by the special judgment of "fire from heaven" (Rev. xx. 7—10).

(3) Rev. xx. 11—15. This is the great and final judg-ment scene.

As to *time*, it is immediately after the thousand years. This marks it off from all others.

---

[1] When Christ or the Church is mentioned it is *"before"* the foundation of the world (John xvii. 24. Eph. i. 4. 1 Pet. i. 20) ; but whenever the Kingdom is in question it is *"from"* the foundation of the world (Matt. xiii. 35; xxv. 34. Luke xi. 50. Heb. iv. 3; ix. 26. Rev. xiii. 8; xvii. 8).

[2] See above, pages 116, 117.

As to *place*, it is before "the great white throne."

The *persons* who appear before it are to be raised from the dead for this special purpose. They lived before the thousand years, but they "lived not again until the thousand years were finished" (*v.* 4). Those who died during the thousand years must also be there, not one will be there who has not died. It is "the resurrection of judgment" (John v. 29) or condemnation.

Those who introduce the *dead* among the living nations in Matt. xxv. do not hesitate to introduce the living among the dead in Rev. xx.

We have thus seen that there are these several judgments: and that while all are still future, we have to rightly divide them as to their order, and nature, and character.

6. *The Truth and Teaching of the CANONICAL Order is to be distinguished from the CHRONOLOGICAL and Historical Order.*

By Canonical order we mean the order in which the teaching comes to us in the Canon of Scripture. That order is more or less Divine, at any rate so far as the Old Testament is concerned;[1] and so far as the order of the Pauline Epistles is concerned.[2]

By Chronological and Historical order we mean the order in which books were written and events happened.

These two may not always be the same in their teaching. One may be *Dispensational*, and the other may be *Experimental*.

All God's "works" are perfect, and so are all His "ways." All can see His works, but He has Himself to make known His own ways; as it is written (Ps. ciii. 7),

> "He made known His WAYS unto Moses,
> His ACTS unto the children of Israel."

(*a*) *The Tabernacle.*—When He ordered the making of the Tabernacle He began with the Ark of the Covenant (Exod. xxv. 10); then the Mercy Seat (*v.* 17); then the Table (*v.* 23); then the Candlestick (*v.* 31); then the Tabernacle

---

[1] See *The Names and Order of the Books of the Old Testament*, by the same author.

[2] See *The Church Epistles*, by the same author.

(ch. xxvi.); then the Altar of Burnt Offering, and the Gate (ch. xxvii. 1, 9, 16). But that was the *historical* order, as originating only from God's side. He begins with and from Himself. But those for whom it was given, and who approached to receive its benefits and its blessings, experimentally, began at the other end, with the Gate; and then went on to the worship of God, ending with the communion of the Mercy Seat.

(*b*) *The Great Offerings.*—It was the same with the four Great Offerings (the Sin and Trespass Offerings being reckoned as one). God begins (Lev. i.) with the whole Burnt Offering, setting forth the value of Christ's offering in relation to Himself; descending by the Meal Offering (Lev. ii.), the Peace Offering (Lev. iii.), the Sin and the Trespass Offering (Lev. iv., v.), to the deepest needs of His people. But His people began at the other end, and approached with the sin offering first, as setting forth the experimental sense of their need (Ps. xxxii. 1, 2).

(*c*) *The Four Gospels.*—So, also, as it required four Great Offerings to set forth all the various aspects of Christ's death, so it required four Gospel records to set forth His earthly life; and it would be as reasonable to attempt to make the four Offerings into one as to vainly attempt to "harmonize" the four Gospels into one; as though there were any want of "harmony" in them.

(*d*) 1 *Samuel.*—It is well known that objections have been made against the text of the Book of Samuel because all the events are not in chronological order. But where is it said that they are? And why should they necessarily be so?

A human author arranges his matter as he pleases; and after bringing up his subject to a certain point, may go back and bring up some other matter to the same point.

Or he may introduce a later event and record it where it is desirable to bring out a certain contrast by way of emphasizing it, leaving it to the reader to discover his reason for doing so, and thereby fixing the lesson more surely on his mind.

A human author, we repeat, may do this; but the Holy Spirit of God may not do it, forsooth, without having objections raised against Inspiration!

Notably is this the case with 1 Sam. xvi. 1 to xviii. 30.

Here the commentators do not hesitate to charge the Text with being corrupted, interpolated or transposed; and charges of contradictions and discrepancies are levelled against the genuineness and authority of Scripture.[1]

Why not recognize the fact that we have four events the Chronological and Historical order of which is as follows:

    (1) 1 Sam. xvi. 1—13. The Call of David by God.
    (2) xvii. 1—xviii. 4. The Call of David by Saul.
    (3) xvi. 14—23. David enters Saul's house.
    (4) xviii. 5—30. David leaving Saul's house.

This being the historical order, why may not the Holy Spirit arrange them in such order that He may call attention to His secret movements which were shaping the whole history? And why may He not alternate DAVID and SAUL in order to emphasize the coming of the Spirit on David, and the departing of the Spirit from Saul? In order to show this we have the four events in their spiritual significance and teaching, according to the following:

Structure of Canonical Order: 1 Sam. xvi.—xviii.

A | xvi. 1—13. DAVID'S Call by God. The Spirit coming upon him.
    B | xvi. 14—23. SAUL: The Spirit departing from him.
A | xvii. 1—xviii. 4. DAVID'S Call by Saul.
    B | xviii. 5—30. SAUL: The Spirit departing from him.

Here, instead of the bare historical facts and exoteric events, we are taken to the esoteric reason for them all. That which explains them is the underlying counsel of God, who had rejected Saul, and taken His Spirit from him.

Thus we have the double lesson; and we retain the latter without losing the former.

If we compare the outward historical order with the inner and spiritual teaching we see at once why

---

[1] Dr. Adam Clarke questions "the authenticity" of the verses which concern this subject, and quotes Pilkington and Kennicott, who suppose it "to be an interpolation of some rabbinical writer, added at a very early period to the Hebrew Text," and a proof of "the carelessness or infidelity of transcribers." But, surely, to put these passages down, thus, to knavery is to charge the writers also with the folly of children!

ch. xvi. 14—23, where the Spirit departs from Saul, is
brought out of its chronological place, and placed in close
juxtaposition with xvi. 1—13, where the Spirit comes upon
David.

(e) " *The Words of Jeremiah.*"—Few books have suffered
more from this treatment than the Prophet Jeremiah.

It is not disputed that the chapters as they are given
to us in Scripture are not necessarily given in their
Historical and Chronological order.

This is so obvious that there is no hint of it given in
the text. Even the natural man can easily arrange the
chapters according to their chronology.

But in this case again the *experimental* teaching depends
entirely on the *canonical* order of the chapters. And the
canonical order can be shown only by its structure:

The Prophecy of Jeremiah as a whole.

A | i. 1—3. Introduction.

   B | i. 4—19. Jeremiah's commission given.

      C | ii.—xx. Prophecies addressed to the
         Jews (Josiah).

         D | xxi.—xxxv. History, etc. (Jehoia-
            kim) (*Not in chronological order.*)

            E | xxxvi. Baruch. His mission
              to Jehoiakim.

         D | xxxvii.—xlv. History, etc. (Zede-
            kiah). (*In chronological order.*)

      C | xlvi.—li. 64-. Prophecies addressed to
        the Gentiles.

   B | li. -64. Jeremiah's commission ended.

A | lii. Appendix.

It will be seen from the above structure that it is the
history connected with Jehoiakim which is not given in
its chronological order.

The member D is specially set in contrast with the
member *D*, and ZEDEKIAH'S history, being in chronological order, emphasizes and calls our attention to the
fact, that it is JEHOIAKIM'S history which is *not in chronological* order.

And why should it be? Who was Jehoiakim? Was
it not he who cut up the words of Jehovah with a pen-
knife? Why should not his history be cut up with the

pen? What does it matter how his history is treated? Note the contrast between him and king Josiah. Josiah, when the book of the law was found and the king heard the words of the law, rent his clothes (2 Chron. xxxiv. 14, 19, 21, 30) and submitted himself to it. He reigned with honour, and when he died he "was buried in one of the sepulchres of his fathers, and all Judah and Jerusalem mourned for Josiah" (2 Chron. xxxv. 24).

On the other hand, Jehoiakim, who refused to hear the word of the LORD, and cut it in pieces, was "buried with the burial of an ass, drawn and cast forth beyond the gates of Jerusalem"; and his dead body was "cast out in the day to the heat and in the night to the frost" (according to the prophecies in Jer. xxii. 18, 19; xxxvi. 30).

And, if any doubt remains as to the reason why this lesson of the prophecy of Jeremiah should not be lost, and its experimental teaching hidden and marred, let the structure of the Canonical portion connected with Jehoiakim be carefully studied; and its perfection be duly noted.

It is as follows:

D (*Jer. xxi.—xxxv.*). *The Canonical History connected with Jehoiakim.* (*Not chronological.*)

  D | F | xxi. Defeat and Captivity proclaimed.
        G | xxii.—xxiii. 8. Promise of the BRANCH.
           H | xxiii. 9—40. Whirlwind. False Prophets. Rejection.
               J | xxiv. Figs. Discrimination. (Captives and Remnant.)
                  K | xxv. 1—11. Time: Seventy years.
                     L | xxv. 12—38. Nations (The Cup).
                       M | xxvi. Proclamation in the Court of Jehovah's House.
                     L | xxvii. Nations. (The Bonds and Yoke.)
                  K | xxviii. Time: Two years.
               J | xxix. Figs. Discrimination. (Captives and Remnant.)
           H | xxx., xxxi. Whirlwind. The Book. Restoration.
        G | xxxii., xxxiii. Promise of the BRANCH.
     F | xxxiv., xxxv. Defeat and Captivity proclaimed.

Is it not clear why this, the Canonical order, is so
perfectly constructed? And is not the *Experimental*
teaching exhibited by it shown to be of far greater
importance than that of the mere Chronological and
Literary order?

(*f*) *The Pauline Epistles.*—In our work on the Church
Epistles we have set forth the experimental teaching of
their canonical order: and have shown that they are presented to us in the order in which we are to study them.

In them we have the fulfilment of the Lord's own promise, given in John xvi. 12—15: "I have many things to
say unto you, but ye cannot bear them now. Howbeit,
when He the Spirit of truth (*lit.*, shall have) come, He
will guide you into all the truth. He shall not speak of
(*or* from) Himself; but whatsoever He shall hear, that
shall He speak: and He will shew you things to come.
He shall glorify me: for He shall receive of mine, and
shall shew it unto you. All things that the Father hath
are mine: therefore said I, that He shall take of mine,
and shall shew it unto you."

That is to say, that had the Lord spoken them then
His disciples would not have been able to bear them.

Whatever may be the force of the word "bear," the
contrast is between what they could not do "now," at
that time, and what they would be able to do at some
later time.

Time, therefore, does enter into the interpretation of
words.

There could be no doctrine until the facts had taken
place on which they were based.

There could be no Epistles until the Gospel history had
been accomplished.

There could be no doctrine of Redemption or Atonement until His blood had been shed; and He, as a corn
of wheat, had fallen into the ground and died (John
xii. 24).

"The things of Christ" were the doctrines concerning
Him which were afterward "taken" and revealed by the
Holy Spirit in the Epistles specially addressed to churches
as such. If not, Where, and How, and When, has this
Divine promise ever been fulfilled? Where has He guided

us into "all the truth"? Where are we to look for this truth except in these Epistles which were written when He, the Spirit of truth had come?

Those who neglect the teaching of the Epistles reject these words of Christ. They "cannot bear them," even now. They put themselves back into a Dispensation which has passed away, and refuse to bear the words now that they have been spoken and written for our learning.

Many, thank God, are heeding what has since been revealed. Many are rejoicing in these "things of Christ" which the Spirit of truth has received, and has shown what God has made Christ to be unto us, and what He has made us to be "in Christ." Many are reading and studying the Epistles which the Spirit of truth has addressed to the churches by the Apostle Paul.

We have spoken of some of the Dispersion Epistles under the heading of rightly dividing of the subject-matter (pp. 72–78), according to which Paul's Epistles must be divided off from those other Epistles which are not addressed directly to the Church of God.

We are specially concerned now, therefore, with

The Pauline Epistles.

Besides the group of Epistles addressed to the Dispersion (1 and 2 Peter, and James), there is another group of General Epistles (1, 2, and 3 John and Jude); and yet another group of Pauline Epistles.

These groups, whatever may be their order in the ancient Greek manuscripts, always consist of the same Epistles, and are thus preserved distinct and separate from the others.

In some MSS. the *Dispersion* group follows the Acts; and is followed by the *General* group, concluding with the *Pauline* group.

In the Pauline group the order of the Epistles varies to this extent; the Epistles addressed to churches (in which we include Romans and Ephesians, though they are not specifically so addressed) are always found together, and in the order in which we have them in our Bibles to-day. No Greek MS. has ever yet been seen in

which this order varies. But in some MSS. the other
Pauline Epistles do vary; the Pastoral Epistles sometimes preceding and sometimes following the Epistle
to the Hebrews. We believe that the proper place of
Hebrews is last, both canonically and chronologically,
thus closing up Judaism effectually and cutting it off
completely.

Many have observed the importance of the epoch
marked by the Destruction of the Temple in A.D. 70, and
the wonderful effect it must have had on Judaism and
Christianity. This epoch is marked in the New Testament
by the Epistle to the Hebrews, written in A.D. 68.

In our work on *The Church Epistles* we have dealt
only with their Canonical order; but their Chronological
order is not without its own direct teaching.

The Holy Spirit of God has specially preserved and
given them to us in their Canonical order, because that
is the order in which we have to learn their truths, which
are *experimental*, and are therefore more important for
our spiritual life.

That Canonical order is as follows :—

A¹ | ROMANS. *Doctrinal.* Dogmatic Instruction (in
which Paul was alone in writing).

    B | CORINTHIANS. Reproof for *practical* failure
as to Romans' teaching. (Paul, Sosthenes,
and Timothy).

        C | GALATIANS. Correction for *doctrinal*
failure as to Romans' teaching. (Paul
and all the brethren).

A² | EPHESIANS. *Doctrinal.* Dogmatic instruction.
(Paul alone in writing).

    B | PHILIPPIANS. Reproof for *practical* failure
as to Ephesians' teaching. (Paul and
Timothy).

        C | COLOSSIANS. Correction for *doctrinal*
failure as to Ephesians' teaching.
(Paul and Timothy).

A³ THESSALONIANS. Praise and thanksgiving for a
model church, manifesting the fruits of Paul's
teaching in Acts xvii. 1-3, in holiness of life and
missionary zeal (Paul, Silvanus, and Timothy).

These are the *experimental* lessons of the Canonical order.[1]

But the Chronological order is equally a fact, and it has its own special teaching for us, which is *Dispensational*.

These Epistles are not given to us in this order, because the Dispensational teaching is not so important or so essential to our salvation.

The experimental teaching, which is essential, is ensured to us by the *Canonical* order in which we receive them; but the Dispensational teaching of their *Chronological* order has to be sought out, by rightly dividing them according to the *times* when they were respectively written.

Both orders are divine; and they have their distinct and separate teaching.

This element of *time*, in interpretation, reminds us that Paul never saw any of John's writings! None of the churches to whom he addressed his Epistles had ever yet seen John's Gospel! That Gospel, therefore, cannot be necessary to the understanding of the Epistles, or to the formation of churches.

Not until some twenty years after Paul's death was John inspired to write. How real must have been his inspiration to give us those verbal conversations of the Lord with Nicodemus, the woman of Samaria and others at which John himself was not present, even though he was a disciple at the time.

All this shows us that we are not to read subsequent revelations into previous writings. The "not yet" of Heb. ii. 8. and the "cannot now" of John xvi. 12, must be allowed to have their full weight in the interpretation of the Scriptures of truth; and, especially in the Epistles of Paul, if we are to "understand the Scriptures."

The churches whom he addressed could not fail to rightly divide the words of truth which they received. They could not mix up the four Gospels with the Prison-Epistles. The Thessalonians could not confuse their teaching with what was written long after to the Ephesians, or to the Hebrews; and which they had never seen.

But we now have "All Scripture" and our responsibility is therefore greater

---
[1] See *The Church Epistles*, by the same author.

If we do not rightly divide "all Scripture" according to the times, when, and as it was written, it will be impossible for us to be guided into "all truth."

Even where this dividing of the Word of truth according to its subject-matter is carried out, there has been failure to carry it out fully with reference to its dispensational or chronological teaching.

And as so very few thus fully observe this all-important precept, and fulfil this great requirement of the Divine Word, it is all the more necessary that we should make an attempt to do so, in some measure, here, and now.[1]

The Chronological order is as follows, according to the generally received dates :—

1 Thess.	A.D. 52	from Corinth.
2 Thess.	,, 53	,, ,,
1 Cor.	,, 57	from Ephesus (spring).
2 Cor.	,, 57	,, ,, (autumn).
Gal.	,, 57	from Corinth (winter).
Romans	,, 58	,, ,,

Acts xxviii. 25, 26 (A.D. 62).

Ephesians	A.D. 62	} spring	} From Prison
Colossians	,, 62		in Rome.
Philippians	,, 62	autumn	
1 Timothy	,, 67	from Corinth.	
Titus	,, 67	,, ,,	
2 Timothy	,, 68	from Prison in Rome.	

It is obvious that we must not read into the Acts or Paul's earlier Epistles that which was revealed to him later, while in prison in Rome.

Up to Acts xxviii. Peter's offer of the kingdom (Acts iii. 19—21, R.V.) was still open.

Stephen (A.D. 33) sees the Lord Jesus still standing (Acts vii. 55), for He had not yet "sat down" at the right hand of God (Heb. x. 12, A.D. 68).

Isaiah vi. had been twice quoted by Christ as not yet fulfilled, Matt. xiii. 15 (Mark iv. 12. Luke viii. 10) and John xii. 40.

---

[1] We must refer our readers here to two separate pamphlets on this subject, viz., *The Pauline Epistles* and *The Good Deposit;* or in *Things to Come,* April and May, 1907, and subsequent numbers.

Not until Acts xxviii. 25, 26, was Paul commissioned to pronounce this threatened judicial blindness, for the third, and last time.

It is obvious that not until after Acts xxviii. could any declaration of the Mystery have been made. Until then nothing could be said which would be incompatible with the possible acceptance of Peter's offer.

However, we must refer the reader to our separate pamphlet on this subject; and to pages 165, 166, above, where we have spoken of the possibility of there being some further revelation in Phil. iii.

Enough has been said on this whole subject of rightly dividing the Dispensational truth and teaching to show the importance of obeying the precept in these various particulars.

Part II: THE WORDS

Part II: THE WORDS

PRELIMINARY REMARKS

Having considered the study of the WORD as a whole, we now come to the study of the WORDS of which it is made up.

The Lord Jesus said, not only, "I have given them Thy WORD" (John xvii. 14); but, "I have given unto them the WORDS which Thou gavest me" (*v.* 8).

In the former of these two solemn statements λόγος (*logos*) is used; in the latter it is ῥῆμα (*rhēma*).

There is this difference between the two: λόγος (*logos*), generally speaking, is taken as meaning a *word* as made up of letters; and ῥῆμα (*rhēma*), a *saying* as made up of words.

It is worthy of note, that it is in this latter connection our Lord speaks of all that He uttered as being given to Him by the Father to speak : He spake nothing of, or from, Himself.

Seven times did He declare this great and solemn fact:[1] so that those who charge our Lord with ignorance of what He said, or with knowingly accommodating Himself to the traditional belief of the people, are charging this home upon God Himself; for the words of Christ were, He says, "not mine, but the Father's which sent me."

The "Higher" critics, therefore, who say that David did not write Psalm cx. really "make God a liar."

But this is not our point here, though it would be unwise to pass it by.

---

[1]
1. "My doctrine is not Mine, but His that sent Me" (John vii. 16).
2. "As My Father hath taught Me I speak these things" (John viii. 28).
3. "Why do ye not believe Me? He that is of God heareth God's words" (John viii. 47).
4. "The Father which sent me, He gave Me a commandment what I should say and what I should speak" (John xii. 49).
5. "The words that I speak unto you I speak not of Myself" (John xiv. 10).
6. "The word which ye hear is not Mine, but the Father's, which sent Me" (John xiv. 24). And here—
7. "I have given unto them the words which Thou gavest Me" (John xvii. 8).

The "Word" as a whole, Christ speaks of in His last prayer to the Father as "THY WORDS"; and the matter, and the words of which it is made up, are the words given Him, by the Father, to speak.

Whether "sayings" or "words," a revelation, in writing, is impossible apart from words; hence the importance of studying, not merely the Word as a whole, but the actual words in which it is given to us.

When, of course, we speak of the "*words*" it must be borne in mind that we mean Hebrew and Greek words; for in these, the original languages, have the words been given to us.

We cannot hold the Spirit of God responsible for the way in which individual men have chosen to translate the original words in their respective languages.

It was truly said by Archbishop Whately that "the Bible consists of the Old Testament in Hebrew and the New Testament in Greek; and a translation of them is only an *Interpretation* according to the best judgment of the translator."

Each, doubtless, has done the best he could, and has brought to bear upon the work his highest powers.

But, unless he has been guided by principles such as those which we have laid down in the first part of this work, his best efforts will be of little avail for us; for he will have given us only his own judgment and his own views.

Those views are, very largely, traditional. He comes to the work of Bible study with his views already more or less fixed. These have been derived from what he has first, and already, received from a man like himself. He may perhaps be more widely read in what others before him have said, but still he is more or less tied and bound by traditional views.

It is surprising, when we really come to examine ourselves closely in this matter, how much of what we already believe has been "received by tradition from our fathers." How little has actually been derived from our own direct personal study of the Word of God itself. We believe what we have received from man; and we do our best to get it confirmed by the Bible. When we are unable to get the confirmation we are in search of, then we find what we call a "difficulty." But the difficulty is not in the Word of God itself; it is in our own minds. The real difficulty is in giving up our own views because we fail to make the Bible conform to them. It does not, at first, occur to our minds that we may have to abandon some of our views if we would get rid of the difficulty.

Even where there is no difficulty, and our view is indeed in accord with the Word of God, we shall find it better to study the Word of truth afresh, and learn it again *direct from the Scriptures.*

This is what we must do if we would really profit by the Word so as to enjoy it. It is better for the truth to hold us, than for us to hold the truth. The two things are very different.

Hence the importance of our great subject, how to study the "WORDS which the Holy Ghost teacheth." (1 Cor. ii. 13.)

As to the original words we must consider them further on. Though, in one sense, that consideration should logically come first, yet, as we are writing for English readers, we may well defer the Hebrew and Greek words to our section on "The Usage of Greek Words" (Canon III.), and "The Place of Various Readings" (Canon XII.), in which we shall put our English readers in possession of all that is essential for them to know.

Our concern now is with the words in the English versions: and our object is to see how far they accord with the words in the original, without a specific knowledge of that original. That is to say, how far an English reader may, by observing certain principles, which we propose to lay down, find out for himself the meaning of the original, and discover the mind of God, who is revealing Himself therein.

Our task is not easy, because often, while we are discussing one particular principle, the passage in question may require the application of several of these principles, or Canons, in order to our full and proper understanding of it.

We would therefore lay down our first great principle that the meaning of words is to be gathered from the scope of a passage, and not the interpretation of a passage from the words.

CANON 1

The Meaning of Words Is to Be Gathered From the Scope of the Passage; and Not the Scope from the Words

1. *"Private Interpretation."*—A passage which furnishes a good illustration is 2 Pet. i. 20: "No prophecy of the Scripture is of any private interpretation."

These words, taken by themselves, would present no difficulty to a Roman Catholic, because they appear to agree with the tradition he has received. But they present a grave difficulty to a Protestant who has been taught, and who believes, that God's word is for all.

> "Hear, O heavens, and
> Give ear, O earth,
> For Jehovah hath spoken."

This word from Isa. i. 2 sums up the ground of our belief; and this is why this text was printed by the Reformers on the title-page of the early editions of our English Bibles.

The question which here presents itself is: How is this apparent difficulty to be solved.

We are studying the "Words," and we desire to know what these two words "private," and "interpretation" mean.

Our first principle now comes in to help us: and it affirms that the meaning of these words must be gathered from the scope of the passage in which we find them. The application of our first Canon to this particular passage is intended only as an illustration of the way in which it may be used to elucidate other passages.

When we speak of the "Scope" we mean—*what it is all about;* the one subject which is being treated of, or written about. This will always furnish a key to the meaning of the *words* employed.

This is not quite the same as "The Importance of the *Context*," which forms the subject of our third Great Principle or Canon, because the Context has to do with the interpretation and sense of a passage as distinct from the actual meaning of its separate *words.*

On examination of this particular passage (2 Pet. i. 20) in which our words occur, we find that the verse forms part of a larger context the Scope or subject of which is *not what Scripture means,* but *whence it came.*

This is evident from the most cursory reading of the whole passage. There is not one word about the meaning, but a great deal about the *origin* of prophecy ; not a word about its interpretation, but about its *source.*

That this is the scope is quite apparent from the mere surface of the passage ; and it is borne out by the *Structure,* which is the subject of the second great principle we wish to lay down (see Canon II., below).

This is sufficient to put us on the right track to find out the meaning of the words "private" and "interpretation." And our business, therefore, is to see if they can have a meaning more in harmony with the general scope of the passage.

As to the word rendered "private" we find that it is ἴδιος (*idios*) and that it occurs 114 times.[1] Out of these 114 times we find that it is nearly always rendered one's *own;* "his own sheep," "his own servants," "his own house," "his own country," etc.; but not once is it rendered "private," except in this passage. This shows us that the rendering "private" is sufficiently abnormal to be suspected ; and that it would be more consistent to render it *one's own* (or lit., *of its own*).

As to the word rendered "interpretation" we shall find that it occurs nowhere else; neither in the New Testament, nor in the Septuagint. It is ἐπίλυσις (*epilusis*). We have no guide to its meaning as we had with the word "private." As this noun occurs nowhere else we must go to the verb ἐπιλύω (*epiluō*), which is made up of the preposition ἐπί (*epi*), *upon,* and λύω (*luō*), *to loosen.* We find Xenophon using it of *letting* dogs *loose upon* the ground to chase a hare. Another Greek writer uses it of *breaking open* a letter bearing upon a certain subject. So that its usage is perfectly clear so far. In the New Testament

---

[1] This is easily seen, at a glance, by consulting our Lexicon and Concordance.

this verb occurs only twice (Mark iv. 34 and Acts xix. 39). From Mark iv. 34 it is evident that it will bear the A.V. rendering *expound*,[1] but it will also bear a larger meaning. He spake publicly "with many such parables," but "when they were alone," He *broke open* the casket which hid His real meaning; He *unfolded* the treasures that were therein; He *let them loose* as it were and displayed them before the eyes of His disciples.

In Acts xix. 39 the Town Clerk said "If ye enquire anything concerning other matters, it shall be *made known* (or *shown*) in a lawful assembly."

Any of these meanings will do here in 2 Pet. i. 20, 21, and it will be seen how they harmonise with the one matter which is the subject, or scope, of the whole passage.

"Getting to know, this, first:—that not any prophecy of Scripture springs[2] from its own unfolding,

[Why ?]

For, not by the will of man was prophecy at any time brought forth—

[How then did it come?]

But being borne along by holy spirit,[3] men spake from God."

Thus, the words are brought into harmony with the scope, or subject of the whole passage; and we see how they refer to the *origin* and *source* of the prophetic Word, and not to its meaning or interpretation.

2. "*The Spirits in Prison*."—1 Pet. iii. 19 is another passage which has been wholly misinterpreted and misunderstood, because it has been taken, not only apart from the Context, but apart from the larger question, *viz.*, the *scope* or subject of the whole chapter.

This verse does not stand alone. It is not an illuminated text we hang on a wall; but is made up of words

---

[1] Just as *private* will bear the meaning of *one's own:* inasmuch as what is *one's own* is private; and what is private is *one's own*.

[2] γίνομαι (*ginomai*), *to begin, come into being, begin to be, become arise, happen*.

[3] πνεῦμα ἅγιον (*pneuma hagion*), *Divine power from on high*. See *Word Studies on the Holy Spirit*, republished by Kregel Publications, pp. 26-34.

which God has placed in immediate connection with other words, on which they depend for their right understanding.

The question we have to ask ourselves, as to the whole chapter, is this: What is it about? What is the great subject which is being treated of?

The smaller passage itself commences at verse 18 with the word "FOR." "For Christ Himself also suffered, the just for the unjust." Verse 19 is therefore part of a *reason* which is being given to explain or illustrate something which has been already said. It is not a new and independent subject which is being introduced.

We must ask therefore, What is this something which has been said, and has to be thus illustrated, and explained?

It requires only care and common sense to see, what the Translators themselves saw, when they put at the head of the chapter "*exhorting all men to unity and love, and to suffer persecution.*" This is right so far as it goes, but it is not all. On reading the whole passage we do indeed see that it is an exhortation to suffer persecution, and especially if the suffering and the persecution be for "well-doing." "*It is better, if the will of God be so, that ye suffer for well doing than for evil doing.*" This is the scope. This is what it is all about. This is verse 17; and then, verse 18 goes on to give us the reason why it is "better"; "For." What follows, must be interpreted by the sense of this *scope*. It is to show us why it is BETTER to "suffer for well-doing."

Now, verse 19 about "the spirits in prison" is usually taken by itself apart from the scope as referring to people who have died, and as teaching that after death they have "a second chance."

But our simple question is, *In what way would this be a reason for, or proof* of the fact that it is "better to suffer for well doing than for evil doing"?

If these were dead men, they must have been evil doers, or there would be no reason for their needing this "second chance." It would, therefore, be an excuse for *evil doing*, seeing that they have this hope to lean upon.

We can see at once, that this common interpretation must be wrong, as it is inconsequent and illogical. It has no connection with or relation to what has gone before; and takes no account of the word "For" which introduces this statement.

We have, therefore, still to look for a *reason*, why "it is better to suffer for well doing, than for evil doing."

The reason given is that Christ suffered for well-doing. All he did was "just." He "suffered for the unjust," to bring us to God. That was "better." But "He was put to death in the flesh." What then? Where does the "better" come in? What happened after that? Ah! He had a glorious resurrection. He was "made a quickening spirit" (1 Cor. xv. 45). "He was put to death indeed as to the flesh." He was "quickened" (or made alive again) as to spirit.[1]

What does *made alive* mean? What can it mean but resurrection? How can anyone who has died be made alive again except by being raised from the dead?[2]

It is the very expression used in 1 Cor. xv. 45. "It is sown a natural (Greek, *psychical* or soulical) body; it is raised a spiritual body." And so also it standeth written, the first man Adam "became, or, *came to be*, a living soul";[3] "the last Adam was made *to be* a quickening spirit." How? The verses that follow go on to explain that this was in resurrection.

But here, in 1 Pet. iii. there is more than resurrection. It was that which made it "better" for Christ to have suffered for well-doing. He had a glorious triumph as well. He went in His resurrection body (ἐν ᾧ, *en hō, by*, or, *in which*) and made proclamation[4] of it to "the in-prison-spirits."

What and who can these be? To answer this question we have to go a little further afield. But not far. The

---

[1] All the Critical Greek Texts omit the article here.

[2] As in Rev. xx. 5, where the rest of the dead *lived again*, only in resurrection after the thousand years.

[3] The Greek has the Preposition εἰς (*eis*) in both clauses. Its use in this connection is Hebrew idiom, and expresses the *object in view*. Man was made *for*, or *as*, or with a view to his being a living soul. See Acts xiii. 22, "he raised up unto them David *to be their* king," i.e., *as* their king. So Acts vii. 21, "for her son"; Acts xiii. 47, "*to be* a light," i.e., as, or for, a light; xix. 27, "*to be* despised"; Greek, to be "reckoned *for* naught." Compare Rom. ii. 26, *for* circumcision; ix. 8, *for* the seed.

[4] The word is κηρύσσω (*kērussō*), *to herald*, i.e., *to proclaim* as a κῆρυξ (*kērux*), *a herald*, not εὐαγγελίζω (*euangelizō*), *to preach the Gospel*.

same Peter tells us over leaf, in 2 Pet. ii. 4, of the angels that sinned in the days of Noah, and who are now cast down to Tartarus and there "delivered into chains of darkness to be reserved unto judgment." And when we read further in Jude 6 (a remoter context) of the same historical fact—the sinning and imprisonment of these angels; and when we remember that angels are spirits, and are so called in Heb. i. 7 and 14, then we are at no loss to understand that the triumph of Christ was so great that, in His resurrection body, He went and made proclamation of it; and it reached to the limits of creation; even the angels now in prison for their sin.

Any one can see that verses 20 and 21 are a parenthetical clause, and that the Relative "which" at the beginning of verse 20 introduces a digression about these angels, in order to tell us what their sin was (*viz.*, "disobedience"), and when their sin was[1] (*viz.*, "in the days of Noah"). And having come round to "the resurrection of Jesus Christ" (at the end of the digression), to the point where we started in verse 18, we are led on now to the end of the Triumph, beyond resurrection; ever to ascension and exaltation and glory, "angels and authorities and powers having been made subject unto Him" (*v.* 22).

Here was triumph indeed. Here we see the reason of the "For" in verse 18. Yes! It is indeed "better to suffer for well-doing than for evil-doing." It was "better" for Christ, the just; and, it will be better for us. We also shall have a resurrection. If we are judged (according to the will of men) and put to death in the flesh, it is only that we might live again in resurrection (according to the will of God) in our spiritual bodies, as Christ did. This is the argument in 1 Pet. iv. 6. It is in view of this blessed hope that the Gospel was preached to them that are now dead. This is why it is preached to us; to show us why it is "better to suffer for well-doing."

If we ask, why these "in-prison spirits" should have this proclamation made to them, we have only to follow up the clue already given in the nearer and remoter contexts.

---

[1] Not when this proclamation of Christ was.

They took part in the gigantic plot to corrupt and destroy the whole human race. The *nature* of their sin is clear from Jude 6. The *time* of it is also given in 2 Pet. ii. 4, 5, and here, in 1 Pet. iii. 20. The *object* of it we have in Gen. vi. The great promise and prophecy had gone forth in Gen. iii. 15, that "the seed of the woman" should come into the world, and should finally crush the head of the Old Serpent.

Satan's object therefore was to frustrate this counsel of God.

Having as yet no clue as to the line by which "the seed of the woman" should come into the world, his first effort was to corrupt and destroy the whole human race. This he carried out as described in Gen. vi. and Jude 6. "The sons of God" were angels; "the angels who sinned." All beings who are the direct creation of God are called his "sons." Adam was "a son of God" (Gen. v. 1. Luke iii. 38). We are not. By nature we are sons of Adam begotten in his likeness (Gen. v. 3). The New nature in us makes us "sons of God," because that is God's own new-creation work (Eph. ii. 10. 2 Cor. v. 17. Rom. viii. 14—17). For the same reason also, angels are called "sons of God," because they are the direct creation of God. In the Old Testament the expression always has this meaning. Before Adam was created "the morning stars sang together, and all the sons of God shouted for joy" (Job xxxviii. 7). An angel was sent to the lions' den to shut the lions' mouths (Dan. vi. 22), as another was sent to the fiery furnace to deliver Jehovah's servants; this angel is called "a son of God" (for there is no article).

They cannot (in Gen. vi.) be the seed of Seth, as is generally taught, because they are contrasted with "the daughters of MEN"; which shows they must be of a different nature.

We know from Gen. vi. how nearly that great plot succeeded; how the whole earth was corrupted [1] (Gen. vi. 11, 12).

All, except Noah's family, were tainted with this uncanny and unholy breed called "*Nephilim.*" Noah was

---

[1] שָׁחַת (*shāchath*), *to ruin, lay in ruins, to make good for nothing.* Hence שַׁחַת (*shackath*), *a sepulchre, corruption.*

tamim, i.e., "without blemish," as the word for "perfect" here is generally rendered elsewhere. All had to be destroyed by the Flood; but the angels who sinned are "reserved," in "chains" and "in prison" (1 Pet. iii. 19. 2 Pet. ii. 4. Jude 6), for their judgment at a yet future day.

The aim of Satan was to corrupt, and so secure the destruction of the whole human race. And his plot would have succeeded but for the direct interposition of Divine judgment.

"The seed of the woman" ultimately came into the world. The Word of God was fulfilled; and now, though His heel had been bruised, and He suffered and died, yet God raised Him from the dead, the token that Satan's head shall in due time be crushed.

This glorious triumph had to be heralded forth. Those who had taken part in that awful plot had to learn that the designs of Satan, their lord and master, had failed. This was the reason why Christ, having risen from the dead, went and proclaimed His glorious triumph.

This is why it is "*better to suffer for well-doing than for evil-doing.* FOR Christ also suffered" [for well doing], "the just for the unjust." And, it was "better" for Him; for He has triumphed gloriously: and it is "better" for us also; for we are thereby saved eternally.

Not merely saved through[1] the judgment (as the digression shows); not saved by means of material water; but by the "suffering" of that perfect sacrifice, which has made the comers thereunto "perfect as pertaining to the conscience" (Heb. ix. 9; x. 1), and given them "the answer of a good conscience toward God" (1 Pet. iii. 21).[2]

Thus we see how the *scope* (or one great *subject*) of the whole passage determines for us the sense in which we are to understand the words which are employed in it; and we see also how this is the only sense which gives cogency and consistency to the whole argument.

Moreover the scope of this passage is in harmony with *the scope of the whole Epistle.*[3] We see and are shown

---

[1] This is the force of διασώζω (*diasōzō*). See its only occurrences: Matt. xiv. 36. Luke vii. 3. Acts xxiii. 24; xxvii. 43. 44; xxviii. 1, 4; and here 1 Pet. iii. 20.

[2] See, on the whole subject, two pamphlets by the same author: *The Spirits in Prison*; and, *The Sons of God.*

[3] See the Structure, below, under Canon II., pages 216-219.

throughout how it is "better to suffer for well doing than for evil doing."

In ch. i. 7 the trial of our faith is to be found unto praise and honour and glory at the appearing of Jesus Christ.

In ch. i. 11 the subject of prophecy was that Christ's sufferings were to be followed by glory.

In ch. i. 13 we are, in our trials, to "hope to the end for the grace that is to be brought unto us at the revelation of Jesus Christ."

In ch. i. 19—21, when Christ's sufferings were over, and the "precious blood" was shed, God "raised Him from the dead and gave Him glory."

In ch. ii. 20 they are asked, "What *glory* is it if when ye be buffeted for your faults ye shall take it patiently? but if, when ye do well and *suffer* for it, ye take it patiently, this is acceptable with God."

In ch. ii. 21—24 Christ's example is given to prove this. He suffered for well-doing, and when he died he committed His spirit[1] unto Him who judgeth righteously (ch. ii. 23; comp. Luke xxiii. 46). And all this was done in order that we, having died to sins, might live again[2] unto righteousness, in newness of life here, and of resurrection life which the righteous Judge shall give us in that day (2 Tim. iv. 8).

In ch. iv. 6, though they might be judged indeed according to the will of men, in the flesh; they might *live* again in resurrection life according to the will of God, in their spiritual bodies.

In ch. iv. 13 they are to rejoice that inasmuch as they were partakers of Christ's *sufferings*, they would be glad also with exceeding joy when Christ's glory should be revealed.

In ch. iv. 19 if they suffered, and this suffering was according to the will of God, they were to commit themselves (in well-doing) to God as to a faithful creator, who was thus able to re-create them in resurrection.

---

[1] "*himself*" is in italics both in A.V. and R.V. R.V. margin suggests "*his cause*"; but Luke xxiii. 46 shows us what it was He committed to the Father —as connected with the glorious resurrection—which was His reward in consequence.

[2] ζάω (*zaō*), *to live*, especially in resurrection life, real or typical. John v. 25; xi. 25. Rev. i. 18; xx. 4.

In ch. v. 1 Peter himself was a witness of this great truth, for he had been a witness of Christ's *sufferings*, and would be a partaker of His *glory* also when it shall be revealed.

Finally, in ch. v. 10, they are reminded that though they may "*suffer* awhile," yet, the God of all grace has called them unto eternal *glory*.

There can be no question, therefore, as to what is the *scope* of the Epistle as a whole; neither can there be any doubt as to the scope of the particular passage (ch. iii. 18—22), where the resurrection, ascension, and glorification of Christ after His sufferings, proved that it was "better to suffer for well-doing than for evil-doing." A triumph it was. And, a triumph so great, that He went and proclaimed it to the in-prison spirits in Tartarus to show them that all this triumph was in spite of the Satanic plot referred to and recorded in Gen. vi. and in which they had so great a share, so great a guilt, and so great a condemnation. This is the triumph of Col. ii. 14, 15.

3. *Testament and Covenant.*—Heb. ix. 15—23 [1] affords another example, showing how the scope of a passage will furnish us with the meaning of the word διαθήκη (*diathēkē*), *covenant*.

In the A.V. it is consistently, but, as we shall see, wrongly rendered by our word "testament." The R.V. is certainly inconsistent, for in verse 15 it twice renders it "covenant," and in verses 16 and 17 it twice renders it "testament"; while in verses 18 and 20 it twice again has the word "covenant" (one of the two being put in italics; as the word "testament" is similarly supplied in italics).

All this confusion speaks loudly to us, and tells us that there is something, here, that needs explanation. The note also given by the Revisers tells us that they were perfectly aware of their inconsistency: for against each of the occurrences of the word in question they say in the margin:

> "The Greek word here used signifies both *covenant* and *testament*."

---

[1] See below, Canon II,, pp. 220—223, our reason for giving these verses as the context or scope.

This statement may be true of Greek classical authors, but this passage is in God's Word.[1] Greek writers knew nothing of God's covenants with Noah and Abraham, and Israel and David. Here, it is entirely a question of what is the subject or scope of the passage. *What is it all about?* This is the question we have to ask. And if we look at the whole passage from verse 15 to verse 23, we see at once that the one great subject is a contrast between the NEW Covenant (*v.* 15), and the OLD Covenant (*vv.* 19—22).

This should settle the question for us, once for all. We have no right within the compass of a few verses to *change the subject* of our own arbitrary will. It is a serious matter so to do, and it leads to grave conse- quences. Here, it quite changes the scope, and affects the translation of the whole passage.

(1) In verse 17 ἐπὶ νεκροῖς (*epi nekrois*) is rendered in the A.V. "after men are dead," and in the R.V. "where there hath been a death." But the Revisers' note against this, in the margin, is "Gr. *over the dead.*" This shows that, having *changed the subject* they are forced to do violence to the translation, and to abandon the plain meaning of the Greek. The marginal note is a confession of this.

(2) In other ways both Versions are compelled to adapt their translation of the words to suit the new subject which they have introduced.

ὁ διαθέμενος (*ho diathemenos*) means *the appointed;* and here, the appointed *sacrifice*, by which all covenants must be made. It is masculine in Gender in order to agree not with the Greek word θύσια (*thusia*), sacrifice, but with the Hebrew thought (זֶבַח) (*zavach*), sacrifice, which is masculine).

The word *diathemenos* is the participle of διατίθημι (*diatithemi*), *to appoint* (see Luke xxii. 29. Acts iii. 25.

---

[1] διαθήκη (*diathēkē*) occurs 280 times in the Septuagint, and is used always of a covenant. This must be its meaning throughout the N.T. The late Dr. Hatch, in his *Essays in Biblical Greek* (Oxford Press, 1889), says, "The attempt to give it in certain passages its classical meaning of 'testament' is not only at variance with its use in Hellenistic Greek, but is probably also the survival of a mistake: in ignorance of the philology of later and vulgar Latin, it was formerly supposed that 'testamentum,' by which the word is rendered in the early Latin versions as well as in the Vulgate, meant 'testa- ment' or 'will'; whereas, in fact, it meant also, if not exclusively, 'covenant.'"

Heb. viii. 10 and Heb. x. 16; the only places where the verb occurs); and it is specially used of *making a covenant* (Heb. viii. 10 and x. 16).

We have said enough to enable us now to give the words their true meaning and force according to the scope; and we are not compelled to adapt them to a different subject.

The scope of Heb. ix. 15—23 is the same as that of Exod. xxiv. 5—8, which describes the old covenant-making.

"For where a covenant [is made, the] death of the appointed [sacrifice] is necessary to be brought in: for, a covenant [is] confirmed [only] over dead [victims or sacrifices]; since it hath no force while the appointed [sacrifice] is living."

The change of the scope in the A.V. and R.V. necessitates the bringing in of the word "men"—about which there is not even a hint in the Greek. All is about covenants and sacrifices.

This will be seen when we look at this passage again, below, where we shall see its scope made more clear by its structure. (See pp. 220—223.)

We see sufficient here to illustrate our first Canon: that the scope of the passage must determine the meaning of the several words employed in it.

4. Another example of a different character is found in Gen. xxiv. 63: "And Isaac went out to meditate in the field at the eventide."

This is a case in which the context must give us the meaning of the word שׂיחַ (*sūach*), which is rendered "meditate," "or, *to pray*," in the margin.

That translators are perplexed is clear. The R.V. has "meditate," the Syriac has "to take a walk." Gesenius suggests *to go to and fro* in the field (to muster the flocks)! We get the rendering "meditate" from the Vulgate's "*ad meditandum*."

But even granting that the word "meditate" would serve, is there any thing to show us what sort of a meditation it was likely to be?

It is clear that chapter xxiv., long as it is, is only a digression introduced in order to give us the mission of Eliezer, to seek a wife for Isaac.

The last event, immediately before that mission was the burial of Sarah, Isaac's mother (Gen. xxiii. 19).

The next thing we read of Isaac is his going forth in the field to meditate. This is followed immediately by his reception of Rebekah : "And Isaac brought her into *his mother Sarah's tent,* and took Rebekah, and she became his wife ; and he loved her : and *Isaac was comforted after his mother's death* " (ch. xxiv. 67).

Is there nothing in this context to show us what is the meaning of the word rendered "meditate"?

Yes, it sends us again to the Lexicon and to the Concordance. There we find that usage connects it with being *bowed down.* Ps. xliv. 25 (26), "Our soul is *bowed down* to the dust." Lam. iii. 20, "my soul . . . is humbled in me" (marg. "Heb. *bowed*").[1]

Why was Isaac "comforted after his mother's death"? Comfort is for those who mourn. Isaac was therefore still mourning the death of his mother ; and he went out into the field to be alone, and to give vent to his grief.

He did not go out either to pray or to think out some problem ; but to seek in solitude comfort and relief.

5. " *The Lord's Day.*" Rev. i. 10.—Here, the whole scope of the passage in which we find these words is concerning judgment. The nine verses which precede lead up to it, and the whole subsequent subject of the book has to do with the coming of the Lord in judgment.

This can have no more to do with a day of the week than with a day of the month ; but it does have to do with "the Day of the Lord."

That this meaning of the expression is not only in agreement with the scope of the book, but with all the known facts of the case, can be tested and proved.[2]

---

[1] Compare also Ps. vi. 6, "I am bowed down with my *groaning*"; 1 Sam. i. 15, a *sorrowful* spirit ; Prov. xxiii. 29, "Who hath *melancholy*" (not "babbling"!); R.V. has "complaining."

[2] See above, pp. 158, 159. Also a pamphlet on this subject entitled, *The Lord's Day : Is it a Day of the Week or the Day of the Lord?* by the same author.

CANON 2

The Scope of a Passage May Best Be Discovered by Its Structure

I. INTRODUCTORY: THE HISTORY AND IMPORTANCE OF
THE SUBJECT.

Every Word of God is pure; and His words, like all His works, are perfect. Perfect in order, perfect in truth, perfect in the use of number, perfect in structure.

"The works of Jehovah are great: sought out of all them that have pleasure therein" (Ps. cxi. 2).

Those who seek out His works find wondrous treasures; and see perfection, whether revealed by the telescope or the microscope. Neither of these exhaust those wonders. Both are only relative, and limited by human powers of sight.

It is the same with that most wonderful of all His works—His WORD. Use what powers of human intellect we may, we find that we know only "in part" (1 Cor. xiii. 9). Pursue any line of truth as far as our human minds can go, and we come to a wall of adamant, which we can neither mount over, pierce through, nor pass round; we return baffled, but solemnized by the fact that we know "in part."

We shall not be surprised therefore to find literary perfection as well as spiritual perfection. For there is perfection of literary form, as well as perfection of spiritual truth.

The correspondence between parallel lines must always have been visible even on the surface to any one who carefully observed the Scriptures even as literary compositions.

Josephus,[1] Philo Judæus, Origen, Eusebius, Jerome, Isidore, among the Ancients, professed to have discovered metres in the Hebrew original. They were followed by

---

[1] See the references to the writings of these men in Bishop Jebb's *Sacred Literature*, p. 10.

others among modern scholars, some of whom agreed with them, while others refuted them.

In spite of Bishop Lowth's Larger and Shorter Confutations, which showed that all efforts to discover the rhymes and metres which characterize common poetry must be fruitless, some few writers have persevered in such attempts even to the present day.

"Bishop Lowth was the first to put the whole subject on a better and surer foundation; reducing the chaos of mediæval writings to something like order. His works were based on one or two who had preceded him, and had laid the foundations on which he built with such effect that he came to be universally recognised and appealed to as the ultimate and classical authority in these matters." [1]

But, as we have said, Bishop Lowth built on the foundations laid by others. [2]

Abravanel, a learned Jew of the fifteenth century, and Azariah de Rossi [3] in the sixteenth century, were the first to demonstrate and illustrate the phenomena exhibited in the *parallel lines* of Holy Scripture.

Azariah de Rossi published, in 1574–5, in Mantua, his celebrated work which he called מאור עינים (*Meōr Enayîm*), or, *The Light of the Eyes*. It was a remarkable work and almost an encyclopedia of biblical literature in itself. Several of its chapters have been translated and published separately, in Latin and English. One chapter (ch. lx.) was sufficient to kindle Bishop Lowth's enthusiasm; and he translated it in his *Preliminary Dissertation* to his last great work, his translation of Isaiah (London, 1835). But, before this, Lowth had already used De Rossi's wonderful work to such purpose that in 1753 he published his *Prælections on the Sacred Poetry of the Hebrews*. This caused quite a sensation in the biblical world, and soon became of European fame.

Meanwhile Christian Schoettgen (born 1687) had published in 1733–42 his *Horæ Hebraicæ et Talmudicæ* (2 vols.

---

[1] Bishop Jebb, *Sacred Literature*, p. 15.

[2] Rabbi Bon Isaac ben Jehudah, a celebrated Spanish-Jewish statesman, philosopher, theologian, and commentator, born 1437. His commentaries anticipate of what has been advanced as new by modern theologians (Kitto, *Enc. Bib.* article by C. D. G.).

[3] Azariah Min Ha-Adonim, as the Jews call him, was born in Mantua, 1513.

4to), at Dresden and Leipzig; Bishop Lowth does not appear to have known of this work, for it anticipates him, and under the heading "Exergasia Sacra" it lays down the very doctrine which it remained for Lowth to improve and elucidate. Schoettgen lays down ten canons, and he illustrates each with three examples.

Bishop Jebb (born 1775 at Drogheda) published his *Sacred Literature* in London, 1820: and, until Thomas Boys began to write in 1824, Jebb's work had remained the last word on the subject. It was a review of Lowth's work and "an application of the principles so reviewed" to the illustration of the New Testament.

But both these works of Bishops Lowth and Jebb were almost entirely confined to the verbal correspondences in parallel lines; and never proceeded beyond short stanzas; and, even then, did not rise beyond what Lowth called "*parallelism*" and Jebb called "*Sacred Composition.*"

It was reserved for Thomas Boys to raise the whole subject on to a higher level altogether, and to lift it out of the literary parallelism between *words* and *lines;* and to develope it into the *correspondence between the subject-matter* and truth of the Divine Word.

In 1824 Thomas Boys soon followed up Bishop Jebb by publishing his *Tactica Sacra*, and in 1827—30 his *Key to the Book of Psalms.*[1]

While the successive works of Bishops Lowth and Jebb were enthusiastically and generally received, yet the works of Thomas Boys not only had to fight their way through much opposition, but are now practically unknown to Biblical students. Whether it is because they afford such a wonderful evidence of the supernatural and miraculous in the Bible, and such a proof of the Divine Authorship of the Word of God, that they are therefore the special object of attack by the enemies of that Word (both Satanic and human) He alone knows. But so it is.

---

[1] This was only a description of his principles of *Correspondence*, which he applied to some sixteen Psalms. It was the privilege of Dr. Bullinger to edit Thomas Boys's manuscript; and, from pencilled notes in Boys's Interleaved Hebrew Bible (Boothroyd's Edition with Commentary), to complete and publish, in 1890, the whole of the Psalms with a Preface, and Memoir by his friend the Rev. Sydney Thelwall (who had been a personal friend of Boys), then Vicar of Westleigh, North Devon. An Introduction and Appendix were added by Dr. Bullinger as editor. This work was called *A Key to the Book of Psalms* to preserve a continuity with Boys's own title.

Bishop Jebb, however, we are thankful to say, in the Second Edition of his *Sacred Literature* (1831), does recognize Boys's work in a note on page 74. He says, "Since the publication of *Sacred Literature*, this peculiarity of composition has been largely and happily illustrated, in his *Tactica Sacra*, by the Rev. Thomas Boys."

In 1851 Richard Baillie Roe made a great effort to revive the subject by publishing *An Analytical Arrangement of the Holy Scriptures according to the principles developed under the name of Parallelism in the writings of Bishop Lowth, Bishop Jebb, and the Rev. Thomas Boys.*

This appears to have shared the same fate as all the others. Roe's book gives us too much as well as too little. It gives too much of dry analysis, and too little of the end for which it is made. Moreover, it is not improved by departing from Boys's simplicity; and serves only to complicate the subject by adding much that is arbitrary in arrangement. It may be said of Roe's method, that what is true is not new; and what is new is no improvement.

The facts being as thus stated, it shows that the subject has either not yet been grasped nor understood by Bible students; or, that it makes too much for the Inspiration and Divine Origin and Authority of the Word of God; and that there are spiritual powers, working with the human, whose one great object is to make the Word of God of none effect (Eph. vi. 12 and 17).

And yet, we may say that, no more powerful weapon has yet been placed in our hands outside that Word, which is "the Spirit's sword." It affords a wondrous proof of Inspiration; it gives us a clearer and more comprehensive view of the scope of the Scriptures, than the most learned and elaborate commentaries can ever hope to do; and it is capable of even turning the scale in doubtful, doctrinal, and critical questions.

By its means the student is led to views and truths, and reflections which, without it, would never have occurred to him. And it is not too much to say that until the Correspondences of the Biblical Structure are duly recognized we shall never get a correct translation or a true interpretation of many passages which are to this day dark and confused in both our Versions, the R.V. as well as in the A.V.

Preaching on another subject, Bishop Lowth truthfully and feelingly observed that "It pleased God, in His unsearchable wisdom, to suffer the progress of the Reformation to be stopped *mid-way;* and the effects of it to be greatly weakened by many unhappy divisions among the reformed." [1]

The same may be said of the Law of Correspondence in the Structure of the Word of God, so wonderfully discovered and developed; and yet, needing to-day almost to be rediscovered, and certainly to be developed in its application to the whole Word of truth.

Parts of the world, remaining yet unexplored, are eagerly sought out without stint of labour or money. Would that the same zeal could be seen applied in the interest of this great subject.

ii. THE PRINCIPLES GOVERNING THE STRUCTURE OF SCRIPTURE.

Having said thus much on the History and Importance of the Structure of Scripture, it is necessary that we should present an account and description of it in some kind of order more or less complete.

We do not propose to wade through all the Divisions and Subdivisions which have been suggested or laid down in connection with Parallelism as it relates to *Lines.* Our general object is to understand the Word of truth; and our special object is to consider how we may, by its means, arrive at the scope or subject of a particular passage.

The laws which govern this Parallelism of lines we will re-state as briefly as may be consistent with clearness. The main principles are as follows:—
Parallel Lines are:—

(1) COGNATE [2] or GRADATIONAL, where the same thought is expressed in different or progressive terms:—

> "*Seek* ye *Jehovah,* while He may be *found;*
> *Call* ye upon *Him,* while He is *near.*"—(Isa. lv. 6.)

---

[1] *Sermons and Remains of Robert Lowth, D.D.,* p. 78.
[2] This is Bishop Jebb's improvement of Bishop Lowth's word "synonymous, as including *different* as well as practically *equivalent* terms.

(2) ANTITHETIC or OPPOSITE, where the terms or subjects are set in contrast:—

> "*Faithful* are the *wounds* of a *friend;*
> But *deceitful* are the *kisses* of an *enemy.*"
> —(Prov. xxvii. 6.)

(3) SYNTHETIC, or CONSTRUCTIVE, where the terms or
subjects correspond in a similar form of construction,
either as equivalent or opposite. (As in Ps. xix. 7—10.
Isa. xliv. 26—28.) It discriminates and differentiates between the thoughts, as well as the words; building up
truth by layers, as it were, placing one on the other.

> "O the happiness of that man,
> Who hath not *walked* in the *counsel* of the
>   *ungodly;*
> And hath not *stood* in the *way* of *sinners;*
> And hath not *sat* in the *seat* of the *scornful.*"
> —(Ps. i. 1.)

(4) INTROVERTED, where, whatever be the number of
lines, the first line is parallel with the last; the second
with the penultimate (or next to the last); the third
with the antepenultimate (or next but one to the last);
and so throughout, until we come to the two corresponding lines in the middle.

This was the discovery of Bishop Jebb; and could not
be seen until a larger number of consecutive lines were
examined.

> "Make the *heart* of this people fat,
>   And make their *ears* heavy,
>   And shut their *eyes:*
>   Lest they see with their *eyes,*
>   And hear with their *ears*
> And understand with their *heart.*"—(Isa. vi. 10.)

Here, the correspondence is manifest.

It was, however, as we have said, reserved for Thomas
Boys to lift the whole study out of the sphere of *words*
and *lines;* and see the Law of Correspondence between
subjects and *subject-matter.* Instead of occupying us with
lines he bade us look at what he designated *members.*
These members consisted of *verses,* and whole *paragraphs.*

And the larger paragraphs were soon seen to have their own peculiar structure[1] or expansions.

This brings us to the consideration of what we have called the Structure of Scripture.

Most of our readers will be acquainted with the practice of marking their Bibles by ruling lines connecting the same word or words as they recur on the same or the adjoining page. The words recur, because the *subject recurs;* and the Law of Correspondences not only explains the practice of such Bible markings, but shows why it can be done.

The principles and phenomena of the Laws of Correspondence are exceedingly simple, however perplexing they may appear to the eye at first sight. A little attention will soon make all clear to the mind as well as to the eye.

There are practically only two ways in which the subject is repeated:—

    1. By Alternation.
    2. By Introversion.

1. *Alternation.*

This is where two (or more) subjects are repeated alternately.

(*a*) We call it *Simple Alternation* where there are only *two* subjects each of which is repeated in alternate lines. Thus:—

$$
\begin{aligned}
&\text{A}\mid \text{———————} \\
&\quad \text{B}\mid \text{———————} \\
&\textit{A}\mid \text{———————} \\
&\quad \textit{B}\mid \text{———————}
\end{aligned}
$$

Here, the letters are used quite arbitrarily, and merely for the convenience of reference. Thus, the subject in the passage marked with an Italic letter (*A*) is the same as the subject in the passage marked with the corresponding Roman letter (A); while the B subject is the same as the *B* subject, the similar Roman and Italic letters indicating their similar, opposite and contrasted, or common subject.

---

[1] The reader will find further elucidation on this subject in *Figures of Speech*, by the same author.

(*b*) Where the two subjects are repeated more than once we call it *Repeated Alternation,* and indicate it thus :—

$$A^1 \mid \text{————}$$
$$B^1 \mid \text{————}$$
$$A^2 \mid \text{————}$$
$$B^2 \mid \text{————} \text{-}$$
$$A^3 \mid \text{————}$$
$$B^3 \mid \text{————}$$

And so on: all the members marked A corresponding in subject; and the members marked B corresponding in like manner. There is no limit to this repetition.

(*c*) Where there are more than two subjects alternating then we call it *Extended Alternation;* and there will be as many pairs, or sets of members, as there are subjects (unless, of course, these are repeated, when it would be a *Repeated Extended Alternation*):—

$$A \mid \text{————}$$
$$B \mid \text{————}$$
$$C \mid \text{————} \text{—}$$
$$A \mid \text{————}$$
$$B \mid \text{————}$$
$$C \mid \text{————}$$

2. *Introversion.*

This is where the subjects are repeated, not in alternation, but in introversion; *i.e.* from opposite ends. In this case there will be as many subjects as there are pairs of introverted members. Suppose we have an example of four subjects. This will give us eight members, in which the 1st will correspond with the 8th; the 2nd with the 7th; the 3rd with the 6th; and the 4th with the 5th. Thus:—

$$A \mid \text{————}$$
$$B \mid \text{————}$$
$$C \mid \text{————}$$
$$D \mid \text{————}$$
$$D \mid \text{————}$$
$$C \mid \text{————}$$
$$B \mid \text{————}$$
$$A \mid \text{————}$$

Now, with these few simple facts and phenomena, it is possible to have a very great variety. For they are practically unlimited, and can be combined in so many ways, and in such varying numbers, that there seems no end to the variety. But, all conform to the above simple laws, in which there is no exception.

iii. EXAMPLES OF EACH PRINCIPLE.

We will give an example of each kind: premising (1) that 1- indicates the first part of a verse, -1 the latter part, and -1- a middle part; (2) that all the larger members have their own special Structures, in which the Correspondences of each may be expanded and exhibited.

We give the examples from the Psalms because they are not encumbered with the human chapter divisions.

Simple Alternation.

Psalm xix.

A | 1—4-. The Heavens.
   B | -4, 6. In them (בָּהֶם) "The Sun."
A | 7—10. The Scriptures.
   B | 11—14. In them (בָּהֶם) "Thy Servant."

Repeated Alternation.

Psalm cxlv.

A¹ | 1, 2. Praise promised. From me, to Jehovah Himself.
   B¹ | 3. Praise offered.
A² | 4—7. Praise promised. From others and me for Jehovah's works.
   B² | 8, 9. Praise offered.
A³ | 10—12. Praise promised. From others, and His works, for Jehovah's kingdom.
   B³ | 13—20. Praise offered.
A⁴ | 21. Praise promised from me and others, to Jehovah Himself.

Introversion and Extended Alternation Combined.

Psalm cv.

A | 1—7. Exhortation to praise.

  B | 8—12. Basis of praise. Covenant in promise. ⎱

      C a | 13. Their journeyings.

          b | 14, 15. Their prosperings.

              c | 16. Their affliction.

                  d | 17—22. Mission of deliver-
                  ance (שָׁלַח). Joseph.

> History. Patriarchs.

      C | a | 23. Their journeyings.

          b | 24. Their prosperings.

              c | 25. Their affliction.

                  d | 26—41. Mission of deliver-
                  ance (שָׁלַח). Moses and
                  Aaron.

> History. The nation.

  B | 42—45-. Basis of praise. Covenant performed.

A | -45. Exhortation to praise.

In order to discover the structure of a particular passage it is necessary that we begin to read the portion of Scripture very carefully, and note the subject. We mark it A | —.

We read on *until the subject changes,* and we note and indent it thus B | —.

So far there can be no difficulty. But when we come to the next change we may find either a third subject, in which case we must further indent it and mark it C | —, or, we shall find the first subject again (as in Ps. xix. above). If it be the latter, then we know that we are going to find an *alternation* (and this, either simple as in Ps. xix. above, or repeated as in Ps. cxlv. above), and we must mark it *A* | — and put it beneath the A | —. If it is a repetition of the second subject, then we know that it is going to be an *Introversion,* and must mark it *B* | — and place it under the B | —.

Let us take, as a working example, "The Prophecy of Zacharias," in Luke i. 68—79; this being a passage of Scripture complete in itself, and not a human or arbitrary division.

We read verse 68 with the object of finding and noting its subjects:—"*Blessed be the Lord God of Israel; for he hath visited and redeemed his people.*" Here, the subject may be either "Visited" or "Redeemed." So we give the place of honour to the former of these two words, and write it down, thus:—

A | 68. Visitation.

We then read the next verse, "*And hath raised up a horn of salvation for us in the house of his servant David.*" Here there can be no doubt that the subject is *Salvation.* This we must mark "B," and set it down, indented, thus:

B | 69. Salvation.

So far all is clear. But we know not, as yet, what the subject of the *third* member is to be. If it is *Visitation* we must set it down under "A" and mark it with an italic "*A.*" Then we read slowly on:—"*As he spake by the mouth of his holy prophets, which have been since the world began.*" It is manifest that we have, as yet, no repetition of either of the subjects in "A" or "B." If it had been that of "A," it would be a *Simple* or *Repeated Alternation.* If it had been that of "B," we should know that it was going to be an *Introversion.* But, it is a fresh subject, which is clearly, "Prophets." So we must mark it "C," and write it down, indenting it still more, thus:

C | 70. Prophets.

Even now, there is nothing to tell us what the Structure is going to be. So far as we can see, it may be an *Extended Alternation* by the repetition of "A," "B," and "C"; or it may be an *Introversion* to be marked "C," "B," and "A." So we must read on:—"*That we should be saved from our enemies, and from the hand of all that hate us.*" Here, we still have no *Repetition:* but we find a new subject, which is clearly "Enemies." So we must mark it "D," and write down (still further indenting it) thus:

D | 71. Enemies.

If the subject is a *Repetition* of any of the above subjects, we know that we are going to have an *Alter-*

nation of some kind, or an *Introversion.* So we must still read on:—" *To perform the mercy promised to our fathers, and to remember his holy covenant.*" Here, there can be no doubt that we have again a new subject, and that it must be *Covenant.* So we put it down, as before, and still further indent it, thus:

E | 72. The Covenant.

We can now be sure that we are going to have either a very *Extended Alternation* or an *Introversion.* So we must still read on, closely scanning every word, in order to get the clue. We find it in the next verse (*v.* 73):—" *The oath which he sware to our father Abraham.*" Here, at length, we get one of our subjects *repeated,* as we were bound to do before long. It is the subject of " E," where the word " Covenant" is repeated in the synonymous word " Oath," thus indicating the sureness and certainty of the Covenant. We must mark this " *E,*" and write it down under the " E," thus:

E | 73. The Oath.

All we have to do now is to read on, and we soon discover that we have an *Introversion,* of great beauty, which we may now easily complete and set out, as follows:

Introversion.

The song of Zacharias (Luke i. 68—79).

  A | 68. Visitation.
    B | 69. Salvation.
      C | 70. Prophets.
        D | 71. Enemies.
          E | 72. The Covenant.
          E | 73. The Oath.
        D | 74, 75. Enemies.
      C | 76. Prophet.
    B | 77. Salvation.
  A | 78, 79. Visitation.

By practice and observation we shall soon surmount the initial difficulties; and in course of time the study and formation of structures will become increasingly easy and happy work.

iv. The Advantages and Importance of the Structures Will be Seen

(*a*) In telling us what a particular passage of Scripture is all about. In other *words*, what is the *Scope* or the *Subject* of the passage we are studying.

(*b*) This will give us the key to the meaning which we are to put upon the *words* which are employed (as we saw under Canon I.).

(*c*) In a case of doubt, the subject which is clearly stated in *one* of the members will inform us as to what it *must* be in the corresponding member, where it may not be so clearly stated.

(*d*) As the sense generally reads on from one member to its corresponding member, it will practically place the intervening member or members in a parenthesis. We shall therefore have to read on from "A" to "*A*" and from "B" to "*B*," etc., in order to get connected sense, instead of apparent confusion. This may be seen from any of the above examples, especially Ps. cv. But we may append another beautiful example:

Hebrews i., ii.

A | i. 1—2-. God speaking.
> B | i.-2—14. The Son. God. Better than Angels.
A | ii. 1—4. God speaking.
> *B* | ii. 5—18. The Son. Man. Lower than Angels.

Here, ch. ii. 1 ("*A*") reads on from i. 2- ("A"), and ch. ii. 5 ("*B*") reads on from ch. i. 14 ("B").

(*e*) Corroborative evidence is sometimes thus obtained for the support or otherwise of a various reading.

v. Illustrations of these Advantages.

But the chief importance of this branch of our subject lies in the fact that the *Structure* gives us the *Scope*, and the Scope will give us the key to the meaning of the words.

It will be interesting if we now apply the principle involved in this our Second Canon to our First Canon, and to the same passages there considered. We shall thus see how the *Structure* of the passages which furnished the several illustrations under Canon I. does indeed give us their *Scope:* which, in turn, gives us the meanings of the words in 2 Pet. i. 20, 21 and 1 Pet. iii. 18—20.

(*a*) " *Private interpretation*" (2 Pet. i. 20, 21). As the Epistles come to us as a whole, without division into chapters, we must not be guided by these human divisions at all in looking for the Structure; neither may we arbitrarily take a few verses, and say: these form a member by themselves. We must show that these verses in question stand in their own special place and have their own proper correspondences in the Epistle as a whole. In looking, therefore, for the structure of 2 Pet. i. 20 we must first find the Structure of the whole Epistle, and see where this particular verse comes in; so that we may know of what subject it forms part; and with what other member it has its correspondence.

The 2nd Epistle of Peter as a whole.

(*Combined Introversion and Extended Alternation.*)

A | i. 1—4. Epistolary. Introduction. Grace and know-
ledge to be increased. Christ, "God and Saviour."

    B | i. 5—11. Exhortations and Reasons.

        C | a | i. 12—15. Peter.

                b | i. 16—21. Apostles and prophets.

                    c | ii. The wicked, etc.

        C | *a* | iii. 1. Peter.

                b | iii. 2. Prophets and apostles.

                    c | iii. 3—13. The wicked, etc.

    B | iii. 14—17. Exhortations and reasons.

A | iii. 18. Epistolary. Conclusion. Grace and knowledge
to be increased. Christ, "Lord and Saviour."

We thus see that ch. i. 20 forms part of a larger member (marked "b") which has for its subject "Apostles and prophets."

This one member (b, i. 16—21) is capable of a wonderful expansion, from which we see that it consists of two distinct parts: *Apostolic witness* (*vv.* 16—18); and, *the Prophetic word* (*vv.* 19—21).

These two, on careful examination, are seen to have a similar construction : Alternately negative and positive.

2 Peter i. 16—21.

(Simple Alternation Combined with Introversion.)

The Apostolic Witness (vv. 16—18).

b D d i. 16.   *What it was NOT.*   "Not cunningly devised (or self-originated) Myths."

e i. -16.   *What it WAS.*   A vision of the power and coming of Christ (Comp. Matt. xvi. 28, and xvii. 1—5).

E i. 17, 18.   *How it CAME.*   Voice came $(\phi\acute{\epsilon}\rho\omega)$ from the excellent glory. Voice came $(\phi\acute{\epsilon}\rho\omega)$ from heaven. "Heard" and "made known."

The Prophetic Word (vv. 19—21).

D e i. 19.   *What it IS.*   A light to be well-heeded till the Day of Christ's coming shall dawn ; and He, the Day Star, shall arise.

d i. 20.   *What it is NOT.*   Not of its own revealment. Not self-originating.

E i. 21.   *How it CAME.*   Not brought $(\phi\acute{\epsilon}\rho\omega)$ by the Will of Man; but brought $(\phi\acute{\epsilon}\rho\omega)$ by *pneuma hagion*, or "power from on high." "Heard," and "spoken."

From this we see the obvious contrast standing out very clearly between the self-originated myths that came by "the will of man"; and the Divine and heavenly Visions and revelations sent and received, and seen and heard from God in heaven.

This revelation is further seen to concern Christ's Coming. In "e" it is the Vision of it, as fore-shown in the Transfiguration: in "e" it is the grand reality of it, of which the Transfiguration was only a typical Vision. The former was believed on *the Apostolic Witness:* the latter was to be believed on the testimony of *the Prophetic Word.*

Further, the great subject, as to *How the Apostolic Witness* and the *Prophetic Word* came is strongly emphasized
by the repetition of the same verb φέρω (*phero*), *to bring*
or *bear*. We have it twice in each of the two corresponding members (E and *E*), showing us how the
human *Witness* and the Divine *Word* were both *brought*
to us from heaven; and did not originate from any
man or men on earth, as did the cunningly-devised
myths.

It is this fact which stamps the Apostasy of the
present day. Those who profess to be in the Apostolic
succession *turn away* their ears from the prophetic
Word; and, while they declare that many of its records
are myths, are themselves "turned unto" the myths[1] of
man's devising.

We may add, in order to complete this passage, the
following Expansions, verbatim:—

The Expansion of *D* (2 Peter i. 19, 20).

The Prophetic Word.

(*Introversion*—Six Members.)

D | f | And we have more sure, the prophetic word (written
prophecy);
    g | to which ye do well to take heed,
      h | as to a light shining in a dark place,
      h | until the day dawn, and the day star arise,
    g | in your hearts;
  f | this knowing first, that no prophecy of scripture
came of *its* own disclosure.

Here, we observe, that the subject of "f" and "*f*"
is the Prophecy. In "f" it is spoken of as a whole; in
"*f*" in part, a particular prophecy. In "g" and "*g*" we
have Exhortation as to our duty with regard to it. In
"g" we are exhorted to take heed to it; and in "*g*" *how*
we are to take heed—*viz.*, in our hearts. Lastly, in "h"
and "*h*" we have the Prophetic Word again. In "h"
its character (a light in a dark place); and in "*h*" its

---

[1] So the Greek word rendered "Fables" in 2 Tim. iv. 4.

duration and object (until the day dawn, etc.). Then in verse 21 we have the reason given.

The Expansion of *E* (2 Peter i. 21).

The Reason.

(*Introversion.*)

E | i | For not by the will of man
   k | was prophecy, at any time, borne in,
   k | but by the Holy Spirit, borne along,
  i | spake the holy men of God.

Here again we have in "i" and "*i*" man's relation to the Prophetic Word; in "i" negative, in "*i*" positive. While in "k" and "*k*" we have its origin; in "k" negative, and in "*k*" positive.

The above two Structures may be now explained by the following Key:

THE KEY TO *D* AND *E*.

The Prophetic Word. (2 Peter i. 19, 20.)

(*Introversion.*)

D | f | The prophetic word as a whole.
   g | Exhortation (general) to take heed to it.
    h | Its character: a light in a dark place.
    h | Its duration: until the Day dawn.
   g | Exhortation (particular): to take heed to it in our hearts.
  f | Prophecy in particular.

The Reason. (2 Peter i. 21.)

(*Introversion.*)

E | i | Man's part in it. ⎫
   k | How it did not come. ⎬ Negative.
   k | How it did come ⎫
  i | Man's part in it. ⎬ Positive.

Thus the *scope*, or great subject, of 2 Peter i. 16—21 is gathered from its *structure;* and it is seen to be, not what Scripture *means*, but whence it *came:* and it is concerned not with the *interpretation* of Scripture, but with its *origin*, as already shown above (pp. 186—188).

(*b*) "*The spirits in prison*" (1 Pet. iii. 18—22). To understand this expression the Structure is necessary to give us the scope of 1 Pet. iii.

Verse 19 does not stand by itself, but forms part of a larger member; and that member has its own *Scope*, or subject, which will give us the meaning of the expression—"The in-prison spirits."

This member is not to be arbitrarily delimited, but must be found from

The Structure of 1 Peter as a whole.

(*Combined Introversion and Extended Alternation.*)

A | i. 1, 2. *Epistolary.*

    B i. 3—12. *Introduction.* Giving out the great subject. "The End." Glory, after suffering for a season (ὀλίγον, *oligon*).

        C a | i. 13—ii. 10. *General Exhortations* in view of "*the End*" (i. 13). Grace to be brought at Revelation of Jesus Christ.

           b | ii. 11—iv. 6. *Particular Exhortations* as to "sufferings" to be followed by "glory" (ii. 20; iii. 17—22).

        C a | iv. 7—19. *General Exhortations* in view of "*the End*." Joy to be brought at Revelation of Christ's glory.

           b v. 1—9. *Particular Exhortations* as to "sufferings" to be followed by "glory" (v. 1).

    B v. 10, 11. *Conclusion.* Embodying the great subject. "The End." Glory after suffering awhile (ὀλίγον, *oligon*).

A | v. 12—14. *Epistolary.*

From this structure it is perfectly clear that the *Scope* and subject of the whole Epistle is only one. This Scope is given in the words of ch. iii. 17.

        " It is better to suffer for well doing than for evil doing."

This truth is enforced and illustrated and emphasized again and again throughout the Epistle.

The verses which follow (iii. 17—iv. 6)[1] are added as *the reason*, which is given in proof of this statement of the Scope of this Epistle. The word "FOR" introduces it, and thus tells us that we have arrived at the very kernel of the whole Epistle. Not some passage which we are to explain as best we can and as though we wished it were not there: but which we are to embrace as all-important, and as though it were indispensable, as it is, to the subject of the Epistle.

But here again we must go back; for though we see that these verses (iii. 17—iv. 6) occur in the member "b," yet we see also that they form only *a part* of that member.

It is necessary for us, therefore, to go back, and see whether it is really an integral part, and whether the break in the whole member (ii. 11—iv. 6) really does occur at iii. 17.

Expansion of "b" (1 Peter ii. 11—iv. 6).

(*Extended Alternation.*)

b | D | ii. 11.   *Exhortations* (Personal).

     E | ii. 12.   *Calumnies*: and how to refute them.

        F   ii. 13—iii. 7.   Submission to man for the Lord's sake: "The will of God" (ii. 15). Reason: "For" (ii. 21), and Example of Christ in His sufferings.

  D | iii. 8—15.   *Exhortations* (General).

     E | iii. 16.   *Calumnies:* and how to refute them.

        F | iii. 17—iv. 6.   Submission to man for the Lord's sake : "The will of God" (iii. 17). Reason : "For" (iii. 18), and Example of Christ in His glorification.

The Correspondence of these members, each to each, is exceedingly exact and minute. From this we see that the last member *F* does actually commence with iii. 17, the "For" corresponding exactly with the "For" in ch. ii. 21: each "for" introducing the example of Christ.

---

[1] We cannot break off at end of ch. iii. for ch. iv. begins "Forasmuch then," which shows that it follows in close continuation of ch. iii.

Now we are, at length, in a position to examine the further delimitation of this member *F* (iii. 17—iv. 6): which is as follows:—

The Reasons for Submission to the Will of God
(1 Peter iii. 17—iv. 6).

(Simple Alternation Combined with Introversion.)

F | G | c   iii. 17. Reason for *our suffering* here, in the flesh, "if the will of God be so."

d   iii. 18-. Reason for *Christ's suffering* here as to His flesh, "put to death."

H | iii. -18—22. *Christ's glory* which followed. (Resurrection, Triumph, Glory, and Dominion).

G | d | iv. 1-. Reason for *Christ's suffering* here, in the flesh.

c | -1—5. *Our suffering* here in the flesh, at the "will of man," by "the will of God."

H | iv. 6. Reason for *our glory* which shall follow. Though judged in the flesh according to the "will of man," we shall live again in resurrection according to the "will of God" (Compare *v.* 19).

Here we see the beautiful contrast between our *suffering* and Christ's; our *glory* and Christ's. This leads us up, naturally, to Christ's example, which follows verses 18—22, with which we are now concerned.

We see, from the above Structure, that these particular verses are located in the member "H," the subject of which is the Example of Christ in His glorification, corresponding with His example in ch. ii. 21, which was Christ in His suffering.

In H (ch. iii. 18—22) the two examples are combined in order to connect the sufferings with the glory; and to show that Christ's glorious triumph which followed was the reason why it is better to suffer here, and now. (Compare ch. iii. -18, with ch. iv. -6.)

This is the triumph referred to in Col. ii. 14, 15, where, having "spoiled principalities and powers, he made a show of them openly, triumphing over them in it."

The Triumph of Christ (H, 1 Peter iii. 18—22).

(*Introversion and Extended Alternation.*)

H | J | e | iii. -18. *The Resurrection* of Christ.

      f | 19. *Result.* πορευθείς (*poreutheis*), *having gone* (to Tartarus, 2 Pet. ii. 4) He made proclamation of His Triumph to the in-prison spirits or angels.

        g | 20-. The *insubjection* of spirits in the days of Noah (Gen. vi. 2 Pet. ii. 4. Jude 6).

          K | -20. *Noah saved then.* Ark the type. Material water the means.

          K | 21-. *We saved now.* Baptism the Antitype. Spiritual water the means.

J | e | -21. *The Resurrection* of Jesus Christ.

      f | 22-. *Result.* πορευθείς, *having gone* into heaven, is on the right hand of God.

        g | -22. The *subjection* of angels, authorities, and powers.

Here we come to the direct proof that verses 18—22 have for their subject the "*glory*" of Christ, which followed on His "*sufferings*," forming the reason why "it is better to suffer for well-doing than for evil-doing."

We see also the importance of the Structure in giving us the *interpretation:* for the "spirits" in verse 20 are shown to be "angels" in verse 22: the *insubjection* of the former being set in contrast with the *latter.*

Thus we have another example of our second great principle that the *scope,* or subject, of a passage is to be sought for in its Structure.

We have also some evidence as to the Divine origin of Scripture. For, these Structures are altogether beyond the power of "unlearned and ignorant men" such as Peter was (Acts iv. 13), and are the best possible proofs we can have of Divine Inspiration.

(*c*) "*Testament*" *and Covenant* (Heb. ix. 15—23).—This will furnish us with an illustration of what we have already said on this passage above (pages 195—197).

There we have shown how the meaning of certain words in this passage is determined by its Scope. Now we have to show how the scope, and, therefore, the interpretation of the passage is determined by its Structure.

It is more profitable to show this in the case of passages we have already dealt with above, than to seek for other examples which would only divert our thoughts instead of concentrating them on the further elucidation of passages already in our minds.

When we say that Heb. ix. 15—23 forms a distinct member by itself, the burden of proof devolves upon us; for, we may not make this arbitrary statement: we must show that it is so in fact, and that it has its own separate place in

The Epistle to the Hebrews as a whole.
(*Introversion and Simple Alternation.*)

A | i., ii. Doctrinal Introduction.

B | iii. 1—iv. 13. The Mission of Christ.

C | iv. 14—16. General Application. ($'E\chi o\nu\tau\epsilon\varsigma$ $o\mathring{v}\nu$, "Having therefore") Boldness.

B | v. 1—x. 18. The Priesthood of Christ.

C | x. 19—xii. 29. Particular Application. ($'E\chi o\nu\tau\epsilon\varsigma$ $o\mathring{v}\nu$, "Having therefore") Boldness.

A | xiii. Practical Conclusion.

We are now in a position to see where our particular passage (ch. ix. 15—23) comes in.

It is in the member marked *B* (ch. v. 1—x. 18) that we find it.

We have to see, next, what particular part of that member it occupies, before we can discover its Scope.

Having thus given the Structure of the Epistle to the Hebrews as a whole, we are now in a position to see where the particular passage which we are considering comes in.

We have before remarked that we cannot be guided in this matter by the chapter-breaks, which are entirely and only of human authority, which is no authority at all.

In the case of an Epistle, we are compelled therefore to begin with the Epistle as a whole before we can discover the position of a particular passage or verse.

The Structure of this member *B*, is based on the same model on which the Epistle itself, as a whole, is framed; and it is as follows:

The Priesthood of Christ.

(*B*, Heb. v. 1—x. 18.)

(Introversion, combined with Simple Alternation.)

B a v. 1—4. The Nature of Priesthood in General. $\pi\tilde{\alpha}\varsigma$ $\gamma\acute{\alpha}\rho$ *(pas gar)* "*for every . . .*"

    b v. 5—10. Christ called by God after the order of Melchisedec.

        c v. 11—vi. 20. Digression, concerning Melchisedec as the Type.

    b vii. Christ called by God after the order of Melchisedec.

        c viii. 1, 2. Summation, concerning Christ as the Antitype.

a viii. 3—x. 18. The Efficacy of Christ's Priesthood in particular. $\pi\tilde{\alpha}\varsigma$ $\gamma\acute{\alpha}\rho$ *(pas gar)* "*for every . . .*"

Now we see that the verses we are seeking (Heb. ix. 15—23) form part of a larger member, *viz.*, Heb. viii. 3—x. 18, and that, in the above expansion, it is the member marked "*a*," which is the last member of the above Structure; and further, we see that its subject is the Efficacy and Superiority of Christ's Sacrifice as compared with the Priesthood of Aaron under the Law.

All we have to do now is to get the Scope of this member (*a*, ch. viii. 3—x. 18) by observing its own special Structure.

We have said above that all these larger members have their own peculiar construction; but we must not be tempted nor turned aside from our main purpose; we must confine our attention, in each case, to the particular members involved in our search: and continue this until we narrow the whole question down to the passage we are examining, and are able to locate the verses (ch. ix. 15—23) and thus discover their scope.

We are now in a position to do this by expanding the member "*a*," above, which we shall find to be as follows:—

The Efficacy and Superiority of Christ's Priesthood.
(*a*, Heb. viii. 3—x. 18).

(Extended Alternation.)

a | d | viii. 3—6. Christ's Priesthood. "A more excellent ministry," "a better covenant" on "better promises."

e | viii. 7—13. The Old and New Covenants compared and contrasted.

f | ix. 1—5. The Earthly Sanctuary a copy of the Heavenly Pattern.

g | ix. 6—10. The Offerings.

d | ix. 11—14. Christ's Priesthood. "A greater and more perfect Tabernacle." "His own blood."

e | ix. 15—23. The Old and New Covenants compared and contrasted.

f | ix. 24. The Heavenly Sanctuary the pattern of the Earthly Copy.

g | ix. 25—x. 18. The Offerings.

Here we see that our special member which we are tracking out is found in that marked "*e*," ch. ix. 15—23. Thus, at length, we learn that its subject is *The Old and New Covenants Compared and Contrasted.*

This settles its Scope for us. All that remains for us to do now is to confirm it by discovering its own Structure and seeing whether this be really the case.

To see the full force of this it will be well to look also at the member with which it stands in Correspondence, *viz.*, "e," ch. viii. 7—13, which is an Introversion. It also follows the model of the Epistle as a whole.

The Old and New Covenants Compared and Contrasted.
(e, Heb. viii. 7—13.)

(Introversion and Simple Alternation.)

e | h | 7, 8. The First Covenant Faulty.

i | 9. The New Covenant (Negative). Not the same in the making and material.

k | 10. The New Covenant (Positive). Spiritual.

i | 11. The New Covenant (Negative). Not the same in its result and effect.

k | 12. The New Covenant (Positive). Spiritual.

h | 13. The First Covenant Evanescent.

Now we are in a position to look at the member with
which we are specially concerned, and again we notice
that the Structure follows the model of the Epistle as a
whole:—

The Old and New Covenants Compared and Contrasted.
(*e*, Heb. ix. 15—23.)

(*Introversion and Simple Alternation.*)

e | 1 | ix. 15. The Old Covenant related only to "the promise
    | of the eternal inheritance."
       m | 16. Death necessary for its making.
           n | 17. Reason for this necessity.
       m | 18. Blood necessary for its consecration.[2]
          n | 19—23-. Reason for this necessity.
 l | -23. The New Covenant related to "the heavenly
    | things themselves."

It is impossible to miss the great subject of these verses.
It forbids us to ignore its importance, which is so essential
to the whole argument.

To arbitrarily change this subject is to entirely miss its
scope, and to be driven to force a meaning into the words
and expressions which are quite foreign to their Biblical
usage.

(*d*) "*Absent from the Body.*"—2 Cor. v. will furnish us
with another illustration of the importance of the *Structure* in determining the Scope. And we have seen, under
Canon I., the necessity of the *Scope* to give us the meaning of the word, and to show us how indispensable it is
for a right understanding of the whole.

The Structure will show us how much we lose by the
break between the fourth and fifth chapters of the second
Epistle to the Corinthians. Chapter v. commences as
though it began an entirely fresh subject, whereas it begins with the word "FOR," which shows that it is the conclusion of what had been begun towards the end of ch. iv.
That subject is Resurrection as our blessed hope in view
of the perishing of our outward man day by day. As a
comforting conclusion it is added, "FOR we know that if

---

[1] So the Greek, which has the article.
[2] Greek, ἐγκαινίζω (*enkainizō*), *to dedicate* (see ch. x. 20).

our earthly house of this tabernacle were dissolved, we have a building of God, an house not made with hands, eternal, in the heavens." This is one of the "things unseen," and which are "eternal"; at which, and for which, we are to "look."

Where the real literary and logical breaks occur can be discovered only from the Structure.

As a matter of fact, 2 Cor. v. forms part of a member which runs from 2 Cor. iii. 1—vi. 10; but we must not make such an arbitrary statement without producing the evidence, so that others may judge for themselves as to its accuracy.

To prove this we must first give

The Structure of 2 Cor. as a whole.

A | i. 1, 2. Salutation.
    B | a | i. 3—11. Thanksgiving.
       | b | i. 12. Paul's Ministry.
             C | i. 13—ii. 13. Epistolary.
    B | *a* | ii. 14—17. Thanksgiving.
       | *b* | iii. 1—vi. 10. Paul's Ministry.
             C | vi. 11—xiii. 10. Epistolary.
A | xiii. 11—14. Salutations.

Without going into the exquisite beauties of C and *C*,[1] we note that the small portion in which the expression "Absent from the body" occurs is the member marked *b* (ch. iii. 1—vi. 10). We must dissect and expand this member, which will be seen to be as follows:

The Character of Paul's Ministry.

(*b*, 2 Cor. iii. 1—vi. 10.)

b | c | iii. 1—3. Commendation (Positive).
      d | iii. 4, 5. Trust in God.   God's Sufficiency.
         e | iii. 6—18. The Ministry of the New Covenant.[2]
           f | iv. 1—v. 11. Support under Afflictions.
      c | v. 12, 13. Commendation (Negative).
        d | v. 14—18-. Love of Christ.   All of God.
          e | v. -18—vi. 2. The Ministry of Reconciliation.
            f | vi. 3—10. Approval under Afflictions.

---

[1] Which may be seen in *Figures of Speech*, p. 388, and *The Church Epistles*, p. 100.

[2] For the structure of this member, see *Word Studies on the Holy Spirit*, republished by Kregel Publications, pp. 138-140.

We are thus narrowing down the issue, which is now seen to lie in the member marked "f" (ch. iv. 1—v. 11).

The subject of this member is Support under afflictions; and its Structure is a repeated alternation, as follows:

Support under Afflictions.

(2 Cor. iv. 1—v. 11.)

f | g^1 | iv. 1—6. Confidence (Neg.). "We faint not."

$\quad$ h^1 | iv. 7—15. Grounds. "Earthen vessels." The working of death in them (iv. 12), with pledge of Resurrection (iv. 14).

$\quad$ g^2 | iv. 16-. Confidence (Neg.). "We faint not."

$\quad$ h^2 | iv. -16—v. 5. Grounds. "Earthly house." The working of afflictions (iv. 17), and the working of God, in Resurrection (v. 5).

$\quad$ g^3 | v. 6—11. Confidence (Pos.). "We are confident."

We need not pursue these expansions further, though we might well do so.

We can see very clearly now, that the wonderful ground of support of Paul and Timothy in their afflictions was the consideration of the "unseen" things, as out-weighing the "things seen"; so that though the "earthen vessels" of their bodies were dissolved there was the "excellency of the power" of God which would be put forth in Resurrection.

It is thus seen how the break between chapters iv. and v. destroys the connection: in fact, breaks in two the *one* member, "h^2" (ch. iv. -16—v. 5), which has only one subject, *viz.*, Resurrection, as the ground of the confidence, and the reason for not fainting in their labours of ministry.

We might have included this under the head of rightly dividing the Word of truth as to its literary form, as shown by the division into chapters (pages 34, 35). We might also have included it under the heading of the importance of the Scope of a passage (Canon I.). We might have included it under the heading of the importance of the Context (see below, Canon III.). It belongs to all three; but considering that the Structure is necessary to the crowning proof, we have given this illustration here.

It is little less than a crime for anyone to pick out
certain words and frame them into a sentence, not only
disregarding the Scope and the context, but ignoring the
other words in the verse, and quote the words "absent
from the body present with the Lord" with the view of
dispensing with the hope of Resurrection (which is the
subject of the whole passage), as though it were unnecessary; and as though "presence with the Lord" is
obtainable without it!

Apart from the doctrine involved, and apart from the
teaching of Tradition (true or false), it is a literary fraud
thus to treat the words which the Holy Ghost teacheth.

We see therefore, for it must be clear to us, that the
Scope of a passage is the key to its words; and that the
Structure of a passage is the key to its Scope.

This will show us the importance of our second Canon.

How great must be our loss if we fail to use this key
to the wonderful words of God.

Like all His works they bear the minutest searching
out.

All the works of God are perfect. And the microscope
and telescope can both be used to examine them; though
neither of them can ever exhaust the wonders of God's
works. In both directions an increase of the power of
the lens will reveal new beauties and fresh marvels.

The Word of God, being one of His works, must have
the same phenomena: and nothing exhibits these phenomena like the Study of its Literary Structure.

To us, God's Word is the greatest and most important
of all His works. If we understand all His other works
(which no one does or can) and yet know not His Word,
our knowledge will not carry us beyond the grave.

But we must not lose sight of the great underlying
lesson, and the great outcome of the whole of this subject,
which is this: If the external form be so perfect, what
must the inward truth be: if the setting be so valuable,
how valuable must be the jewel: if the literary order be
Divine, how solemn must be the warnings, how important
the truth, how faithful the promises, how sure the words
of which the Word is made up.

CANON 3

The Biblical Usage of Words Is Essential to Their Correct Interpretation

Next to the Scope of a passage in determining the meaning of words must be placed the Biblical *usage* of words, as distinct from the meanings put upon them by lexicons, dictionaries, and commentaries.

These are too often based on etymology merely, or on the meaning put upon words by tradition; or on their usage at some time other than the time at which they were written or spoken.

The *usage* of words is prior in time, as well as in importance, to all dictionaries.

Indeed, in all languages, the dictionary has to be compiled directly from such usage, and is, in fact, only a record of it, so far as it can be gathered.

Hence the value of such a work is in direct proportion to the number of examples which it gives of usage by different writers recognized as standard authorities.

In the case of many words, *changes* of usage can be traced through different periods of time.

Words in a living language are like coins which are in constant use; and, as coins not only differ in value between different countries, but change their own values at different periods in the same countries; so it is with words; there is a constant change in value when measured by their purchasing power.

The greatest possible care, therefore, is required in dealing with "words," especially when they are the "words which the Holy Ghost teacheth."

It is necessary that we should get not only the exact equivalent in changing words from one language to another, as we do in changing coins; but that we should know the relative value of the same words (or coins) in the same country at different periods of its history.

Over and above this, we read in Psalm xii. 6:

a | The *words* of Jehovah are pure words,

   b | As silver *tried* in a furnace:

a | [*Words*] of the earth,

   b | *Purified* seven times.

The Holy Spirit has used words pertaining to this world. He has not spoken with "the tongues of angels" (1 Cor. xiii. 1), but with "the tongues of men." In using men's words, and words pertaining to this world, He has used them in all perfection.

The Hebrew Old Testament we must regard as consisting only of Divinely chosen and inspired words, as we have no literature that goes behind it.

With the Greek of the New Testament the case is different, for there is the whole of Greek classical literature behind it.

It is intensely interesting to notice that while there are 97,921 words used by the classical Greek writers,[1] the Holy Spirit has chosen and used only 5,857 in the Greek New Testament.[2]

So that there are 92,064 Greek words which the Holy Spirit has never used at all.

That is to say, out of all the Greek words used in Greek Classical Literature the Holy Spirit has used only one in sixteen, or six per cent.!

Those He has used, He has, in many cases, used in a *higher* sense.

Some He has used in a *different* sense.

While others,[3] again, He has *coined* Himself.[4]

It is unnecessary for us to consider those words He has never used at all.

There are five distinct divisions under which this subject of *usage* of words may be profitably considered:

    i. Where English words have gone out of use altogether.

    ii. Where the usage of English words has been changed.

    iii. Where the usage of Greek words had become changed:

        (*a*) By God;

        (*b*) By man.

---

[1] This is the number of words treated in Liddle and Scott's Standard Greek Lexicon, 8th Edition, 1901. (It consists of 1774 pages.)

[2] This is the number of words treated in Thayer's (Grimm's Wilke's) Greek-English Lexicon to the New Testament.

[3] See ἐπιούσιος (*epiousios*), Matt. vi. 11 and Luke xi. 3, and separate pamphlet on *The Lord's Prayer*, by the same author.   Also σκανδαλίζω (*skandalizō*), *to cause to stumble* (Matt. xi. 6), *Figures of Speech*, p. 73.

[4] These should, of course, be deducted from the 5,857 mentioned above.

iv. Where different, but concurrent usages of Greek words should be observed in the English.
v. Where a uniform usage of Greek words should not be departed from in the English; English words obsolete.

i. WHERE ENGLISH WORDS HAVE GONE OUT OF USE ALTOGETHER.

In the English language certain words and expressions which were common in the seventeenth century have gone out of use altogether, and require explanation before they can be correctly interpreted.

The following are examples of words and expressions which have become obsolete:—

All to brake (Judges ix. 53) is the Anglo-Saxon *tobrecan*, which meant *to smash.* "All to brake," therefore, was used in the sense of *to completely smash* or *break.*

Away with (Isa. i. 13), meant *to tolerate.*

Come at, meant *to come near* (Num. vi. 6).

Do to wit (2 Cor. viii. 1), meant *make to know, to certify.*

For to do, meant *in order to do* (Deut. iv. 1).

Full well (Mark vii. 9), meant *with full knowledge.*

Go to (Jas. iv. 13), meant *come now.*

Trow (Luke xvii. 9), meant *to suppose* or *imagine.*

Wist (Luke ii. 49. Mark xiv. 40), is the past tense of the Ang.-Sax. *wit, to know. Unwittingly* (Josh. xx. 3), meant *unknowingly.*

Very (Gen. xxvii. 21. Prov. xvii. 9. John vii. 26; viii. 4), meant *true, real.*

These are only examples. There are many other such words for the Bible student to search out.

ii. WHERE THE USE OF ENGLISH WORDS HAS BECOME CHANGED.

Another class of words, which have not themselves become obsolete, but of which the *usage* has become entirely changed during the centuries, requires careful discrimination.

We are familiar with some of these changes, notably in the word

Prevent, which originally meant *to precede* or *go before,* but now means *to hinder.* The importance of this is seen in such a passage as 1 Thess. iv. 15, "We shall not precede those who are fallen asleep." So R.V. (See also Job iii. 12. Ps. xvii. 13 (marg.); lix. 10; lxxix. 8; lxxxviii. 13; xcv. 2 (marg.); cxix. 148. Amos ix. 10).

It is a strange commentary on fallen human nature to see words thus changing their usage; for this change is uniformly in one direction; it is *always a change for the worse.* We never find a word acquiring a higher meaning! It is always down, down, like fallen and falling man himself, who thus drags down with him the meanings of the words he uses.

How, for example, did the change in the usage of this word "prevent" come about? And why? It was because whenever one man got before another, it was generally for his own advantage, and to the hindrance, hurt, and loss of the other; hence the word came to have this new and lower meaning.

Other words may be studied with advantage, *e.g.,* boor, pagan, brat, imp, bombast, oversight, wretch, vagabond, craft, inquisition, impose, meddle, impertinent, garble, equivocation.[1]

---

[1] The same may be seen in the word *apology,* which was used of *a defence,* as in *Jewel's Apology* (i.e., *Defence) of the Reformation.* But, because man's defences of himself are usually so poor, the word has come to mean a mere *excuse.*

Our word *censure* was used simply of *judgment,* which might be favourable or otherwise; but, inasmuch as such judgments have generally proved to be unfavourable, the word is used, to-day, only of *blame.*

Our word *story* was originally short for *history,* but because so many histories and stories are what they are, the word has come to mean that which is not true.

Knave was originally a boy, especially a *servant boy;* but his character has served the purpose of changing the usage of the word to describe what he so often proved himself to be. In Scotland a *knave-bairn* was a boy-child. Wyckliffe rendered Exod. i. 13, "If it be a knave child, sle ye him." While Paul calls himself "a knave of Jesus Christ."

Cunning meant merely *knowing;* but because knowing people generally know too much, or use their knowledge to a bad purpose, it has come to have its present usage.

Subtle meant *finely-woven;* hence, *fine, accurate, clever.*

Villain meant a servant of a villa, or of a country or farm-house. The house has kept its good meaning, but the man has lost it.

But in this section we are dealing with English words where the fall is not so great, but where the old meaning has gone out.

To take in, was the act of hospitality (Matt. xxv. 35), but it stands on the border line, and is used of what it more often is than is not, *viz.*, to deceive.

Adventure, meant *to go* (Acts xix. 31. Deut. xxviii. 56).

Artillery, meant any instruments made by *art;* hence, weapons of any kind (1 Sam. xx. 40).

Assay, meant *to attempt, to try* (Job iv. 2).

By and by, meant *immediately*. This change is very important in the interpretation of Luke xxi. 9.

Charity, meant *love;* not from the Greek χάρις *(charis)*, but from the old French *charitet*, which meant *dearness*. This dearness of affection has resolved itself into the mercenary act of *giving money;* which has passed into our word *charity*, which no longer, therefore, represents the Greek word *charis*.

Beeves, was the plural of *beef*, the Norman-French for an ox (Num. xxxi. 33).

Parasite meant, in Greek, *a sacred granary;* but it is a word which has sunk low indeed, seeing that in Shakespeare's time he was able to write:

> " ' Most smiling, smooth, detested parasites,
> Courteous destroyers, affable wolves, meek bears,
> You fools of fortune.'

Yet in Greece, where it originated, *parasite* was once a highly respectable word. The original parasites were 'all honourable men; in repute alike for their learning and integrity.' They held positions of trust in Church and State, for which they had salaries and a table furnished them by the State. This latter fact led to their name, and ultimately to the downfall of the word. For long, however, the profession of parasite was an honourable one, and so great was the public confidence in them that *a sacred granary*, the *Parasitium*, containing corn for the service of the gods, was placed in their charge. Mural inscriptions recording the services of the parasites were placed in the temples, and some of them obtained the civic crown of gold. Presently, however, the word began to be used for those who fed at the expense of others. The hungry tribe sank yet lower in public estimation, and became the toadies and syco-phants at great men's tables."—*The Globe* (London, Eng.), April 23, 1907.

Inn, again, is another example of a word which has seen better days. It is "now applied only to low places and the better sort of public-house in which travellers are entertained; it formerly signified *a great house, mansion*, or *family palace*." Yet, in London, it still retains some signs of its former grandeur in Lincoln's Inn, formerly the residence of the Earls of Lincoln, and Gray's Inn, once the mansion of the noble family of Gray. Clement's Inn takes its name from Clement, the Dane on whose burial place a church was subsequently built. Thavie's Inn was built by John Thavie in 1347. Clifford's Inn was denomi-nated from Robert de Clifford, 1309; and Furnival's Inn, from Sir William Furnival, 1388.

Bonnet, was used of a man's head-dress (Exod. xxviii. 40), but to-day it is used only of a woman's (except in Scotland).

Carriages (Acts xxi. 15), was used of what was carried. To-day it is used of that which carries.

Clouted, meant *patched* (Josh. ix. 5).

To ear, meant *to plow* (1 Sam. viii. 12. Isa. xxx. 24). And *earing* meant *plowing* (Gen. xlv. 6. Exod. xxxiv. 21); and *eared* meant *plowed* (Deut. xxi. 4).

Earnest, meant *a pledge,* but of the same kind (2 Cor. i. 22. Eph. i. 14). A pledge might be of a different kind, and hence in that case it would not be an earnest. An earnest is to show that one is, as we say, "in earnest," or serious.

Fast, was used in the sense of *near,* or *close by* (Ruth ii. 8).

Libertine, was used originally of a class of freedmen among the Romans; but even in those days it came to be used (as now) of the licentious use of this liberty (Acts vi. 9).

Lusty, meant *vigorous* (John viii. 44. 2 Tim. iv. 3. 1 John ii. 16). *Lust* meant desire; but to-day it is used of one particular kind of desire.

Naughty, meant *worth nought, worthless* (Prov. vi. 12; xvii. 4. Jer. xxiv. 2). Now it is used to gloss over any evil, or evil of some special kind.

Nephew, was used of a grandson (Judg. xii. 14. Job xviii. 19. Isa. xiv. 22. 1 Tim. v. 4).

Occupy, was used of carrying on any business or trade. This usage is still preserved in the noun *occupation* (Luke xix. 13).

Penny, was used of any piece of money (Matt. xx. 2). Even silver money was called a *penny.* This usage is still preserved in our expression "to turn a penny." The word originally meant a *little pledge* or token, then *any coin.* Then it was used of a *day's wage* (Matt. xx. 2). In Luke x. 35 of two days' wage. Now, usage confines it to one particular coin, the twelfth part of a shilling. But that is not the usage in the New Testament.

Presently, meant *immediately* (1 Sam. ii. 16. Prov. xii. 16. Matt. xxi. 19; xxvi. 53. Phil. ii. 23).

Publican, was the Latin *publicanus,* or tax-gatherer (Matt. ix. 10, &c.). To-day it is used only of a vintner.

Quick, is the Anglo-Saxon *cwic*, *alive*, as opposite to
being dead (Lev. xiii. 10, 24. Num. xvi. 30. Ps. lv. 15;
cxxiv. 3. Isa. xi. 3. Acts x. 42. 2 Tim. iv. 1. Heb. iv. 12.
1 Pet. iv. 5). To-day we use it in the sense of *lively*, as
the opposite to slow.

Quicken, means *to make alive* (Ps. lxxi. 20; lxxx. 18;
cxix. 25, 37, 40, 88, 107, 149, 154, 156, 159; cxliii. 11.
Rom. viii. 11).

Quickened, means *made alive* (Ps. cxix. 50, 93. 1 Cor. xv.
36. Eph. ii. 1, 5. 1 Pet. iii. 18).

Quickeneth, means *maketh alive* (John v. 21; vi. 63.
Rom. iv. 17. 2 Cor. iii. 6 (marg.). 1 Tim. vi. 13).

Quickening, means *making alive* (1 Cor. xv. 45).

Simple, meant *one fold, without guile, open, artless*. But
because such an one says and does what more worldly-
wise people would conceal, he is considered foolish. Hence
the changed usage of the word. (See Ps. xix. 7; cxvi. 6;
cxix. 130. Prov. i. 4, 22, 32; vii. 7; viii. 5; ix. 4, 13; xiv. 15,
18; xxi. 11; xxii. 3. Ezek. xlv. 20. Rom. xvi. 18, 19).

Simplicity, has a similarly changed usage (see 2 Sam.
xv. 11. Prov. i. 22. Rom. xii. 8. 2 Cor. i. 12; xi. 3).

Sottish, meant *dull, heavy, stupid* (Jer. iv. 22), but because people are made so by intoxicants, it is used of
dullness so caused.

Vagabond, meant *a wanderer* (Gen. iv. 12, 14. Acts xix.
13). Our modern usage testifies to the character of most
wanderers.

Silly, is the Anglo-Saxon for *inoffensive, harmless;* but
because persons who are such are regarded as an easy
prey for designing persons, the word has come to be used
of those who are easily duped. (See Job v. 2. Hos. vii. 11.
2 Tim. iii. 6).

It will be seen from these examples how important
it is that we should have due regard to these changes of
usage in our own English language.

As we have exactly the same phenomena in the Greek
(as in all *living* [1] languages) it will be necessary to consider
this under our next heading.

---

[1] This is why Latin is used in all scientific terminology, because, being a
dead language, the meaning of its words is fixed, and cannot now be changed
by flux of time, or by use.

iii. Where the Usage of Greek Words had become Changed.

Greek being a living language, its words (like coins) became changed in usage.[1] Some words were thus changed by the Holy Spirit, and were purified as silver is purified in a furnace; and used in a higher, a better, nobler and a different sense from that in which man had ever used them.[2]

We will consider first the

(1) Changes of usage made by God, the Holy Spirit—

ἀρετή (*aretē*). Man used this only of *manhood* or *manly prowess*, but the Holy Spirit uses it in the far higher sense of Divine *glory* and of what God could praise. The only occurrences in the N. T. : Phil. iv. 8. 1 Pet. ii. 9. 2 Pet. i. 3, 5.

ἦθος (*ēthos*) was used only of the *haunt* of an animal, but it came to have the moral meaning of *custom*, or *character* (1 Cor. xv. 33).

ἄγγελος (*angelos*) was the Greek word for any *messenger*, also for a messenger of the gods. But the Holy Spirit takes it up, and purifies it, by using it as a *messenger* from God, and "the Angel of the LORD."

χορηγέω (*chorēgeō*) meant simply *to supply* or *furnish a chorus*. But the Spirit uses it of the Divine supply of all his people's needs (1 Pet. iv. 11).

ἐκκλησία (*ecclesia*) was used, by the Greeks, only of *a town's meeting* of its citizens (Acts xix. 39). But the Spirit uses it of the assemblies of God's elect.[2]

παράκλητος (*paraklētos*) was used only of *a legal assistant* or *helper*. But Christ uses it of the Holy Spirit or "Comforter" within us that we may *not* sin (John xiv. 16, 26; xv. 26; xvi. 7). And the Spirit uses it of Christ as the Advocate with the Father if we *do* sin (1 John ii. 1).

σκάνδαλον (*scandalon*) was used only of *a snare* to catch animals; but in the New Testament it is used in

---

[1] Similar changes are taking place to day: χρόνος (*chronos*), which, in Ancient Greek, meant *time*, is used in Modern Greek of *a year;* and καιρός (*kairos*), which meant *season*, is now used of *weather!*

[2] See above, pp. 227 228.

a moral and spiritual sense of that which causes anyone to stumble or fall (Matt. xi. 6); a sense in which the Greeks *never* used it.[1]

But there are other

(2) Changes of usage, made by man.

The Greek language was in use some four centuries before Christ, and had a wonderful literature. But, in the course of time the laws which operate to affect and change the usage of words wrought the same inevitable changes in many Greek words.

For this reason classical Greek usages are no infallible guide to the usage of Biblical Greek.

The vast moral and spiritual nature of the subject-matter of the New Testament necessitated of itself many changes, quite apart from those which were produced by the changes of time.

The Septuagint Version (of the Hebrew Old Testament into Greek) marks many of these changes. But within the last few years the evidence from this source of information has been vastly increased by the multitude of *papyri* which have been discovered, and dug up, in Egypt. These are daily increasing in number, and are being bought up for deposit and study in the principal libraries of Europe. Some students are engaged in their discovery, others in their translation, while others (like ourselves) are at work in applying them to the language of the Greek New Testament. All these are rendering great service to God's Word by making their discoveries public.[2]

These *papyri* are in Greek, and belong, for the most part, to the first and second centuries before and after Christ. They are therefore of the utmost importance in enabling us to discover the exact sense and usage of Greek words at that period.

These *papyri* consist of documents of all kinds ; exactly what would be found centuries hence in a house, buried suddenly to day in sand, or put away in tombs. There

---

[1] The noun is always translated *offence* in A.V., except Rom. xi. 9. 1 Cor. i. 23, and Rev. ii. 14, where it is "stumbling-block"; Rom. xiv. 13, where it is "occasion to fall." The Verb σκανδαλίζω *(scandalizō)* is always rendered *offend*.

[2] Notably Professor Deissmann, of Heidelberg; Professor Flinders Petrie, of Oxford, and others.

are business-letters, love-letters, contracts, estimates, certificates, agreements, accounts, bills of sale, mortgages, school-exercises, receipts, bribes, charms, litanies, tales, magical literature, pawn tickets, and every sort of literary production.

All these are of inestimable value in enabling us to arrive at a true knowledge of many Greek words of which our translators, and, indeed, the Revisers, did not possess; having merely the help of lexicons, which gave the usage of words *only in classical Greek*.

It is impossible for us, in a small work like this, to give anything like even a general view of so vast a subject. We can only indicate the existence and nature of such a field of study, and give a few examples by way of illustration of its usefulness in connection with this our third Division, which concerns the changes of usage in Greek words brought about by man, but used by the Holy Spirit.

We must take them at random, and cannot even attempt to observe alphabetical or other order.

The word ζωοποιέω (*zōopoieō*), was used in classical Greek as meaning *to produce live offspring;* but the usage became in N. T. Greek *to make alive again*, either of spiritual or of resurrection life (John v. 21; vi. 63. Rom. iv. 17; viii. 11. 1 Cor. xv. 22, 36, 45. 2 Cor. iii. 6. Gal. iii. 21. 1 Tim. vi. 13. 1 Pet. iii. 18).

πάροικος (*paroikos*), which meant *neighbour*, had come to mean *sojourner* (Acts vii. 6, 29. Eph. ii. 19 (*foreigner*). 1 Pet. ii. 11 (*strangers*)).

πράκτωρ (*praktōr*), which is literally *a doer* of anything, came to mean the man who *did* the most objectionable thing, viz., *the tax-collector.* But the *papyri* show us that it came to have a still lower meaning. The tax collector was the one who put them into prison; hence, it came to be used of *the jailor !* The word occurs twice (Luke xii. 58), and should not be rendered "officer," but *jailor.*

πήρα (*pēra*), is rendered "scrip" in the A.V., and "wallet" in the R.V., but commentators are quite undecided as to whether it means a "portmanteau" or a "bread-bag"; though the latter seems superfluous after the word "bread."

The following are the passages :—

Matt. x. 10, "Heal the sick, raise the dead, cleanse the lepers, cast out devils: freely ye have received, freely give. Provide neither gold nor silver, nor brass in your purses: nor scrip (R.V. 'wallet') for your journey, neither two coats, neither shoes, nor yet staves."

Mark vi. 8, "And commanded them that they should take nothing for their journey, save a staff only: no scrip (R.V., 'wallet'), no bread, no money in their purse."

Luke ix. 3 (compare x. 4 and xxii. 35, 36), "Take nothing for your journey, neither staves, nor scrip, (R.V., 'wallet'), neither bread, neither money, neither have two coats apiece."

But a special meaning is made known to us by an ancient stone monument. A Greek inscription of the Roman period[1] has been discovered at Kefr-Hauar in Syria, in which a "slave" of the "Syrian goddess" speaks of the begging expeditions he has undertaken for the "Lady." This heathen apostle—who speaks of himself as "sent by the Lady"—tells with triumph how each of his journeys brought in seventy *bags*. Here he uses this word πήρα. It means, not *bags* filled with provisions and taken on the journey, but *a beggar's collecting bag*. This is evidently the meaning in the passages cited above: and when we connect it with the context in St. Matthew, we learn the Lord meant that they were not to earn money, and they were also not to beg. The nature of the Lord's commission is at once seen from what is involved in this interpretation of the word πήρα (*pera*). In the days of early Christianity the mendicant priest of the ancestral goddess wanders through the Syrian land; from village to village the string of sumpter animals lengthens, bearing his pious booty to the shrine, and the Lady will not be unmindful of her slave. In the same land, and in the same age, was One who had not where to lay His head, and He sent out His apostles with the words :

"Freely ye received, freely give. Get you no gold, nor silver, nor brass in your purses: no *wallet* (or *beggar's collecting bag*) for your journey."

---

[1] Published in the *Bulletin de Correspondance Hellénique*, 1897, p. 60. Compare *Die Christliche Welt*, 1903, p. 242, etc.

He who sent them had "all power" to provide for their supply.

πρεσβύτερος (*presbuteros*), which meant one *older* in years, is, in the *papyri* always used of *official position*, civil as well as religious (just as we use our word "alderman"). This is its usage in the New Testament.

ἀναγινώσκω (*anaginōskō*), meant *to persuade;* then, *to know well, gather exact knowledge;* then, *to read.* But later usage extended this reading *to reading aloud with comments, with a view to persuade.* This is its meaning in the New Testament. (See Matt. xxiv. 15. Mark xiii. 14. Luke iv. 16. Col. iv. 16. 1 Thess. v. 27. Rev. i. 3, etc.)

ἀποστοματίζω (*apostomatizō*), meant *to dictate* to a pupil what he was to write or recite. But its later usage was *to examine* by questioning on what had been taught. This is its usage in Luke xi. 53: "They began to urgently press him and *question* him about many things" [as though he were their pupil]. They were not seeking for information, but for grounds of accusation.

γράφω (*graphō*), *to write*, is always used in the *papyri* of legal, official, and documentary writing. The perfect γέγραπται (*gegraptai*), *it standeth written*, always implies an appeal to authoritative, incontestable authority, definite and regulative.

In this we see the position held by Holy Scripture over oral tradition. In this, too, we may see a reference to the certainty and nature of the revelation of the Mystery (or secret) in the γραφῶν προφητικῶν (*graphōn prophētikōn*), *prophetic writings*, of Rom. xvi. 26 (compare Eph. ii. 20 · iv. 11, and 2 Pet. i. 20, etc.). We may also see in this a reason for Paul's desire to have "the parchments" which he asked Timothy to bring with him (2 Tim. iv. 13): for, Bible truth is based on *documentary evidence*, and not on oral tradition.

ἀπέχω (*apecho*), *to have from, to receive* or be [distant] *from.* But the *papyri* show that it was the common form of giving a *receipt in full.* This is its usage in Matt. vi. 2, 5, 16. Luke vi. 24, and Philem. 15, which shows that when the scribes prayed they did it to be seen of men; men had seen them; they had got their *receipt*, therefore, in full; and there was nothing more for them to receive: no real answer to their prayers to be expected,

The rendering "reward" (A.V. and R.V.) conveys no sense.

βεβαίωσις (*bebaiōsis*), *confirmation.* In the *papyri* it is the *guarantee* of the seller to the buyer as to the validity of the sale (Phil. i. 7. Heb. vi. 16, where it is rendered " confirmation ").

τὸ δοκίμιον (*to dokimion*), *the trial* or *trying.* In the *papyri* this is always used as an adjective, meaning *genuine, tested,* and is found especially on pawn-tickets and marriage-contracts in the sense of *certified.* This is its usage in the N. T., which had come to denote the *result of trial,* and had been changed from the act or process of trial. Hence 1 Pet. i. 7 means "your tried or genuine faith"; and Jas. i. 3, "your tried or tested faith enables you to be patient."

δίκαιος (*dikaios*), *just,* or *righteous,* is used in the *papyri* of *that which comes up to the required stan- dard* expected or looked for. It is used of a horse, of cattle, of a cubit; as it is used in the Septuagint (Prov. xi. 1) of "a just weight."

This is its New Testament usage, showing that God's righteousness, when it is bestowed, brings its recipient up to the standard which God Himself requires and looks for. The saved sinner is therefore by it "made meet for the inheritance of the saints in light" (Col. i. 12), and hence can be declared " complete in Christ."

ἱλαστήριον (*hilasterion*) comes to us through the Septua- gint; where, in Exod. xxv. 17 (Heb. 16), "thou shalt make a כַּפֹּרֶת (*kapporeth*), *cover,* of pure gold." This word *kap- poreth* (*cover*) is rendered ἱλαστήριον ἐπίθεμα (*hilastērion epithema*), *propitiatory cover,* because the *cover,* on which the blood was sprinkled, was the means of propitiation.

The word in Heb. ix. 5 must retain this usage, and be rendered "the cherubim of glory shadowing the *propi- tiatory* [cover]." By the figure, Metonymy, the *result* (propitiation) is put for the *means* by which it was ob- tained (the *cover* of the ark on which the blood was sprinkled). That was what the cherubim shadowed, not the propitiation itself.

So that the word can be taken in this sense here; as it must be in the other passage where it occurs, Rom. iii. 25: " Whom God hath set forth as His propitiatory gift."

In the *papyri* and on inscriptions and monuments this word is used in the sense of votive or propitiatory gift.

So here, Christ was God's propitiatory gift, the gift of Divine love. Not man's gift to God; but God's gift to man.

The rendering of *hilastērion* by "mercy-seat" is quite wrong. The R.V. puts in the margin, "Gr. *the propitiatory*"; but, not seeing the Figure of Speech, nor knowing of the *usage* of the word in the *papyri*, the Revisers did not add the noun, "cover," after the adj. "propitiatory"; and with the A.V. rendered "propitiatory" in Rom. iii. 25 as a noun, "propitiation."

The saints of God in Rome would hardly know the technical "mercy-seat," but they would know the common usage of the word at the time as being *a propitiatory gift.*[1]

εὐεργέτης (*euergetēs*), meant a *well-doer*, but our Lord uses it in Luke xxii. 25 in the particular and almost technical sense which recent discoveries have revealed. The word had been restricted from the extended sense of *well-doing* to the limited and special sense of a *well-doing on behalf of the public*, which deserved the public recognition of one as being a BENEFACTOR.

The discoveries of inscriptions and coins, added to the literary evidence already available, establishes this special usage of the word in our Lord's days.

πλῆθος (*plēthos*), is generally rendered *multitude*. In the *papyri* it has a technical usage applying to associates in a community or congregation. This appears to be the usage in Luke i. 10; xix. 37. Acts ii. 6; iv. 32; vi. 2, 5; xv. 12, 30; xix. 9; xxi. 22.

μικρός (*mikros*), *small, little*. In the *papyri* this word is used in the sense of *junior* in contrast with μέγας (*megas*), *great*, which is used as *senior*. This is clearly the sense in Mark xv. 40; and it is a question whether it is not also in Matt. xi. 11; xviii. 6, 10, 14. Acts viii. 10; xxvi. 22.

κυριακός (*kuriakos*), the *Lord's*, is used in the *papyri* of what is imperial, and especially pertaining to the κύριος (*kurios*), *the Lord, as Ruler.*[2]

---

[1] In 1 John ii. 2; iv. 10 it is the noun ἱλασμός (*hilasmos*), *propitiation*.
[2] See pamphlet on *The Lord's Day*, by the same author.

χειρόγραφον (*cheirographon*), *hand-writing.* In the *papyri* this is the technical term for *a bond* or *certificate of debt.* Many have been found; some of them are scored through and thus cancelled. This is the sense in Col. ii. 14, where only it is found.

ἄδολος (*adolos*), occurs only in 1 Pet. ii. 2 and is rendered *sincere.* In the *papyri* the usage is in the sense of *unadulterated*, referring to food.

σφραγίζω (*sphragizo*), *to seal.* In the *papyri* it is used of delivering property into the possession of the receiver. To seal a thing to a person was used of delivering and securing that thing to him, sealing being the last thing done prior to such delivery. Thus we read "Seal the wheat and the barley," *i.e.*, seal [the sacks containing] the wheat and the barley [and deliver them].

This is the usage in Rom. xv. 28. Eph. iv. 30.

χάραγμα (*charagma*), *a mark.* In the *papyri* this word (1) is always used of a mark connected with the emperor; and (2) it always contains his name or effigy, and the year of his reign. (3) It was necessary for buying and selling. (4) It was technically known as *charagma.*

It is found on all sorts of documents, even on "a bill of sale." In Acts xvii. 29 it is rendered "graven." Elsewhere it is used only of the "mark" of the Beast (Rev. xiii. 16, 17; xiv. 9, 11; xv. 2; xvi. 2; xix. 20; xx. 4). He will be the Overlord in that day!

ἀναπέμπω (*anapempō*), *to send up.* This word is used in the *papyri* of *sending up to a superior authority.* This is the usage in Luke xxiii. 7, 11, 15, and Acts xxv. 21.[1]

It is also used of *sending up* with pomp and dignity.

βιάζομαι (*biazomai*), *to use force* or *press with violence.* Commentators tell us that it occurs only twice in the New Testament, and that it *must*, in the former of the two passages, be taken as a Passive. The former passage is Matt. xi. 12, "the kingdom of heaven suffereth violence." The latter is Luke xvi. 16, "every man presseth into it."

But the meaning of the word, and the interpretation of both passages is settled for us by an inscription found

---

[1] Here all the Critical Greek Texts prefer this word to the simple πέμπω (*pempō*), *to send by an escort.* See below under Canon VIII., Sect. 1 (Matt. viii. 5 and Luke vii. 1).

in a temple near Sunium,[1] built not earlier than the imperial period which commenced in B.C. 24.

It was founded by Xanthus the Lycian as a sanctuary.

In this inscription certain ceremonial purifications are prescribed as a condition of entrance into the temple; and it goes on to say that no one may sacrifice in the temple without permission from its founder. Then the regulation continues :—

$$\dot{\epsilon}\grave{\alpha}\nu \; \delta\acute{\epsilon} \; \tau\iota\varsigma \; \beta\iota\acute{\alpha}\sigma\eta\tau\alpha\iota$$
"*But if any one forces* [*his way in*]
$$\dot{\alpha}\pi\rho\acute{o}\sigma\delta\epsilon\kappa\tau o\varsigma \; \dot{\eta} \; \theta\upsilon\sigma\acute{\iota}\alpha \; \pi\alpha\rho\grave{\alpha} \; \tauo\hat{\upsilon} \; \theta\epsilon o\hat{\upsilon}$$
his offering is not pleasing to the god."

This settles the usage of the word in the two passages:

Matt. xi. 12, "But from the days of John the Baptist until now the kingdom of heaven forces itself [on the people], and the pushful seize on it."

Luke xvi. 16, "Since that time (John's) the kingdom of God is announced [as good news] and every one forces [his way] into it."

Thus, both passages harmonize; the usage in both is the same; and, both accord with the usage which obtained in the New Testament period.

κατάκριμα (*katakrima*), is an important word, occurring only three times in the New Testament.

Rom. v. 16, "The judgment was by one offence unto *condemnation.*"

Verse 18, "As by one offence [judgment came] unto all men for *condemnation.*" Rom. viii. 1, "There is therefore now no *condemnation* to them that are in Christ Jesus."

In deeds of sale found among the *papyri* this word is found in its legal usage. It is used of a *burden* on land, such as debts, taxes of all kinds, arrears, and all payments of every kind. All are mentioned, but the effect of the legal document is to declare that the land sold is *free from all burdens of every kind.* Note the bearing of this in such passages as Rom. viii. 1.

---

[1] Sunium is a promontory at the S.E. extremity of Attica, Greece, now known as Cape Colonna. It contains to-day the ruins of a temple measuring 44 by 98 feet. Twelve columns are still standing.

ὑπόστασις (*hupostasis*), rendered "substance" in Heb. xi. 1, is used in the *papyri* in the sense of *title-deeds*. This shows that believing what God has said and promised, is our *title-deed* for which He has caused us to hope.[1]

iv. WHERE DIFFERENT BUT CONCURRENT USAGES OF WORDS SHOULD BE OBSERVED IN THE ENGLISH.

Quite apart from age or clime there are many Greek words which the Holy Spirit Himself uses in different connections, and with varying meanings. These can be easily seen, observed, and classified; and our English renderings can and must be made to conform to them.

Unlike our last division (No. iii. above) this is work for the English reader, who is at no disadvantage with the Greek scholar, provided he uses our *Lexicon and Concordance to the English and Greek New Testament*.[2] It is designed for English readers; and, though the Greek words are given, the truth can be gained without looking at them; for they are numbered, and the reference is to the meaning given under that number.

The use of that book will enable the student to find out, at a glance, under the English word, the Greek word which is so translated. The index will tell him whether the word is translated otherwise elsewhere; and, if so, under what renderings he can find them. At this stage he will be able to use more readily the *Englishman's Greek Concordance*[3] and easily make out a list of all the occurrences of the word in question.

It is here that his real study of this branch of our subject will begin. For now he must turn to every passage, and note *how* the Holy Spirit uses the word; and when he has all the data before him he will soon discover whether the usage is uniform; or whether there is more than one sense in which the word is employed.

This part of the study requires a spiritual understanding (1 John v. 20. 1 Cor. ii. 14), common sense, and strength

[1] Other words will be found in our *Figures of Speech* (pp. 850—856) and in Diessmann's *Bibelstudien* (Marburg, 1895) and *Neue Bibelstudien* (1877). Also in *Essays in Biblical Greek*, by the late Professor Hatch, of Oxford.

[2] Published by Longmans & Co., 39, Paternoster Row.

[3] Published by Bagster & Co.

of mind to follow the leading of God's Word in spite of all that has been imbibed and "received from the fathers by tradition."

When difficulty is experienced in receiving the truth of God, it is because we try at the same time to hold on to tradition, and try to combine the two. But the moment we let tradition go all will become easy. It is not the simple truth that is difficult, but it is the endeavour to hold on to the traditional belief as well as the simple truth. Let one of the two beliefs go, and either will be easy; it is the effort to hold both that creates the real difficulty.

Let us illustrate this by looking at the word

1. *"Parousia."—*παρουσία *(parousia).*—This word furnishes us with an excellent and useful example, showing the necessity of discriminating between its different usages.

Many take it as a proper noun, and speak of *"The Parousia"* as though it always refers to one separate and distinct act, *viz.,* the coming of the Lord as revealed in 1 Thess. iv.

The next step is that, when they find that this same word is used of the coming of Christ in Matt. xxiv., "immediately after the Tribulation of those days," there is no alternative but to interpret 1 Thess iv. as being after the Tribulation.

Thus, trouble and confusion is created; and the loss of the blessed hope and waiting for God's Son from heaven is shrouded in darkness.

But all is made clear, the moment we discriminate between the various *usages* of the word *parousia.* There is no dispute about the meaning of the word. All are agreed that its only meaning is *presence;* and when translated *coming* it always denotes the actual *presence* of the person who thus comes.

From our *Greek and English Lexicon and Concordance,* page 977, we find that παρουσία *(parousia)* occurs twenty-four times; and that it is rendered twice *presence,* and twenty-two times *coming.*

Our object, now, is to find out how the Holy Spirit uses it; and whether the teaching of some is correct, who tell us that it refers always to the coming of Christ *for* his Saints *before* the Tribulation, and not the coming of Christ *with* His saints, *after* the Tribulation.

No one can help us in making this discovery; neither do we need any help beyond collecting all the data, and looking closely at every passage, and noting the different usages.

Having got our complete lists of twenty-four Texts, we read each (with its context, of course), and we find that:—

(*a*) *Six* times it is used of the *presence* of INDIVIDUALS, and that it is always their personal, bodily *presence*.

> 1 Cor. xvi. 17, Stephanus.
> 2 Cor. vii. 6, 7, Titus.
> 2 Cor. x. 10, and Phil. i. 26; ii. 12, Paul.

(*b*) *Six* times it is used of Christ's *presence* in the air, when He comes forth thither to meet His raptured saints, before the Great Tribulation (1 Thess. ii. 19; iii. 13; iv. 15; v. 23. 2 Thess. ii. 1, and 1 John ii. 28). We note that all but one of these six are in the Epistles to the Thessalonians.

(*c*) *Eleven* times it is used of Christ's *presence* on earth, when *with* His Church He comes unto the earth, in the Day of the Lord, "Immediately after the Tribulation of those days" (Matt. xxiv. 3, 27, 37, 39. 1 Cor. xv. 23. 2 Thess. ii. 8. Jas. v. 7, 8. 2 Pet. i. 16; iii. 4, 12).

(*d*) *Once* it is used of the *presence* of "that lawless one," who shall be destroyed by the glorious advent of Christ (2 Thess. ii. 9).

Here are all the usages; and we see, at once, that it is not correct to speak of "*The Parousia*" as though it related only to Christ; or to His coming as being one single act; or to one part only of that coming.

We note that there is one chapter (2 Thess. ii.) where the word is used of *three* distinct acts of being present:—

There is the *presence* of Christ in the air *before* the Tribulation (2 Thess. ii. 1) and our gathering together unto Him there;

There is the *presence* of the Lawless one on the earth *during* the Tribulation (2 Thess. ii. 9);

And there is the *presence* of the Lord on the earth, in all His glory, by which the Lawless one will be destroyed. This will be *after* the Tribulation (2 Thess. ii. 8).

If we are not careful to distinguish these various usages of the word *parousia,* we shall only create confusion in the Word, and trouble in our own minds. We shall find ourselves taking a passage which speaks of the Lord's *presence* on earth *after* the Tribulation, and interpreting it of His *presence* in the air *before* the Tribulation; and, if we thus take the word *parousia* as being used of the latter, then we shall interpret 1 Thess. iv. by Matt. xxiv., and not only take the Church through the Tribulation, but we shall defer the realization of the Rapture of 1 Thess. iv. until *after* the Tribulation, and take all the blessedness out of it. We shall give a flat contradiction to 1 Thess. v. 4, which categorically assures us that "the Day of the Lord shall not overtake us as a thief"; and plunge ourselves into that very "darkness" which the same word declares that we are "not in."

2. *Pneuma,* spirit.—The word πνεῦμα (*pneuma*), *spirit,* is a word of the greatest importance.

When we have made out our complete list (as before we made of Parousia) we find that there is practically little or no difference as to its *translation;* for it is rendered *spirit* every time, except John iii. 8, where it is rendered *wind;* Rev. xiii. 15, where it is rendered "life" (marg. *breath*); Matt. xxvii. 50 and John xix. 30, where it is rendered *ghost.*

In this case, though there are different usages, they are all confined to *interpretation* and not to translation.

We need not say more on this word here, for in our work, *The Giver and His Gifts, or, the Holy Spirit and His Work,*[1] we have given a complete list of all the occurrences of the word *pneuma;* and have set out, in an exhaustive manner, all the data.

Fourteen different usages are given, and classified lists are appended, from which the reader can gather *for himself* all that can be learnt from those lists.

[1] *The Giver and His Gifts, or, the Holy Spirit and His Work,* republished by Kregel Publications as *Word Studies on the Holy Spirit.*

It is used of (1) God, (2) Christ, (3) the Holy Spirit, (4) the Operations of the Spirit, (5) the New Nature, (6) Psychologically, (7) of Character, (8) by *Metonymy* for what is not of the body, (9) by *Synecdoche* for one's self, (10) Adverbially, (11) of Angels, (12) of Demons, (13) of the Resurrection Body, (14) in combination with the word "holy," without the article.

The usages of this word are so important that it requires a separate volume for their full treatment.

One great fact may be noted here, *viz.*, that the expression πνεῦμα ἅγιον (*pneuma hagion*), *holy spirit*, occurs *fifty* times (out of 388), and it always refers to *the gifts and operations* of the Holy Spirit, and never to the Holy Spirit, *the Giver*.

The evidence is simple and clear. In Luke xxiv. 49 the Lord Jesus calls "the promise of my Father" (for which the apostles were to tarry in Jerusalem), "power from on high."

In Acts i. 5 He calls this same promise "*pneuma hagion.*"

Therefore *pneuma hagion* is "power from on high."

This proves that *pneuma hagion* is *what is given*, and not the Giver.

If further proof is needed, then it is furnished by that crucial passage, Acts ii. 4, "And they were all filled with *pneuma hagion*, and began to speak with other tongues as THE SPIRIT gave them utterance."

Here the Giver and His gifts are quite distinct. What was given was "the gift of tongues." The Giver, who "gave," was "The Spirit."

Nothing could be clearer than this.

Unfortunately the A.V. and R.V. have, in all these fifty occurrences of *pneuma hagion*, arbitrarily inserted the article, and used capital letters for "Holy Spirit," so that the English reader is entirely misled, and is compelled to understand that it is the Person who is meant; while he is kept quite uninformed of the fact that it means *His gifts and operations*.

The subject is so important, and the information so difficult to be obtained, that it will be necessary for us to give a list of the fifty passages. They will repay abundantly any pains that may be taken in their careful study. The reader should take his or her Bible, and mark in the margin every one of these

Fifty occurrences of *pneuma hagion:* Matt. i. 18, 20; iii. 11. Mark i. 8. Luke i. 15, 35, 41, 67; ii. 25; iii. 16; iv. 1 (first); xi. 13. John i. 33 (second); xx. 22. Acts i. 2, 5, 8; ii. 4 (first), 33, 38; iv. 8 (25¹), 31; vi. 3,¹ 5: vii. 55; viii. 15, 17 (18¹), 19; ix. 17; x. 38, 45; xi. 16, 24; xiii. 9, 52; xix. 2 (twice), 6. Rom. v. 5; ix. 1; xiv. 17; xv. 19. 1 Cor. ii. 13¹; vi. 19; xii. 3 (second). 2 Cor. vi. 6. 1 Thess. i. 5, 6. 2 Tim. i. 14.¹ Titus iii. 5. Heb. ii. 4; vi. 4. 1 Pet. i. 12. 2 Pet. i. 20. Jude 21.

Some of the above passages are very important, and will be found most instructive if studied in the following order: Acts vi. 3. Luke xi. 13. John xx. 22. Acts viii. 15, 17, 19, 20.

3. *Church.*—We have already considered this word under "Dispensational Truth and Teaching" (Part I., chap. III., pp. 145—148). But there is something further to be learnt from the *usage* of the word ἐκκλησία (*ecclēsia*), of which it is generally the translation.

This rendering is unfortunate, considering the fact that our English word "church" has also, itself, several usages.

It is important therefore that we should carefully adjust the two usages, and rightly adjust and appropriate the one to the other.

The Greek word *ecclesia* means *a convocation* of persons *called out.* Hence, *an assembly* of persons so called out.

It is used (1) of Israel as a People *called out* from the rest of the nations (Gen. xxviii. 3); (2) of the Tribal Council of Simeon and Levi, a smaller company, *called out* from each Tribe (Gen. xlix. 6); (3) of an assembly of Israelites *called out* for worship or any other purpose (Deut. xviii. 16; xxxi. 30. Josh. viii. 35. Judg. xxi. 8. 1 Kings viii. 65. 1 Chron. xxix. 1. Acts vii. 38); (4) any assembly of worshippers as a *congregation* (Ps. xxii. 22, 25. Matt. xvi. 18; xviii. 17. 1 Cor. xiv. 19, 35. Gal. i. 13. Heb. ii. 12.); (5) of separate assemblies in different localities (Acts. v. 11; viii. 3. 1 Cor. iv. 17, etc.); (6) of the Guild or Company of

---

¹ These verses are the subjects of Various Readings, and our larger book should be consulted.

Ephesian Craftsmen (Acts xix. 32) as distinct from the population of Ephesus; (7) of a Town's meeting (Acts xix. 39).

Then there is the special Pauline usage, which was quite different from any of the above. Other assemblies consisted of *called out ones* from Jews, or from Gentiles (as in Acts xix.); but this new Body is called out from *both* and yet consists of neither (Gal. iii. 28; vi. 15). This calling out is the Secret (or Mystery) which was hidden in God, and never revealed to men until the administration of it was committed to the Apostle Paul.[1]

The usage of the English word "church" is just as varied. It is used (1) of any congregation, (2) of a particular church (as Rome or England), (3) of the Ministry of a church, (4) of the Building in which the congregation assembles, (5) of Church as distinct from Chapel, (6) it is used of the Church as distinct from the world, and (7) it is used in the Pauline sense, of the Body of Christ.

This shows us the extreme care with which we should note the usage of words.

4. *"Elements" or "Rudiments."*—The Greek word στοιχεῖα (*stoicheia*) has at least two different usages, one *material*, and the other *moral*.

It is used of what is material in 2 Pet. iii. 10, 12; of the material elements of which creation, or this world, is made up.

In the other five passages it is used of the moral and religious ordinances which make up *the outward acts of religion*, with all its rites and ceremonies.

Four times it is used in the Epistles which are addressed to churches; twice in Galatians and twice in Colossians, these two being the Epistles which are written to correct errors in doctrine. Galatians corrects errors in connection with the doctrine as taught in the Epistle to the Romans concerning justification, Colossians being written to correct errors in doctrine as taught in the Epistle to the Ephesians concerning the Mystery.

In these, the outward ordinances of *Religion* are contrasted with the spiritual truths of *Christianity* (as distinct from Religion).

---

[1] See above, Part I., Chap. III., § iv. (pp. 141—143).

The A.V. renderings show the confusion of thought in the mind of the Translators. In Gal. iv. 3 and 9 they render it "elements" in the text, and "rudiments" in the margin.

In Col. ii. 8 and 20 they render it "rudiments" in the text, and "elements" in the margin.

The R.V. agrees with the A.V. translation in Colossians; and in all four passages renders the word "rudiments" in the text, and "elements" in the margin.

The *usage* of the word in the Church Epistles is seen to be peculiar to them, and this fact must be borne in mind in the interpretation of these four passages.

5. *Saints.*—The word ἅγιος (*hagios*), *holy*, is when in the plural ἅγιοι (*hagioi*) always translated *saints.*

Of course it means the same, *holy*, i.e., or, *holy ones*, except that it is left to be inferred from the context who *the holy ones* are who are so designated.

A brief examination of the usages of the plural, *hagioi*, will show us that they are *four* in number.

Of course, ordinary readers, who are, as a fact, more familiar with the New Testament usage; and, as a matter of selfishness, more prone, as well as accustomed, to interpret *everything of the church!* will have neither the inclination to study its usage, nor the willingness to part with the meaning which they have appropriated to themselves.

This is sufficient to show us the necessity of studying the usage of this word "saints."

(1) It is used of *Angels* (Deut. xxxiii. 2).

"Jehovah came from Sinai,
    And rose up from Seir unto them;
    He shined forth from mount Paran,
    And He came with ten thousands of holy [ones]:
    From His right hand went a fiery law for them."

Here, it is evident that the word "angels" should be supplied after the word holy, thus "holy [angels]" for these celestial beings are meant. This is proved by a reference to Ps. lxviii. 17; where, in a reference to the same Divine descent at Sinai, the word "angels" is used instead of "holy ones," as another name for them.

(2) It is used of *Israel* in the very next verse (Deut. xxxiii. 3).

> "Yea, He loved the People;
> All His holy ones are in Thy hand."

Here the word is used of the People of Israel. For the preceding words are—"This is the blessing wherewith Moses the man of God blessed the children of Israel before his death."

It is a blessing which is yet to receive its full consummation when the Lord shall have come again, and the People of Israel shall know Him to be their Divine Redeemer, their King, and their God.

(3) It is used also of individuals and other godly Israelites, as in Pss. xvi. 3; xxxiv. 9; lxxxix. 5, 7; cvi. 16. Hos. xi. 12.[1]

(4) It is used in the Church Epistles specially of the members of the one Spiritual Body, whose holiness is that of Christ; and whose saintship therefore, though enjoyed on earth, is higher than that of any other created beings, being merged in their higher title, "the sons of God."

This is its usage in the commencement of the Epistles, as in Rom. i. 7. 1 Cor. i. 2, etc.

With this key, Bible students will have no difficulty in determining what the usage of the word is in any particular passage; for the Context alone is the all-sufficient guide as to what it must be.

We need not go through all the passages where the word "saints" occurs; this would be doing the work which it should be our readers' pleasure and profit to carry out.

One or two passages may be doubtful; in which case it may be well to come to no conclusion, but to wait for further light.

A few other passages will receive a new interpretation and lead to a change in our traditional views.

---

[1] The English word "saints" represents quite a different Hebrew word in 1 Sam. ii. 9. 2 Chron. vi. 41. Pss. xxx. 4; xxxi. 23; xxxvii. 28; l. 5; lii. 9; lxxxv. 8; xcvii. 10; cxvi. 15; cxxxii. 9, 16; cxlv. 10; cxlviii. 14. Here the Hebrew word is חָסִיד (*chasid*), *pious, Godly.*

With Matt. xxv. 31 before us we shall find that several passages which we have been in the habit of referring to the Church of God, really refer to angelic beings.

"When the Son of Man shall come in his glory, and all the holy angels with him, then shall he sit upon the throne of his glory" (Matt. xxv. 31).

Here we have the word "angels" associated with the word "holy" (pl.), which leaves us in no doubt.

In harmony with this passage we must take 1 Thess. iii. 13. "To the end he may establish your hearts unblameable in holiness before God, even our Father, at the coming of our Lord Jesus Christ with all his holy [angels]."

On the other hand, in 2 Thess. i. 10 the word "saints" is used synonymously of "all them that believe," and in *contrast* with "the mighty angels" of verse 7, because

"At the revelation of the Lord Jesus from heaven" (*v.* 7), those who have been troubled now will be at "rest."

This revelation in judgment (*v.* 10) will take place "when *He shall have come* to be glorified amid His saints on earth (Israel), and wondered at (in that day) amid all raptured believers."

In Jude 14 the word "saints" clearly refers to angels; "Enoch also, the seventh from Adam, prophesied of these, saying, Behold, the Lord cometh with ten thousands of his saints to execute judgment upon all."

In Rev. xv. 3 the word "saints" should be "ages" according to the R.V., or "nations" according to the R.V. margin. The Structure (*Introversion*) requires "nations."

v. Where a Uniform Usage of Greek Words should not be Departed from in the English.

It is not always that Greek words have different usages. The vast majority have one uniform usage; and this must not be departed from in the English, and cannot be ignored without serious loss.

Even where it does not lead to a misunderstanding or a wrong interpretation of a passage, it creates great and unnecessary confusion.

1. *Withhold,* κατέχω (*katechō*). Who would imagine that "let" and "withhold" of the A.V.; and "restrain" of the R.V. in 2 Thess. ii. 6, 7, are all the rendering of one and the same Greek word?

The word κατέχω (*katechō*) occurs nineteen times, and is rendered by thirteen different English words.

Who is to help us in coming to a true interpretation of this word, and of the passages in which it occurs?

There is no help outside the Word of God.

It is rendered *hold fast* three times, and *hold* three times, so that these are the most frequent renderings.

The only way of finding and testing the correct rendering is to look at every one of the passages and see if the one rendering *hold fast* can be consistently used. It will not follow that this word will be the very best according to our English idiom; and we need not make it the uniform rendering. We may use other words more in harmony with the genius of the English language so long as we keep the uniform sense *hold fast* in our mind:—

> Matt. xxi. 38, "*let* us *seize on* his inheritance" (let us hold fast).
> Luke iv. 42, "and *stayed* him, that he should not depart" (held him fast).
> Luke viii. 15, "having heard the word *keep* it" (hold it fast).
> Luke xiv. 9, "with shame *to take* the lowest place" (to hold).
> John v. 4, "of whatsoever disease *he had*" (he was held).
> Acts xxvii. 40, "and *made* towards shore" (held their course toward).
> Rom. i. 18, "*who hold* the truth in unrighteousness"[1] (hold fast).
> Rom. vii. 6, "having died to that by which we were *held*" (so marg. and R.V.).
> 1 Cor. vii. 30, "as though they *possessed* not" (held nothing fast).

[1] This is done in cases where any may "hold the truth," and where *the truth does not hold them.* In that case such may continue to act unrighteously; *e.g.,* when the proprietor of a journal, who holds the truth, allows an editor or writer to regularly teach what he knows to be error; and this for the sake of gain. *That* is holding the truth in unrighteousness; and, unfortunately such a thing is not unknown even in religious journalism.

1 Cor. xi. 2, and *keep* the ordinances" (hold them fast).

1 Cor. xv. 2, "if ye *keep in memory* what I preached" (hold fast).

2 Cor. vi. 10, "and yet possessing all things."[1]

1 Thess. v. 21, "prove all things, *hold fast* that which is good."[2]

2 Thess. ii. 6, "ye know what *withholdeth*" (holds [him] fast).

2 Thess. ii. 7, "only he who now *letteth*" (he who now holdeth *fast*).[3]

Philem. 13, "I would have *retained*" (held fast).

Heb. iii. 6, "if we *hold fast* the confidence."

Heb. iii. 14, "if we *hold* the beginning of our confidence" (hold fast).

Heb. x. 23, "let us hold fast the profession of our faith."

Thus, we see, that *hold fast* is, and must be, the only correct rendering in 2 Thess. ii. 6, 7. This gives us, therefore, the key to the true interpretation of that prophecy.

2. *Temptation.*—πειράζω (*peirazō*), *tempt;* πειρασμός (*peirasmos*), *temptation.*—These words are of frequent occurrence. The latter word occurs twenty-one times, and in all but one is rendered *temptation.*

But the usage of *peirasmos* in the Bible is always in the sense of *trial:* hence specially of *trouble* or *tribulation,* because it is that which really *tries* a man better than anything else.

Our English word "temptation" meant, originally, much the same: *to stretch out, handle, try the strength of.*

This is stated to be the object of *trial* (Deut. viii. 2).

In the Old Testament the word is used of the troubles themselves (Deut. vii. 19; xxix. 3. Compare Wisdom iii. 5; xi. 10. Sirach ii. 1. Judith viii. 24—27).

---

[1] The context shows that this rendering could not be improved, though the idea is there.

[2] Here the correct rendering occurs in one of the very Epistles where we have the wrong rendering, 2 Thess. ii. 6, 7.

[3] This is Satan, who *holdeth fast* to something. What it is may be suggested in Rev. xii. 9—xiii. 1, *viz.,* to his position in the heavenlies; from whence when he is cast out, he stands upon the sand of the sea, and "the man of sin" is revealed in his appointed season.

This is also clearly its use in Luke viii. 13: "in time of *trial*, or trouble (not temptation in the sense of enticement, as we now use the word almost exclusively) fall away." (So Matt. xiii. 21, and Mark iv. 17.)

In Acts xx. 19 Paul is evidently alluding to what he calls, in 2 Cor. xi. 26, the "perils by mine own countrymen."

In Heb. ii. 18. 1 Pet. i. 6. Rev. iii. 10 the meaning is the same.

From all this we see that in the Lord's Prayer the word should be *trial* or *tribulation*, viz., the Great Tribulation.[1]

In Matt. iv. 1. Mark i. 13, and Luke iv. 2 the physical sufferings of our Lord are meant (compare Heb. iv. 15).

3. *Poor*, πένης (*penēs*).—The words used for and rendered "poor," πένης (*penēs*), πραΰς (*praüs*), πτωχός (*ptōchos*), and ταπεινός (*tapeinos*), all mean *oppressed*.

Our Western idea of being *poor* has come to mean being *without money*, because the condition of the poor in modern times has lost the one great characteristic of the poor in past centuries, and of present times still, in the East.

But the Biblical usage of the word has not changed, though customs have.

In the Greek civilization the word had much the same meaning as that in which we use it to-day, because *oppression* was not then associated with poverty.

But the Bible deals with and describes Eastern conditions, and hence though in classical Greek πένης (*penēs*) meant *poor* as opposed to rich, πτωχός (*ptōchos*) meant *destitute* as opposed to affluent, and πραΰς (*praüs*) meant *easy-tempered* as opposed to violent, yet in the Bible these words are all used of *the oppressed class* of any country: the *peasantry* or *fellahin*, who then, as now, lived quiet lives and were the victims of constant oppression, ill-treatment, and plunder at the hands of their autocratic rulers.

This is the meaning of the words *poor* and *meek*.

---

[1] See our separate pamphlet on *The Lord's Prayer*, pp. 12—15, by the same author.

See Ps. x. 9; xxxvii. 14, "He lieth in wait to catch the
poor;" or Ps. xxxv. 10:

"All my bones shall say, LORD, who is like unto Thee,
　　Which deliverest the *poor* from him that is too strong
　　　　for him,
　　Yea, the *poor* and needy from him that spoileth him."

This is why God is represented so often as the deliverer
of the poor, or *oppressed* (Pss. xii. 5; xxxiv. 6; xxxvii. 10,
11; xl. 17; lxxii. 4, 13; lxxvi. 9; cxlvii. 6).
　In the New Testament this usage is the same.

4. *Paradise,* παράδεισος.—Paradise is an Oriental word,
and was apparently first used by Xenophon to indicate
the parks of the Persian kings. It originally meant an
enclosed park, planted with trees, and stocked with game.
In such paradises eastern monarchs were wont to take
their pleasure in hunting.
　But the Holy Spirit has exalted it, and used it in a
sense higher than that in which man had ever used it.
For "the Paradise of God" is the "garden" which God
planted in Eden for man's blissful abode. And when the
curse shall have been removed, the whole earth will be
a paradise where God shall again dwell with man.
　The Bible knows no other Paradise. The Greek word
παράδεισος occurs in the Septuagint twenty-eight times.
In nine it represents the Hebrew word "Eden"; and in
nineteen places the Hebrew word גן (*gan*), *garden.* In
English it is rendered *Eden, Garden, Forest, Orchard.*
　The Hebrew word *Eden* occurs sixteen times; and
Garden, is used of Eden, thirteen times in Genesis; and six
times in other passages of "the Garden of God" (see Gen. ii.
Neh. ii. 8. Eccles. ii. 5. Song iv. 13).[1]
　It is man who has changed the usage of the word from
its only Biblical usage, and dragged it down and fastened
on it the meaning given to it in Babylonian, Jewish, and
Romish traditions.

5. "*Sheōl*" and "*Hades.*"—Here, again, the Biblical
usage of these words is uniform, and we must refer our

---

[1] See further in *The Rich Man and Lazarus*, by the same author.

readers to our separate pamphlet on this subject, in which will be found every passage in the Bible where these words occur, with their renderings.

These renderings are so various that, they are not only confusing to the mind, but misleading as regards the truth.

The Hebrew *Sheol*, and the Greek *Hades* are rendered thirty-one times *the grave*, thirty-one times *hell*, three times *pit;* sixty-five times in all. Four times *the grave* is put in the margin for *hell*, which increases the rendering *the grave* to thirty-five times and reduces the rendering *hell* to twenty-seven times.

On the face of the matter, this gives the preference to *the grave*, not " A grave," for which there are other words : but "THE grave," for which there is no other word. Grave-dom, or *the state of the dead* as being in the dom-inion of the grave, is the idea associated with the word. Not the *act* of dying, but *the state of the dead*, the present condition of death.

The Old Testament Biblical *usage* must settle the meaning of the heathen (*i.e.*, the Greek) usage of the word *Hades*, because the Holy Spirit *uses* it of His own Hebrew word *Sheol* in Acts ii. 27 by quoting Ps. xvi. 10.

From these last two passages it is clear that *Sheol* or *Hades* is the place where "corruption" is seen (Acts xiii. 34—37); and from which Resurrection is the only exit (Rev. xx. 4, 5). Those who are raised in the First Resurrection "live and reign with Christ a thousand years." Of those who are not raised then it is written they "LIVED NOT AGAIN until the thousand years were finished."

This is conclusive as to the Holy Spirit's own usage of these words.

6. *"Mystery,"* μυστήριον *(mustērion)*.—This English word is a transliteration of the Greek word μυστήριον *(mysterion)*, but its usage by us to-day in no sense corresponds with the meaning of the Greek word.

The Greeks used it of *a secret*, pure and simple; a secret which can be perfectly well understood when made known ; whereas we use the word "mystery" of what cannot be understood at all; and is past comprehension even when it is revealed. Thus our usage of the word to-day is *quite different* from the Biblical usage.

We must be careful, therefore, not to read our present usage of the word into the past usage. Not so very long ago the word was used in its true sense. This was in legal language, when an apprentice was articled in order to learn the "mysteries" or *secrets* of a certain trade or business. This is the sense also in which we still use it when we speak of the Greek "mysteries," *i.e.*, the *secrets* of that religion into which persons were initiated. This is the usage of the word in the Greek Testament, and in our transliteration of it.

No matter what the context may relate to, the *usage* of the word is uniformly *secret.*

(*a*) It is used in connection with the *duration* of Israel's blindness (Rom. xi. 25). That blindness itself was not a secret : for it was clearly foretold in Isa. vi. 9, 10. But the *duration* of that blindness was not revealed (Isa. vi. 11. Rom. xi. 25).

(*b*) It is used in connection with the rejection of the kingdom, the fact of its remaining in abeyance, and the duration of that abeyance. The Lord revealed this secret to the Apostles "in the house" (Matt. xiii. 11, 35), while it was still hidden from the people "out of the house." (Compare verses 1 and 36.)

In this revelation, the duration of this present interval between "the sufferings and the glory" was also kept secret (1 Pet. i. 10, 11).

Hence, the secrets which the Lord then revealed, concerned the kingdom only ; and all that He said about it must be read on, leaping over this (as yet, to them, secret, and unknown) present interval : and taking up the kingdom again, as though such interval had no existence.

(*c*) It is used in connection with the counsels and purposes of the lawless one (2 Thess. ii. 7), which, though *secret,* were already beginning to work themselves out.

(*d*) It is used in connection with the word *Ecclesia.* There was nothing to show that that word was going to be used in a sense altogether different from any in which it had before been used.[1]

---

[1] See above, pp. 141—149 ; 248, 249. Also our pamphlet on *The Mystery.*

(*e*) It is used also, and specially of "*the great secret*" (1 Tim. iii. 16. Rom. xvi. 25, 26. Eph. iii. 1—11. Col. i. 24—27).

This secret does not refer to the fact that Gentiles were to be blessed with Israel. That was never a secret, but was revealed to Abraham at the moment of his own call (Gen. xii. 3; xxii. 18; xxvi. 4, etc. Compare Pss. lxxii. 17; lxvii. 1, 2; xviii. 49. Deut. xxxii. 43. Isa. xi. 10; xlix. 6. Luke ii. 32).

Thus though the connections are different, the meaning and usage of the word are uniform; and the translation and usage of it in English should be uniform also.

7. "*At hand*," ἐνίστημι (*enistēmi*).—The word ἐνίστημι (*enistēmi*) occurs seven times, and though its usage is uniform, it is rendered in four different ways in English. One of them is of great importance, and most misleading. The word means *to be present*, and is so rendered in Rom. viii. 38. 1 Cor. iii. 22; vii. 26. Gal. i. 4. Heb. ix. 9.

In 2 Tim. iii. 1 it is "perilous times *shall come*": *i.e.*, be present.

But in 2 Thess. ii. 2 it is rendered "at hand," in connection with "the Day of the Lord" as being "now present" (R. V.).

The interpretation of the verse is thus shown to be that the Day of the Lord could not then have been present, inasmuch as the foretold Apostasy had not taken place, and the Man of Sin had not yet been revealed.

This being the case they were not to be troubled or disturbed in their mind.

On the other hand, however, if that had been the case, and the Day of the Lord had set in, there was every reason why they should have been troubled; for, the Apostle's word would in that case have failed; the revelation made in 1 Thess. iv. would not have been fulfilled; and the comfort would have been given in vain. That day would have overtaken them as a thief, which he had assured them should not be the case (1 Thess. v. 4). And they had not "gathered together" unto Christ in the air as He had promised them.

The rendering "at hand" makes the whole context of none effect.

The English expression "at hand" occurs in twenty other places, but in not one of them is it the Greek word *enistēmi* as in 2 Thess. ii. 2.

8. *"Depart,"* ἀναλύω, *analuō.*—The word rendered *depart* in Phil. i. 23 must be taken in the same sense as that in which it is used in the only other passage where it occurs; *viz.,* Luke xii. 36: "when he shall RETURN from the wedding." It does NOT mean *to depart,* in the sense of setting off from the place where one is, but *to return* to the place that one has left. The verb does not occur in the Greek translation of the Canonical books of the Old Testament, but it does occur in the Apocryphal books; which, though of no authority for the establishment of *doctrine,* are invaluable as to the use and meaning of *words.* In these books, this word always means *to return,* and is generally so translated.[1]

This settles for us the uniform usage of the word rendered "depart" in Phil. i. 23, and shows that it must have the same rendering as it has in Luke xii. 36.

It was the return of Christ and to be with Him for which the Apostle longed; and this longing pressed him out of the other alternatives of living or dying.

It was not his personal gain of which he was thinking, but the gain to the Gospel. The Scope of the whole passage is the Gospel. The argument is that, If his imprisonment had turned out for the "furtherance" and gain of

---

[1] See Tob. ii. 9. "The same night I *returned* from the burial."

Judg. xiii. 1. "Now when the evening was come, his servants made haste *to depart*" (*i.e.,* to return to their tents).

1 Esd. iii. 3. "They ate, and drank, and being satisfied *they went*" (*i.e.,* returned) "*home.*"

Wisd. ii. 1. "Neither was there any man known to have *returned from* .the grave."

Wisd. v. 12. "Like as when an arrow is shot at a mark, it parteth the air, which immediately *cometh together*" (returneth) "again."

Wisd. xii. 14. "The spirit when it is gone forth *returneth* not."

Ecclus. iii. 15. "As the ice *melteth away*" (*i.e.,* returneth to water) "in the fair warm weather."

2 Macc. viii. 25. "They pursued them far; but lacking time, they *returned.*"

2 Macc. ix. 1. "Antiochus *returned* and came away with dishonour from the country of Persia."

2 Macc. xii. 7. "He went backward, as if *he would return* to root them all out of the country of Joppa."

2 Macc. xv. 28. "Now when the battle was done, returning again with joy they knew," etc.

the preaching of the Gospel, what might not the gain be by his death.

It ought to be added that there are no less than twenty-two Greek words rendered "depart" some one hundred and thirty times: but this one word ἀναλύω (*analuō*) occurs only twice, and in one of these it is rendered "depart" and in the other "return." If this is not convincing evidence as to what should be the correct rendering in Phil. i. 23, we know not what evidence is required.

We have the noun ἀνάλυσις (*analysis*) in 2 Tim. iv. 6, but it has the same meaning, *returning* or *dissolution;* *i.e.*, the body *returning* to dust as it was, and the spirit *returning* to God who gave it.

9. *"Leaven."* ζύμη (*zumē*).—The usage of this word is uniformly in a bad sense throughout Scripture.

(1) It must be put away at the Passover (Exod. xii. 15).

(2) It must not come into contact with any sacrifice (Exod. xxxiv. 25. Lev. ii. 11; x. 12).

(3) It is likened to the corrupt doctrines of the Pharisees and of the Sadducees (Matt. xvi. 6); and of Herod (Mark viii. 15).

(4) The Corinthian Church was commanded to purge out corrupt persons (1 Cor. v. 7) because "a little leaven leaveneth the whole lump" (*v.* 6); and

(5) It is used of "malice and wickedness" (1 Cor. v. 8).

In the face of this, How can anyone dare to use "leaven" in a sense totally opposite, and interpret it of that which is good in itself and in its workings and effects?

The supposed exceptions are—

(1) Lev. xxiii. 17. From verses 9—14. The wave-sheaf or first-fruits was to have no leaven. But in verse 17 the "Two wave loaves" offered fifty days after were to have leaven with them. This distinction was made because the "wave-sheaf" represented Christ the first-fruits in resurrection, without sin (1 Cor. xv. 23); while the two wave-loaves represented those who were endued with His gifts (fifty days later, Acts ii. 1—4): but who had sin

262 BIBLICAL USAGE ESSENTIAL TO INTERPRETATION:

and corruption in them. This is why leaven was used in the two wave-loaves and not in the wave-sheaf.[1]

(2) Amos iv. 4, 5. But here the offering "a sacrifice of thanksgiving with leaven" is what is described as the multiplying of transgression.

(3) Matt. xiii. 33. The Parable of the Leaven hidden in three measures of meal. It is one of seven parables which all have to do with the "Kingdom," and therefore not with the Church. This we have already seen under our chapter on "Dispensational Truth and Teaching."

The Kingdom was proclaimed by John the Baptist, by Christ, and by Peter. But since it was finally rejected, it is in abeyance, and is not recognized as having any place in Scripture.

"We see not yet all things put under Him" (Heb. ii. 8), who is now "henceforth expecting till his enemies be made his footstool" (Heb. x. 13).

Till that day, the Kingdom has no place on earth, and it must not be read into those Scriptures which concern the present position and portion of the "Church ot God."

The Scriptures relating to the Kingdom must be confined to the Kingdom period which is before and after this present Church-Interval: they must be read on from its rejection in the Acts of the Apostles to the coming of the King; leaping over this present Dispensation as though it had no existence.

Only thus shall we understand the Seven Parables of Matt. xiii.

The Kingdom was proclaimed by John the Baptist and Christ: The seed was sown. But from that moment the enemy (likened to the "fowls of the air") was on the watch, not only to catch it away, but to sow and mingle tares with the good seed. The tares appear, but nothing more is said about them "till the harvest": nothing is done till "the time of harvest." "The harvest is the end of the age": *i.e.*, after the present Dispensation.

The mustard-tree, rooted in the earth, gives shelter for the same "fowls of the air" (Rev. xviii. 2).

---

[1] See a separate pamphlet on *Leaven* by the same author.

The leaven follows immediately to illustrate the inward corruption (as the mustard-tree shows the outward).

If the leaven be taken here in a good sense it would reverse the whole course and point and scope of the previous teaching; and this parable would be the very opposite of the others.

It cannot mean the preaching of the Gospel in this present Dispensation; for the woman *hides* it, but the Gospel is proclaimed *openly*.

The usage of the word "leaven" here must be taken in this sense; and thus, uniform with all the other passages where the word occurs.

CANON 4

The Context Is Always Essential to the Interpretation of Words

i. THE IMPORTANCE OF THE CONTEXT SHOWN.

We have already seen something of this in the consideration of the Structure of the Word and the Words of God.

The *order* of the words is as perfect as the truth revealed by them, and contained in them.

This order is Divine: and it is nothing less than a crime for any human hand to subvert that order, either by ignoring it or changing it.

Beware of any teacher to whom the context is not manifestly essential. Beware of any teaching that is not based upon it.

Some passages of Scripture derive their chief importance from some remarkable words employed; others derive their chief importance from some wonderful truth revealed; while others derive their chief importance *from the place where we find them.* Every passage has its own importance in this last respect. When we find a passage in its own particular place, there is a Divine reason why it is there, and also why it is not in any other place.

It is essential to our understanding of the "words" to find out why they are where we find them. It is essential to our enjoyment of the words that we should discover not only what they mean, but why they are not in any other passage. If we would find the words and the Word of God to be a delight to us, instead of a perplexing jumble, we must have special regard to the Context.

If this be disregarded, then a word, a sentence, or a verse, may be taken out from its context and interpreted of something quite foreign to its original intent.

We have all heard the proverbial saying that "the Bible may be made to prove anything." Exactly so; but this, very often, is only when, and because, a verse is taken apart from its context: otherwise it could never be made to teach anything different from the context in which God has set it.

Every sentence and every verse has something going before it and something following after it. We call this the context. This is regarded as being essential even in the case of human writers. How often are complaints made by public speakers and writers that only *a part* of what they have said is quoted; whereas, if the whole had been given, or even the sentence that preceded or followed, quite a different complexion would have been given to the point referred to.

If this be so important where man is concerned, how essential it must be when we remember that, in the case we are considering, it is God's context and not man's.

How great must be the presumption if we disregard or disturb that context.

Yet this is constantly done in order to prop up some tradition.

Let us illustrate this by giving a few examples of error arising from a disregard of the context.

ii. Examples of Error arising from a Disregard of the Context.

1. Isa. lii. 8, "They shall see eye to eye."

The context shows that this means the *seeing* of one another personally "face to face," and not the agreement with one another in opinion or judgment.

2. Hab. ii. 2, "That he may run that readeth it."

> "Write the vision
> And make it plain upon tables,
> That he may run who readeth it."

The reason given in the next verse (*v*. 3) shows that the verb רוּץ (*rūtz*) is to be taken in its sense of *hasten*, or *flee:* *viz.*, that he who reads of the coming troubles may flee from them.

It does not mean that he may be able to run *while* he reads it; but flee *when* he reads it.

3. Ps. ii. 8, "Ask of me, and I shall give thee the heathen for thine inheritance, and the utmost parts of the earth for thy possession."

How often have we heard these words quoted on missionary platforms and in pulpits, as though, by missionary efforts, the reign of Christ here spoken of as the one subject of the psalm is to be brought about.

But this is *not* to be the way in which that glorious reign is to be inaugurated. Many are the Scriptures which state this unmistakably. Judgment, not grace, is to be the means employed. " Worse and worse" is to be the character of the coming days, until they are like "the days of Noah," which will end up in the Great Tribulation. Then, without any interval or break of any kind, " IMMEDIATELY after the Tribulation of those days . . . then shall appear the sign of the Son of Man in heaven . . . and they shall see the Son of Man coming in the clouds of heaven" (Matt. xxiv. 29, 30).

This exactly accords with Ps. ii. as is shown by the words that immediately follow verse 8 :

> "Thou shalt break them with a rod of iron ;
> Thou shalt dash them in pieces like a potter's vessel" (*v.* 9).

But, these words of verse 9 are never quoted at missionary meetings, because it is all too plain that it is not such means as these that missionary societies use, or profess to use. Their agents proclaim the good news of "the grace of God." They are not sent out to break the "heathen." They are not commissioned to "dash them in pieces like a potter's vessel."

And so the context of *this ninth verse is prudently left out!* And the quotation always stops short at the end of the eighth verse !

This is very clever ; but is it right? It is one way of "dividing the Word of truth." But, Is it "RIGHTLY dividing" it ?

It is dividing it for a purpose ; and that purpose is manifest. It is done in order to make the Scripture appear to give a Divine support to the tradition of men, that the work of the Church and the Gospel is to bring about the Millennium ; and that, by their means the earth is to be "full of the knowledge of the LORD as the waters cover the sea" (Isa. xi. 9).

But here again the context forbids such an application, for verses 3 and 4 state that it is to be by righteous judgment that He will "SMITE the earth with the rod of his mouth, and with the breath of his lips shall he SLAY the wicked."

If the context, which is always essential, had been duly noted and considered, it would have been impossible for Ps. ii. 8 ever to have been distorted, and have an interpretation given to it which is contrary to the whole teaching of the Word of truth.

4. Another example of error arising from disregard of the context is seen in Matt. xxii. 32:

"God is not the God of the dead, but of the living."

Quoted thus, apart from the context, as an independent statement, the words are at once placed, by those who hear them, *in the context of their own traditional belief;* instead of in the context of God's Word, and in connection with the rest of the words of the Lord Jesus.

Misquoted as above by being taken thus, apart from their context, they are used to teach that the dead are not dead at all, but that they are alive. This is exactly what the Old Serpent said in Gen. iii. 4 when he gave the lie to what God had said (Gen. ii. 17).

But, as in the two cases already cited, not only are the words thus perverted from their meaning, but the logical sequence of the whole context is suddenly broken off, and ends in a bathos. There is no conclusion to the Lord's words. He set out to prove the truth of resurrection, which, among other things, His opponents, the Sadducees, denied:

"Then came the Sadducees which say that there is NO RESURRECTION" (*v.* 23).

They propound a hypothetical case of the woman with the seven husbands, and ask therefore

"IN THE RESURRECTION whose wife shall she be of the seven?" (*v.* 28).

The Lord replies by saying:

> "Ye do err, not[1] knowing the Scriptures nor the
> power of God.   For IN THE RESURRECTION
> they neither marry nor are given in marriage."

He goes on to refer to Scripture:

> "But as TOUCHING THE RESURRECTION OF
> THE DEAD, have ye not read that which was
> spoken unto you by God, saying, I am the God
> of Abraham, and the God of Isaac, and the God
> of Jacob? God is not the god of the dead, but
> of the living."

Is it not clear that these words are used by the Lord
in order to prove the fact and truth of resurrection? How
could this argument prove that the dead would rise again
if He meant that the dead are alive *now*?

Surely the logical conclusion is that, If God is "the
God of the living," the dead Abraham, and the dead Isaac,
and the dead Jacob must live again,[2] in resurrection, in
order to have God's promise to them fulfilled.   God had
promised to each of these three patriarchs, that not only
their seed, but that *they themselves*, should possess the
land, and therefore, to do this, they must "live again."

"TO THEE, and to thy seed"

was the promise made to Abraham (Gen. xiii. 15), to Isaac
(Gen. xxvi. 3), and to Jacob (Gen. xxviii. 13),

It is a matter of history that neither of them ever
possessed the land (Heb. xi. 13), and never had more than
a sepulchre there.   That sepulchre they *purchased* and
there they were buried (Gen. xlix. 29—33); but it was not
the promised gift.

How then can God's promise to these three patriarchs
be fulfilled except by resurrection? The argument of the
Lord proves, unmistakably, the necessity of resurrection
if God is to fulfil His promise to them, and to be faithful
to His word to Moses at the Bush.

---

[1] Greek, μή (*me*), *not*, used subjectively ; *i.e.*, not wishing to know the
Scriptures.

[2] Compare Rev. xx. 5, "the rest of the dead lived not again until the thousand years were finished," which proves that they cannot be alive during the
thousand years, while they remain "dead."

Apart from the context the Lord's argument is shorn of its conclusion and robbed of its point; while God's promise is made to fall to the ground, and the hope of resurrection lost. And all this because a sentence is wrested from the context in which the Holy Spirit of God has placed it.

These are good examples of how a short sentence may be perverted by a violation of this canon.

It will be noticed how these examples point to the fact that it is only traditional beliefs that seem to require such a treatment of Scripture, and that this treatment is practically confined to them. This explains why so many of our examples are connected with these strongholds of tradition. Unable to find Scriptural support for the traditions of men, resort must perforce be had to a few isolated passages which are thus forced apart from their Divine context for this special purpose.

5. "*Observe and do.*"—Another example may be seen in Matt. xxiii. 3, where the context clearly tells us whether the translation should be "observe and do" as a *command*, or "ye observe and do" as a *statement*.

In the Greek the second person plural Indicative Mood is exactly the same as the Imperative. There is nothing therefore to guide us, as to which Mood should be read, but the context. Now, the context of the immediate passage, and the context of the whole Gospel, leads us to expect that the Lord cannot possibly be thought of here as enjoining obedience to the teaching of the Scribes and Pharisees. On the contrary, He was always uttering the most solemn warnings against them and their teachings. We must, therefore, read them as being in the *Indicative* Mood; *as stating a fact*, and not as enjoining a precept. This is still more clear if we observe that the word translated "sit" is not in the Present Tense, but in the Past: "*have taken their seat.*"

With these two notes we must translate the passage as follows:

"The Scribes and Pharisees have seated themselves in Moses' seat: all things, therefore, whatsoever they bid you, *ye observe and do:* but *do not ye* according to their works."

The word "therefore" is very significant. It is *be-cause* "they have taken their seat in Moses' seat" that ye observe and do whatever they bid you. But, the injunction is "*Do them not.*" And then in verses 4—33 the most weighty reasons are given why they should *not* do them. How, then, can we go out of our way, gratuitously to create a difficulty, by taking the Mood as being the Imperative, and make the Lord command them to do the very things He was about to condemn?

The Chief Priests and Elders who had thus arrogated to themselves the authority of Moses, shortly after this used it to bid the people "that they should ask Barabbas and destroy Jesus" (Matt. xxvii. 20—23). Are we to suppose, for one moment, that in observing to do this bidding the people were acting in conformity with the Lord's words in ch. xxiii. 3? This consideration by itself is quite sufficient to condemn the "reading" riveted on the Greek by the Revisers' text; quite apart from the Critical evidence which can be adduced in favour of the Received Text.

There is another and overwhelming reason for this understanding of the Lord's words; and that is the concluding reason given why they are not to do the works which the Scribes and Pharisees commanded, "for they say and do not."

Can the argument be: Do the works (which they command) because they do them not?

Surely there is no sense in such an argument. But rather it is: "Do not ye the works (*which they command*), for they do not do them themselves"; which clearly shows how grievous their heavy burdens were.

This is the continuation of the Lord's argument; and it is the only logical conclusion from His words as recorded in the context.

6. John vi. 37, "Him that cometh unto me I will in no wise cast out." This verse is indeed divided; but wrongly, not rightly, divided by quoting only a part of it as though it were the whole.

How often do we hear the promise—"Him that cometh unto me I will in no wise cast out." But how seldom do we hear the first half, which is an integral part of the sentence. "All that the Father giveth me shall come to me: AND him that cometh unto me I will in no wise cast out."

The reason for the mangling of this verse is the same reason why, when the Lord stated the same truth in verse 65, "No man can come unto me, except it were given him of my Father; FROM THAT TIME many of his disciples went back, and walked no more with him."

Wherever this same truth is proclaimed to day, the same result will follow; and this, in spite of all the talk about "the teaching of Jesus," which is only an excuse for attempting to get rid of the teaching of the Holy Ghost by Paul.

7. Acts xvi. 31, "Believe on the Lord Jesus Christ and thou shalt be saved."

This is an example of how a *special* and personal injunction is detached from its context, put forth, and used as a general and universal command.

The quotation generally stops here, because the words "thou and thy house" would show the *special* nature of the command. The context shows that it was given to one who was under deep conviction of sin. The jailor had seen himself in the presence of God. His one *thought* was that the prisoners had fled. His one *act* was that "he drew out his sword and would have killed himself:" for he knew what his fate would be in the morning (Acts xii. 19).

But there was One who knew what he *thought*, and the voice said, "We are all here." There was One who could see in that darkness what he was going to do, and the voice said, "Do thyself no harm." "THEN he *called for a light*, and sprang in, and came trembling and fell down," and asked, "What must I do to be saved?"

To all such in similar circumstances; to all who thus fall down and ask such a question, this is the right answer. But it is no command at all to those who are not under conviction of sin. Such have first to believe God as to their lost and ruined condition.

There are other passages, however, which are not so serious, where mistakes are made and errors are fallen into through partial quotations, where a part of a verse is used to upset the teaching of the other part, or of the immediate context.

8. Rom. viii. 28, " All things work together for good."

These words are often taken by themselves, as though they were an independent statement; a statement moreover which is contrary to fact.

Sometimes the words that follow are added, "to them that love God."

But very seldom do we hear the next sentence: "to them that are the called according to his purpose."

9. 1 Cor. iii. 17, " Him shall God destroy."

"If any man defile the temple of God, him shall God destroy; for the temple of God is holy, which temple ye are."

It is well for us first to note the fact that the words "defile" and "destroy" represent but one and the same word in the Greek. In both clauses the word is φθείρω (*phtheirō*), *to spoil* or *corrupt*. That this is the meaning may be seen from 1 Cor. xv. 33. 2 Cor. vii. 2; xi. 3, etc.

But, the pronoun rendered "him" is τοῦτον (*touton*), *this*. To what noun does the pronoun "this" refer? The context alone can help us.

It cannot be "this" man, or "him" as in A.V.; because verse 15 distinctly states that "he himself shall be saved."

It can be, therefore, only "this" thing that the man builds on the one foundation as stated in verse 12. Whatever man's building-work may be—good, bad, or indifferent; "gold, silver, precious stones, wood, hay, stubble;" grand, imposing, insignificant, or mean, whatever it may be, it will be burnt up (*vv.* 13—15).

"Ye are God's building" (*v.* 9).

"Ye are the temple of God" (*v.* 16).

"Which temple ye are" (*v.* 17).

That temple is God's building (Eph. ii. 21). It is "one body" (Eph. iv. 16). It is a spiritual unity (Eph. iv. 3, 4).

If any man builds any other "temple," or makes any other "body," or creates any other "unity," it is

corporate; and it "defiles God's building"; and "this" it
is that God will destroy.[1]

10. 2 Cor. v. 8. "Absent from the body."

In this case a few words are taken out of their context
and used as a motto or proverbial expression; and are
quoted as conclusively settling a disputed question. We
have already considered this illustration under Canon 11.
(pp. 223—226), where we showed the Scope of the Passage
from its Structure. We wish to show now, how these
words can be explained by simply heeding the context.

Again and again we hear :

> "Absent from the body,
> Present with the Lord "

quoted as though it asserted that the moment a believer
is "absent from the body" he is "present with the Lord."

But this is what it does not say. Many will be surprised to hear that no such collocation of words occurs
in Scripture : and that 2 Cor. v. 8 reads

> "We are willing rather to be absent from the body,
> and to be present with the Lord,"

which is quite a different thing ; because the whole context from 2 Cor. iv. 14 down to this verse, is wholly
occupied with the subject of *Resurrection*, and a longing
and desire not to die, or to be unclothed (*v.* 4), but "to
be clothed upon" with our heavenly and glorious resurrection body.

While we are in this body we are "absent from the
Lord." That is why we so earnestly desire to be alive
and remain till His coming, that we may be clothed upon
with our house[2] which is from heaven.

---

[1] See a separate pamphlet entitled *God's Building*, by the same author .

[2] The word here rendered "house" is οἰκητήρι ν (*oikētērion*), which is used
of the spirit-body which we shall have in resurrection. The word occurs only
here and in Jude 6, where it is rendered "habitation," and is used here of
whatever that word may mean when used of angels or angelic beings in Jude 6.
The word οἶκος (*oikos*) is used of our present human body or *house* (2 Cor. v. 1).
It is also used of our resurrection body in the same verse, but there it is
specially distinguished as being "not made with hands." This shows that
the meaning of *oikētērion* in verse 2, is a spirit-body, because it is not made
with human hands, but "a building of God," "which is from heaven."

We ourselves are very willing to be *thus* "absent from the body"; nay, we are desirous of it, because, when we are, we shall then have our *oikētērion* in which we shall be "at home with the Lord."

We have precisely the same teaching in the word "SO" in 1 Thess. iv. 17. "SO shall we ever be with the Lord." The Greek is οὕτως (*houtōs*), *thus, in this manner: viz.* by Resurrection, and Ascension; raised and "caught up to meet the Lord in the air, SO shall we ever be with the Lord."

It will be noticed again that it is tradition which thus requires such perverted misquotations. This is because the errors of tradition are produced by ignoring the context. We have another:

11. "To die is gain," (Phil. i. 21), constantly cited as though it were a separate, independent, and dogmatic categorical statement of Divine truth; whereas it is nothing of the kind. It is not even a complete sentence. The verse says:

"For to me to live is Christ,
And to die is gain."

The **very** word "For" should be sufficient to show that the statement is not independent; but that it depends on what has been before said, and is added as a reason for it.

What has been said before? What is the context all about?

A very cursory reader will at once see that it is all about the "gain" of the Gospel. That is what the Apostle was so deeply concerned about. He was in prison, and yet he wanted them to "understand that the things which happened unto me have fallen out rather unto *the furtherance of the Gospel*." And he goes on to show that the one effect of his bonds on many of the brethren had been to make their confidence to increase, so that they were "much more bold to speak the Word without fear."

Paul rejoiced at this, notwithstanding that some did it of contention and others from love.

It made him bold also, and bold enough to say that he did not care what happened to himself; he did not mind whether he lived or died. Christ would be magnified in his body (*v.* 20) in either case. "The furtherance of the Gospel" was the one thing he cared about; not his own personal "gain." He never thought of that. It ruins the whole scope of the chapter to introduce the thought, yea, the slanderous thought, and charge him with such selfishness, as though he were thinking only of his own personal gain. It is a gross injustice to the Apostle, as well as a perversion of his words, thus to bring against him a charge of which he was not only innocent, but which is foreign to the context.

It also mars and breaks up the logical sequence of the Context, considered merely as literary matter. The argument is this; If my bonds have resulted in the furtherance of the Gospel, what might not my death produce? Christ is preached through my bonds; so He may be magnified through my body, whether by my living or dying, "For to me to live will be Christ; and to die [will be His] gain." In either case He will be magnified. The gain will be His.

But though his death might result in Christ's gain, it might not be their gain; for to abide in the flesh would be more needful for those to whom he wrote.[1]

12. Phil. ii. 12. We have a similar example in the next chapter: "Work out your own salvation with fear and trembling."

These words are quoted as a general instruction applying to everyone universally. Whereas the preceding context shows that they are part of an exhortation for these Philippian saints to do this working in the Apostle's absence as they had always done in his presence.

Moreover the context which follows gives the reason why they should, and why they could, do this *working out;* "FOR it is God which worketh in you both to will and to do of his good pleasure."

What that work is, is added in verse 14. "Do all things without murmurings and disputings." That is how they would work out that salvation which they had in Christ, during the Apostle's absence.

We must not dismiss this negative branch of our subject without a reference to the two pernicious practices

---

[1] See above, under Canon III., Section v. 8; the word "Depart.

which may be termed *Text-mangling* on the one hand,
and *Text-garbling* on the other.

13. *Text-mangling* is common on illuminated wall-texts,
motto-cards, birth-day books, and almanacs.

The practice is to take a few words (for the space is
often very limited) regardless of the context in which
they may be found; regardless also of their proper interpretation. Hence, passages are often selected which may
give false peace to those who stand in need of conviction
of sin; or they may disturb the peace of those who
need assurance; or they may remove others from the
ground of grace to the ground of works. Sometimes
also this practice causes the words of God to be treated
as Shakespeare is often treated by advertisers, comic
artists, and others, who are thus able to show at once their
intimate knowledge of Shakespeare and their cleverness
in twisting his words to an end and for a purpose which
Shakespeare never dreamed of. , This is done in order to
attract attention by showing the absurdity of making
Shakespeare recommend some "buttons," "pills," or
"soap" of which he never heard.

This practice may be innocent and amusing when it is
confined to a human author; but, when it is brought into
use in dealing with the words of God, the practice cannot
be too strongly reprobated as being an insult to God, and
pernicious to man.

Just in this same way we might quote, or rather mis-
quote, the words of Truth:

"There is no God" (Ps. xiv. 1).

"Hang all the law and the prophets" (Matt. xxii. 40).

"Woe unto you lawyers" (Luke xi. 52).

All these are true, if taken in connection with the
context in which they stand; but not otherwise. Apart
from their context these and others may form complete
sentences, but they may make either nonsense or false
sense.

We have actually seen the following short sentence as
a wall-text:—
"Thou shalt not drink wine"
as though this was a general command demanding universal obedience.

But it is taken from the Minor Prophets, where it forms part of Divine threatening of judgment:

"Thou shalt eat, but not be satisfied; . . .
Thou shalt take hold, but shalt not deliver . . .
Thou shalt sow, but thou shalt not reap;
Thou shalt tread olives, but thou shalt not anoint thee with oil;
And sweet wine, but shalt *not drink wine*" (Mic. vi. 15; compare Zeph. i. 13).

Not only are these words thus wrested from their proper context and meaning; but, by so doing, they are set in flat contradiction to Amos ix. 14, where exactly the opposite prophecy is given by way of blessing:

"They shall plant vineyards
And drink the wine thereof."

On the other hand, there are texts which are of such universal and eternal application, and which so touch the conscience, that they could not fail to be of untold blessing to thousands, if they were chosen for this purpose.

How seldom, if ever, do we see such passages as these plainly printed and prominently exposed:

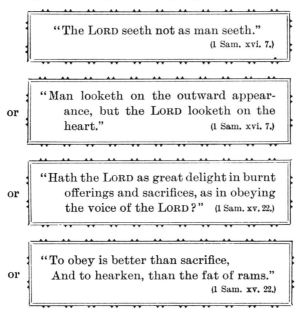

"The LORD seeth not as man seeth."
(1 Sam. xvi. 7.)

or "Man looketh on the outward appearance, but the LORD looketh on the heart." (1 Sam. xvi. 7.)

or "Hath the LORD as great delight in burnt offerings and sacrifices, as in obeying the voice of the LORD?" (1 Sam. xv. 22.)

or "To obey is better than sacrifice,
And to hearken, than the fat of rams."
(1 Sam. xv. 22.)

The governing principle in this matter should be that, what is put out for general observation should be in perfect harmony with, not wrenched from, its context, and universal and eternal in its application.

14. *Text-garbling* differs from *Text-mangling* in that a passage is not only taken out of the context in which God has set it, but it is placed in *another context* in which He has not set it. This, to say the least, is an act of the grossest impertinence.

There are some writers who are specially addicted to this habit, and string a number of texts together as though they occurred exactly in this order in God's Word. True, the references may be given with each verse; but unwary readers may not notice or heed this; hence they will read on from one to the other as though they are reading the words as God has given them.

There is one book, especially, in our mind, which does this, and leads many to do this "daily," every day of the year: but whether in each case it gives daily light is another matter.

If it comes to merely stringing texts together, this can easily be done; we could say:

"Judas went and hanged himself" (Matt. xxvii. 5).
Go and do thou likewise" (Luke x. 37).

This shows the absurdity to which such a principle can be reduced.

We do not deny, of course, that it is *possible* for a well-taught and well-read spiritually-minded student of the Word of truth to do this with effect. Great light may be thrown often on a passage by putting it alongside another, thus letting one Scripture be its own Divine comment on another. That is quite a different thing altogether from the ill-considered practice of dislocating a passage from its own context and putting it into another.

What we are speaking of is the *habit* of garbling Scripture by bringing texts together, regardless as to whether such displacement affects in any way the special interpretation which they have in their own respective contexts.

It may be that, with due regard to this point, the truth and teaching of each of two such passages may be enhanced. But the practice is one which requires much spiritual discernment, great care, long experience, special knowledge of the context, extensive knowledge of Scripture, and a recognition of the principle involved in the important distinction between *interpretation* and *application*, dealt with in Canon X. below.

iii. EXAMPLES OF TRUTH AND TEACHING RESULTING FROM A DUE REGARD TO THE CONTEXT.

We come now to another part of this subject, as to the context being essential.

What we have said above is negative and destructive rather than positive and constructive. We have shown some of the mistakes arising from a disregard of the context; and have seen some of the evils resulting from this dangerous practice.

We now have a happier branch of this subject, *viz.*, we have to show some of the advantages of giving heed to the context; and the blessing, truth, and teaching resulting from a careful observation of the context, not only in the removal of difficulties, or in the explanation of so-called "discrepancies," but in the manifestation of the perfections of the Divine Word.

We shall divide this branch of our subject into two parts—

(*a*) The Nearer Context, and

(*b*) The Remoter Context.

From one point of view, the Word of truth, coming as it does, as a whole, from one and the same Divine Author, *is its own context.* That is to say, a particular passage is to be regarded not only in the relation it bears to its own nearer or remoter context; but, in the relation which it bears to the Word of God as a whole.

It may not be intended *to teach* science, chronology, or history, either Assyrian, Babylonian, Palestinian, or Egyptian, as such; but, everything that it records will be in perfect harmony with whatever is true of any or all of these. *Scientia* means *knowledge*, and nothing in

Scripture will be found to contradict what we really *know*, which is true science. Much that goes by the name of "science" is only hypothesis; and, in much more, supposition is so mixed up with knowledge that the result is vitiated.

All must be brought to the bar of the Divine Word. That Word as a whole is the context for its every part. All that is outside the two covers of the Word of God must be judged by what is within. We must not reverse this process and judge what is within by anything that may come to us from without.

With this understanding we will look at a few illustrations, which show how certain passages may receive light; how certain difficulties may be removed, how new beauties may be revealed by having regard to this, our fourth canon or principle, that the context is always essential.

Let us take, first, passages which are illuminated by

(a) *The Nearer Context.*

By this we mean what we may find and read on the same page, or opening; or at the most on the pages or in the chapters near to it.

[By the Remoter Context we mean that which is separated from it by some chapters at least; or even by other books of Scripture.]

1. In Gen. xxxv. 2, we read Jacob's command, "Put away the strange gods (Heb., *the gods of the stranger*) that are among you, and be clean and change your garments."

This looks, at first sight, as though Jacob and his family had become idolaters. It is true, we read of the "*teraphim*" which Rachel had taken away when she fled with Jacob from her father's house (ch. xxxi. 19); but it does not appear that they were for worship. More probably they were of silver or gold, and were taken as valuables in lieu of the balance of wages still owing by Laban to Jacob.

It is hardly credible that idolatry could have been common in Jacob's household as the command in Gen. xxxv. 2 would seem to imply.

We have not far to look before we find the explanation. Only a few verses before (ch. xxxiv. 26—29) we read how the sons of Jacob had just captured the city of Shechem and taken their cattle, and "all their wealth, and all their little ones and their wives took they captive, and spoiled even all that was in the house."

Here then we have the explanation of these strangers and their strange gods. Here also we see why Jacob gave this command not only "unto his household," but "to all that were with him."

2. In 2 Kings iv. 13 Elisha asks "a great woman" of Shunem (who had befriended him): "Behold, thou hast been careful for us with all this care; what is to be done for thee? *Wouldest thou be spoken for to the king or to the captain of the host?*"

This sounds strange, when, from the previous history, we should hardly suppose that Elisha was on sufficiently good terms with Jehoram king of Israel to have any grounds for holding out such hopes to this woman. And yet he could not be trifling with her after all her care of him.

What then is the explanation? We find it in the immediate context. Chap. iii. 16, 17 tells how he had just by a miraculous supply of water saved the armies of Israel and enabled them to defeat their enemy.

Elisha might well therefore presume that he had some ground on which he could appeal for a favour to the king; or at any rate to "the captain of the host."

3. In Dan. v. 30 we read, "In that night was Belshazzar the king of the Chaldeans slain. And Darius the Median took the kingdom."

In ch. vi. 1, we read, "It pleased Darius to set over the kingdom *an hundred and twenty* princes which should be over the whole kingdom."

In Esther i. 1—3, we read that Ahashuerus (a subsequent king of Persia) "reigned from India even unto Ethiopia, over *an hundred and seven and twenty* provinces."

Here, if princes necessarily imply provinces, there appears to be a discrepancy as to which no explanation is vouchsafed by the historian: the fact being stated as well known and needing nothing beyond its statement.

However, in Dan. viii. 4, the Nearer Context, we find that Daniel had a vision in the reign of Belshazzar, showing the nature and character of the impending change, and the rise of the Medo-Persian kingdom.

It is pictured as "a ram pushing westward, and northward, and southward; so that no beasts might stand before him" (Dan. viii. 1—4).

This can mean only that, in the early days of its existence, the Medo-Persian kingdom would extend its boundaries, and receive accessions of empire.

This is exactly what we find from Esther i. 1—3, where the one hundred and twenty provinces of Dan. vi. 1 had increased to one hundred and twenty-seven in the subsequent reign of Ahashuerus.

4. Eph. iii. 15, "The whole family in heaven and earth." This is another illustration of quite a different character. But first we must ask what is the sense in which we are to take the word "family." It is an unfortunate rendering of the Greek $\pi\alpha\tau\rho\iota\acute{\alpha}$ (*patria*), and yet it is so difficult to suggest a better, that the only alternative is to try and understand it. Our English word "family" takes its meaning from the lowest in the household; from *famulus*, the servant, and not from the father. The Latin *familia* was the household of servants. But the idea of *patria* is Hebrew, and is *a group or class of families* all claiming a common descent from one $\pi\alpha\tau\acute{\eta}\rho$ (*patēr*), or father. The twelve tribes were divided into *patria*, and these again into οἶκοι (*oikoi*), houses. Joseph was of the house and family of David. The word occurs only here, Luke ii. 4, and Acts iii. 25. It denotes *a clan* all descended from a common stock.

So much for the meaning of the word. Now for the meaning of the verse: "Of whom the whole family (R.V. every family) in heaven and earth is named."

This verse is always understood of "the Church of God;" and is taken to mean that one part of it is already in heaven, and the other part is on earth.

But this is not an illuminated wall-text, or a text from a birthday book, or from an almanac. It occurs in the middle of an Epistle which has something to say about the names, and about the naming of these families.

God has many families, in heaven and on earth, both in this world and in the world to come. But we, with our usual selfishness, can see only one Family; and that must, of course, be the Church, for that is the Family *we* belong to. Thus we bring everything round to ourselves; especially if there is blessing, mercy, or glory attached to it.

In Eph. i. 21 we have the names of some of these "Families":

" Principalities,"	"Thrones,"
" Powers,"	" Angels,"
" Might,"	and
" Dominions."	"Archangels."

These belong to "heaven above" and to "the world to come." Two of them are again mentioned in Eph. iii. 10, *viz.*, the "Principalities and Powers," to whom God is manifesting now His manifold wisdom by means of the Church, using it as His object-lesson. The Church must, therefore, be distinct from these families in heaven.

What these heavenly families may be we do not know. Others are mentioned in Rom. viii. 38. Col. i. 16. 1 Pet. iii. 22,[1] but the Greek words employed reveal no more to us than the English words. For words that pertain only to "this world" cannot contain any information as to the "world to come."

Other "names that are named" are referred to in Eph. i. 21.

And yet in spite of all this when the R.V. correctly renders πᾶσα πατριά *(pasa patria) every family* (Eph. iii. 15) an outcry is made because Eph. iii. 15 has been heretofore wrongly limited and restricted to the Church; and that verse has been used as a proof that part of the Church is in heaven and part of it is on earth. On this unwarranted limitation the non-Scriptural (not to say un-Scriptural) terms of "church militant" and "church triumphant" are based.

But the text reads, "Of (*or*, by) whom every family in the heavens and upon earth is named."

---

[1] From Eph. vi. 12 we gather that there are similar classes of spirit-being who are evil and fallen, opposing and conflicting with the good and unfallen (See Col. ii. 15).

We know this only because we are here told of it. No further explanation is given. We have the key to the interpretation in the Nearer Context (Eph. i. 21). We have "every family that is named" in chap. iii. 15, and "every name that is named" in chap. i. 21. It seems very inconsistent to translate "every name" in ch. i. 21, and "the whole family" in ch. iii. 15. But out of this inconsistency flows the error; and on this inconsistency is built up the figment of part of the Church being in heaven and part on earth. Those who believe in and teach an "Intermediate state" must get over this difficulty as best they can. For our own part we see no difficulty at all; but only a simple revelation as to unseen realities.

We have here in Eph. iii. 15 and i. 21 a universal truth; but those who limit it to the Church of God not only lose that great truth, but they get error in its stead.

Rightly divided, the families in heaven consist of Principalities, Powers, Might, Dominions, Thrones, Angels and Archangels, while the families on earth are Israel and the Church of God.

All the promises of God to the Church are made concerning heavenly things; all the promises made to Israel, the other earthly family, have to do with earth and earthly things.

Presently the Church will take its place in the heavens, and will be the chiefest of every family in heaven, while Israel will be *the Family on Earth*. The object in the Epistle to the Ephesians is to show how the risen Christ has been given and made the Head over all things to (*or* for) the Church. He is and will be the centre of all things in heaven and on earth, both to the Church and to Israel.

Join together what God has put asunder; fail to divide rightly or to recognize the distinction between these families; allow ourselves to be misled by tradition and deceived by partisan teachers that there is only one family (part of it in heaven and part on earth), and we shall not only lose some of the most wonderful truths of the Word of God, but we shall find ourselves in the mists and clouds of darkness and error.

Rightly divide the Word of truth, giving due heed to the Context, and there will be opened out to us whole vistas of separate truths, which will all converge and unite in magnifying the Word of God, and in glorifying the Christ of God.

(b) *The Remoter Context.*

By this we mean that the Word of God, being one whole, is its own Context, for every separate passage, quite apart from all that is outside its own covers; and each passage has to be read in reference to the whole book.

Each passage stands, not only in its own *immediate* Context, but it stands also in the Context of the Bible as a whole; and is to be read, and explained, and understood, and interpreted in the light of the rest of Scripture.

An inexplicable verse, or act, or fact may find its solution in some other part of Scripture. For all of it is God-breathed. All has one Author. The Bible is not a "Symposium" of many authors; for though there are many writers there is only one Author, the Holy Spirit of God.

He has used various mouths to speak and various pens to write; He has "spoken at sundry times, and in divers manners:" but it is the same God who has spoken.

When we realize this great fact, we shall perceive the all-pervading presence of that one Author in all parts of the Word, which was written as holy men of old spake from God as they were moved by that same Spirit.

If any doubt the truth of this fact they will soon be convinced as they consider the Illustrations which we propose to give them.

1. Gen. xix. and xiv. *The cities and the city.*—Look, for example, at Gen. xviii., where Abraham pleaded with God for Sodom that the city might be spared in the day of His judgment.

God had told him that He would destroy the cities (*v.* 20) Sodom and Gomorrah. Gen. xix. speaks of "the cities." But Abraham prayed only for "the city." No reason is given. And, for aught that is said in these two chapters, we might conclude that he was influenced solely by feelings of humanity. But on referring back to ch. xiv. 12, we learn that his nephew Lot and his family dwelt in Sodom, and thus we see a special reason why

Abraham should thus feel so acutely, and intercede so earnestly for deliverance of that city.

We may further learn that God has more than one way of answering prayer.

When we are in difficulty, danger, or trouble, we see a way out of it, and we ask God, very "definitely," to deliver us by that way.

All the time He has many ways of delivering us, each better than the one *we* can see.

No greater evil could happen to us than for God always to answer our prayer and grant our definite request.

Here, in this history, Abraham could see only one way of delivering his nephew Lot; so he prays that God would avert His judgment from Sodom and spare "the city."

God did not grant his request, but he delivered Lot out of the midst of the overthrow; and thus answered Abraham's prayer, though not in the way Abraham had asked.

2. In Gen. xxiv. 24 Rebekah is said to be "the daughter of Bethuel the son of Milcah, which she bare unto Nahor."

From verse 15 we learn that Nahor was Abraham's brother. But there is nothing in all this chapter to explain to us how it was that a *grand-daughter* of Abraham's brother could be old enough to marry Isaac, Abraham's son; in other words, how Rebekah of the *third* generation could marry Isaac who was of the *second* generation.

We have to go back to Gen. xviii. 11, 12, quite a remote context, and there we read that Sarah, Abraham's wife, was "*old and well stricken in years,*" before Isaac was born.

This quite accounts for what otherwise would be a difficulty. Dr. Blunt refers to such an example as this for quite a different purpose. In his work on *Undesigned Coincidences* he uses these and similar examples as an argument for the veracity of the Scriptures.

We refer to the same examples with quite a different object, *viz.*, to show how, in a difficulty which we meet with in a particular passage, we find the solution in a remote Context, and often in a mere passing parenthetical statement.

3. Gen. xxxvii.   *The Ishmaelites and Midianites.*—In Gen. xxxvii. 25 Joseph's brethren "lifted up their eyes and looked, and, behold, a company of Ishmaelites came from Gilead with their camels bearing spicery and balm and myrrh, going to carry it down to Egypt."

In verse 28: "Then there passed by Midianites merchant-men: and they [Joseph's brethren] drew and lifted up Joseph out of the pit and sold Joseph to the Ishmaelites for twenty pieces of silver."

In verse 36: "And the Midianites sold him into Egypt unto Potiphar an officer of Pharaoh's."

In ch. xxxix. 1: Potiphar "bought him of the hands of the Ishmaelites which had brought him down thither."

Grave charges have been brought against the Text on account of these and other so-called "discrepancies" by the "Higher" Critics of the present day. But it will be found that most of these objections are contained in the writings of the French and English Atheists and Deists of the eighteenth century, though the cursory reader may be quite sure that no writer or editor would be so ignorant, or would be so careless, as to make such blunders, if blunders they are.

Moses and his readers knew the facts so well that there could be no possibility of the record being misunderstood.

It is rather an evidence of veracity and accuracy that the interchange of names should thus be made, without any attempt to explain it. A later editor would be sure to have noted the phenomenon presented in the Text, and have made some effort to correct or explain it.

It is in the remoter Context of Judges viii. 24 that we learn from a parenthetical remark, connected with quite another subject, that the Midianites, whom Gideon had just defeated, "had golden earrings[1] because they were Ishmaelites."

Thus it must have been a well-known fact as shown by this parenthetical remark that all Midianites were Ishmaelites, but all Ishmaelites were not Midianites.

---

[1] נֶזֶם (*nezem*), *a ring*, from נָזַם (*nāzam*), *to bore.* Hence, any ring as worn in the *ear* or the *nose.* It appears to be a *nose-ring* in Gen. xxiv. 47. Isa. iii. 21. Prov. xi. 22. Ezek. xvi. 12; and an *ear-ring* in Gen. xxxv. 4 and Exod. xxxii. 2. In certain passages it is doubtful where the ring was worn, the part of the body not being named. See Judg. viii. 24, 25. Job xlii. 11. Prov. xxv. 12. Hos. ii. 13.

But if we enquire further, and ask how this could be, we have to go to another context altogether, even to two Scriptures earlier than Gen. xxxvii.

We find our first clue in Gen. xvi. 11, 12, where we learn that ISHMAEL was the son of Abram, by his wife Hagar: while from Gen. xxv. 2 we learn that MIDIAN and MEDAN were Abraham's sons by his wife Keturah. So that Ishmael and Midian were half-brothers, and doubtless shared the same countries and the same life. Hence, in Gen. xxxvii. there was no need to add any explanation of this fact, because it would be a matter of common knowledge.

But we, approaching Gen. xxxvii. from its own standpoint, are left to discover the fact; and we do so, from the remoter Context of Judges viii. (where a parenthetical remark solves the whole difficulty), and from Gen. xvi. 11, 12, and xxv. 2.

Thus, it is clear, from Gen. xxxvii., that while the caravan at a distance was seen and known to be Ishmaelite, a closer inspection showed that there were Midianite merchantmen travelling with the company, and were known by wearing the same nose- or ear-rings, which we see from Judges viii. were the distinguishing badge of all Ishmaelites.

We could hardly find an example which more clearly shows the importance of the Canon we are considering, and affords evidence of the exceeding value of carefully studying and marking the Context, however remote it may be, for the purposes of interpretation.

4. Exod. vi. 16—20. *Moses's Parents.*—Another Illustration is found in the case of the parents of Moses.

From Exod. vi. 16, 18, 20 we learn that his father Amram was the *grandson* of Levi, and that he married Jochebed the *daughter* of Levi.

This looks as though there must have been a great disparity of age, belonging as they did to different generations.

But it is not until we look in the book of Numbers that we find there, in the remoter Context, the solution of the difficulty. There we read, in Num. xxvi. 59, that "the name of Amram's wife was Jochebed, the daughter of Levi, *whom her mother bare to Levi in Egypt.*"

Thus, Jochebed of the first generation would be about the same age as Amram of the second.

Dr. Blunt cites this to show that, as the object of Num. xxvi. 59 was not to explain this matter, we have an undesigned coincidence which establishes the veracity of the Scriptures. We cite it to show the importance of always noting and heeding the context.

5. Num. xvi. 1. *The Sons of Kohath and Reuben.*—In Num. xvi. 1 we read of the rebellion of Korah, Dathan, and Abiram, the sons of *Kohath* and *Reuben*.

Nothing is said as to why these should have joined together in the conspiracy. But in the remoter context of Num. iii. 29 we find that the tents of Kohath were pitched on the South side of the Tabernacle; and from Num. ii. 10 we find that the camp of Reuben was on the same (South) side also.

These statements are not made to *explain* how it was that Kohathites and Reubenites conspired together; but so it was, and so the difficulty is explained.

6. Num. xvi. 27. *The Sons of Korah.*—Again, from this chapter, Num. xvi., it reads as though all shared the same judgment.

But, in the nearer context we find the "sons" of Dathan and Abiram mentioned in verse 27. Korah himself and his "men" who conspired with him and his goods are mentioned also; but no mention is made of Korah's sons.

Then, in the remoter context, ten chapters later, we read in ch. xxvi. 11, "notwithstanding the sons of Korah died not."

Doubtless, therefore, they obeyed the call of Moses and Aaron (ch. xvi. 24) and "gat up" out of the Tabernacle which these rebels had set up; and so were delivered.

These "sons of Korah," thus rescued as brands from the burning, monuments of the grace of God, were in later days conspicuous in the prominence given to them and their descendants in the worship of the Temple, the "true Tabernacle" under David and Hezekiah.

7. Josh. iii. 15. *Jordan overflowing in time of harvest.*—In Josh. iii. 14—17 we have the crossing of the Jordan

described, and the parenthetical remark that it was in "the time of harvest" (*v.* 15).

In Josh. iv. 19 we read that it was also on "the tenth day of the first month." This was the season of the Passover, and of *barley* harvest, seven weeks before the Feast of Weeks, when the wheat harvest was celebrated (Exod. xxiii. 14.   Lev. xxiii. 15).

But, according to Exod. ix. 31, this was also the time of the *flax* harvest.

How wonderful, then, and how simple is the truth of the narrative in Josh. ii. 6, where we are told that Rahab hid Joshua's two spies beneath "*the stalks of flax.*"

8. 1 Sam. xiii. 19.   *No smith found in Israel.*—A brief statement in 1 Sam. xiii. 19 explains many circumstances when read in the light of remoter contexts.   There we read "*there was no smith found throughout all the land of Israel,*" and the reason is given as the result of the rigorous law of the Philistines, who oppressed Israel at that time, and held them in subjection.

This explains how it was that Ehud "made him a dagger. which had two edges"; and made it himself (Judg. iii. 16).

Shamgar had to use an *ox-goad* in his attack on the Philistines (Judg. iii. 31).

Samson "had nothing in his hand," no weapon, when he slew the lion (Judg. xiv. 5, 6).

There was not "a shield or spear seen among forty thousand in Israel" (Judg. v. 8).

In the days of Israel's liberty we read of men that "drew the sword;" but in the days of their oppression we read of *the sling and the stone* (Judg. xx. 2, 15.   1 Sam. xvii. 40) and other ignoble weapons.

Dr. Blunt cites all these as arguments for the veracity of Scripture.

We use them for another purpose; to show the necessity of having due regard to the remoter contexts of the Word of God in order to understand parenthetical remarks which are made, and left, without any explanation being given in the immediate context.

9. 1 Sam. xvii. 4.   "*Goliath of Gath.*"—In 1 Sam. xvii. 4 and 2 Sam. xxi. 18—22 "Gath" is spoken of and emphasized

as the city of Goliath, and of his brother and sons. It is mentioned incidentally, as needing no explanation.

But the explanation is found in the remoter context of Josh. xi. 21, 22, where we read of the utter destruction of the Anakim (or giants); and it is added that "there was none of the Anakim left in the land of Israel: only in Gaza, in *Gath*, and in Ashdod there remained."

10. 1 Kings xvii. 9. "*A little oil in a cruse*."—In 1 Kings xvii. 9 Elijah is commanded to get him to *Zarephath which belongeth to Zidon*, and dwell there; where a widow woman was to sustain him.

He goes to Zarephath and meets the widow, who says: "As the LORD thy God liveth, I have not a cake, but an handful of meal in a barrel, and *a little oil in a cruse*."

This Zarephath (in the New Testament called Sarepta) belonged to Zidon.

Now, from the remoter context (Josh. xix. 24—28), we find that the district of Zidon fell to the lot of *Asher;* and if we turn to another context, still more remote (Deut. xxxiii. 24), we learn that in the blessing of the Tribes by Moses it is written: "And of Asher he said:

Let Asher be blessed with children,
Let him be acceptable to his brethren,
And *let him dip his foot in oil*."

If this last sentence means anything, it denotes an abundance of olive trees and of oil, as the special characteristic of Asher's blessing.

This is just what we find in 1 Kings xvii. 9, where after three years and a half of drought there is still a little oil left; and that in the store of a widow who was probably only a small proprietor.

11. 2 Chron. xvii. 1. "*Jehoshaphat strengthened himself against Israel*."—The histories of Jehoshaphat king of Judah, and of Jehoram his son, furnish us with several illustrations.

There is first the nearer context, 2 Chron. xvii. 1, "And Jehoshaphat strengthened himself against Israel."

This is meant to exhibit the enormity of his sin when, in ch. xviii. 1, he married his son Jehoram to Athaliah, the daughter of Jezebel; who afterwards did for Judah what Jezebel had done for Israel.[1]

12. 2 Chron. xxii. 11, 12. *Joash, Jehosheba and nurse hidden six years in the Temple.*—The history of Jehoram goes on to tell us how he slew all his brethren (ch. xxi. 4); how the Arabians came and destroyed all his children, and left him "never a son, save Jehoahaz (*or* Ahaziah) the youngest of his sons" (ch. xxi. 17).

Then we are told that, when this Ahaziah died, his mother Athaliah "arose and destroyed all the seed royal of the house of Judah" (ch. xxii. 10).

We are told also how the infant Joash was rescued by Jehosheba, the wife of Jehoiada, the High Priest (ch. xxii. 11, 12); and how she and the nurse and the child were hid in the house of God for six years.

We marvel how such a thing could be; for, for aught that is said there, the worship of the Temple was still going on, and the difficulty of hiding these three for so long a time looks as though the thing were impossible.

If we had no regard to the remoter context we should see here an insuperable difficulty; but when we read the whole context we find that, like most of our other difficulties, they are made by ourselves!

It is not until we reach chapter xxiv. that we learn *what had previously taken place.*

Not until those six years had run their course, and Athaliah was slain, and Joash sat upon the throne of Judah, not until then does it come out (and even then, not at all for the purpose of solving our difficulty or removing our perplexity) that *in the previous reign* the house of God had been broken up, and all the vessels removed to the temple of Baal which had been established in Judah (ch. xxiv. 7).

Not until Joash begins to reign are we told this, and even then it is only to explain why Joash set himself to repair it by preparing timber and stones and masons and carpenters for the work (ch. xxiv. 12—14), and not to explain why Jehosheba, Joash, and his nurse found the house of the LORD such a safe hiding-place. These large

---

[1] See a pamphlet on *Jehosaphat: a Lesson for our Times,* by the same author.

preparations made by Joash for the repairs show the extent of the breaches which had been made; and tell us how that ruined and deserted Temple was *the safest place in the whole kingdom.*

13. 2 Chron. xxi. 10. *The revolt of Libnah.*—Another circumstance, mentioned quite parenthetically in 2 Chron. xxi. 10, and without any apparent object, throws a flood of light on the whole history when we compare it with its remoter context in the book of Joshua.

The revolt of Edom from under the hand of Jehoram king of Judah (2 Chron. xxi. 8—10) is not recorded as fulfilling prophecy; but it did, as we shall see if we look at the still more remote context of Gen. xxvii. 40.

The parenthetical remark in 2 Chron. xxi. 10 merely states the fact that at "the same time also did Libnah revolt from under his (Jehoram's) hand; because he had forsaken the LORD God of his fathers."

What is this remark thrown in here for? To tell us to look and see where and what Libnah was. We have to go back as far as Josh. xxi. 13, and there we find that Libnah was one of the cities of the Priests.

This tells us that when Jehoram and Athaliah broke up the Temple of God, and set up the house of Baal, the priests held aloof, and must have conspired to restore Joash to the throne as soon as the convenient time should come.

This explains why Jehoiada the High Priest had the chief part in the restoration of Joash and the execution of Athaliah, and the slaying of Mattan her priest of Baal (2 Chron. xxiii. 14—16).

This is why the priests took such a prominent part in collecting the money to repair and restore the House of the LORD (ch. xxiv. 4—11).

So that these references to the remoter context reveal all these truths, explain these difficulties, and throw a flood of light on the whole history.

14. 2 Kings xviii. 13, 14. *The depletion of Hezekiah's Treasury.*—In the history of Hezekiah we read (2 Kings xviii. 13—16) that his treasury had been depleted by the demands of the king of Assyria; for he had not only

given him what was in his own house, but he was reduced to the necessity of stripping the gold from the doors of the Temple.

Yet in Isa. xxxix. 2 we find Hezekiah showing the emissaries of Babylon all "the house of his precious things, the silver, and the gold, and the spices," etc.

No attempt is made to explain how this could be after so short an interval; and that interval covered by his sickness, and the siege of Jerusalem.

But there is one short passage, 2 Chron. xxxii. 22, 23, introduced there quite independently of all else:

"Thus·the LORD saved Hezekiah and the inhabitants of Jerusalem from the hand of Sennacherib the king of Assyria, and from the hand of all other, and guided them on every side. *And many brought gifts unto the LORD to Jerusalem, and presents to Hezekiah king of Judah: so that he was magnified in the sight of all the nations from henceforth."*

In addition to these presents there must have been vast spoils after Sennacherib's army had been destroyed, if we may judge from another remote context, in 2 Kings vii. 15, where, when the Syrians fled, "all the way was full of garments and vessels which the Syrians had cast away in their haste."

15. Isa. lxii. 4, 5. *Thy land shall be called Hephzibah.*—
In Isa. lxii. 2 we are told that in the day of Israel's future and coming glory both People and Land will be called by "a new name which the mouth of Jehovah shall name."

In verses 4, 5 we read of the giving of this new name:

"Thou shalt no more be termed 'Forsaken'; neither
    shall thy land any more be termed 'Desolate':
But thou shalt be called '*Hephzi-bah*' (i.e., *my delight
    is in her*)
And thy land '*Beulah*' (i.e., *married*).
For Jehovah delighteth in thee,
    And thy land shall be married.
For as a young man marrieth (i.e., *possesseth*) a
    virgin, so shall thy sons marry (i.e., *possess*) thee:
And as the bridegroom rejoiceth over the bride, so
    shall thy God rejoice over thee."

Now, when we remember that Isaiah prophesied in the days of Hezekiah, we may well conclude that this prophecy synchronized with the marriage of Hezekiah with his wife *Hephzibah* (2 Kings xxi. 1).

As to when this took place we have no record; but we do know that at the time he was stricken unto death (in the fourteenth year of his reign) he had no son; nor was Manasseh born until three of those miraculously added fifteen years had run their course.

The marriage of Hezekiah therefore occupies an important, not to say a solemn, place in his history; and might well be thus used in connection with another solemn crisis in the miraculous future history of Israel.

16. Jer. xiii. 18. *"Say . . . unto the Queen."*—In Jer. xiii. 18 we read "Say unto the king and unto *the Queen,* Humble yourselves, sit down; for your principalities shall come down, even the crown of your glory."

There is nothing in the prophecy to enable us to identify either the king or the queen. But in the remoter context of 2 Kings xxiv. we find that in the second of three invasions of Nebuchadnezzar, "Jehoiachin the king of Judah went out to the king of Babylon, he, and *his mother*, and his servants, and his princes and his officers; and the king of Babylon took him in the eighth year of his reign" (*v.* 12); and in verse 15 we read:

"And he carried away Jehoiachin to Babylon, and *the king's mother*, and the king's wives, and his officers, and the mighty of the land, those carried he into captivity from Jerusalem to Babylon."

Dr. Blunt suggests that as Jehoiachin was only eighteen and had reigned only three months (*v.* 8), the queen dowager held a position of some influence, which is sufficient to explain the reference of Jehovah to her by Jeremiah.

17. Mark xiv. 51, 52. *The young man who fled from Gethsemane.*—In Mark xiv. 51, 52, we read of the young man who followed Christ, and when they attempted to take him prisoner "he left the linen cloth and fled from them naked."

There is no indication here as to the identity of this young man.

But from the remoter contexts we learn .

(1) That the Lord was sleeping out at Bethany, each night during that last week (Luke xxi. 37; xxii. 39. Compare Matt. xxvi. 6). He would be staying there with Lazarus and Martha and Mary.

(2) On this night they would be watching for the Lord's return. And seeing the lights in the garden below the mount, what more natural than that Lazarus should go down to see what the tumult was about.

(3) We know from John xii. 10 that "the chief priests consulted that they might put Lazarus also to death." We read of *no one else* whom they wished to take, or to kill. All His disciples seem to have been quite safe. The reason for the decision to put Lazarus to death is given in John xii. 9—11.

(4) The linen cloth betokens considerable wealth. This the family possessed, judging from Matt. xxvi. 7, the purchase of *the very precious ointment* which excited the cupidity of Judas.

This garment must have been put on hastily and loosely, for it was left in the enemies' hands unceremoniously.

All these different contexts unite in helping us to identify this young man with Lazarus whom the Lord had raised from the dead.

18. John xxi. 15. "*Lovest thou me more than these?*"— In John xxi. 15 there is nothing to show us whom or what the Lord referred to by the pronoun "these": "Lovest thou me more than these?"

But in the remoter context of Matt. xxvi. 31, 33 and Mark xiv. 27, 29, we have the words of Peter, to which the Lord, doubtless, referred: "*All ye* shall be offended because of me this night . . . Peter answered and said unto him, Though all shall be offended because of thee, yet will I never (*i.e.*, in no wise) be offended."

From this it is clear that the pronoun "these" refers to Peter's fellow disciples; and the ellipsis must be sup-

plied, not "Lovest thou me more than [thou lovest] these";
but, Lovest thou me more than these [love me].

19. Acts ii. 16. "*This is that*."—Acts ii. 16—21 is an
illustration which affects the *remoter* context as well as
the *nearer*, because it is a quotation from Joel ii. 28—32.[1]
This fact makes àll the difference.

"This is that which was spoken by the prophet Joel"
(Acts ii. 16). There is nothing in these words to tell us
what is "this" and what is "that." The word "this" is
emphatic; and the word "but," with which the new argument begins, sets what follows in *contrast*, not in correspondence. It does not begin with the word "For," but
with the word "But." This points to the fact that the
quotation is intended to show that their enemies' charge
(that they were drunk) would not stand. So far from
such signs and wonders proving they were drunk, Peter
asks, What about the prophecy of Joel? He prophesied
of similar scenes "in the last days."

Peter does not say that these were the last days, but:—
"this is what Joel says" of those days. Will those scenes
(he argues) lie open to the same charge of drunkenness?
Certainly not! Then, how can these men be charged with
drunkenness now, especially "seeing it is but the third
hour of the day."

Peter is not expounding Joel. Nor is he saying that
that prophecy was then fulfilled. He does not say "then
was fulfilled"; or, "as it is written." He merely calls
attention to what Joel said of a similar scene, which is to
be fulfilled "in the last days."

That this is so is clear the moment we turn to the
prophet Joel, and read what Jehovah there speaks by
him.

To understand Joel's prophecy it is absolutely necessary
for us to see exactly what is the subject of it. What Dispensation is he speaking about? Is it about the Christian
Dispensation, or is it the Dispensation of Judgment which
shall follow it? Is it all about the Jew? or about the
Gentile? or, is it about the Church of God?

[1] Hebrew Text, iii. 1—5.

The Structure will give us the Scope. It is exceedingly simple :—

The Prophecy of Joel, as a whole.

A | i. 1—3. The Call to hear.

   B | i. 4—12. The evil which had come upon the Land and the People.

A | i. 13—ii. 17. The Call to Repentance.

   B | ii. 18—iii. 21. The evil removed from the Land and the People

We see, from this, what the prophecy of Joel is all about. It describes the fulfilment of the last clause of "the Song of Moses" in Deut. xxxii.,[1] which finishes up with the solemn but gracious assurance in *v.* 43 :

> "Rejoice, O ye nations, with *His People:*
> > For He will *avenge* the blood of His servants,
> > And will *render vengeance* to His adversaries,
> > And will be merciful unto His Land and to *His People.*"

So the member *B* (Joel ii. 18) begins—

> "Then will Jehovah be jealous for *His Land;*
> And pity *His People.*"

"THIS," therefore, is "THAT." This is the scope, or the subject-matter, or context of Acts ii. 16. It concerns Jehovah's "Land" and Jehovah's "People," and not "the Church of God." Peter addresses these "people": he says, "Ye men of Judea" (*v.* 14), "Ye men of Israel" (*v.* 22). He calls "the house of Israel" (*v.* 36) to this very *repentance* to which Joel calls in view of "the last days." For national repentance is ever declared to be the condition of national blessing.

But the key to the correct understanding of Peter's quotation lies in the word "afterward" of Joel ii. 28. After what? No one can tell us but Joel. We ourselves cannot tell apart from his prophecy.

We see that ch. ii. 28 is part of the member we have marked *B* (ch. ii. 18—iii. 21), the subject of which is *the*

---

[1] For the structure of "the Song of Moses" see *Commentary on Revelation*, republished by Kregel Publications, p. 470; or *Things to Come*, Vol. X., p. 55.

evil (of B, ch. i. 4—12) *removed from the Land and the People.*

The removal of this evil is elaborately set forth and described. The member *B* is no mere conglomeration or jumble of words and phrases. It has its own Structure as follows :—

Expansion of *B*. (Joel ii. 18—iii. 21.)

B   a^1 | ii. 18, 19.   Blessings bestowed.   (Temporal.)

     b^1 | ii. 20.   Evil removed.   (Judgment prophesied.)

   a^2 | ii. 21—29.   Blessing bestowed.   (Temporal and Spiritual.)

     b^2 | ii. 30, 31.   Evil removed.   (Accompanying Judgment signs.)

   a^3 | ii. 32.   Blessing bestowed.   (Spiritual.)

     b^3 | iii. 1—16-.   Evil removed.   (Fulfilment.)[1]

   a^4 | iii.-16—18.   Blessings bestowed.   (Spiritual and Temporal.)

     b^4 | iii. 19.   Evil removed.   (Judgment executed.)

   a^5 | iii. 20, 21.   Blessing bestowed.   (Spiritual.)

These "*Blessings bestowed*" must be read on from one to the other; and the "Evil removed" must, in like manner, be connected; the members relating to the "*Evil removed*" being treated as parenthetical to the members which treat of "*Blessing bestowed*," and the "*Blessing bestowed*" members being treated as parenthetical to the "*Evil removed*" members.

From the above Structure we see that ch. ii. 28 is contained in the member marked "a^2," and is not a separate member to be treated parenthetically; but it

---

[1] The expansion of "b^3" (iii. 1—16) is just as perfect and beautiful :—

```
b³ | c¹ | d¹ | iii. 1, 2-  Assemblage.
   |    |      e¹ | -2—6.  Judgment.
   |    |           f¹ | 7, 8.  Threatening.
   |    c² | d² | 9—12-.  Assemblage.
   |    |      e² | -12.  Judgment.
   |    |           f² | 13.  Execution.
   |    c³ | d³ | 14 .  Assemblage.
   |    |      e³ | -14.  Judgment.
   |    |           f³ | 15, 16.  Threatening.
```

connects the Spiritual blessing with the temporal, and shows that it follows on from it.

This Spiritual blessing is introduced by the words:

> "And it shall come to pass AFTERWARD that I will pour out my Spirit upon all flesh (*v.* 28).

After what?

After the Temporal blessings of
> The former and latter rain (*v.* 23).
> The fulness of the threshing floors and of the wine and oil-presses (*v.* 24).
> The plenty[1] and satisfaction (*v.* 26).
> The entire and perpetual removal of shame (*vv.* 26, 27).
> When Jehovah shall be "in the midst of Israel" (*v.* 27).

It is "afterward"; after all these temporal blessings, that these Spiritual blessings shall be bestowed.

This is "afterward"; *when* the Spirit shall be poured out "upon all flesh."

The most cursory reader must see and know that the Spirit was NOT poured out upon *all flesh* in Acts ii., but only on those then present: that none of these wondrous and great signs had been shown: that deliverance was not manifested in Mount Zion and in Jerusalem; for the Land and the People were still in the power of the Romans.

This word "AFTERWARD" thus shows that the prophecy of Joel in Acts ii. is not quoted in order to prove that this Pentecostal scene was the fulfilment of it; but in order to show that, as that future scene could not be ascribed to drunkenness, so neither could this Pentecostal scene be so ascribed.

At least, a child could see that Acts ii. is not the fulfilment of Joel ii.; but it is hopeless for those to see it whose eyes are blinded by believing the tradition of those who persist in saying that "the Church was formed at Pentecost."

---

[1] Heb., "Eat to eat and be satisfied." The infinitive of the verb following its own finite, *i.e., eat and eat* is most expressive and emphatic.

They not only say this with great assurance; but they lay it down as an article of faith; and are ready to excommunicate any who do not believe it.

But this is only the Tradition of the Brethren; not even the Tradition of the Fathers   though it just as surely makes void the Word of God.

There can be no mistake about Joel's word "afterward." The Holy Spirit by Peter interprets it as of "the last days."   The Hebrew is not the simple אַחַר ('āchar), *after* (Gen. v. 4),[1] but it is this, compounded with כֵן (kēn), *so*, or *thus* (Gen. i. 7), referring always to what follows. It is אַחֲרֵי־כֵן ('acharey-kēn), *after that* (Gen. vi. 4; vii. 14; xxiii. 19; xli. 30. 1 Sam. ix. 13, etc., etc.).

It is thus perfectly certain that the word "this" in Acts ii. 16 refers *to what follows,* and *not to what precedes:* to the yet future events prophesied by Joel, and not to the events then taking place at Jerusalem.

The word "this" is an emphatic pronoun. But there is no similarly emphatic pronoun for the word "that." It is simply the article with the perfect passive participle:— "This (that follows) is what has been said by the prophet Joel." Not "this" (which has happened); for, in that case, what could be the "this"? This apparent drunkenness? There was no "this," preceding. It would be these events; these phenomena; these Pentecostal scenes. But it is *Singular,* "this," agreeing with the Scripture about to be quoted from Joel.

The word "*this*" could not, and cannot, refer to these Pentecostal scenes; for no gift of tongues was spoken of by Joel.

It could not refer to the pouring-out foretold by Joel, because here, this pouring-out was only on the Apostles; whereas Joel speaks of it being poured upon "all flesh." There is not a word said in Acts ii. about any of their "sons and daughters" prophesying; or of their "old men" dreaming dreams; or of their "young men" seeing visions; or of their "servants and handmaids" receiving spiritual gifts.

In fact there is in Acts ii. no *fulfilment* at all of Joel's prophecy, either implied or expressed.

---

[1] In these and all similar references to the meaning of a word in the Original we give **the First Occurrence** of it. See Canon V., Part II.

There is nothing beyond the argument that the charge
of drunkenness could no more be brought against these
present Pentecostal scenes than against those yet future
scenes connected with the blessings to be bestowed upon
Israel, prophesied of by Joel, as what should take place
"afterward": *i.e., after* all those temporal blessings have
been bestowed on Israel's Land and on Israel's People.

20. 1 Cor. xi. 10.   *"Power on her head."*—"For this
cause ought the woman to have power (see margin) on
her head because of the angels."

"Power" is put by *Metonymy* for the vail which was
the symbol of being under her husband's power.

For this we have to go to the very remote context of
Gen. vi. 1, 4, where we learn by comparing 2 Pet. ii. 4 and
Jude 6 the reason for this injunction. (See Canon I.,
pp. 192, 193 above, and notes on "angel" and "spirit,"
pp. 191, 219.)

21. Gal. iii. 15—17.   *The four hundred, and the four
hundred and thirty years.*—The subject of these verses
is the "promise" or unconditional Covenant which God
made with Abraham.

This was four hundred and thirty years before the
giving of the Law (Exod. xii. 40).

When the four hundred years are mentioned they are
reckoned from Abraham's "seed," which was Isaac, who
was not born till thirty years later (Gen. xv. 13[1] and
Acts vii. 6).

22. Gal. iii. 20.   *"God is one."*—"Now a mediator is not
a mediator of one, but God is one."

Verse 19, compared with the remoter contexts of Acts
vii. 53. Deut. xxxiii. 2. Ps. lxviii. 17. Heb. ii. 2, shows that
the Law was given by a mediator.

Now where there is a mediator there must be two
parties to a covenant.

But in Gen. xv. there was only one party; and that was
God. When Abraham was about to take part in making the
Covenant according to the custom (Jer. xxxiv. 18, 19), God
put him to sleep (Gen. xv. 12), and passed between the
pieces Himself, alone (*v.* 17).   He was "one;" one party,

---

[1] See above, under Parentheses, p. 58.

alone in the "promise." That Covenant is not only prior to the Law as to time, but was superior to it because it was unconditional.

23. Heb. xii. 17. *"No place of repentance."*—"For ye know how, afterward, when he would have inherited the blessing, he was rejected : for he found no way to change his [father's] mind (see margin) though he sought it carefully with tears."

To what does the pronoun "it" refer? What was "it" that Esau sought so carefully?

The context (and especially the remoter context of Gen. xxvii. 34, 36, 38) clearly shows that it was the "blessing" which he sought.

CANON 5

The First Occurance of Words, Expressions, and Utterances Are Generally Essential to Their Interpretation

This is a law we have long since noticed, and have never yet found it to fail. The first occurrence of a Word, or an Expression, or an Utterance is the key to its subsequent usage and meaning; or at least a guide as to the essential point connected with it.

We propose to consider this Law as illustrated in these three classes:—

i. Words.
ii. Expressions.
iii. Utterances.

i. WORDS.

1. *Prophet.*—The first occurrence of the word Prophet is in Gen. xx. 7, and is used by God to Abimelech king of Gerar, of Abraham—

> "Now therefore restore the man his wife; for he is a prophet and he shall pray for thee."

This first occurrence of the word shows that it is used in a very different sense from that in which we use it to-day.

Of course, even apart from this, our present usage is of no account in determining the Biblical usage.

We use it of one whose sole mission is to *foretell* future events.

But, here, it is used in connection with Abraham, who foretold nothing; and of whose prophecies, as such, we have neither mention, allusion, or record.

The only thing associated with the prophet, in Abraham, here, is *prayer!*

This first occurrence, therefore, speaks to us if we have ears to hear; and, being so contrary to our current usage, tells us to search further and see what it teaches us in connection with its other occurrences.

We soon learn from Exod. vii. 1 that the same God calls Aaron, Moses's "prophet." This takes us a step further; and leads to another question: How could one man be another man's "prophet"? The answer is found in Exod. iv. 16, where God, referring to the same matter, says of Aaron, to Moses, "He shall be thy spokesman."

Here, then, we learn that the essential interpretation of the word "prophet" is *spokesman*. So that the prophet was one who spoke FOR God, whether by way of Exhortation, Instruction, Reproof, Warning, Correction, Reprobation, or Judgment. Foretelling was only a very small part of his duties.

There was "no prophet greater than John the Baptist" (Matt. xi. 9—11). He prophesied that Christ should baptize with *pneuma hagion*, but where are his prophecies, as we understand the word, to-day? Not one is recorded. But he was God's *spokesman*, prepared, equipped, and sent forth by God to prepare the way of the Messiah (Luke i. 13—17, 76—79).

The prophet, therefore, was essentially *God's spokesman;* and his sole mission was to speak only those words which were given him to speak.

In this sense Moses was the great prophet typical of the Lord Jesus. Seven times in the closing words of Exodus we find the refrain associating Moses's words and deeds with his obedience, "*as the Lord commanded Moses*" (Exod. xl. 19, 21, 23, 25, 27, 29, 32).

Even so the Lord Jesus was "the prophet like unto Moses." Why? Not because of His foretelling future events, but because "He whom God sent speaketh the words of God" (John iii. 34. Compare John iii. 32; vii. 16, 26, 28; xv. 15, etc.).

For the same reason "prophets" were bestowed upon the Church at the beginning (Eph. iv. 11); "*for (πρός, pros*) the perfecting of the Saints *with a view to* (εἰς, *eis*) the work of the ministry for (εἰς, *eis*) the building up of the body of Christ." (See above, pages 53, 54.) This was the special object of the New Testament prophetic ministry (compare Eph. ii. 20. Rom. xvi. 26, "prophetic writings," 2 Pet. i. 19, "the prophetic[1] word").

The work of these prophets was specially connected with the making known the "Mystery" or the great secret, which had been "hid in God." (See above, p. 257.)

---

[1] In both these passages the Greek has the adjective, not the noun.

It is a great mistake to suppose that Eph. ii. 20 refers to the Old Testament Prophets; and that the Church is built upon them! There is abundant evidence as to the New Testament order of Prophets; and that they were charged with quite a different mission, though they were God's spokesmen: Barnabas (Acts iv. 36), Stephen (Acts vi. 10, 15), Agabus (Acts xi. 28; xxi. 10), Silvanus, Silas, and Judas (Acts xv. 32), Manaen and Lucius of Cyrene (Acts xiii. 1), Timothy (1 Tim. vi. 11; 2 Tim. iii. 17), the daughters of Philip (Acts xxi. 9), and others, unnamed (Acts viii. 17; x. 44—46; xix. 6).

The Exhortations addressed to and connected with the prophets are also special. "Despise not prophesyings" shows that the word "spirit" in the preceding clause refers to the spiritual gift of prophesying (1 Thess. v. 20); and "Quench not the spirit" means, Do not stifle or suppress such spiritual gifts in others.

Examples of this prophetic power in action and teaching, etc., are seen in Acts v. 4; xiii. 2; xxi. 1—14. 1 Cor. xiv. 24, 25. 1 Tim. i. 18; iv. 1.

Thus, the first occurrence of the word "prophet" leads us into all this line of teaching, and shows us that the Preposition πρό (*pro*), *before*, is not used with regard to *time*, but to *manner;* not to speaking beforehand, or telling-before, but *telling forth.*

Moreover, we may note there was no place for the ministry of prophets till the priests had failed in their mission, which was to teach the Word of God. When the priests became absorbed in their ritual, then God raised up prophets as His spokesmen. Hence a prophet was known as a "Man of God" (see page 314 below).

2. "*Hallelujah*."—This Hebrew word occurs twenty-eight times, and is eleven times transliterated "Hallelujah," or, according to the Greek spelling in the New Testament, "Alleluia"; and is nineteen times translated, "Praise ye the Lord."

But our question now is to ask, Where is the first occurrence of this word? and by it to discover not merely the meaning of the word, but its significance and interpretation.

It is found first at the end of Ps. civ.; and, its position there leaves us in no doubt as to its true interpretation. It is associated with praise for deliverance from, and for the destruction of, enemies—

"Let sinners be consumed out of the earth,
And let the wicked be no more.
Bless Jehovah, O my soul,
Hallelujah" (Ps. civ. 35).

Its first occurrence in the New Testament is in precisely the same connection (Rev. xix. 1, 3):—

"HALLELUJAH,
Salvation, and glory and honour, and power
Unto the Lord our God.
For true and righteous are His judgments:
For He hath judged the great whore which did corrupt the earth with her fornication,
And hath avenged the blood of His servants at her hand.
And again they said HALLELUJAH."[1]

The word is thus associated with the thought of judgment: not necessarily every time; for praise must be rendered for many things: but this is its first great theme.

This thought will not be repugnant to those who "rightly divide the Word of truth," and understand such "praise." Though it is out of harmony in this Dispensation of grace, it is quite in keeping with the past Dispensation of works and the coming Dispensation of Judgment. (See pages 110, 111.)

3. "*Selah.*"—The first occurrence of this word furnishes us with the key to its meaning.

All explanations of it which have been given, and have been derived from sources *outside the Word of God*, are worthless. They are only what men have thought; and have never risen above musical notation.

No meaning has hitherto been suggested that is worthy of the dignity of the Inspired Word; or that is connected with the truth, teaching, or subject-matter of the Scriptures.

---

[1] This is the Figure *Epanadiplosis*. See *Figures of Speech*, page 245.

Some have said that it always marks the end of a Strophe; others that it marks the beginning. Both are wrong, being only a part of the truth; and, as is so often the case in other departments of Bible study, when a part is put for the whole the result is error instead of truth.

The word *Selah* may be derived from one of two roots: either from סָלָה (*sālāh*), *to pause*, and, though this may well apply to the pausing of the heart and mind to dwell on the words of God, yet man seems unable to rise above the thought of the musical instruments pausing, while the voices go on. On the other hand, some derive it from סָלַל (*sālal*), *to lift up;* but they limit this to lifting up the voices in song, and do not rise to the lifting up of the heart.

The word *Selah* occurs seventy-four times in the Old Testament: seventy-one times in the Book of Psalms and three times in the Prophecy of Habakkuk.

Of these it occurs several times in the middle of a verse; which is a proof that it need neither commence nor end a Paragraph or Strophe.

The key will be furnished by its first occurrence, in Ps. iii., where it occurs three times—

> (1) Between verses 2 and 3.
> (2) Between verses 4 and 5.
> (3) Between Psalms iii. and iv.

Here, it will be seen that the word is used as a *connecting link*, calling our attention to what has been said, and bidding us to associate it with what immediately follows.

This may be for various purposes:

> (1) It may be by way of *contrast*.
> (2) It may be by way of further *explanation*.
> (3) It may be to mark a *cause*, or an *effect;* or,
> (4) It may be at the end of a Psalm, in which case it connects the two Psalms and tells us that they relate to the same authorship, or have the same subject-matter.

In this first occurrence (Ps. iii.) we have three of these usages.

The first *Selah* (between verses 2 and 3) contrasts what the many said of David:

"There is no help for him in God,"

with what David could say to the LORD:

"But Thou, O Jehovah, art a shield for me."

Here the "many" are thus put into contrast with the one; and, while the many knew the Divine being only as "God" (the creator),[1] David knew Him as "Jehovah," his Covenant God, the God to Whom he stood in a covenant relation.[2]

The second *Selah* (between verses 4 and 5) marks and connects the cause and effect. It is a practical exhibition of the truth afterwards revealed in Phil. iv. 6, 7.

"Let your requests be made known unto God,
And
God's peace . . . shall keep your heart and mind."

This is what David experienced, practically, in that terrible night, in his flight from Jerusalem:

"I cried unto God with my voice,
And He heard me out of His holy hill.
Selah
I laid me down and slept; I awaked:
For Jehovah sustained me."

The third *Selah* (between the two Psalms iii. and iv.) connects not merely the two verses (Ps. iii. 8 and iv. 1), but the two Psalms, as such. It tells us that Ps. iv. relates to the same time, and to the same circumstances in David's life: and gives us further details as to what the cry and the prayer was that is referred to in Ps. iii.

Having thus got the key to the *usage* of the word *Selah*, which is of far greater importance than its Etymology or Lexical meaning, we can apply it to all its other occurrences.

It is, in fact, another example of our third Canon (page 227 above), where the Biblical usage of words is

---

[1] The first occurrence of the word "God," in Gen. i. 1, shows that this is the essence of its meaning.

[2] This is shown by the first occurrence of Jehovah, in Gen. ii. 4, at the commencement of the section (or *Toledôth*), "the generations of the heavens and the earth," when God (as Jehovah Elohim) comes into Covenant relation with Adam, whom He had created.

considered as being essential to their correct interpretation.[1]

4. *"Jerusalem."*—The first occurrence of the word "Jerusalem" is in Judg. i. 7, 8. And in one sentence the whole subsequent history of centuries is condensed.

"The children of Judah had fought against Jerusalem, and had taken it, and smitten it with the edge of the sword, and set the city on fire."

This is in strange contrast with its name:—*The Vision of Peace!* But it is in accordance with its history.

It has been a history of sieges. Some twenty-seven times has it been besieged, three times has the city, and twice its temple, been destroyed by fire.[2]

But it is yet to be the centre and symbol of peace. Peace shall be the eternal character and blessedness of Jerusalem, in spite of her past history, as foreshadowed in the first occurrence of the name. (See Ps. cxxii. 6—8; cxxv. 5; cxxviii. 6. Isa. xxxii. 17; liv. 12; lx. 17; lxvi. 12. Hag. ii. 9.)

5. *Numbers.*—The Spiritual Significance of numbers is seen in their first occurrence.

One is associated with Deity (Gen. i. 3, 4). "God is light" (1 John i. 5).

Two is associated with Separation and Division (Gen. i. 6—8), though afterwards it is associated with *union* in testimony (Deut. xvii. 6. Rev. xi. 3).

Three is associated with resurrection in Gen. i. 9, when the earth rises up out of and above the waters; and fruit arises out of the earth.

Four is associated with the earth when (Gen. i. 14—19) the Sun and Moon were established as light-holders, to "give light upon the Earth."

Five is associated with grace, in the gift of life, in the creation of living creatures; and in the production of life out of the waters of the great deep.

Six is associated with the creation of Man (Gen. i. 26—31). Man was created on the *sixth* day; and hence six

---

[1] For further examination and study of all the *Selahs* the reader may consult Part II. of the work on *The Psalm-Titles*, by the same author .

[2] See *Number in Scripture*, republished by Kregel Publications, pp. 236-240.

is man's "Hall-mark"; and, with its multiples, is stamped upon all that characterizes man as falling short of God; or in opposition to or defiance of God.

Goliath was 6 cubits high; his spear's head weighed 600 shekels of iron; and he had 6 pieces of armour enumerated.

Nebuchadnezzar was similarly marked. His image was 60 cubits high, and 6 cubits wide, while 6 instruments of music called for its universal worship.

The Beast is marked by the threefold combination of 666 (Rev. xiii).

Seven is associated with Divine Blessing and Rest (Gen. ii. 1—3), and is thus the mark of the Spirit of God as "the author and giver of life," and blessing, and rest. Hence it is that this number is so frequent in Scripture, as being the "Hall mark" of the Spirit's authorship of "the Word of life."

Eight is a new first and, like the Number Three, is associated with newness, especially in resurrection, which took place on "the first day of the week." It first occurs in Gen. v. 4 in the number of the years of Adam, the end of the first man. "The second man" began his resurrection life on the eighth day. Hence the association of the number with resurrection.

Nine occurs first in Lev. xxv. 22, and is used of *the end of full time.* Inasmuch as the fulness of time issues in judgment for good or evil, so *nine* becomes the symbol or *hall-mark* of all that stands connected with judgment.

Ten is the great cardinal number, completing one order and commencing a new one. Hence it is used of ordinal perfection, and is so used in its first occurrence in Gen. xxiv. 55.

Twelve is associated with service, rule, and Government. "Twelve years they *served*" (Gen. xiv. 4). Henceforth we find 12 and its multiples connected with *Government* both in heaven and on earth. It is the factor in the heavenly Signs, Constellations, and Measurements. It is the factor in all earthly enumerations that have to do with government.[1]

Thirteen first occurs in Gen. xiv. 4 also, "Twelve years they served Chedorlaomer and the thirteenth year they

---

[1] See *Number in Scripture*, republished by Kregel Publications, p. 253.

rebelled." So that ever after, in Scripture, the Number 13, and every multiple of it, is associated with *rebellion, apostacy,* and *disintegration.*[1] It is universally a number of evil omen: but those who go back for the origin of anything never go back far enough. They go back, in their own imagination, to the Twelve Apostles and our Lord as making 13; but the first occurrence of the number takes us back to the Divine usage of the Word, Gen. xiv. 4.[2]

6. *The Divine Names and Titles* are determined in the same way by their first occurrence.

GOD (Gen. i. 1). "In the beginning God *created*." Hence whenever we meet with the name of God we may always associate with it the thought of the *Creator*, and its appropriate use by His *creatures* (see p. 309).

LORD or Jehovah (Gen. ii. 4) first occurs as the special title used in the first of the Eleven *Toledōth* or "Generations." It is the Creator standing *in Covenant relation*, and in communication with those whom He had created.

Most High, or *Elyon*, occurs first in Gen. xiv. 18, and is associated with God as being "the possessor of Heaven and Earth." This is the essence of the meaning wherever we afterwards find it; and this will give the Scope of the passage in which we find it.[3]

ii. EXPRESSIONS.

The same is true not only of separate *Words*, but of a combination of words in such expressions as "Son of Man," "Man of God," "Day of the Lord," etc.

1. *"The Son of Man."*[4]—This expression is first met with in Psalm viii. And if we wish to know what its distinctive significance is we must note its associations.

There we find, from the first and last verses, that it is "the earth" which is in question, and that it is "dominion" in the earth which is the scope of the

---

[1] See *Number in Scripture*, republished by Kregel Publications, pp. 205-233.

[2] See further information as to this and other numbers in *Number in Scripture*.

[3] See *The Divine Names and Titles* for a complete view of the subject by the same author.

[4] See *Divine Names and Titles*, p. 140.

Psalm as a whole. It is universal dominion over all the works of God's hands.

This then is the special thought to be borne in mind whenever we subsequently meet with this title.

Not "a son of man," for every mortal being is that, as a descendant of Adam. Ezekiel is constantly so called. "A son of man" is the converse of "a son of God."

There is just the same difference between "a son of God" and "the Son of God" as there is between "a son of Man" and "the Son of Man."

"The Son of Man" is the special title of the Lord Jesus, in connection with His right and title to universal dominion in the earth; and as having had all things placed as a footstool for His feet, when the time comes for Him to exercise that right.

At the present moment, according to the Divine Counsels "we see NOT YET all things put under Him" (Heb. ii. 8); but we shall see them in due time, when "He shall come whose right it is" to reign (Isa. xxxii. 1. Ezek. xxi. 27).

It was as "the Son of Man" that He came unto His own dominion. But His own people "received Him not" (John i. 11), hence His title is associated with His humiliation.

The first New Testament occurrence is full of significance. It is in Matt. viii. 20; where we are told that "the Son of Man" had not where to lay His head on that earth which was His by right.

This title, in perfect harmony with that first occurrence, is used eighty times in the four Gospels, not once in the Church Epistles; once in Acts vii. 56; once (and then only as a quotation) in the Epistle to the Hebrews. It does not reappear until the Apocalypse, twice (ch. i. 13; xiv. 14). There, at the crisis, when the moment arrives for executing judgment in the *earth*, He is seen and described as "the Son of Man"; no longer in humiliation, no longer wearing a crown of thorns, but "having on His head a golden crown" (Rev. xiv. 14—16).

The fact that this title never once occurs in the Epistles that are addressed to churches speaks loudly to those who have ears to hear; for it declares that we, as the members of the Body of Christ, have no more connection with Him by the title of "the Son of Man," than had the Syro-Phœnician woman with Him as "The Son of David" (Matt. xv. 21—24). Hence, it follows, that the Church of God must be rightly divided off, and excluded from all portions of those Scriptures where the Lord Jesus bears this title of "the Son of Man." The use of that title is sufficient proof in itself that the Scope of all such passages where it occurs is *dominion in the earth;* and not glory in the heavens.

2. *"The Man of God."*—We find this expression used twice of Timothy in the New Testament (1 Tim. vi. 11. 2 Tim. iii. 17). And if we ask for the exact essence and force of the expression; and what is the teaching conveyed in it, we have to ask for its first occurrence.

We find it in Deut. xxxiii. 1: "This is the blessing wherewith Moses the man of God blessed the children of Israel before his death."

This blessing is a great prophecy: and Moses, in this Book, is spoken of as being that Prophet, like unto whom Christ was to be hereafter raised up (Deut. xviii. 15).

This title "Man of God" came to be the popular description or title of the prophet, and we meet with it, as being so used, throughout the historical books of the Old Testament. What this teaches us will be further seen under our next Canon, as to the importance of the *place,* in Scripture, where we meet with certain expressions, in addition to the first place in which we find it.[1]

3. *"The Day of the Lord."*—This we have already considered in part, under Part I. § iv. (p. 158). It only remains, here, to show that what we have there said is based upon what we learn from its first occurrence.

We meet with it first in Isa. ii. 11, 12.

"The lofty looks of man shall be humbled,
    And the haughtiness of men shall be bowed down,
    And the LORD alone shall be exalted in that Day.
    For the Day of the LORD of hosts shall be upon
        every one that is proud," etc.

---

[1] See a pamphlet on *The Man of God*, by the same author.

Here we have the essence of the expression. Whatever may be the marks and accompaniments of that Day; whatever may be its judgments and plagues and terrors, they have all only one twofold object;

The abasement of Man and

The exaltation of God.

This is their object and this is the great and final result.

Now, it is "Man's day" (1 Cor. iv. 3, margin). Man is judging. But "the Lord's Day" is coming, when He will be the judge. John is carried away by the Spirit and shown the future judgment scenes in the visions which are described in the Apocalypse: so that we can there read about the unveiling and exaltation of Christ, and the abasement of man in that day.[1]

iii. UTTERANCES.

1. *The first Utterance of the Old Serpent.*

In Gen. iii. 1 the Old Serpent is introduced to us as already fallen, and his first words are intended to impress us with the fact that, the special sphere of his activities is not the *criminal* sphere; not the sphere of *immorality*; but it is the *Religious* sphere: it is the sphere which has the *Word of God* for the great object of attack.

The first utterance of Satan, as the Old Serpent, was to question the truth of the Word of God. "He said unto the woman,

> *Yea, God hath said ye shall not eat of every tree of the garden,*"

It is not certain whether this should be a question or a statement. The woman's answer appears to regard it as a statement, by meeting it with a denial and an explanation.

And the woman said unto the Serpent

> "*We may eat of the fruit of the trees of the garden,*" etc,

---

[1] See the pamphlets *The Lord's Day* and *Four Prophetic Periods*, by the same author.

But we are concerned now with the subject of Satan's first utterance.

It is about the Word and truth of God. God had spoken. Shall man believe what He has said?

This fact speaks to us if we have ears to hear.

It bids us look for Satan's sphere of influence to-day, not in the Police Courts, but in the Pulpits; not in the Newspapers, but in Sermons; not on the Stage, but in our Universities; not in our streets, but in the Professors' Chairs at our Theological Colleges.

Time was when Infidels carried on a platform campaign of lectures against the Word of God. In our day this has practically ceased. There is no further need for it; the work is more effectually done in the Pulpit by Theological Infidels, who have "turned away their ears from the truth and are turned unto myths" (2 Tim. iv. 3, 4). Treating the Word of God as "unhistorical" and its records as "fables," they teach the myths of men instead of obeying the command to "Preach the word."

This is what we learn from this first utterance of the Old Serpent.

With this we ought to couple

2. *The First Ministerial Utterance of the Lord Jesus.*

We have it in Matt. iv. 4; immediately after His consecration for His office of Prophet.

The Old Serpent comes to the Second man, the last Adam, not in a garden of delights, but in the wilderness. He questions again the truth of God's words, the echo of which, "This is my beloved son," had scarcely died away:—"*If thou be the Son of God.*"

What are the words of the Lord's reply.

"IT IS WRITTEN."

This is the Lord's first ministerial utterance.

Could language tell us more pointedly and plainly that we are again on the same battle-field in which the truth of God's Word is at stake?

"It is written." What was written? What can be written but *words?* How can it be possible to have *writing* apart from *words?*

And yet there are those that tell us that the Bible "*contains* the Word of God," but that it "is not the Word of God." That its thoughts are inspired, but not its words. But again we ask, How can thoughts be written down without words? It is by words, and only by words that thoughts can be made known.

When Milton dictated his poems to his amanuensis, did he communicate his *thoughts* and leave his *words* to the choice of another? Are not the actual *words*, and even the spelling and rhythm of them, vital to the whole matter? Are not the choice of the words and the scanning of their syllables the very essence of what made the result Milton's, and not that of his amanuensis?

"IT IS WRITTEN."

This is an utterance which settles such questions for ever; and closes the mouth of Satan and all "his ministers" (2 Cor. xi. 15).

At least, it closed the mouth of Satan; though men's mouths will be open and vent their blasphemies until they are closed in judgment.

Three times did the Lord Jesus use that first utterance, "It is written," and three times did He utter *no other than the words written*, until He dismissed the Old Serpent with the rebuke: "Get thee hence, Satan."

Is it not as significant as it is remarkable, that when the Lord delivered up His trust, having finished the work which was given Him to do, He again, three times, referred to God's Word written, in John xvii.:

"Thy word is truth" (*v.* 17).
"I have given them Thy Word" (*v.* 14).
"I have given unto them the words which Thou gavest me" (*v.* 8)?

Does not this fact speak to us? Surely the fact that the Lord's ministry began and ended with a three-fold reference to the Word of God emphatically assures us that—

THE BEGINNING AND END OF ALL MINISTRY IS
THE WORD OF GOD.

3. *The first utterance of the Lord as the Son of Man.*

This also is important, as distinct from this first official and ministerial utterance.

He must have spoken from the time that all children speak. But not one syllable has the Holy Spirit written down until twelve years had passed by; and then, not another until eighteen years later.

Only one utterance of the Lord Jesus through all those thirty years of His earthly life as the Son of Man.

It was this:

> "Wist ye not that I must be about my Father's business?" (Luke ii. 49).

It was in the form of a question which Joseph and Mary could neither understand—nor answer.

It was a rebuke; for Mary had spoken of "thy father and I." The Lord speaks of "I" and "My Father."

No utterance could have more fully, completely or beautifully summed up His whole mission—which had been, centuries before, written "in the Volume of the Book," concerning Him (Ps. xl. 7. Heb. x. 7).

> "Lo I come to do Thy will, O my God."

And, when we compare with this His last recorded utterance as the Son of Man, no language can describe its fulness of meaning, its significance, and its importance:

> "It is finished."

What was finished? *The Father's business which He came to be about!*

4. *The First Questions in the Old and New Testaments.*

We have already seen (page 315) that the words of the Old Serpent in Gen. iii. 1 are, probably, not to be regarded as a question.

In that case the first question in the Old Testament is put by Jehovah Elohim to the lost sinner (Gen. iii. 9)—

> "Where art thou?"

This question reveals to Adam his lost and ruined condition; and makes way for the promise of the needed Saviour which is given in verse 15.

Then the first question in the New Testament (Matt. ii. 2) is put by those who are seeking that Saviour—

> "Where is He?"

In these two questions we have the object of the two Testaments. The Old, which ministers law and condemnation, is intended to convict the sinner of his sin and to show him his need; the New, which ministers grace, is intended to bring peace and blessing in the gift of the Saviour whom God has provided, anointed, given, and sent.

"Where is He?" Where is that Saviour who has been promised? Where is the Saviour of whom I, as a lost sinner, have discovered my need?

5. *The Holy Spirit's first Interpretation of Prophecy.*

The first interpretation of a prophecy written in the Old Testament and fulfilled in the New must furnish us with a key to the interpretation and understanding of all other prophecies.

It occurs in Matt. i. 22, 23, and the way in which the Holy Spirit, who inspired it through Isaiah, records His own fulfilment of it by Matthew must needs be full of instruction.

We have gone into this very fully in our work on *Number in Scripture* (pages 63—67), so that it is not necessary to repeat it here. We only recommend the study of this first example of interpretation as being a guide to the way in which we should approach the interpretation of other prophecies.

CANON 6

The Place Where the Passage Occurs Is Often Essential to Its Full Interpretation

Some passages of Scripture derive their chief importance from the *revelation* of a great truth which is made in them.

Some derive their chief importance from certain *words* employed in that revelation.

But others derive their chief importance from the *place* where we find them written.

It is well, therefore, for us always to notice and see whether this last is the case with any passage which we may be considering.

We must ask: Why is this passage or verse here? Why is it in this Book, or in this Epistle? Why is it not in some other Book or Epistle?

This, it will be seen, is closely connected with our Canon IV. as to the Context being always essential to correct interpretation: for, the examination of the place where a Scripture is written involves giving this attention to the Context.

Yet it is distinct; for it has a special object in view, instead of a general object.

Let us give a few illustrations.

1.—2 Tim. iii. 16, 17: "All Scripture is given by inspiration of God, and is profitable for doctrine, for reproof, for correction, for instruction in righteousness; that the man of God may be perfect, thoroughly furnished unto all good works."

This passage is remarkable for all three of the reasons given above.

It is remarkable for its wondrous revelation of the claim that the Scriptures are the *gift of God;* and that they are "God-breathed."

It is remarkable also for certain *words* employed in this revelation of truth:

Especially for the word θεόπνευστος (*theopneustos*), *God-breathed*, which is rendered by the five English words, "given-by-inspiration-of-God."

It is remarkable also for the expression "the man of God," which is the Hebrew idiom for the prophet, as being God's "spokesman" (compare Exod. vii. 1 with iv. 16),[1] and needing, therefore, the God-breathed Scriptures so that he may know what to say for Him for whom he speaks as His spokesman.

It is remarkable also for the word ἄρτιος (*artios*), rendered *perfect*, but meaning *fitted* as perfectly as a joint is *fitted* in its socket.

Also for the word ἐξαρτίζω (*exartizō*), *to fit out*, used of fitting out a vessel for sea, which must take everything, on every voyage, which experience has shown may by any possibility be needed.

All this teaches us that only the man of God who thus has the profitable God-breathed Word is thus *fitted out*, prepared and equipped for every emergency as God's prophet or spokesman.

But our particular question now is not confined to the *revelation* of truth, however important, or even to the *words* employed, however interesting, but to the *place* where we find both.

Why is this passage given to us here in this third chapter of Paul's second Epistle to Timothy?

Why not in one of the other four chapters? Why not in the first Epistle to Timothy? or in some other Epistle?

The answer to these questions leads us to "search" this Epistle, and track out that reason.

In doing this we note, in chapter i. 15, the falling away of some who turned away from the Apostle Paul and his teaching; and we note also the Divine provision for such a trial in his unfeigned faith in God (*v.* 12), who would never turn away from him.

In chap. ii. 18 we read of those "who concerning THE TRUTH have erred," and note the Divine provision of comfort in the fact that "The foundation of God standeth sure, having this seal, The Lord knoweth them that are His" (*v.* 19). Those secured on that foundation will not so "err."

---

[1] See above, pp. 304, 305.

In chap. iii. 8 we read of those who "resist THE TRUTH." What is the Divine provision for an emergency like this? We have it introduced in the fourteenth verse: "But continue thou in the things which thou hast learned and hast been assured of"; going on and leading up to the verses we are considering as to the profitableness of the God-breathed Word for God's spokesman, fitting him out for this special conflict with those who oppose and withstand the truth.

The fact of this passage occurring here, as the Divine provision for this conflict, speaks to us, if we have ears to hear; and it says:

"When men 'resist the truth,' do not trust in your own wisdom, but in the Scriptures of truth. If they will not believe God, they will not believe you. If God's Word will not conquer them, be sure yours will not. Remember how the Lord Jesus engaged in His conflict by using this Sword of the Spirit: 'It is written.'"

The reason why so many fail in silencing those who "resist the truth" is because they depend on the logic of their argument, or the neatness of their retorts, or the smartness of their replies, or the cleverness of their answers, instead of on *the power of the Word of God*.

The fact of this passage occurring here speaks to us and says: "Open the book." Close your own mouth, and quote and use the words of God, the Sword of the Spirit, in meeting resistance to His truth.

In ch. iv. 4 we read of those who would "turn away their ears from THE TRUTH, and be turned unto fables," and we note that the Divine provision in such a condition of things is our one and only duty to "Preach the word." Nothing more, nothing less, nothing different. And this, all the more diligently and earnestly, for the reason given, because "the time will come when they will not endure sound doctrine," but "will turn away their ears from the truth." At such a time we are not to seek for something which men *will endure*, but to "Preach the Word."

Thus, in this brief epistle, we have a complete directory for these last "perilous times" in which our lot is cast; and a Divine provision for all our needs. We have:

God's faithfulness toward us for our comfort (i. 12).
God's foundation beneath us for our security (ii. 19).
God's Word within us for our defence (iii. 16).
God's crown before us for our hope (iv. 8).

And thus we have:

Unfeigned faith for our Possession.
Divine security for our Position.
The God-breathed Word for our Protection, and
The crown of righteousness for our Prospect.

2.—Matt. xi. 28: "Come unto me, all ye that are heavy-laden, and I will give you rest."

How often are these words used, and interpreted, as being addressed to sinners, to come and be saved.

But what is the interpretation of them, when looked at in the light of the question as to *where* we find them?

If we go back in the chapter to verses 2, 3, we find John the Baptist wondering whether Christ were indeed He that should come.

In verses 16—18 the Lord upbraids the people respecting both John and Himself, and for saying that John was possessed by a demon, and that Himself was a glutton and a drunkard.

In verses 20—24 he upbraided the cities of Chorazin, Bethsaida, and Capernaum, and said "Woe unto thee," "Woe unto thee."

Then, in verse 25, we read, "AT THAT TIME Jesus answered and said, I thank thee, O Father, Lord of heaven and earth, because thou hast hid these things from the wise and prudent, and hast revealed them unto babes. Even so, Father: for so it seemed good in thy sight."[1]

In other words, at the moment when (humanly speaking, of course) His mission was ending in failure; when He and the kingdom were being alike rejected, and His testimony not believed, "at that time," and at such a time, the Lord Jesus found His REST *in the Father's*

---

[1] This passage might have been considered under Canon VIII. below—The Importance of Accuracy in noting Marks of Time.

will. Here was rest indeed, in not seeking or desiring to accomplish anything that was not in the Father's will.

Then, turning to His "weary and heavy-laden" servants and disciples, He speaks, in order that they may find their rest where He found His, and says:

"Come unto me, all ye that labour, and are heavy-laden, and I will give you rest. Take my yoke upon you and learn of me: for I am meek and lowly in heart: and ye shall find rest unto your souls. For my yoke is easy and my burden is light."

He alludes not to their sins, but to their service: not to their guilt, but to their labour; not to their conscience, but to their heart; not to their repentance, but to their learning of Him; not to their finding forgiveness of their sin, but to their finding rest in His yoke.

This fact, again, speaks to us if we have ears to hear, and it says: "If you would find rest in your service, and be without care; be free from the heavy burden of responsibility as to the results of your testimony, and enjoy peace, the peace of God, in the midst of what man might call, and we might regard, as failure, then you will find your rest where Christ found His, in submission to the Father's will, and say: "Even so, Father, for so it seemeth good in Thy sight."[1]

3.—1 Cor. xvi. 22: "If any man love not the Lord Jesus Christ, let him be Anathema. Maran-atha."

"*Anathema*" means *accursed*.

"*Maran-atha*" means *the Lord cometh*.

This verse, though it speaks of *love*, is not written in John's Epistles.

Though it speaks of a *curse*, it is not written in the Epistle to the Galatians.

Though it speaks of the Lord's *Coming*, we do not find it in the Epistle to the Thessalonians.

No! it occurs in this first Epistle to the Corinthians.

And, not at the beginning, or in the middle, but at the end. And right at the end, immediately before "The Grace of our Lord Jesus Christ." In fact, the very last verse of the Epistle proper. What lesson does its position

---

[1] See further, on this passage, under Canon VIII., below, "The Importance of Accuracy": marks of time.

here have for us? Surely the place where we find it gives
the verse a fulness of meaning, both by interpretation and
application, which it would not possess if it occurred in
any other part of Scripture.

It owes its chief importance, and all the solemnity of
its lesson, entirely to the fact that we find it here, and
nowhere else.

It bids us, therefore, look at the Epistle as a whole;
there we see, on the very surface, that the Epistle is full
of reproof for practical errors in life and walk:

(1) There is reproof for their divisions, envyings, strifes,
and contentions (1 Cor. i.—iii.), which are further particularized as including debates, envyings, wrath, strifes, back-
bitings, swellings, tumults (2 Cor. xii. 20).

(2) There are errors of life, and sins of uncleanness
(1 Cor. v.), further particularized in 2 Cor. xii. 20, 21, as
including fornication and lasciviousness.

(3) There is brother going to law with brother before
the ungodly (1 Cor. vi.).

(4) There is the wounding of the weak brother's conscience (1 Cor. viii.).[1]

(5) There is the questioning of Paul's apostleship
(1 Cor. ix.).

(6) There are errors in ritual (1 Cor. xi.).

(7) There are errors in the use of gifts (1 Cor. xiv.).

(8) There are errors in doctrine (1 Cor. xv.).

But when it comes to the end of the Epistle, and all
is viewed in the light of *Maran-atha*—the Lord cometh,
not one of these things is mentioned.

It does not say, "If any man be not moral in his life,"
"If any man be not correct in his ritual," or "orthodox
in his creed"; but, "if any man love not the Lord Jesus
Christ."

This fact speaks to us and tells us that a man may be
perfectly moral and yet have no love for Christ. He may
be correct in ritual, and orthodox in creed, but he may
have a heart as hard as a stone, and as cold as ice toward
the person of the Lord Jesus Christ.

It is not that these errors are made light of. God
forbid! but, that if a man have no error, and yet have
no love, he will be accursed when the Lord cometh.

---

[1] See further on this point, page 328, below.

In the light of that day, *love* will be the true test; loyalty will be the true token of acceptable service.

It was even so with the "Last words of David," when at the end of his reign he summed up and numbered his "mighty men" and set forth their service. In 2 Sam. xxiii. all is enumerated, wonderful deeds are recorded, marks of devotion are cited.

The boldness of one through whom "the LORD wrought a great victory" (*v.* 10), though "the men of Israel had fled" (*v.* 9).

And of another who defended David's rights when "the people fled from the Philistines" (*vv.* 11, 12).

But among the mighty men and servants of David there were those who were noted for military prowess, political wisdom, and diligent service, whose names are not enumerated in this list. Yes, their *names* are mentioned, but they themselves are *not numbered*.

JOAB'S name is there, three times : as the brother of Abishai (*v.* 18), as the brother of Asahel (*v.* 24); but he himself is not numbered, though "Nehari . . . armourbearer to Joab" is (*v.* 37).

AHITHOPHEL'S name is there; but he is not numbered: though we find "Eliam the son of Ahithophel" (*v.* 34).

ABIATHAR the high priest, David's friend (1 Sam. xxii. 23), is neither named nor numbered; though "Uriah the Hittite" is.

What does all this say to us but exactly what we have in 1 Cor. xvi. 22: "if any man love not."

It is not might, nor courage, nor wisdom that constitutes true service; but it is loyalty and love.

Ahithophel failed in his loyalty when Joab stood firm : for Joab and Abiathar remained loyal during Absalom's rebellion, but failed in the rising of Adonijah.

Thus was their service truly appraised, and their hearts tested. The test was not the skilfulness of the hand, or the wisdom of the head, but the loyalty of the heart (Jer. ix. 23, 24).

This is the great lesson which is impressed upon us by the place where we find the words: "If any man love not the Lord Jesus Christ let him be anathema, Maranatha." These are "the last words" of that first Epistle to the Corinthians.

No One Passage to Be Interpreted in a
Sense Repugnant to Others That Are Clear

This Canon is laid down in the twentieth of "the Thirty-nine Articles of Religion" of the Church of England.

That article treats of "*The Authority of the Church.*" It says: "The Church hath power to decree Rites or Ceremonies, and authority in Controversies of Faith: and yet it is not lawful for the Church to ordain any thing that is contrary to God's Word written, *neither may it so expound one place of Scripture that it be repugnant to another . . .*"

With the claim here made as to "The Authority of the Church" we are not now concerned; but we cannot deny that, in the latter clause quoted, we have a very important principle laid down: a principle which we shall do well ever to bear in mind in our study of the "words which the Holy Ghost teacheth."

This principle is true: because, as no one text *is* repugnant to another, it is clear that to explain one as being so repugnant, is what cannot lawfully be done.

If one passage appears to be repugnant to others, then there is something amiss either in the translation of it, or in our understanding of it.

In either case it behoves us to examine it and see where the fault lies. The one, apparently more difficult passage, must be understood, explained, and interpreted by the others which are quite plain and clear.

If this method be not possible, then the difficult passage must be left unsolved for the present, with the prayer that God will, in His own time, bestow the needed grace and light. But in no case must we allow that one difficult passage to disturb all the others which are clear; nor must we give heed for a moment to any false teaching which Tradition may have founded upon its misunderstanding or perversion of that one passage, whether through ignorance or malice.

1. We may apply this Canon to the Scripture concerning "the Rich man and Lazarus."

Without entering at all into the question of the interpretation of this Scripture, we would merely call attention to many other passages of Scripture which are perfectly clear and plain as to Man and Death, and to the condition of man "after death." These do not at all agree with what this Scripture seems to teach.[1]

What then is our duty as humble students of, and firm believers in, the truth of all and of every part of God's Word?

Are we to believe one and leave the others?

Are we to explain the one to our own satisfaction, and then explain the others away?

This is clearly impossible, though it is what the majority of Bible readers do!

If we cannot reconcile them, then let us wait for further light, and "with meekness, and all lowliness, with long-suffering, forbearing one another in love," "let each esteem other better than ourselves," and let us each suffer long with other fellow-believers, who think they see a way of interpreting all that is said on this subject in Scripture, in harmony with Scripture, and with satisfaction to their own consciences before God.

The same principle applies, of course, to other subjects.

2. We have an example in 1 Cor. viii. 11 and Rom. xiv. 15.

These two passages furnish us with a valuable example as to how our Canon No. VII. should be used.

1 Cor. viii. 11.—"Through thy knowledge shall the weak brother perish for whom Christ died?"

Rom. xiv. 15.—"Destroy not him with thy meat, for whom Christ died."

It will be at once observed that these two passages appear to be repugnant to many other passages which speak of the eternal preservation of the saints, and which assure them that they can "never perish," and that nothing can separate them from the love of God (Rom. viii. 38, 39).

The many passages which speak on this wise are perfectly clear. The repugnance to them is contained in these two passages (Rom. xiv. 15 and 1 Cor. viii. 11).

---

[1] See pamphlets on this subject, by the same author, entitled *The Rich Man and Lazarus*, and *Sheol and Hades*.

According to our present Canon we must not attempt to make the many yield to these two; but, if we can, we must find an explanation of them which shall put them in harmony with the many.

If we cannot do this, then we must wait till further light can be obtained; or until such discoveries are made which will enable us to harmonize the two with the many.

While we are thus waiting, we will say something which may tend to remove their apparent repugnance.

(1) The number of various readings in the Greek, and the many conflicting expositions of the commentators, show us that some difficulty has been experienced in the Text, with which transcribers, as well as translators, have had to cope. Their struggles are all too painfully evident. There is scarcely a word in 1 Cor. viii. 11 which is not the subject of a various reading in the Greek.

(2) We will first suggest what may prove a key; and then see whether the Structure of the two passages, and the Scope, will bear out and support it; or whether, on the other hand, they will condemn and overthrow it.

We suggest that the reading of the MS. known as "D" should be taken as having been the primitive reading. Notwithstanding the fact that the numerical weight of the MSS. is not in its favour, it is quite possible that the MS. "D" may represent a *reading* more ancient than MSS. which are themselves older.[1]

(3) There are two verbs which are much alike, and which, in fact, differ only in having one "l" instead of two ("ll"): ἀπολύω (*apoluō*), and ἀπολλύω (*apolluō*).

Apoluō (with one "l") means *to put away;* as in Matt. i. 19; v. 31, 32; xix. 3, 7, 8, 9. Mark x. 2, 4, 11, 12. Luke xvi. 18 (twice).

Apolluō (with two "ll's") means *to destroy.*

The former verb is that which is written in the MS. known as "D(2)."[2] It is called the *Codex Claromontanus,* and is now in the National Library at Paris (No. 107).[3] Tischendorf believes it to be of the sixth century, and

---

[1] On the whole subject of Various Readings, see Canon XII.
[2] See pp. 409, 410.
[3] This MS. is to be distinguished from D (1) (see p. 410). D (1) contains the Gospels and Acts; while D (2) contains the Pauline Epistles and Hebrews.

Dr. Tregelles says "it is one of the most valuable MSS. extant; none of the Texts published by Tischendorf is so important, with the single exception of the Palimpsest Codex Ephræmi."

It is noteworthy that we have the same confusion of readings in Rom. xiv. 15 as well as in 1 Cor. viii. 11. This difference of reading, therefore, must have been introduced at a very early date.

The one reading is μή ἀπολύται (*mē apolutai*), **do** *not put away, separate not, do not put out.*

The other reading is μή ἀπόλλυται (*mē apollutai*), **do** *not destroy.*[1]

We will give the two passages separately, as the authorities are not the same for each.

In 1 Cor. viii. 11 the reading "Do *not put away*" (or "put out") is supported by "D" (see above), and was the original reading of that MS.; while the other reading is the subject of four various readings, showing the perplexity of the transcribers.

The question is, How did all these Various Readings arise? There must surely have been some ancient original authority which was copied by Codex D, and this may have been a reading older than some of the MSS. which were written earlier than "D."

We are quite aware that this is conjecture; but it is not without foundation. It is not as though we invented the idea out of our own head. It is something more than that; and the difference between the two spellings, with "L" or "LL," is so slight, that an error once made might well come, by being copied and re-copied, to be the recognized reading. But, if originally an error, the fact of its multiplication has no bearing on the point, or weight in the argument.

There seems, then, to be room for another line of proof.

(1) There is the whole analogy of New Testament teaching as to the eternal preservation of God's Saints to which these two passages seem to be repugnant. Indeed, it seems as though a Pelagian copyist might well be tempted to add another "l," when, by so doing, he could so easily obtain a proof of his doctrine.

---

[1] But even this is the subject of divergences in the MSS. which favour it.

(2) Then there is the Scope of each of the two passages to be considered according to our first Canon. If one reading suits the Scope perfectly, and the other is quite out of harmony with it, that would be a very weighty piece of evidence, sufficient of itself to settle the matter.

To take 1 Cor. viii. 11 first, it is obvious that the Epistle is directed against the Divisions, Separations, Strifes, and Contentions of 1 Cor. i.—iii. Then, further, we have the truth of the one spiritual Body of Christ set forth, from which there can be neither amputation nor separation (1 Cor. xii.).

The whole of this eighth chapter is directed as a warning against doing anything that would be a stumbling-block to a brother.

One point is dealt with concerning which enquiry had been made by the Saints at Corinth; *viz.*, the eating of meat offered to idols, about which there were evidently differences of opinion likely to lead to, and end in, Division and Separation.

These are dealt with, in the manner shown by the Structure : for we must apply our second Canon in order to find the Scope.

Two points are treated of :—

(1) The *knowledge* of different brethren (*vv.* 1—8).
(2) The *liberty* in the use of this knowledge (*vv.* 9—13).

1 Cor. viii.[1]

Things enquired of Paul.

(1) *The knowledge of different brethren* (*vv.* 1—8).

A | 1-. " Touching things offered to idols."
  B | -1, 2. The possession of knowledge.
    C | 3. God's knowledge of the believer.
      D | a | 4-. Idols are nothing.
         | b | -4. There is one God.
      D | a | 5. Idols are many.
         | b | 6-. There is one God.
    C | -6. The believer's knowledge of God.
  B | 7-. The possession of knowledge.
A | -7, 8. Concerning " a thing offered to an idol."

---

[1] For the place of this member in the Structure of the Epistle as a whole, see *The Church Epistles* (p. 91), by the same author.

(2) *Liberty in the use of this knowledge* (1 Cor. viii. 9—13).

E | 9. Care lest liberty to eat causes stumbling.
    F | c | 10-. Influence of thy *"knowledge"* on the weak brother.
        d | -10. Effect of *example* on the conscience of a weak brother (singular).
    F | c | 11. Result of *"thy knowledge"* in the putting away of the weak brother.
        d | 12. Result of the *example* on the consciences of the weak brethren (plural) who have put the brother away.
E | 13. Care lest liberty to eat causes stumbling.

Here, all seems quite clear. The abuse of knowledge leads to a bad influence on a weak brother, who is "put away" in consequence; and it leads also to trouble of the weak brethren, who have put him away.

The fact that Christ died for such an one should be sufficient to make them use the care which is enjoined.

In Rom. xiv. 15 the reading *Do not put away* is supported by the MS. described above, known as D³ (the small numeral denoting the work of a corrector in Cent. viii.).

Another Codex, known as L, the *Codex Angelicus Romanus*, a MS. in the Anglican Library of the Augustinian Monks in Rome.

A Lambeth MS. (No. 1,182), Cent. xii., known as "a."

A British Museum MS. (Add. MSS., No. 11,837) known as "h," and dated 1157.

A Trinity Coll. Camb. MS. (B. x. 16) known as "k," and written about 1316.

Another Codex, known as *Codex Leicestrensis*, of about Cent. xii., known as "m."

To find the scope of the passage in which Rom. xiv. 15 occurs, we must, according to our Canon II., first find its place in the Epistle as a whole.[1] If we do this we find that the member of which it forms a part deals with practical matters:

---

[1] For the Structure of the Epistle as a whole and the place occupied by this member see *The Church Epistles* (p. 23), by the same author.

Rom. xii. 1—xv. 7.

Practical duties.

A | xii. 1—8. Ecclesiastical.

  B | xii. 9—21. Social.

   C | xiii. 1—7. Civil.

  B | xiii. 8—14. Social.

A | xiv. 1—xv. 7. Ecclesiastical.

From this it will be seen that our verse (Rom. xiv. 15) forms part of our *Ecclesiastical obligations*, A (xiv. 1—xv. 7) and may be thus expanded:

A (Rom. xiv. 1—xv. 7), *Ecclesiastical duties.*

A | D¹ | xiv. 1. Reception of the weak.

   E¹ | xiv. 2—23. Our self-denial.

   D² | xv. 1, 2. Our bearing with the weak.

   E² | xv. 3, 4. Christ's self-denial.

   D³ | xv. 5—7. Our mutual reception of one another.

The scope of this member is at once clearly seen. And the place occupied by our passage is discerned. It is in the member E¹, and the subject of it is *Our exercise of self-denial.*

"If on account of thy meat thy brother is grieved, thou walkest no longer according to love. Do not grieve him, do not *separate* (or put away) with thy meat him for whom Christ died."

It will be seen that the word "Destroy not" is altogether out of harmony with the whole scope of the chapter. Moreover, we have in verse 20 the correlative word to the one we suggest: *viz.*, καταλύω (*kataluō*), to *throw down*. The difference between *apoluō* and *kataluō* is at once seen. *Apoluō* is to *throw out; kataluō* is *to throw down.*[1]

"For meat do not *throw down* or *upset* the work of God" (*v.* 20). What work of God? "God's building"

---

[1] See Matt. xxiv. 2. Mark xiii. 2. Luke xxi. 6. Acts v. 38, 39, etc.

(1 Cor. iii. 9).   This is corrupted and *defiled* when we build any thing on to the one foundation. It is *thrown down* and injured to that extent, when we *throw out,* or put away, any weak brother whom God has built upon that foundation.

Thus we see that these two passages, which seem to be repugnant to many passages which are perfectly clear, are capable of an explanation which not only sets them in harmony with all the others, but shows that the explanation is in harmony with the full context and structure of both passages.

The word is not "*Do not destroy*": but it is "*Do not put away,*" or "*Do not separate.*"

CANON 8

The Importance of Accuracy in the Study of the Words of Scripture

This canon will be conceded by all as one of the first magnitude. Accuracy is everywhere demanded, and in every department of life, and in every branch of service.

How many calamities and disasters have occurred from a want of accuracy. The want of accuracy in under-standing a word of command led to the disastrous cavalry charge at Balaclava. Want of accuracy or the misunder-standing of a word in a correspondence has led to the separation of close friends or the miscarriage of impor-tant business.

Inaccuracy is no less disastrous in the reading and study of the Word of God.

It is said of a poorly-informed preacher in southern Illinois, that he took his text from Luke xiv. 4, and read it out "And he took him, and held him, and let him go." The preacher was trying to explain the difficulty thus created, when a daring interrupter called out, "*My* Bible says, 'He *healed* him, and let him go.'" As may be imagined, the proposed exegesis was brought to a sudden close.

But there are many popular difficulties of which this is a typical example; and which might all be ended as suddenly, if a similar remark were made.

How long shall we hear of the Fall as having been brought about by the eating of an *apple?* And how soon would the fiction vanish if we would exclaim, "*My* Bible doesn't say apple."

How long shall we hear about Jonah's being swallowed by the *whale?* when we could stop it by simply saying "*My* Bible doesn't say *whale.*" Jonah i. 17 says, "The LORD had prepared a great fish."[1]

---

[1] The Lord Jesus used the word κῆτος (*kētos*) in Matt. xii. 40. It is a pity that any ground was given to the cry of the Infidel and the Higher Critics by translating it "whale" in the A.V. But it is unpardonable of the R.V. to perpetuate it, when it puts in the margin "Gr. *sea-monster*," though the words of Jonah i. 17, "a great fish," were ready to their hand. Why not have put "sea monster" or "great fish" in the Text?

How long are we to hear about the sin of the children of Israel by command of God, as *borrowing* without intention of returning the property of the Egyptians (Exod. iii. 22; xi. 2; xii. 35, 36)? Our A.V. seems to say this, and has thus provided material for scoffers. The R.V. rightly translates the Hebrew שָׁאַל (*shā'al*), *to ask :* and out of one hundred and sixty-eight occurrences it is only six times rendered in the A.V. *borrow;* while in all the other one hundred and sixty-two passages it is rendered *ask, beg, require,* or some similar word. (See Ps. ii. 8, "Ask of me," etc.: this, surely, cannot mean "Borrow of me"?)

The same want of accuracy in reading the sacred text has led to the mistakes of artists as well as of theologians. For *angels* are always represented as women instead of men; and in the piercing of the Lord the heart is always represented as being on the right side instead of on the left.

Similar are the mistakes of interpreters.

"Ye do ALWAY resist the Holy Ghost" (Acts vii. 51) is quoted to prove that men can successfully withstand the Spirit, instead of stumbling at His words.

While "Ye WILL NOT come unto me" (lit., "will not to come": John v. 40) is quoted to prove that men will to come; and this, in spite of Phil. ii. 13.

And in 1 Cor. xvi. 1, the injunction to lay by in store, that there be "no collection," is used to support the modern practice of having a collection at every service.

The Lord's Supper, in spite of its being so called, and being instituted as *part of a meal*, is ordered by all Romanizers to be taken in the morning, fasting.

"Blood and Fire," which is a description of the judgment of the great Day of the LORD (Joel ii. 30), is adopted as the symbol of salvation by His grace.

Instead of hearing what the Spirit saith to the churches we are commanded by man to hear what the Church says to us; and to heed "the voice of the Church."

The same want of accuracy leads those who set themselves up as "Higher" Critics to forget that it is the Word of God which is to be their critic, or judge. (Heb. iv. 12, "discerner." Gr. *critic* or *judge.* Compare John xii. 48, and see *Number in Scripture*, p. 70.)

These and many other examples are sufficient to emphasize the importance of accuracy in our reading of Scripture if we would avoid falling into mistakes and blunders of any kind.

Examples and illustrations abound where this canon may be applied. We cannot pretend to make the list of those we give exhaustive; we offer them only as specimens.[1]

We will divide them into two classes: where the principle may be used

> i. In the removal of difficulties.
> ii. In the revelation of truths.

i. ILLUSTRATION OF ACCURACY APPLIED TO THE REMOVAL OF DIFFICULTIES.

1. *The Ammonite and Moabite.*—In Deut. xxiii. 3 it is declared that "an Ammonite or Moabite shall not enter into the congregation of the LORD." And it is urged that it was in contravention of this, when Ruth not only entered into the congregation, but into the genealogy of our Lord (Ruth iv. 13—22. Matt. i. 5).

But if we read Deut. xxiii. 3 accurately, we find that the word is masculine מוֹאָבִי (*mōābī*), *Moabite*, while in the Book of Ruth it is *feminine*, and she is called מוֹאָבִיָּה (*mōabīyah*). (Ruth i. 22; ii. 2, 6; iv. 5, 10.)

2. *Zedekiah and Babylon.*—In Jer. xxxii. 4 and xxxiv. 3 King Zedekiah was told that he should see the king of Babylon, and "speak with him mouth to mouth, and his eyes shall behold his eyes," and should go to Babylon.

In Ezek. xii. 13 it is as distinctly said that he should not see Babylon, though he should die there.

If we read these two passages accurately, we shall see how both are true as recorded in 2 Kings xxv. 6, 7, where we are told that Zedekiah was brought to the king of Babylon at Riblah, and spoke with him; that he was tried and then condemned, had his eyes put out, and bound with fetters of brass and was taken to Babylon. Thus, though he died there, he never "saw" it.

---

[1] We do not repeat here any examples given in our pamphlet on this same subject and under the title of this Canon.

This apparent difficulty might have been given under Canon IV. as being explained by a reference in the Remoter Context.

3. *Omer and Homer.*—In Exod. xvi. 36, we are told that "an omer is the tenth part of an ephah."

In Ezek. xlv. 11 an ephah is said to be the tenth part of apparently the same measure.

But if we read the two passages accurately we find the former is spelt "omer," and the latter is spelt "homer." And though the letter "h" is often treated with scant respect in speaking, it is well to give it its place when we find it in writing. The difference compels us to look at the Hebrew, where we find that in Exod. xvi. the word is עֹמֶר (*'omer*), while in Ezekiel xlv. the word is חֹמֶר (*chomer*).

Thus we have two totally different words denoting two different measures.

4. *The Going of Balaam.*—In Num. xxii. 22 we read that "God's anger was kindled because he (Balaam) went" with the princes of Moab.

It is supposed that this anger was out of place, because God had said, "Rise up and go with them" (*v.* 20). But it does not seem to be noticed that *a condition was attached* to this permission, *viz.:* "*If the men come to call thee.*"

No such coming and calling is mentioned; and it is quite gratuitous for any one to assume that this condition was fulfilled, when such assumption *creates* the very difficulty to which objection is made.

5. *God's command concerning sacrifices.*—In Jer. vii. 22, 23, we read: "I spake not unto your fathers, nor commanded them in the day that I brought them out of the land of Egypt, concerning burnt offerings and sacrifices; but this thing commanded I them, Obey my voice, and I will be your God."

It was through reading this inaccurately that the late Professor Mivart left the Church of Rome and gave up his belief in the Bible. He supposed (as many have done before and since) that God *did* command sacrifices.

If Leviticus be read accurately it will be seen that God did not "COMMAND" the offering of sacrifices. The very essence of all offerings was that the act should be *voluntary*, "of his own voluntary will." This being the case, God did then lay down the *conditions* on which they should be brought and offered. Hence the book of Leviticus begins by saying, "IF any man of you bring an offering unto the LORD, ye shall bring," etc. (Compare Lev. i. 2, 3, 10, 14; ii. 4, 5, 7, 14; iii. 1, 6, 7, 12; iv. 32, etc.).

It was essential that all sacrifices should be of the offerer's "*own voluntary will*" (Lev. i. 3). What Jehovah commanded "in the day that He brought them out of Egypt" was to "diligently hearken to the voice of the LORD;" and "Do that which is right" in His sight; and "Give ear to His commandments; keep all His statutes." This was the command "in the day that He brought them out of Egypt" (see Exod. xv. 26).

This inaccurate reading not only *creates* the difficulty; but misses the very scope of Jer. vii. 22, 23.

6. *Hearing and not hearing the voice.*—In Acts ix. 7 we read, "The men that were with him (Saul) stood speechless, hearing a voice, but seeing no man."

In Acts xxii. 9 "they heard not the voice of him that spake to me."

In this case it is the Greek that has to be read accurately. The verb ἀκούω (*akouō*), *to hear*, is the same in both passages, but it governs two cases of the noun which follows it.

It takes the *Genitive* case of the *sound* which is heard; and it takes the *Accusative* case of the *words* or *matter* which is heard.

In Acts ix. 7 "the voice" that was heard is in the *Genitive* case (φωνῆς, *phōnēs*).

In Acts xxii. 9 "the voice" that was *not heard* (*i.e.*, the matter) is in the *Accusative* case: so that while the men with Saul heard the sound of the voice, they did not hear the words that were spoken. (Compare Luke xi. 28.)

7. *Standing and falling to the earth.*—But there is another difficulty in these passages besides the hearing and not hearing.

There is the difficulty between Acts ix. 7, "the men that journeyed with him stood speechless," and Acts xxvi. 14, "and when we were all fallen to the earth."

This difficulty is removed the moment we read the passage accurately and notice that the word ἵσταμαι (*histamai*) has another meaning besides *standing erect* on one's legs. It means to remain *motionless in whatever position one may be.*

It is rendered *abode* in John viii. 44; *continue* in Acts xxvi. 22 (R.V. stand); *stanch* in Luke viii. 44. Hence it is used of *standing fast* (1 Cor. vii. 37. Col. iv. 12. 2 Tim. ii. 19).

More to the point is the Septuagint of 1 Sam. xxviii. 20, where it is said of Saul that he "made haste, and fell *motionless* upon the earth." No one would think of rendering this, he "fell standing." [1]

So that the two passages taken together mean that "the men that journeyed with him" fell to the ground and remained speechless; or were motionless as well as speechless.

8. *Spoken and written.*—In Matt. ii. 23 we read: "He came and dwelt in a city called Nazareth; that it might be fulfilled which was spoken by the prophets, He shall be called a Nazarene."

This being inaccurately read, search is made in the prophets for any such prophecy.

But none can be found.

The Hebrew word נֵצֶר (*nētzer*), a *branch*, is then taken, and an attempt is made to identify it with "Nazarene." But even if this could be established (which it cannot be) it would not solve the difficulty which has been created; for the word *nētzer* is used of Christ, only in Isaiah; and it says prophetS.

If we read the verse accurately we notice that it says "spoken," and not *written.*

Some prophecies were written and not spoken. Some were spoken and not written; others were both spoken and written.

---

[1] Homer, in reference to one thus fallen, says: "he fell from his car ... and then, for a long time remained he *motionless*"; (not standing on his legs *after he had fallen!*). *Iliad,* v. 585.

There is all the difference, surely, between τὸ ῥῆθεν (*to rhēthen*), *that which was spoken*, and ὁ γέγραπται (*ho gegraptai*), *that which standeth written*.

Even granting that by a figure of speech, what is written is sometimes said to be spoken, there is no necessity arbitrarily to introduce the hypothesis when such introduction actually creates the difficulty.

9. *Jeremiah the Prophet.*—The same application of accuracy in reading the words of a Scripture solves the precisely similar difficulty in Matt. xxvii. 9. The prophecy as to the "thirty pieces of silver" was first "spoken by Jeremiah the prophet," and afterwards written down by Zechariah.

And yet, having arbitrarily substituted in their minds the word "written" instead of "spoken," commentators are at their wits' end to explain the difficulty they have themselves created.

One says "Matthew quoted it from memory" (Augustine, followed by Alford); another speaks of it as a "slip of the pen" on the part of Matthew.

Another thinks that Jeremiah is put for the whole body of the prophets (Bishop Lightfoot).

Another thinks that the passage was originally in Jeremiah, but the Jews cut it out (Eusebius and others).

Another thinks that it may have been in another writing of Jeremiah which is now lost (Origen and others).

Another, (Bishop Wordsworth) believes that the mistake was made on purpose, so that we should not trouble ourselves as to who the writer was, but receive all prophecy as coming direct from God.

We make no comment on these, but only mention them to show the shifts to which expositors are driven in order to get out of the pit which they have digged themselves.

The solutions which are suggested are a greater obstacle to faith than the original difficulty; even if it were real instead of being only apparent.

10. *The sending of the Centurion* (Luke vii. 3, 6 and Matt. viii. 5).—In Matt. viii. 5 it reads as though the centurion came himself to the Lord; and in Luke vii. 3, 6,

it reads as though he sent others and remained behind himself.

The difficulty is removed the moment we read the Greek accurately, and note that in Luke two different words are used for sending.

In Luke vii. 3 it is the verb ἀποστέλλω (apostellō), which means *to send away from*, the sender remaining behind. This is when he sends "the elders of the Jews."

In verse 6 the centurion "sent friends," but here it is the verb πέμπω (pempō), which means *to send with*, the sender either accompanying or sending an escort.[1]

From this latter word being used in verse 6 it is clear that the centurion accompanied his "friends." This is where the account in Matthew takes up the narrative, when he says "there came to him a centurion."

We may note further that, in Matt. viii. 13, the Lord said, "Go thy way." But from Luke vii. 10 it appears that the Centurion did not go; his great faith not making it necessary for him to go and verify the Lord's word.

11. *The Inscriptions on the Cross.*—The variation between these in the four Gospels has given rise to charges which detract from the claim of the Gospels to the accuracy involved in inspiration;[2] while the defences and explanations have been little less injurious in their effects.

The inscriptions are as follows:

1. Matt. xxvii. 37, "This is Jesus the King of the Jews."
2. Mark xv. 26, "The King of the Jews."
3. Luke xxiii. 38, "This is the King of the Jews."
4. John xix. 19, "Jesus of Nazareth the King of the Jews."

---

[1] In John xx. 21 we have both words in one verse: "As my Father hath *sent* me (apostellō), even so *send* I you (pempō)." While in other passages the latter verb is used also of the sending of the Lord Jesus by the Father; yet, here, in John xx. 21, for the purpose of emphasizing the fact that the Lord remains with those whom He sends, the verb πέμπω (*pempō*) is used.

[2] A very moderate statement of the difficulty presents it as follows: "The Evangelists, while fully agreeing in the substance of their narratives, are by no means careful about literal words—as for example, their record of the Inscriptions on the Cross, where no two of them exactly agree."—Rev. J. Paterson Smyth, in *How God Inspired the Bible.*

It is universally *assumed* that there was only one inscription: and, some Interpreters account for the differences by a further supposition that the full and complete version was—

"THIS IS JESUS OF NAZARETH, THE KING OF THE JEWS,"

the four consisting of certain words which formed a part of that whole.

It has been suggested by one[1] that these four, respectively, are in harmony with the special object and scope of the Gospel in which it is found. This is ingenious and would be worthy of Divine revelation if it could be substantiated.

Others suggest that as the inscription was originally in Hebrew, Greek, and Latin, they are the translations of these respectively.

But this involves another assumption, *viz.*, that these three were not only not the same, but were so different as to allow of such various renderings. It also accounts for only three out of the four; and does not explain how the Greek form could be a translation of the Greek!

In all these cases of difficulty it is well to "open the book" and see exactly what is said, and whether there is any ground for the original *assumption* that there was only one inscription, which is the foundation of the difficulty and the cause of its explanations.

Let us begin with Mark xv. 26:

(1) "The King of the Jews." Here we have not a word about a "title" (τίτλος, *titlos*, John xix. 19) being on the Cross at all, or which any one had seen. It is a question of "his accusation." It is the bill of his *indictment*, or the ground or cause of his condemnation, which was His claim to be "the King of the Jews."

(2) John xix. 19. This was written by Pilate, and put upon the cross before it left Pilate's presence. For no one suggests that Pilate went to the scene of the execution and wrote anything there. It was written in Hebrew, Greek, and Latin. The Latin put last as Pilate's language.

This title was read *after the cross was set up;* and became a source of argument between the chief priests

---

[1] The late Rev. James Kelly.

and Pilate (John xix. 21, 22), *before the parting of the garments* (*vv.* 23, 24).

What the final result of this argument was, does not appear from John's Gospel; but it appears from

(3) Matt. xxvii. 37, that it must have resulted in that one being taken down, and another "set up over his head" *after* they had "parted his garments among them" and *after* they had set down to watch him there (*vv.* 35, 36).

(4) Luke xxiii. 38.   This appears to have been a different one again.   For we are not told all that took place.   It is evident from John that the feelings of those concerned were deeply stirred.

The inscription mentioned by Luke was evidently much later, and was seen close upon the sixth hour (*v.* 44), when the darkness fell.   It was put upon or "over him" (*v.* 38, $\dot{\epsilon}\pi$' $\alpha\dot{\upsilon}\tau\tilde{\omega}$, *ep'autō*), and in this order: "Greek, Latin and Hebrew," and *after* the revilings of the people. (Compare *vv.* 35—37 with *v.* 38.)   Matthew's (No. 2) was *before* the revilings.   (Compare Matt. xxvii. 37 with *v.* 39).

If we accurately notice what is written we conclude:

(*a*) That Mark's was only his *indictment*.

(*b*) That John's was the first, written by Pilate and put on the Cross before it left his presence.

(*c*) That Matthew's was substituted for it and placed "over his head" after the dividing of the garments and after the soldiers had set down to watch; but *before* the revilings.

(*d*) That Luke's was the last, put upon or "over him" *after* the revilings, and seen near the sixth hour.

12. *The offering of drink at the Cross.*—A great difficulty has been created by a want of accuracy in discriminating the three different occasions on which drink was offered to the Lord when on the Cross: the assumption being that it was offered only once.

The words of God have to be rightly divided in more senses than one.

There are great differences between the three accounts. If these are *identified* and treated as being different versions of one event, instead of complementary accounts, each supplementing the other, then we shall have what is so glibly called a "discrepancy."

Now read the words accurately and note—

(1) The three *occasions:*

> (*a*) Mark xv. 22, 23, "When they were come unto the place called Golgotha."
>
> (*b*) Matt. xxvii. 34, "When they were come unto Golgotha."
>
> (*c*) Matt. xxvii. 48. Mark xv. 36. John xix. 29. Six hours after the former two, in response to the Lord's cry, "I thirst."

(2) The three *kinds* of drink offered—

> (*a*) 'Wine mingled with myrrh."
>
> (*b*) "Vinegar with gall."
>
> (*c*) "Vinegar."

(3) The three *receptions:*

> (*a*) The first was refused without even tasting it.
>
> (*b*) The second was first tasted and then was refused.
>
> (*c*) The third was "received" after He had called for it.

Thus so far from there being any discrepancy, the absolute accuracy of the Divine word is brought clearly out.

13. *The "others" crucified with Christ.*—Through not reading accurately what is written in the several accounts of the Crucifixion, and being misled by tradition and the mistakes of mediaeval artists, ground has been given for objections to be made as to the truth of the Scriptures; and difficulties have been gratuitously created.

The pictures and tradition give us "two" men who were crucified with Christ. In Matt. xxvii. 44, and Mark xv. 32, it is stated that they *both* reviled Christ: "the thieves also which were crucified with him, cast the same in his teeth." But in Luke xxiii. 39 it is as distinctly stated that it was only "one" of them: and that they were not "thieves," but "malefactors."

Moreover, in Luke, the two were led forth, with Christ, from Pilate's presence; whereas, in Matthew and Mark, they were not brought to the place of crucifixion until after the dividing of Christ's garments.

These are adduced as obvious errors: and it is alleged that both accounts cannot be correct.

The usual defence of the accuracy of these Scriptures is to *assume* that both the men reviled Christ *at first;* but that *afterward* one of them repented.

But this is a pure assumption, and is not only not so stated, but is quite contrary to what is so clearly written : "One of the malefactors which were hanged railed on him, saying, If thou be the Messiah, save thyself and us. But the other answering rebuked him saying . . . This man hath done nothing amiss" (Luke xxiii. 40, 41).

But even if this were not so, and there were nothing against the assumption, there are still other difficulties which require explanation.

In Matthew and Mark they are called δύο λησταί (*duo lēstai*), *two robbers.*

In Luke xxiii. 32, they are called δύο κακοῦργοι (*duo kakourgoi*), *two malefactors.*

This also is supposed to be an inaccuracy. And so it is, if we accept the assumption of Tradition and Painting.

But if we read the accounts, as written in the Word of God, more accurately, we shall have to revise all our views which we have received from the "Traditions of Men."

(1) We start from the alleged discrepancy, and accept the two statements that there were four men crucified with the Lord Jesus—Two Malefactors and Two Robbers.

(2) These words are different; for while a Robber is a Malefactor (or evil-worker), yet an evil-worker is not necessarily a Robber.[1]

(3) It is also the fact that the two Malefactors "were led with him to be put to death and when they were come (Greek, *came*) *to the place* which is called Calvary, there they crucified *him and the malefactors*, one on the right hand and one on the left" (Luke xxiii. 32, 33).

---

[1] There is a difference between κακοῦργος (*kakourgos*), *an evil-worker*, and κακοποιός (*kakopoios*), *an evil-doer*. The former is general, while the latter is worse, in that it is specific. Paul was treated as the former (2 Tim. ii. 9), Christ was charged with being the latter (John xviii. 30).

(4) The two Robbers were not brought till much later. *Not until the garments had been divided* and after they had sat down to watch Him there. "Then," *i.e.*, at that particular moment, *while they were thus watching;* "THEN were two robbers crucified with Him, one on the right hand, and one on the left" (Matt. xxvii. 38. Mark xv. 27).

(5) The two Malefactors would therefore be on the inside next to the Lord; and the two Robbers would be on the outside. Being nearer to Him, the two malefactors could more easily speak with one another, and to the Lord.

(6) John adds his testimony in ch. xix. 18, without any note of time: only of place "where" (not of time, "then"). He speaks generally of the fact: "where they crucified him, and with him, others, two on this side and on that side, and Jesus in the midst." The Greek is clear: δύο ἐντεῦθεν καὶ ἐντεῦθεν (*duo enteuthen kai enteuthen*). In Rev. xxii. 2 we have "*enteuthen kai enteuthen*" translated "on either side." So it should be here in John's other writing (Gospel, xix. 18), "and with him others, two on either side." This is exactly in accord with the other three Gospels, and combines their statements.

(7) But John bears further testimony. He says (ch. xix. 32, 33), "then came the soldiers and brake the legs of the first, and of the other which was crucified with him. But when they came (Greek, 'having come') to Jesus, and saw that he was dead already, they brake not his legs." This shows that the soldiers in approaching Christ passed two of the four men before coming to Him.

(8) Note the two different words translated "other," in John xix. 32: "the first and of the other." The word is ἄλλος (*allos*), which is the *other* (the second) of two *when there are more*.[1]

In Luke xxiii. 32 the word is ἕτερος (*heteros*), "and others also, two, were led with him."[2] *Heteros* is used of and denotes not one of the two malefactors, but both of them, they being one party of two, and the Lord being the other, and different.

---

[1] See Matt. x. 23; xxv. 16, 17, 20; xxvii. 61; xxviii. 1. John xviii. 15, 16; xx. 2, 4, 8 (the 2nd of eleven), and Rev. xvii. 10 (the 2nd of seven).

[2] Matt. vi. 24; viii. 21; xi. 3. Luke v. 7; vi. 6; vii. 41; ix. 56; xiv. 31; xvi. 13, 18; xvii. 34—36; xviii. 10; and xxiii. 40.

It is the same word (*heteros*) in verse 40, because here it is other of the two malefactors; *viz.*, the one who did not "rail on him."

We thus reach the conclusion that there were four others crucified with the Lord Jesus. This fact not only removes all difficulties, but perfectly harmonizes all the four Scriptures, and establishes the Divine accuracy of every word and every expression.

Of course it does not agree with Tradition; and we are quite aware that we shall have to reckon with all Traditionalists for thus upsetting their idol.

14. *The burying of Jacob and his sons.*—The difficulty in Acts vii. 15, 16 arises from confusing two distinct purchases; one by Abraham in Gen. xxiii. 19, and another by Jacob in Gen. xxxiii. 18, 19; and Josh. xxiv. 32.

Abraham's purchase was of Ephron the Hittite in Hebron; a field, with a cave (Maçhpelah) at the end of it, for 400 shekels of silver.

Jacob's purchase was "a parcel of a field" in Shechem, of the sons of Hamor the father of Shechem for 100 lambs.

There can be no confusion between these two.

As to the historical record, the burials in Abraham's sepulchre were Sarah (Gen. xxiii. 19), Abraham (Gen. xxv. 9), Isaac (Gen. xxxv. 29), Rebekah and Leah (Gen. xlix. 31), and Jacob (Gen. l. 12, 13).

The burials in Jacob's field were Joseph (Josh. xxiv. 32), and, according to Acts vii. 16, the other sons of Jacob who were carried over into Sychem.

Acts vii. 15, 16 agrees with this history if we note two simple Various Readings of the Greek supported by most of the Textual Editors (see Canon XII.); and if we remember that the circumstances were so well known to Stephen's hearers that they perfectly understood what he said. Though they were waiting to catch something out of his lips, yet they saw nothing to stumble at.

The two readings are ᾧ (*hō*), *in that which*, instead of ὅ (*ho*), *that* (before Abraham); and ἐν (*en*), *in*, instead of τοῦ (*tou*), *of [the]*, in the phrase "[the father] of Sychem." In which case we read "in Sychem," and do not read the italics "*the father*" or the word "of" before Sychem.

With these changes the verses will read as follows:

"So Jacob went down into Egypt, and died, he, and our fathers, and they [our fathers] were carried over into Sychem, and laid in the sepulchre: he [Jacob] in that which Abraham bought for a sum of money, [and they in that which was bought] from the sons of Hamor, in Sychem."

Thus, Jacob was buried in the sepulchre which Abraham bought; and his sons were afterwards buried in that which Jacob bought. The historic record is perfectly simple and clear; and no difficulty whatever exists, except in the minds of those who create it.

ii. ILLUSTRATIONS OF ACCURACY APPLIED TO THE
REVELATION OF TRUTH.

1. *Words and Expressions.*

"*From above.*"—In Luke i. 3 we read, "It seemed good to me also, having had perfect understanding of all things *from the very first* to write unto you in order."

There is no "very" in the Greek. The R.V. says simply "from the first."

But, when we read this accurately, we note that the word is ἄνωθεν (*anōthen*); and, when we look at all the other passages where it occurs we see that it means here *from above.* That is where Luke got his information from. That is why his understanding was so "perfect."

If the following passages be read carefully this will be seen to be the meaning: Matt. xxvii. 51. Mark xv. 38. John iii. 3, 7, 31; xix. 11, 23. Jas. i. 17; iii. 15, 17.

With two exceptions (Acts xxvi. 5, and Gal. iv. 9) the word always means *from above.* There is no occasion to introduce the idea of time where it is not needed. If the ordinary meaning makes sense, and makes for the Inspiration of God's Word, why arbitrarily take a meaning which destroys the sense? If holy men of old spake from God, who is "above" (2 Pet. i. 21), why give ἄνωθεν a meaning here which makes them speak *from themselves?*

" *Another King*" (Acts vii. 17, 18).—Here we read the words of Stephen: "The people grew and multiplied in Egypt till another king arose which knew not Joseph."

If we read this accurately we notice that the word for
another is ἕτερος (*heteros*), *another*, of a *different* kind;
and not ἄλλος (*allos*), which means *another* of the *same*
kind.[1]

The word points, therefore, to the fact that it was not
another king of the same dynasty, but a *different* dynasty
altogether.

With this agrees Exod. i. 8, not, of course, in the use
of the word *heteros*, which is Greek, but in the Hebrew
"arose," which is קוּם (*kūm*), and means *to stand up*
and occupy the place of another (see Dan. ii. 31, 39, 44;
iii. 24). Moreover the word "new" is חָדָשׁ (*chādāsh*) (for
the meaning of which see Deut. xxxii. 17, and compare
Judg. v. 8).

Josephus says, "the crown being come into another
family" (*Ant.* ii. 9).

The discoveries now made in Egypt prove that this
was the case. The mummy of this very Pharaoh is
to be seen to-day in the Museum at Bulak, and it is
clear that this *Rameses* was the Pharaoh of the Oppression.[2]

He was an Assyrian, and every feature of his face
shows that this was the case, being so different from the
pictures of the Pharaoh who preceded him.

Now we can understand Isa. lii. 4, which has so puzzled
the commentators, who were unable to understand why
the two oppressions, in Egypt and Assyria, should be
mentioned together in the same sentence, as though they
were almost contemporary.

The discoveries in Egypt, and the Accuracy of the
Divine Words, show that this latter was indeed the case.
For in Isa. lii. 4 we read:

"Thus saith Adonai Jehovah,
　My People went down aforetime into Egypt to
　　sojourn there;
　And the Assyrian oppressed them without cause."

---

[1] The force of these may be seen in Matt. ii. 12: "another way" (*allos*).
Matt. iv. 21: "other two brethren" (*allos*). Gal. i. 6, 7: "a different (*heteros*)
gospel, which is not another" (*allos*). Matt. vi. 24: "hate one and love the
other" (*heteros*). Matt. xi. 3: "do we look for another" (*heteros*). Heb. vii. 11;
"another priest" (*heteros*).

[2] While *Menephta*, his son, was the Pharaoh of the Exodus.

These words are now seen to be exquisitely accurate; for that was exactly what took place: Israel did go down into Egypt to sojourn there, but a new king arose, of a different dynasty, and he, an Assyrian, oppressed them without cause.

There is no occasion to assume that Isaiah coupled together two events separated by centuries, when such assumption creates the very difficulty complained of.

"The world that then was" (Gen. i. 2).—The accurate reading in the English of the A.V. Gen. i. 2 will be sufficient to show there is something in the verse which needs explanation; and when we have explained it we shall find that it points to a wonderful exposition of the Creation, and provides a complete answer to all the cavils of Geologists.

This discovery would be impossible if the Revised Version were used, as the Revisers deliberately discarded the use of *italics* in certain cases, one of which was in the case of the verb "*to be,*" which does not exist in Hebrew.

In Gen. i. 2 (A.V.) we read: "And the earth was without form and void; and darkness *was* upon the face of the deep."

Here, it will be seen that, the first "was" is in Roman type, while the second is in *Italic* type. This accuracy tells us that the latter verb, "*was,*" represents the verb *to be;* and that the former "was" must represent a different verb, and not the verb "to be." This is the case; and the verb is הָיָה (*hāyah*), to become, come to pass.

That this is its meaning is clear from the very next verse (*v.* 3): "Let there be light, and there was light." Here the verb for "be" and "was" is *hayah*, and means *become*, while, in verse 4, the verb "*was*" is the verb *to be*, and is in italics.

The same use of "was" (Roman type) and "*was*" (*Italic* type) may be seen in verses 9 and 10; and in verses 11 and 12.

If we enquire further about the verb *hayah* we find it in Gen. ii. 7, "and man *became* a living soul; ch. iv. 14, "it shall *come to pass*"; ch. ix. 15, "the waters shall no more *become* a flood"; ch. xix. 26, Lot's wife "*became* a pillar of salt."

From all this we assuredly learn that Gen. i. 2 should read, "and the earth BECAME without form."

Having made this discovery we now pursue it further; and we "search the Scriptures" to find out whether God has said anything else about the way in which He created the earth. And we find it in Isa. xlv. 18. Here the sentences are heaped together, in order to impress us with the fact that, He who created the earth, ought to know, and be able to tell us, how He made it. Note the words:

> "Thus saith Jehovah that created the heavens;
> Elohim himself that formed the earth, and made it;
> He hath established it,
> He created it not *tohū*."

But this word תֹהוּ (*tohū*) is the very word which is translated "without form" in Gen. i. 2. So that, whatever *tohū* means, it is evident that God did not *create* the earth *tohū*. Therefore it must have *become* so, at some time, in some way, and from some cause which we are not told.

It is clear from this that in Gen. i. 1 we have the record concerning what is called in 2 Pet. iii. 6 "the world that then was." This earth, we are there told also, "being overflowed with water perished." This is exactly what is stated in Gen. i. 1, 2.

So that at the end of the first verse we must put a very large full stop; or draw a line; or leave a blank space, so as to separate verse 1 from what follows in verse 2, which relates to "the heavens and earth which are now" (2 Pet. iii. 7), and which will continue, until the time comes for "the new heavens and the new earth" of 2 Pet. iii. 13, and of many other Scriptures.

When Geologists have settled how many years they require between the first and second verses of Gen. i. there is ample room for all they want, and a large margin beside.

Meanwhile, we may well conclude that all the fossils and remains which are found belonged to "the world that then was," and thus, at one stroke, remove all friction between Geology and Scripture.

Again, we ask, why assume that all the Geological phenomena pertain to the earth "which is now," when it is this very assumption which creates the difficulty?

and compels us to ignore all the phenomena of God's Word
mentioned above?

His Word is misinterpreted, and His works are misunderstood, and the difficulty thus created is charged
against the Scriptures of Truth!

"*The mention of the blood*" in 1 John i. 7 and ii. 1.—
Much may be learnt from accuracy in noting that "the
blood of Jesus Christ" is mentioned in 1 John i. 7 in
connection with "walking in the light;" but it is not
mentioned in 1 John ii. 1 in connection with the commission of sin.

This fact speaks to us, if we have ears to hear, and
tells us that, when we "walk in the light," *i.e.*, when we
have access into His presence, as the High Priest had
(though only on one day in the year), it is entirely in virtue
of that precious blood of Christ which gives us a title
to that access, and preserves us in that presence. The
High Priest could not enter into the Holy of Holies and
see that glorious light of the *Shekinah* which symbolized
the presence of God, without blood; neither can we enter
into and enjoy "fellowship" with God, who is light
(*vv.* 5—7), apart from the merits of that precious blood
of Christ. Then it is that we need those merits; then
it is that we are reminded of them; then it is that the
blood is mentioned.

But, in 1 John ii. 1, when it is a question of sin, there
is no need to mention it at all; for it was once offered,
once for all, and its virtues and merits in the putting
away of sin are eternal in their results. It is "eternal
redemption," "eternal salvation."

Hence, "if any man sin we have an Advocate with the
Father." It does not say "a high priest with God"; for
that title was in connection with the priestly act of
access and approach through blood, but "an advocate
with the Father." This is to remind us that *relationship
has not been broken.* He who is spoken of as "God" in
connection with the access of his sinful creatures, is
spoken of as "Father" in connection with His sinful
"children."

Thus, accuracy in reading shows us that these Scriptures are Divine; for where the Holy Spirit mentions

the blood, man (if he had written it) would surely have
left it out; while, where the Holy Spirit does not mention it, man would certainly have put it in. Indeed he
does so, constantly, in his prayers, and in his writings.

"*Accepted*" *and* "*Acceptable*" (Eph. i. 6 and 2 Cor.
v. 9).—We must accurately note the distinction between
these two words. In the A.V. we have the one word
"accepted" in both passages; but in the Greek they are
different.

The former (Eph. i. 6) is χαριτόω (*charitoō*), *to make
one an object of favour.* This refers to the standing which
God has given us, in Christ, in the heavenlies.

The latter (2 Cor. v. 9) is εὐάρεστος (*euarestos*), *well-
pleasing.* This refers to our state, and our daily walk
and life on earth.

The former relates to the person, the latter to his
actions.

It is one thing for us to be *accepted* in Christ, for
His merits' sake; and it is another thing for our walk
to be *well-pleasing* to God.

The former is the gift of God's grace; the latter is the
fruit of that grace.

It is most important that we should be accurate in
noting this distinction, so that we may be preserved
from legality on the one hand, and from laxity on the
other.

All the children of God have the same standing; the
strongest as well as the feeblest, the oldest as well as
the youngest.

We do not labour to be accepted, but having been
"accepted in the Beloved" we make it our aim (R.V.)
for our walk to be acceptable.

"*Man*" *and* "*men.*"—It is important that we should
be accurate in noticing such a difference between the
singular and the plural; for example, in this case, between "man" and "men," especially in the Divine use
of these words.

"Man," God has written down as lost, ruined, guilty,
helpless, and hopeless; though the world deifies "man";
and exalts him as having within him a part of the Divine.

"Men," God graciously saves; and deals with individual men in mercy, pity, and blessing; though the world thinks little and makes less of individual sinners. They may go to the wall for all that the world cares, when it comes to showing kindness, or giving help.

In this is manifested the difference between God's thoughts and the world's thoughts (Isa. lv. 8).

God declares that "there is no good thing" in man (Rom. vii. 18). The world with one voice, in Pulpit, Platform, and Press, declares that there *is* some good thing in man.

The issue is clear, sharp, and decisive; and the only question is, Do we believe what God says? or Do we believe what man says?

Remembering and Forgetting.—The same difference is manifested in the treatment of man by God, and by the world.

As to our frailties and infirmities the world makes no allowance for them. It does not remember our weaknesses; but holds us responsible for our mistakes however excusable. But God "knoweth our frame; He remembereth that we are but dust" (Ps. ciii. 14).

As to our sins, the world remembers them. After long years they are brought up against us; and the time and the circumstances are remembered, enumerated, and described in all their detail. But God has written of His forgiven people: "Their sins and their iniquities will I remember no more" (Heb. viii. 12; x. 17. Jer. xxxi. 34).

Thus what God remembers, man forgets; and what God forgets, man remembers.

2. *The negative of what is said.*

It is sometimes useful, if not important, to note this; and to put what is said into opposite language.

"Out of the Scriptures" (Acts xvii. 2).—For example, in Acts xvii. 2, where Paul for "three Sabbath days reasoned with them out of the Scriptures," it may be well to note that it does not say, "out of the newspapers" or "out of his own head."

" *Waiting for God's Son from heaven* " (1 Thess. i. 10).—
When we read that the Thessalonian saints were " waiting for God's son from heaven," it is well to note what
they were *not* waiting for.

It does not say that they waited for the "Spirit of
God," but for the Son of God.

It does not say that they waited for "death," for that
comes without waiting for it.

It does not say that they were waiting for Titus with
his armies to come from Rome, but for God's Son to
come from heaven.

It does not say that they waited for the fulfilment
of prophecy, for Nebuchadnezzar's Image, or Daniel's
Beasts, but for "God's Son from heaven, whom He raised
from the dead, even Jesus, which delivered us from the
wrath to come."

2 *Thess. ii.* 3, "Except there come the Apostasy first."
—When it says "that day (the day of the Lord) shall not
come except there come the Apostasy first and that man
of sin be revealed, the son of perdition," we are to note
that it does not say, "till the world's conversion comes,"
but till the Apostasy comes.

It does not say, "the world is not yet good enough,"
but the world is not yet bad enough.

3. *Marks of Time.*

These are of the utmost importance, often pointing
the way to the correct interpretation; giving us the
clue to the explanation of some difficulty; or, bringing out
some hidden truth or beauty concealed in that particular
Scripture.

" *The second day* " (Josh. x. 31, 32).—Here we read:
" And Joshua passed from Libnah, and all Israel with
him, unto Lachish, and encamped against it, and fought
against it. And the LORD delivered Lachish into the
hand of Israel, which took it *on the second day* and smote
it with the edge of the sword."

Thus Lachish seems to be an exception to all the other
cities taken by Joshua at that time. Of Lachish alone
is it said that " he took it on *the second day.*"

This point of accuracy invites our attention: and when we give it by looking more closely into Lachish, we find that—

In 2 Chron. xxxii. 9 "Sennacherib himself laid siege against Lachish, and all his power with him;" while he sent Rabshakeh to Jerusalem with a summons to Hezekiah.

Yet when Rabshakeh returned he "found the king of Assyria warring against Libnah; for he heard that *he was departed from Lachish*" (2 Kings xix. 8). He evidently found Lachish a difficult place to take, as Joshua had done.

We note the further confirmation of this in a reference by Jeremiah to a subsequent assault by another king of Babylon. He says:

"When the king of Babylon's army fought against all the cities of Judah *that were left*, against *Lachish*, and against Azekah; for these defenced cities remained of the cities of Judah" (Jer. xxxiv. 7).

So that when we read in Josh. x. 31, 32, about Joshua taking Lachish on "*the second day*" of the siege, we get a note of time which is not a mere casual remark, but is full of meaning when compared with other references to the same city.

"*Then came Amalek*" (Exod. xvii. 8).—Here we read that immediately after the miraculous supply of water recorded in verses 1–7, "THEN came Amalek and fought with Israel in Rephidim."

No reason is given for this assault on the part of Amalek beyond what may be inferred from the word "Then."

When we consider what is recorded in remoter contexts we gather that in a land of that character, a well of springing water would be a bone of contention, and a possession to be coveted and, if possible, taken by force.

In Gen. xxi. 25 we read of Abraham reproving Abimelech "because of a *well of water* which Abimelech's servants had *violently taken away*."

In Gen. xxvi. 19, 20, we read how Isaac's servants found "a well of springing water, and the herdmen of Gerar did strive with Isaac's herdmen saying the water

is ours . . . And they digged another, and strove for
that also."

In Exod. ii. 17 we read how the shepherds drove a-
way the daughters of Reuel who came to draw water ;
and how Moses helped them.

In Num. xx. 19 we read how Israel offered in vain to
pay for the water as they passed through Edom; also
afterwards how the same offer was made to Sihon the
king of the Amorites.

In Judg. v. 11 Deborah sang of the wells as scenes
of conflict.

No wonder then that such a miraculous supply of
water as at Rephidim should at once become a reason
why Amalek should thus make this assault against Israel
"then."

   "Then will I sprinkle" (Ezek. xxxvi. 25).—

     "THEN will I sprinkle clean water upon you and
          ye shall be clean ;
     From all your filthiness, and from all your idols will
          I cleanse you,
     A new heart also will I give you,
     And a new spirit will I put within you."

When? When Jehovah shall have taken the house of
Israel from among the heathen whither He has scattered
them, and gathered them out of all countries and brought
them "INTO THEIR OWN LAND" (*vv.* 16—24).

If we observe this mark of time, it will effectually
prevent our misinterpretation of this passage, and save
us from taking what is spoken of Israel in a future day
and applying it to the Church of God in the present
day.

   "Then shall the offering" (Mal. iii. 4).—"THEN shall
the offering of Judah and Jerusalem be pleasant unto
Jehovah as in the days of old, and as in former years."

   When? When Jehovah shall have sent His Messenger,
who will sit as a refiner and "purify the sons of Levi
that they may offer unto Jehovah an offering in righteousness" (*vv.* 1—3).

"THEN they that feared Jehovah spake often one to another," etc. (Mal. iii. 16).

When? In a time of apostasy, and neglect of the service and worship of Jehovah. In days of darkness and "perilous times." When the godly are minished; and it is difficult to find the assembly of true worshippers. "THEN" will be the time for believers to meet together, and speak often to one another and "think upon His name" (*vv.* 7—18).

May we not *apply* this Scripture to the condition of things in the present day, without robbing Israel of the *interpretation* of it in a future day?

1 *Thess.* iv. 17.—"THEN we which are alive and remain shall be caught up with them in the clouds, to meet the Lord in the air: and so shall we ever be with the Lord" (1 Thess. iv. 17).

When? When the Lord Himself shall descend from heaven; and when the dead in Christ shall have first risen.

"*Then*" (Matt. xxv. 1).—"THEN shall the kingdom of heaven be likened unto ten virgins, which took their lamps and went forth to meet the Bridegroom."

The word "then" points to the fact that this prophetic parable will have its fulfilment, not now, but at that particular moment in the sequence of events then being revealed by the Lord.

It forms part of the Lord's instruction and teaching as to His coming; and finds its place in His last great prophetic discourse contained in Matt. xxiv. and xxv.

No one part may be taken out from its context, and interpreted apart from it, as conveying a lesson different from that which it was first intended to teach.

In the first place, the whole discourse is wrongly divided from the literary point of view. The Structure and the Scope combine to show that ch. xxv. should begin at ch. xxiv. 29. It consists of two portions of unequal length, answering to the two questions of ch. xxiv. 3. These portions are differently constructed in order to mark their different subjects and scope.

The first part is an *Extended Alternation.* The second part is a *Complex Introversion.*

The questions were two in number.

(1) When ($\pi \acute{o} \tau \epsilon$, *pote*)? and
(2) What ($\tau \acute{\iota}$, *ti*)?

(1) "*When* shall these things (spoken of) be?"
(2) "*What* shall be the sign of Thy coming and of the *sunteleia* of the age (or Dispensation)?"

Answer to the First Question, "When?"

(Matt. xxiv. 4—28).

A | 4—6. Events *heard* of, leading up to the end (*telos*), which is "not yet." Direction to "see that ye be not troubled."

   B | 7, 8. The birth-pangs of the Great Tribulation.

      C | 9, 14. Events leading up to the end (*telos*).

A | 15—20. Events *seen*, sign of the end (*telos*). Direction to "understand it," and "flee."

   B | 21, 22. The Great Tribulation itself.

      C | 23—28. Events ending it.

Thus far we have the Great Tribulation: and the events leading up to, characterizing, and ending it.

Now, in the second part, we have the events following it.

Answer to the Second Question, "What?"

(Matt. xxiv. 29—xxv. 46).

D | a | 29, 30. The Coming of the Son of Man.
    b | 31. The gathering of the elect Remnant of Israel from judgment.

      E | c | 32—41. Parables (General). Fig-tree and Noah.
         d | 42—44. Warning. "Watch."
           e | 45—51. Servants (General).

      E | c | xxv.1—12. Parable(Special). Ten Virgins.
         d | 13. Warning. "Watch."
           e | 14—30. Servants (Special).

D | a | 31. The Coming of the Son of Man.
    b | 32—46. The gathering of the nations for judgment.

From all this, which is pointed out by the word "THEN" in Matt. xxv. 1, it will be seen how impossible it is for us to read the Church of God into the parable of the Ten Virgins without introducing confusion of thought, loss of instruction, and dislocation of our Lord's teaching.

"*Immediately*" (Matt. xxiv. 29).—The word "Immediately" in Matt. xxiv. 29 tells us that there is no interval between the end of the Great Tribulation and the appearing of the Son of Man in His glory, for judgment.

No room for a Millennium therefore, before that glorious Advent.

No place for a thousand years of universal peace and blessing without Christ.

This word "immediately" writes folly on all man's vaunted remedies for the world's sorrows.

It convicts of grossest ignorance all the Church's self-claimed mission to "convert the world" before that Advent.

If the Church is to convert the world, where is the place or possibility of the Great Tribulation?

And, if the Coming of Christ *follows* that Tribulation "immediately," where is there room for the conversion of the world, or for any Millennium before His coming?

The whole argument which is so universally made on behalf of Foreign Missions is radically false. It must be, and can be based on truly Scriptural grounds, without thus mangling and marring the Scriptures of truth. Not only does this want of accuracy in interpreting the Word of God bring it into contempt and make it of none effect; but it deceives the world, and enables the scoffer to ask, "Where are the signs that your mission is being accomplished?"

The Church answers back, that though there are no signs yet; though heathen births far exceed the converts' deaths, yet they are "waiting for an outpouring of the Spirit." Thus they deceive themselves with a false hope, and substitute it for the true hope which God has given, which is, "to wait for God's Son (not God's Spirit) from heaven."

If the Church urges, as it does, that Daniel's prophecies were fulfilled under Antiochus Epiphanes, and that it was

he who set up "the abomination of desolation, spoken
of by Daniel the prophet," it is a sufficient answer to
point out that the Lord speaks of it, in His day, as being
still future, and gives solemn warning to those who shall
see it, to heed it and "understand" it; and adds specific
directions as to what they are to do.

"*Afterward*" (Joel ii. 28).—"And it shall come to pass
AFTERWARD, that I will pour out my spirit upon all
flesh," etc. [1]

After what?

After God has brought Israel back into their own land,
and made it fruitful, and blessed it and them with all
blessings. If we read the previous part of the chapter we
can see plainly enough *when* the pouring out of spiritual
gifts shall take place. The verse immediately before
reads:

> "And ye shall know that I am in the midst of Israel,
> And that I am Jehovah your God, and none else:
> And my people shall never be ashamed.
> And it shall come to pass AFTERWARD," etc.

This shows that Peter could not have been referring to
Joel to show that that prophecy was *then being fulfilled*,
for none of those things had taken place; and none of
those conditions had been enjoyed.

Peter is merely rebutting the charge of drunkenness,
and showing that it could not be true, inasmuch as similar
scenes were spoken of by Joel the prophet. When he
says, "This is that which was spoken of by the prophet
Joel" he can mean only *this* (Sing.) *prophecy* which he
proceeds to quote; not those (pl.) events which were
taking place.

And yet his utterance is so worded that had the
people and their rulers repented, as he exhorted them
(Acts ii. 38; iii. 19—26, R.V.), and as it was required by
the one great condition of the fulfilment of the promise
of Joel ii. 12—17, then the prophecy of Joel ii. 28 (which
Peter quoted) would have been fulfilled: for that will be
the time when the LORD will "be jealous for His LAND
and pity His PEOPLE," as long before foretold in "the
Song of Moses" (Deut. xxxii. 43).

---

[1] On the whole context of this passage, see above, pages 297—302.

"*At that time*" (Matt. xi. 25).—This mark of time we have already referred to under Canon VI. (page 323).

4. *Marks of Reasoning.*

"*Therefore*" (Eph. iv. 1).—"I THEREFORE the prisoner of the Lord beseech you that ye walk worthy of the calling wherewith ye are called."

Why? Ch. iii. being a parenthesis between ch. ii. and ch. iv. (see page 62), we see that the word "therefore" stands connected with ch. ii. 22.

It is the one building "fitly framed together"; the "holy temple" (ch. ii. 21, 22): It is the one body which is likewise "fitly framed together" (ch. iii. 16).

"THEREFORE," endeavour to keep this unity of the spirit (this spiritual unity) which God HAS MADE in Christ.

Seek not to *make* a corporate or bodily unity; but give diligence to KEEP to the spiritual unity which God has made.

To do this will require "all lowliness and meekness, with longsuffering, forbearing one another in love" (*v.* 2).

"*Therefore . . . I charge thee*" (2 Tim. iv. 1).—Here, and in all similar cases where we have such words as "Therefore," "Wherefore," marking logical conclusions of arguments or statements, it is always important for us, in our reading, to be most accurate, and to notice the matter thus introduced and emphasized by the word "therefore." This is the more important, because such words, more often than not, come at the beginning of a chapter, where the break is apt to sever the connection between the argument and the conclusion, between the cause and the effect, or between a statement and its result.

A good example is furnished in 2 Tim. iv. 1. The chapter begins:

"I charge thee THEREFORE, before God and the Lord Jesus Christ, who shall judge the quick and the dead, and by His appearing and His kingdom—Preach the Word" (R.V.).

Why is this charge given? and why is it given here?

The answer to these questions is furnished by the word "therefore." Ch. iii. had ended with a statement as to the wonderful profitableness of the God-breathed Word, fitting out God's spokesman for every emergency (see above, under Canon V., pp. 304, 305, and VI., p. 321). The solemn conclusion is:—

Seeing that the Divine Word is God-breathed;—seeing that it is so profitable,—seeing that it is so necessary to fit out him who thus possesses it,

THEREFORE

"Preach the Word." Note the comparison thus suggested between ch. iii. 16, and ch. iv. 2.

Seeing it is profitable for "doctrine," *therefore* "preach it in season and out of season."

Seeing it is profitable for "reproof," *therefore* "reprove."

Seeing it is profitable for "correction," *therefore* "rebuke."

Seeing it is profitable for "instruction in righteousness," *therefore* "exhort with all longsuffering and doctrine."

All this, and more, is wrapped up in this word "therefore."

Similar examples may be noted, and instruction gained by accurately observing the occurrences of such words.

5. *Numeration*

It is a great question whether we have the correct method of translating numbers. Each nation has its own method of reckoning, and its own idioms of numeration.

We have only to go to the French and to one illustration to see this. Take as an example our simple ninety-seven (97). How is this to be translated into French? Idiomatically, of course, and not literally. The French would be *quatre-vingt-dix-sept*, or four-twenty-ten-seven: *i.e.*,

four twenties . . .	$= 80$
ten	$= 10$
seven	$= 7$
	$\overline{}$
	97

Now, may it not be well to ask whether the Hebrew mode of reckoning was the same as the English; or, indeed, whether it was the same in Old Testament days as it is to-day?

In any case, is it not wiser to ask this question instead of first assuming an answer which may be incorrect, then charging the error on the inspired writers, and then explaining it by talking of "exaggeration," or of "round numbers"?

That is an easy, not to say the usual, way out of difficulties which we ourselves perhaps have created.

1 Sam. vi. 19.—Infidels and Critics have brought charges of error, for example, against 1 Sam. vi. 19:

"And he smote the men of Beth-shemesh, because they had looked into the Ark of Jehovah, even he smote of the people fifty thousand and three-score and ten men" (*i.e.,* 50,070 men).

This is what the A.V. says.

But, Is this what the Word of God says?

The Hebrew of the latter clause reads: "Jehovah smote seventy men, [two] fifties and one thousand."

The word "fifties" is in the Dual number, which means *two fifties.*

So that we have, according to this—

seventy men . . .	70
two fifties	100
one thousand . . .	1,000
or	1,170 men.

There is a slight difference it will be observed. And, as Beth-shemesh was quite a small place, this smaller number would appear to be more correct.

Judg. xii. 6.—Another example might be found in Judg. xii. 6, where we read of the tribe of Ephraim:

"And there fell at that time forty, and two thousand."

This would be . . .	40
and	2,000
or, as we should say .	2,040

This would be more in harmony with Num. xxvi. 37, which gives the total of the second census of Ephraim as 32,500, while the first was not more than 40,500 (Num. i. 33). Not only is the above *more* in harmony, for the other reckoning is *out of all harmony;* as those slain of the tribe would be more than the number of the whole tribe, within about three hundred years.

The Census of Num. i. and xxvi.—This leads to another suggestion which is made by Professor W. M. Flinders Petrie in his *Researches in Sinai.*[1] His suggestion is that in the two Census Lists of Num. i. and xxvi. the word *Eleph, thousand,* should be taken in the sense of *family* or *tent.* He would then reckon, Reuben (Num. i. 21) as "46 *eleph* 500 people": *i.e.,* eleven to a tent.

But the objection to this is (1) that it is not "people," but the "men over twenty years of age"; (2) that the first list works out at 598 *eleph* 5,550 men over twenty years old (not people), whereas it is several times given as 603 *eleph* 3,550 men; which shows that the 598 and 5,550 *must* be reckoned as *thousands,* in order to arrive at the totals as given in Exod. xxxviii. 26. Num. i. 46; ii. 32, *viz.,* 598,000 + 3,550 = 603,550 (compare Exod. xii. 37. Num. xi. 21).

We must therefore conclude that Moses knew more about what he was writing than explorers and critics can imagine.

Our suggestion as given above does not lie under these serious objections, but relates merely to the principle underlying the method of numeration, and the idioms used in stating it.

6. *Names of Persons and Places.*

Accuracy is also required in the study of the names of persons and places. Apart from Scripture evidence we know that, in all countries, many places and persons have the same name; while on the other hand some are known by, and have, several names.

We should expect, therefore, to find these phenomena in the Bible.

---

[1] London: John Murray, 1906; pp. 194—223.

So far from being a discrepancy which amounts to
an objection, it is only a difficulty calling for greater
accuracy and care in our study of the Word.

Moreover, it is an argument for the veracity of God's
Word, in that, what are difficulties to us, are left unex-
plained because the truth as to the facts was perfectly
well known.

(a) *As to Persons.*

1. *The same name was borne by different persons* then,
as now.

This is particularly noticeable in the case of James.

JAMES.—We have to distinguish:

(1) James the son of Zebedee, and brother of John
(Matt. iv. 21; xvii. 1, etc.).

(2) James the son of Alphæus, one of the Twelve
(Mark iii. 18. Matt. x. 3, etc.).

(3) James the Lord's brother (Gal. i. 19. Matt. xiii.
55. Mark vi. 3).

JOHN.—We have to distinguish—

(1) John the Baptist (Matt. iii. 4).

(2) John the Apostle (Mark i. 20).

(3) John Mark (Acts xii. 12, 25; xiii. 5, 13; xv. 37).

(4) John of Acts iv. 6.

SIMON was a name borne by at least ten persons in the
New Testament. There were—

(1) SIMON (Luke ii. 25).

(2) SIMON PETER the Apostle.

(3) SIMON ZELOTES, one of the Twelve (Luke vi. 15.
Acts i. 13). This is the same as SIMON THE
CANANITE (Matt. x. 4. Mark iii. 18), being the
Aramaic for Zelotes, both meaning *Zeal* or
Zealot; the name of a Jewish sect.

(4) SIMON son of Joseph and Mary (Matt. xiii. 55.
Mark vi. 3).

(5) SIMON the father of Judas Iscariot (John vi. 71;
xii. 4; xiii. 2, 26).

(6) SIMON the Pharisee (Luke vii. 40, 43, 44).

(7) SIMON THE LEPER (Matt. xxvi. 6. Mark xiv. 3).

(8) SIMON THE CYRENIAN (Matt. xxvii. 32. Mark xv. 21).

(9) SIMON THE TANNER (Acts ix. 43; x. 6, 32).

(10) SIMON MAGUS (Acts viii. 9, 13).

HEROD was a name borne by seven different persons:

(1) HEROD THE GREAT of whom we read in Matt. ii.
and Luke i. He died in the year of the true
Nativity (B.C. 4). During his last illness he
ordered the slaughter of the children at Bethlehem (Matt. ii. 16—18).

(2) HEROD ANTIPAS, son of Herod I., Tetrarch of
Galilee (Luke iii. 1), the central portion of kingdom of Herod I. He was the half-brother of
Herod Philip I. and abducted his wife Herodias
and married her (Matt. xiv. 3. Luke iii. 19.
Mark. vi. 17). He heard John gladly, but
afterwards beheaded him (Mark vi. 20). This
was the Herod to whom the Lord was sent for
trial (Luke xxiii. 8—12).

(3) HEROD ARCHELAUS, son of Herod I. Ethnarch of
portion of kingdom of Herod I., on account of
whom Joseph turned aside into Galilee (Matt.
ii. 22).

(4) HEROD PHILIP I., son of Herod I., without terri-
tory. Husband of Herodias, who was abducted
and married by Herod Antipas (Matt. xiv. 3.
Mark vi. 17. Luke iii. 19).

(5) HEROD PHILIP II., son of Herod I., Tetrarch of the
N.E. portion of kingdom of Herod I. (Luke
iii. 1). Built Cæsarea Philippi (Matt. xvi. 13.
Mark viii. 27).

(6) HEROD AGRIPPA I., grandson of Herod I., succeeded Philip II. Put James to death, and
Peter in prison (Acts xii.).

(7) HEROD AGRIPPA II., son of Agrippa I., whom he
succeeded in part. The Herod before whom
Paul stood (Acts xxv. 13).

The same name in some cases arises from the fact that
it is a title associated with royalty; just as the words
"Czar," "Kaiser," etc.

ABIMELECH was the common name for the kings of
the Philistines.
AGAG, for the kings of the Amalekites.
CÆSAR, for the emperors of Rome.

PHARAOH, for the kings of the Egyptians, such as Pharaoh Hophra (Jer. xliv. 30); Pharaoh Necho (2 Kings xxiii. 29, 33, 34, 35. Jer. xlvi. 2).

We may learn a solemn lesson from the history of the calamitous and fatal matrimonial alliance of Jehoram the son of Jehoshaphat with Athaliah, the daughter of Ahab and Jezebel.[1]

We find, after this, *the same names being given to members of both families*, showing how close this alliance became, and how the evil leaven worked and permeated the whole mass.

Not only was the house of Jehovah broken up and the vessels thereof taken to the house of Baal, but the two families became alike in their life and their religion.

Care has to be taken by the Bible student in the midst of the confusion created for him by this unholy alliance: and the difficulties caused by it have to be noted and unravelled.

2. *The same person has different names,*[2] or more than one:

ABIEL (1 Sam. ix. 1) is NER of 1 Chron. ix. 39.

ISHUI (1 Sam. xiv. 49) is ABINADAB of ch. xxxi. 2.

ABIMELECH of Ps. xxxiv. (Title) is ACHISH of 1 Sam. xxi. 11. (See above.)

LEVI (Luke v. 27) is the same as MATTHEW.

THOMAS and DIDYMUS are the Hebrew and Greek words respectively for *twins*.

SILVANUS (2 Cor. i. 19. 1 Thess. i. 1. 1 Pet. v. 12) is the same as SILAS (Acts xv. 22, 27, 34, 40; xvi. 19, 25).

TIMOTHEUS (Acts xvi. 1, etc.) is TIMOTHY.

CEPHAS (John i. 42. 1 Cor. i. 12; iii. 22; ix. 5; xv. 5. Gal. ii. 9) is the Aramaic for the Greek PETER. His Hebrew name was SIMEON or SIMON. Hence he was sometimes called SIMON PETER. But there were several who are known by the name of SIMON. (See above, page 367).

---

[1] See the separate pamphlet on *Jehoshaphat: a Lesson for our Times*, by the same author.

[2] Sometimes this is only apparent, as in the case of JESUS, which is the Greek form of JOSHUA (Acts vii. 45. Heb. iv. 8). CHRIST is the Greek for the Hebrew MESSIAH. REMPHAN (Acts vii. 43) is the Greek for CHIUN (Amos v. 26). So in the same way ALLELUIA (Rev. xix. 1, 3, 4, 6) is the Greek form of the Hebrew HALLELUJAH.

Esau's wives.—Perhaps one of the most intricate of
these problems is that of Esau's wives. As infidels and
"higher" critics (which too often mean very much the
same thing) have sometimes referred to this as showing
the human element in an untrustworthy record, it may
be well to say a few words about it.

In Gen. xxxvi. 1—3 we have "the generations of Esau."
This, therefore, is the correct and standard genealogy
which must be our foundation.

Here Esau's wives are stated to be three in number;
and their names are thus definitely stated:

(1) Adah.
(2) Aholibamah.
(3) Bashemath.

(1) As to the first, Adah, she was the daughter of Elon
the Hittite. In Gen. xxvi. 34 she has a second name,
Bashemath, which happened to be the same as that of
the first name of the third wife, and therefore is dropped
here.

(2) As to the second, Aholibamah, she was the daughter
of Anah the Hivite [1] (Gen. xxxvi. 3, 14, 25). In Gen. xxvi. 34
she is called Judith, and her father is called Beeri the
Hittite.[1] Doubtless Anah got this name later on, from
a fact that is mentioned in ch. xxxvi. 24 concerning Anah.
"This is that Anah who found[2] the hot springs[3] in the
wilderness as he fed the asses of Zibeon his father."

This was the origin of his other name Beeri or *the
spring-man*, or the man that discovered the hot springs.

(3) As to the third, Bashemath, she was the daughter
of Ishmael and had a second name Mahalath (ch.
xxviii. 9).

---

[1] In Gen. xxvi. 34 he is called "Hittite." Hittite is the general name, which
includes the Hivite, which is particular. Ch. xxvi. 34 is history, but ch. xxxvi. 2
is genealogy, and is therefore more precise (see Josh. i. 4. 1 Kings x. 29. 2 Kings
vii. 6). In Gen. xxviii. 8 these Hittite wives are called "daughters of Canaan,"
i.e., the general name.

[2] The Hebrew is מָצָא (*mātzā'*), *to happen on, meet with, find, discover* (not
to invent or *find out*).

[3] Hebrew, הַיֵּמִם (*hayyēmim*), *hot springs*. (The Vulgate has *aquæ calidæ*.
Probably the *Calirrhoe* in the Wady Zerka Maein, or Wady el Asha, S.E. of
the Dead Sea.) Hence Anah was called *Beeri*, which would mean *the spring-
man*. It certainly cannot mean *mules*, as the word for mules is פְּרָדִים
(*perādim*). (See 2 Sam. xiii. 29; xviii. 9. 1 Kings x. 25. 2 Kings v. 17. Ps. xxxii. 9).

There is no difficulty, therefore, if we accurately note these different names; and remember that a forger would be perfectly sure to have made all clear, and have left no such matters in doubt; also that women, as a rule, received a second or additional name on their marriage.

3. *Changes in Names.*—In some cases different names came from a definite change, as ABRAHAM for ABRAM (Gen. xvii. 5). BOANERGES for JOHN and JAMES, PETER for SIMON (Mark iii. 16, 17). PAUL for SAUL (Acts xiii. 9). DANIEL and his three companions (Dan. i. 7). JOSEPH (Gen. xli. 45).

4. *The Divine Names and Titles.*—These also need careful discrimination if we would explain difficulties, and see new beauties in the words of God.

There is no need to say anything on the subject here, as the whole subject is referred to above (p. 312); and is fully dealt with in our separate pamphlet on this subject.

(b) *Of places.*

(1) *The same name was given to different places.*

CAESAREA

    (1) Was given to DAN, before called LAISH (see below), and

    (2) Was called CÆSAREA PHILIPPI[1] (Matt. xvi. 13. Mark viii. 27) to distinguish it from CÆSAREA of Palestine, which was on the coast (Acts xviii. 22; x. 1, 24; xii. 19; xxi. 8; xxv. 6, 13).

ANTIOCH was the name of

    (1) A city in Syria (Acts xi. 20—26); and

    (2) A city of Pisidia (Acts xiii. 14).

DAN was the name of a city or country in the north of Palestine (Gen. xiv. 14. Deut. xxxiv. 1), long before the tribe of Dan changed the name of quite another place (before called Laish) to the name of their ancestor, Dan (Judges xviii. 29).

---

[1] Because beautified by Philip the Tetrarch, now known as BANIAS.

BETHSAIDA:

   (1) The city of Andrew and Peter on the N.E
shore of Galilee (John i. 44), called πόλις (*polis*),
a *city*.

   (2) On the W. shore (called κώμη (*kōme*), a
village, Mark viii. 22, 23).

   (3) Of Gaulonitis, Luke ix. 10 (afterwards called
Julias).

BEEROTH:

   (1) In Benjamin, Josh. ix. 1—18. 2 Sam. iv. 2.

   (2) Of the children of Jaakan, Deut. x. 6 (Num.
xxxiii. 31, 32, called Bene-jaakan).

RAMAH:

   (1) A city of Benjamin (Judg. iv. 5; xix. 13.
1 Sam. xxii. 6. Jer. xxxi. 15. Matt. ii. 18).

   (2) In Asher (Josh. xix. 29).

   (3) In Naphtali (Josh. xix. 36).

   (4) In Gilead (2 Kings viii. 29. 2 Chron. xxii. 6).

   (5) The birth-place of Samuel (1 Sam. i. 19;
ii. 11, etc.).

Sometimes these names were so indeterminate that it
was necessary to couple with them some explanatory
word:—

KIRJATH. From *Kir*, a *wall* or *walled*. Hence we
have:

   (1) Kirjath Arba (Gen. xxiii. 2; xxxv. 27. Josh.
xiv. 15; xv. 13, 54; xx. 7; xxi. 11. Neh. xi. 25).

   (2) Kirjath Baal (Josh. xv. 60; xviii. 14).

   (3) Kirjath Huzoth (Num. xxii. 39).

   (4) Kirjath Jearim (Ezra ii. 25. Josh. ix. 17).

   (5) Kirjath Sepher (Josh. xv. 15, 16. Judg. i.
11, 12).

   (6) Kirjath Sannah (Josh. xv. 49).

ARAM (meaning *high*, but translated "Syria"). From
this we have:

   (1) Aram of Damascus (2 Sam. viii. 5, 6).

   (2) Aram-beth-Rehob (2 Sam. x. 6).

   (3) Aram-Zobah (2 Sam. x. 6).

   (4) Aram-Naharaim (*i.e.*, Aram of the two
rivers, translated "Mesopotamia"), (Gen. xxiv. 10.
Compare ch. xxvii. 43).

So that if we note accurately the use of these various names we shall not, like many, jump to the conclusion that there must be a "discrepancy."

The same phenomena are seen in all countries.[1]

(2) *The same place has different names.*

JEGAR-SAHADUTHA was the Aramaic name, but the Hebrew name was GALEED (both having the same meaning) (Gen. xxxi. 47).

LUZ was afterwards called BETHEL (Gen. xxviii. 19).

HERMON was known as SIRION by the Sidonians, and as SHENIR by the Amorites (Deut. iii. 9), also by the name of SION (ch. iv. 48).

EGYPT was known as HAM (Pss. lxxviii. 51; cv. 23), and as RAHAB (Pss. lxxxvii. 4; lxxxix. 10. Isa. li. 9).

JERUSALEM is called ARIEL (*The lion of God*, Isa. xxix. 1), as it had been called JEBUS by the Jebusites (Judg. xix. 10).

BABYLON is called SHESHAK (Jer. xxv. 26).

CÆSAREA in Galilee was called LAISH at first, and was afterwards known as DAN (Judg. xviii. 29. 1 Kings xii. 29). This has to be distinguished from another CÆSAREA, which was on the coast (Acts xviii. 22, see above).

THE LAKE OF GENNESARETH was known also as the SEA OF TIBERIAS, and as the SEA OF GALILEE (John vi. 1, 23). Also as CHINNERETH.

CHARRAN of Acts vii. 2 is the HARAN of Gen. xi.

ARAM is the same as MESOPOTAMIA and SYRIA (Num. xxiii. 7).

MIZRAIM is EGYPT.

LAISH was afterwards called DAN (Judg. xviii. 29).

SINAI is known also as HOREB.

7. *Chronology.*

Accurate reading of the words, as written, will soon make it apparent that there is no Chronology as such in the Scriptures. Years are numbered not as *dates*, but as to *duration*. And when dates are used they are

---

[1] Note the eight "Suttons," and combined with other words, 26 more; the ten "Miltons"; the eleven "Newports"; the eleven "Newtons" and 30 combinations with other distinguishing names.

reckoned as having happened in a certain year from some event, or from the commencement of a reign, or a captivity, etc.: otherwise, the years are reckoned only as being so many, during a certain period. This is the case with

The 120 *years of Gen. vi.* 3.—These are usually taken as referring to one hundred and twenty years of probation before the Flood. But, is this the case? The A.V. reads: "Jehovah said, My spirit shall not always strive with man, for that he also is flesh ; yet his days shall be a hundred and twenty years."

There are several traditional interpretations of this verse, all equally unsatisfactory.

There is the fanciful Rabbinical one which makes it refer to Moses's age.

The popular idea is that it refers to the period of probation between that time and the Flood : another explanation refers it to the altered duration of human life.

But, if we note accurately the words employed another interpretation will be suggested.

(1) The word rendered "man" is אָדָם (*'ādām*), *Adam*. It occurs thirty-seven times in these early chapters of Genesis (from Gen. i.—vi. 3), and is rendered *Adam* nineteen times and *man* eighteen times. It occurs without the article twelve times.[1]

(2) It occurs with the article הָאָדָם (*hā'ādām*), twenty-one times.[2]

(3) It occurs not only with the article, but with this and the very strong demonstrative אֵת (*eth*) four times.[3] *Eth* means *self, this same, this very,* and is quite emphatic.[4]

(4) Nos. 2 and 3 always mean *the man, Adam.*

---

[1] Gen. i. 26; ii. 5, 20 (2nd); iii. 17, 21; iv. 25; v. 1 (twice), 2, 3, 4, 5.

[2] Gen. ii. 7 (2nd), 16, 18, 19 (twice), 20 (1st), 21, 22 (twice), 23, 25; ch. iii. 8, 9, 12, 20, 22, 24; iv. 1; vi. 1, 2, 3.

[3] Gen. i. 27; ii. 7 (1st), 8, 15.

[4] In order that the reader may judge for himself, we give all the above passages in their order, indicating which of the three forms of the word is used in each:—

1. Gen. i. 26.	2. Gen. ii. 20 (1st).	1. Gen. iii. 21.
3. „ i. 27.	1. „ ii. 20 (2nd).	2. „ iii. 22, 24.
1. „ ii. 5.	2. „ ii. 21, 22 (twice),	2. „ iv. 1.
3. „ ii. 7 (1st).	[23, 25.	1. „ iv. 25.
2. „ ii. 7 (2nd).	2. „ iii. 8, 9, 12.	1. „ v. 1 (twice), 2,
3. „ ii. 8, 15.	1. „ iii. 17.	[3, 4, 5.
2. „ ii. 16, 18, 19	2. „ iii. 20.	2. „ vi. 1, 2, 3.
[(twice).		

Where it occurs without the article it is rendered
"Adam," except in Gen. i. 26 and ii. 5, where it is rendered "man."

Where it is used without the article and with the
pronoun and verb in the plural number, as in ch. i. 26, it
denotes *man* or *mankind* as such ("Let us make *man*
(sing.) . . . and let *them* have dominion," etc.).

In Gen. vi. 1 we have *Adam* in the singular with the
article, and it means, "Adam began to multiply, and
daughters were born to them." Here the plural pronoun
shows that Eve is associated with Adam as in ch. v. 2.

In Gen. vi. 3 it must mean *the man Adam*, because it
has the article and is followed by the pronoun and the
verb in the Singular Number: "because that he also is
flesh." The Hebrew is הוּא בְּשַׁגַּם (*beshaggām hū'*), *because
that also he.* This has no sense whatever if it does not
refer to *the man Adam.* To whom does the word "also"
refer if it refers not to him? If men as such were meant, it
would say, "for that they also are flesh": but it says,
"for that he also is." That is to say, Adam had become
like the others. He was flesh as they were. All flesh had
corrupted his way on the earth. Noah and his family
alone had preserved their breed "perfect" (*v.* 8): Hebrew,
תָּמִים (*tāmim*), *without blemish.*[1]

The word "generations" occurs twice in verse 8. The
first time it means Noah's family history (*Toledōth*); but
the second is a different word (*Dōr*), and means his
contemporaries.

This is the third reference to the man Adam's end. In
Gen. ii. 17 it was prophetically announced. In ch. iii. 22—24
he was driven out from the tree of life that he might not
eat and live for ever; and now, here, the actual year of
his death was fixed. He should live 120 years more, but
not for ever.

In Gen. vi. 3 we have a chronological indication of the
date of this announcement. Adam lived, altogether,
930 years. If we deduct from this, these 120 years, we get
A.M. 810 as the date. But the corruption spoken of in
this chapter must have commenced much earlier.[2]

---

[1] And is generally so rendered. See Exod. xii. 5; xxix. 1. Leviticus and
Numbers throughout.

[2] See *Things to Come*, Vol. VIII., pp. 11, 56, 97; xi. 110, 111, 138.

The word rendered "strive" is דוּן (*dūn*). It occurs only here. The Ancient Versions (the Sept., Syriac, Arabic, and Latin) give it the sense of *remaining* or *dwelling*. They are right; and what Gen. vi. 3 actually says is, "My spirit (or, breath of life) shall not always remain in Adam, for that he also is flesh." (Compare Isa. lvii. 16).

"Spirit," here, must mean "breath," or life, as in verse 17; vii. 15, 22.[1]

Both A.V. and R.V. use a small "s" and not a capital letter.

The 400 *years of Gen. xv.* 13 *and Acts vii.* 6 (see above under Canon V. *b.*, pages 58 and 302).

The 430 *years of Exod. xii.* 40 *and Gal. iii.* 17 (see above under Canon V., pages 58 and 302), and
The 450 *years of Acts xiii.* 20, and
The 490 *years of Dan. ix.* 24.

These are part of a larger period: the second of the four periods of 490 *years*, which was the duration of the four hundred and seventy hebdomads, or seventy sevens of years, during which Jehovah stood in special covenant relation with Israel. As these were *covenant* relations, the years when those relations were interrupted were not reckoned in the number of the years of such periods.

Just as, in this present interval, while Israel is *Lo ammi*, ("not my people," Hos. i. 9, 10. Isa. liv. 7, 8), the years are not reckoned, but are deducted from the 490 years.

The *first* of these periods is reckoned from the birth of Abraham (Gen. xi. 26) to the Exodus. But to get these 490 years we must deduct fifteen years. And these were exactly the number of years that Ishmael was in Abraham's house.

The *second* period of 490 years is reckoned from the Exodus (Exod. xii. 40, 41) to the Foundation of Solomon's Temple (1 Kings vi. 1). But to get this 490 years

---

[1] רוּחַ (*rūach*) is rendered *breath* in Gen. vi. 16; vii. 15, 22. 2 Sam. xxii. 16. Job iv. 9; ix. 18; xii. 10; xv. 30; xvii. 1; xix. 17; xxvii. 3, marg. Ps. xviii. 15; xxxiii. 6; civ. 29; cxxxv. 17; cxlvi. 4. Eccles. iii. 19. Isa. xi. 4; xxx. 28; xxxiii. 11. Jer. x. 14; li. 17. Lam. iv. 20. Ezek. xxxvii. 5, 6, 8, 9, 10. Hab. ii. 19.

we must deduct the ninety-three years of the captivities of Judges,[1] and add three years for the building.[1]

The 480*th year of* 1 *Kings vi.* 1 is an *Ordinal* number, and not a *Cardinal* number. It is the four hundred and eightiETH year after the Exodus, omitting the ninety-three years referred to above.

The *third* period of 490 years is reckoned from the Dedication of Solomon's Temple (1 Kings vi. 1) to "the going forth of the Decree to restore and rebuild Jerusalem" (Dan. ix. 24—27. Neh. ii. 1). But to get these 490 years we must deduct the seventy years of the Captivity in Babylon.

The *fourth* period of 490 years dates from the going forth of the Decree (Neh. ii. 1—8), B.C. 454, to the consummation; deducting the years of this present interval, dating from "cutting off of the Messiah" (Dan. ix. 26) to the fulness of the times of the Gentiles (Luke xxi. 24. Isa. lix. 19, 20).[2]

That there are such parentheses in God's reckonings; and the particular parenthesis of this present Dispensation see above under "Rightly Dividing the Word of Truth as to its Times and Dispensations." See Part I., above, pages 100—104.

8. *Synonymous Greek Words.*

The importance of accuracy in discriminating many synonymous Greek words cannot be overrated. This can be done by English readers who know little or nothing of Greek by the use of our Lexicon and Concordance. By means of this the meaning of any Greek word can be seen at a glance, and the different shades of meaning between various words which are similarly translated. Among the most important are the words rendered "world," "wash," "if," "search," "hell," "judgment," "no," and "not."

There are 32 different Greek words rendered "come," 10 "destroy," 18 "receive," 5 "rest" (noun), 8 "say," 13 "see," 12 "deliver," 13 "in," 20 "show," 13 "then," 12 "think," 17 "when," 22 "for," 11 "suffer," 22 "take," 17 "therefore," 14 "call," 12 "behold," 6 "know," 9 "leave,"

---

[1] See *Things to Come*, Vol. II., p. 184, and Vol. IV., p. 104.
[2] See *Things to Come*, Vol. VII., p. 57.

10 "ordain," 14 "make," 7 "master," 7 "mind," 16 "give,"
21 "go," 15 "keep," 5 "pray," 6 "preach," 4 "redeem,"
8 "wash," 12 "perceive," 4 "perfect," 6 "perish," etc.

It will thus be seen that Cruden's *Concordance*, while
indispensable for the purpose of finding a particular
passage, is misleading for finding the sense of it, if we
suppose that in each passage we have the same Greek
word.

Sometimes the same English word occurs only in two
passages, but in each case it may be a different word in
the Greek; *e.g.*, "found," "be spent," "spill," "tidings,"
"victuals," "company with," "censer," "certain" (adj.),
"deceitful," "settle," "unmoveable," "unreasonable,"
"bring word," "eye-witness," "joyfully," "justification,"
"unblameable," "unwise," "be wearied," "young," "as-
sent," "last," "lend," "liberality," "malefactor," "melt,"
"spy," "stay," "make straight," "support," "unawares,"
"mist," "pollution," "powerful," "purification," "quar-
rel," "be quiet," "quietness," "race," "reason," "religious,"
"rust."

Sometimes an English word will occur three times, and
each time represent a different Greek word: *e.g.*, "imagination," "merchandise," "press," "reasoning," "roar,"
"sorcerer," "stand with," "subvert," "swift," "break
up," "trial," "uncircumcised," "unruly," "vehemently,"
"vile," "confer," "brightness," "bring again," "assay."

"Tempest" occurs four times, each time representing
a different Greek word. So also does "throng."

"Purpose" occurs seven times, and six out of the seven
represent different Greek words.

"Stir up" occurs nine times as a rendering of eight
different Greek words.

"Strengthen" occurs nine times, and represents seven
different Greek words.

These examples (taken promiscuously) will be sufficient
to show the importance of accuracy when we sit down
to interpret the "words which the Holy Ghost teacheth."

We can, commend, therefore, the use of our own
*Critical Lexicon and Concordance to the English and
Greek New Testaments*, because all the occurrences of the
English word on which light is sought are given in *one
list*, in which the Greek words are referred to by numbers;

and the correct meaning is seen at a glance. Young's *Concordance* gives as many separate lists of passages as there are Greek words, and each list has to be examined in turn: *e.g.*, if there are twelve Greek words the reader has to wade through twelve separate lists of words. Moreover, the Lexicographical part is very meagre, generally giving only one meaning; and what is more, it is not critical: that is to say, it gives the word which stands in the Textus Receptus, but does not indicate any of the Various Readings which are found in the MSS. or in the Greek Texts of the various printed editions.

Our own work gives, in addition to all this, an Index of Greek Words showing all the various renderings of each, and the number of times such rendering is given.

9. *Synonymous Hebrew Words.*

We have a similar phenomenon in the case of the rendering of Hebrew words.

No less than 66 different Hebrew words are translated "bring," 45 "lay," 49 "make," 24 "think," 74 "take," 23 "run," 24 "keep," 21 "join," 26 "hold," 26 "high," 29 "grief," 23 "grow," 26 "turn," 30 "trouble," 35 "give," 68 "go," 23 "burn," 47 "come," 26 "cover," 25 "deliver," 55 "destroy," 12 "eat," 27 "end," 30 "fail," 24 "fall."

Our English word "know" is used to represent 5 Hebrew words, "judge" 10, "iniquity" 7, "increase" 17, "hear" 4, "haste" 14, "habitation" 11, "prophet" 5, "wicked" 13, "world" 5, "worm" 4, "work" 21, "word" 5, "good" 13, "grave" 8, "guide" 9, "hand" 13, "hard" 14, "heart" 7, "congregation" 4.

The importance of this branch of our subject will be seen in connection with such words as "man," which represents thirteen different Hebrew words, four of which it is very important for us to distinguish, *e.g.* :

אָדָם (*'ādām*), *man* as a created being, and as descended from the first man.

אִישׁ (*'ish*), *a notable man of quality or degree.*

אֱנוֹשׁ (*'enōsh*), *a frail, mortal man.*

גֶּבֶר (*gever*), *a strong or mighty man.*

Sometimes an English rendering is used only twice, and each time it is a different Hebrew word:

"Haven." Gen. xlix. 13 (*coast*). Ps. cvii. 30 (*destination*).

"Apiece." 1 Kings vii. 15 (*one*). Num. vii. 86 (*a spoon*, lit. *each spoon*). 1 Kings vii. 15 (*pillar*, lit. *each pillar*).

"Behead." 2 Sam. iv. 7 (*to take off*). Deut. xxi. 6 (*break the neck*).

"Bunch." Exod. xii. 22 (*a bundle*). Isa. xxx. 6 (*camel's bunch*).

"Cliff." Job xxx. 6 (*anything inspiring terror*). 2 Chron. xx. 16 (*an ascent*).

"Convey." 1 Kings v. 9 (*to place*). Neh. ii. 7 (*to pass*).

"Decrease." Gen. viii. 5 (*to grow less*). Ps. cvii. 38 (*to be few*).

"Enjoin." Est. ix. 31 (*ordain, decree*). Job xxxvi. 23 (*give charge over*).

"Even." Job xxxi. 6 (*righteousness*, lit. *a righteous balance*). Ps. xxvi. 12 (*plain, smooth*).

Sometimes one English word occurs only three times, and each time represents a different Hebrew word:

"Appease." Gen. xxxii. 20 (*cover* or *propitiate*). Est. ii. 1 (*subside*). Prov. xv. 18 (*to still*).

"Deprive." Gen. xxvii. 45 (*to be bereaved*). Job xxxix. 17 (*to cause to forget*). Isa. xxxviii. 10 (*made to miss*, i.e., *to want*).

The Hebrew words for "Tabernacle" must be carefully distinguished; *e.g.*:

אֹהֶל (*'ohel*), *tent*, has regard to the place where the people or congregation assembled.

מִשְׁכָּן (*mishcān*), *tabernacle*, has regard to the place where God dwelt.

The Hebrew words rendered "sin" are also to be distinguished:

אָשָׁם (*āshām*), is *sin* moral or ceremonial committed through mistake or ignorance. Usually translated *trespass*.

חָטָא (*chātāh*), *sin*, as a missing of the mark; a falling short of what ought to be done.

עָוֹן (*'avōn*), *sin*, as to its nature and consequences, *iniquity.*

פֶּשַׁע (*pesha'*), *sin*, as revolting from constituted authority.

שָׁגָה (*shāgah*), *error* through inadvertence.

These examples are taken out at random, merely to serve as illustrations of this branch of our subject.

As to helps for these Old Testament Words, there is Strong's *Concordance*, or Young's. The drawbacks to the latter are stated above (see p. 379).

Far and away the best is *The Bible Student's Guide*, by the late Rev. W. Wilson, D.D., Canon of Winchester, the second edition of which was published by Macmillan & Co. in 1870. It is, unfortunately, out of print, and can now occasionally be obtained second-hand.[1] It is on exactly the same lines as our *Lexicon and Concordance of the Greek New Testament.*

10. *The Genitive Case.*

The importance of accuracy is nowhere so clearly shown as in the interpretation of the word "of."

It is usually the sign of the Genitive case, though it is used also to represent fourteen different Greek words. What these words are and where the renderings are can be seen at a glance (so far as the New Testament is concerned) under the word "OF" in our *Critical Lexicon and Concordance* (pp. 543—546).

In all other cases it is the rendering of the Genitive Case of a noun: and is used by the Holy Spirit in quite a variety of different senses. We propose to present them in *nine* different classes.

We have gone fully into them in our work on *Figures of Speech used in the Bible*, and Appendix B of that work ought to be studied in this connection. We give a brief *resumé* here.

---

[1] We constantly buy up secondhand copies and supply them for ten shillings. If means were forthcoming, we would gladly enter into negotiations with the owner of the copyright for the production of a new edition; or, if health, strength, means, and leisure permitted, we would willingly undertake to prepare one ourselves.

Every Bible student who desires to enjoy the study of the "words" of God must stop whenever he comes to the word "of," and first look at our *Critical Lexicon* and see whether it represents a separate Greek word.

If he finds it does not, then it must be the Genitive Case of some noun; and in that case it belongs to one of the following nine classes.

No one can help him in determining to which of the nine it belongs. Opinions may, and do, differ. The Context and a spiritual instinct will be the best guides.

Sometimes it may be doubtful as to which of two classes it belongs; and it may often be that it belongs to both, and that each may yield a truly Scriptural sense.

(*a*) *The Genitive of Character.*—This is when it is an emphatic *adjective*. The ordinary way of qualifying a Noun is by using an Adjective; but when special emphasis is desired to be placed on the Adjective, the author goes out of his way to use a Noun instead, which is a Figure of Speech called *Enallage*, or exchange. Thus, if we say, "a bright day," the emphasis is on "day," and we mean "a bright DAY." If we say "a day of brightness," we exchange the Adjective "bright" for the Noun "brightness," and thus put the emphasis on "brightness," and we mean "a BRIGHT day."

In the former case we think only of the day as being bright. In the latter case we think of the brightness which characterizes the day.

So, if the Scripture used the Adjective "mighty" in connection with "angels," the emphasis would be on the Noun "angels": "mighty ANGELS," but if attention is called to their power it would say "angels of might," *i.e.,* "MIGHTY angels" (2 Thess. i. 7; see margin).

The following examples will illustrate this:

"Zion, the mount of my holiness," *i.e.,* my **HOLY** mount (Ps. ii. 6).

"A man of understanding" is a WISE man (**Ezra** viii. 18).

"Be to me for a rock of strength": *i.e.,* a **STRONG** rock (Ps. xxxi. 2).

"Men of scorning": *i.e.,* SCORNFUL men (**Prov.** xxix. 8).

"A wild bull of a net:" *i.e.*, a NETTED wild bull (Isa. li. 20).

"My portion of desire:" *i.e.*, my DESIRED portion 'Jer. xii. 10).

"The burial of an ass:" *i.e.*, an ASS'S burial (Jer. xxii. 19).

"A sleep of perpetuity:" *i.e.*, a PERPETUAL sleep (Jer. li. 39).

"The bread of the children:" *i.e.*, the CHILDREN'S bread (Matt. xv. 26).

"The throne of his glory:" *i.e.*, his GLORIOUS throne (Matt. xix. 28).

"The steward of injustice:" *i.e.*, the UNJUST steward (Luke xvi. 8; so xviii. 6, UNJUST judge).

"The body of this death:" *i.e.*, this MORTAL body (Rom. vii. 24).

"Mind of the spirit" and "mind of the flesh"; rendered SPIRITUALLY minded, and CARNALLY minded (Rom. viii. 6.)

"Fathers of our flesh:" *i.e.*, HUMAN fathers (Heb. xii. 9).

"A hearer of forgetfulness:" is a FORGETFUL hearer (Jas. i. 25).

"The word of life:" *i.e.*, the LIVING word (1 John i. 1).

"The word of truth": *i.e.*, the TRUE Word (2 Tim. ii. 15). This is in contrast with the other passages where we have the Adjective, and the emphasis is on "the true SAYINGS" (Rev. xix. 9; xxii. 6), or "the true WORDS" (Acts xxvi. 25). In the one case (2 Tim. ii. 15) the emphasis is on the *character* of what is said; in the others it is on the *matter*.

(b) *The genitive of Origin.*

This marks the efficient cause; the source from which anything has its origin.

"Words of God" is not character (Divine words), but words which come FROM God (Num. xxiv. 4, 16).

"The provoking of his sons and his daughters" means the provocation produced BY the conduct of His people (Deut. xxxii. 19).

"The overthrow of strangers:" *i.e.*, overthrown BY strangers (Isa. i. 7; see margin).

"The Prince of peace:" *i.e.*, the Prince who BRINGS peace (Isa. ix. 6).

"Smitten of God" means smitten BY God (Isa. liii. 4).

"The chastisement of our peace" means the chastisement which PROCURED and GIVES us peace (Isa. liii. 5).

"Taught of the LORD" means taught BY the LORD (Isa. liv. 13).

"Visions of God" means visions FROM God, given by God (Ezek. i. 1).

"Kingdom of heaven," "kingdom of God," means the kingdom which comes FROM heaven, as being "not of" (ἐκ, *ek*), *out of*, or *from* this world (John xviii. 36).

"The obedience of faith" means which SPRINGS FROM faith (Rom. i. 5).

"The righteousness of faith" means which COMES FROM or THROUGH faith (Rom. iv. 11, 13).

"Justification of life" means which PRODUCES or GIVES life (Rom. v. 18).

"Comfort of the Scriptures" means which COMES FROM the Scriptures; or which the Scripture GIVES or ministers (Rom. xv. 4).

"Dangers of waters" means which were occasioned BY waters (2 Cor. xi. 26; R.V., rivers).

"The God of peace," *i.e.*, the God who has MADE peace, and who GIVES peace (Phil. iv. 9).[1]

"The word of his power." This does not mean His powerful word, but that His word is the instrument BY which His power works (Heb. i. 3); or it may be "His POWERFUL word" (character).

"The bond of peace" means the bond which PRODUCES peace. The acknowledgement of the spiritual unity of the one body, which God has already *made* in Christ, and which we are to endeavour to *keep*, is a bond which is productive only of peace. Whereas the attempt to make a corporate unity in sects and denominations is the fruitful source of strifes and divisions (Eph. iv. 3. Compare 1 Cor. i. 10—13; iii. 1—4; xi. 18).

"The mystery of godliness" is the Great Mystery (or Secret), the knowledge of which produces true godliness of life, to which Timothy is exhorted (1 Tim. iii. 15, 16).

---

[1] This differs from "the peace of God" in verse 7, which is the Genitive of "possession" (see p. 385, under Genitive of Possession, Phil. iv. 7).

(c) *The Genitive of Possession.*

This is perhaps the most common, and is generally unmistakable. But there are some cases where it may not be so clear.

"The business of my Father" means my FATHER'S business, which was the Father's will (Luke ii. 49). Here, the emphatic Pronoun "my" stands in marked contrast with the "thy" of verse 48. (See pp. 318 and 404).

"The shield of faith" means Faith's shield, which is Christ (Eph. vi. 16. Compare Gen. xv. 1. Ps. lxxxiv. 11).

"The sword of the Spirit" means the Spirit's sword, which is the Word of God (Eph. vi. 17).

"The peace of God" means God's peace; the peace which reigns with Him, and in His presence, the peace which belongs to Him. Of this peace we shall know something if we make our requests known unto Him (Phil. iv. 6, 7). Compare this with "the God of peace," above (Phil. iv. 9). See p. 384.

"The patience of Christ" (Greek) means Christ's patient waiting (2 Thess. iii. 5 and margin). Compare R.V.

(d) *The Genitive of Apposition.*

In this case the "of" means "that is to say," or "which is."

"The heights of the clouds: *i.e.*, "the heights, *that is to say*, the clouds (Isa. xiv. 14).

"The temple of His body" means the temple, *that is to say*, His body (John ii. 21).

"A sign of circumcision" means a sign, *that is to say*, circumcision (Rom. iv. 11). So "the first fruits of the Spirit" (Rom. viii. 23) means, "the first fruits, *that is to say*, the Spirit." So also:

"The house of our tabernacle" (2 Cor. v. 1).

"The earnest of the Spirit" (2 Cor. v. 5).

"The lower parts of the earth" means the lower parts, *that is to say*, the earth (Eph. iv. 9) in contrast with heaven.

"The breastplate of righteousness" (Eph. vi. 14) means "the breastplate," *that is to say*, "righteousness."

"The cities of Sodom," etc., which means "the cities, *that is to say*, Sodom and Gomorrha" (2 Pet. ii. 6).

(e) *The Genitive of Relation.*

This is perhaps the most interesting of all; and requires
a greater variety in the manner of expressing the particular *relation.*   This must be gathered from the context.   It may be objective, or subjective, or both.   For
example:

"The love of Christ" (2 Cor. **v.** 14).   Is this the love
which Christ bears to us? or is it our love which we bear
to Christ?   No one can decide apart from the context.
Verse 14 seems to show that it means the love which
Christ bore to us in thus dying for us; or, if we judge
from verse 13, it seems to be the constraining power of
love for Christ which made the Apostle to appear to be
beside himself for their sakes.

The following are a few examples:—

"The tree of life" is the tree which PRESERVED life
(Gen. ii. 9).

"The way of the tree of life" is the way LEADING
TO the tree of life (Gen. iii. 24).

"The God of my righteousness" is the God who DE-
FENDS my righteous cause (Ps. iv. 1).   It may be the
God who procures and gives us His righteousness.   This
is true, of course, but the context seems to require *relation* rather than *origin.*

"Sheep of slaughter" (Greek) means sheep DESTINED
FOR slaughter (Ps. xliv. 22.   Rom. viii. 36).

"The fear of the Lord," *i.e.,* the fear or reverence
shown TOWARD God (Prov. i. 7.   Compare Ps. v. 7).

"Little of the earth:" little IN the earth (Prov. xxx. 24).

"The spoil of the poor": *i.e.,* TAKEN FROM the poor
(Isa. iii. 14).

"The sure mercies of David," *i.e.,* PERTAINING TO
David (Isa. lv. 3.   Compare Acts xiii. 34).

"The gospel of the kingdom" means the good news
RELATING to the kingdom (Matt. iv. 23; xxiv. 14).

"Fowls of the air" means fowls which FLY in the air
(Matt. vi. 26).

"Lilies of the field" means lilies which GROW IN
the field (Matt. vi. 28).

"Have faith of God" means have faith WITH RE-SPECT TO God (Mark xi. 22).

"By faith of Jesus Christ," *i.e.*, faith which HAS RESPECT TO Jesus Christ (Rom. iii. 22).

"They have a zeal of God" means a zeal FOR God (Rom. x. 2).

"Obedience of Christ" means obedience RENDERED TO Christ (2 Cor. x. 5).

"Every joint of supply" (Greek) means every joint which MINISTERS supply (Eph. iv. 16).

" The afflictions of Christ" means the afflictions UNDER-GONE FOR Christ (Col. i. 24).

"Reproach of Christ" means reproach SUFFERED FOR Christ (Heb. xi. 26).

"Conscience of God" (Greek) means conscience TO-WARD God (1 Pet. ii. 19).

" The word of my patience :" My word which ENJOINS patience, or patient waiting (Rev. iii. 10).

" The testimony of Jesus" means testimony CONCERN-ING Jesus ; or perhaps the testimony which He gave (Gen. of Origin). (Rev. xix. 10.)

(f) *The Genitive of the Material.*

When the genitive denotes the material of which any-thing is made, the words " made of" have to be substituted for it, *e.g.* :—

"Coats of skins," *i.e.*, made out of skins (Gen. iii. 21).

" An ark of gopher wood " (Gen. vi. 14).

" A cake of barley-bread " (Judg. vii. 13).

" A house of cedar " (2 Sam. vii. 2).

" A rod of iron " (Ps. ii. 9).

" This head of gold " (Dan. ii. 38).

(g) *The Genitive of the Contents*

Denotes that with which anything is filled.

"A bottle of wine" means a bottle or skin FILLED WITH wine (1 Sam. xvi. 20).

"A cup of cold water:" a cup CONTAINING cold water (Matt. x. 42).

" Waterpots of water " (Greek), *i.e.*, water-pots FULL OF water (John ii. 7).

This is the Genitive which always follows the verb *to fill :* while the vessel filled takes the *Accusative* case, and the one by whom it is filled is put in the *Dative* case.

"They were all filled OF *pneuma hagion* (*i.e.*, with the gift of speaking with tongues), and began to speak with tongues as the Spirit [the Giver] gave them utterance" (Acts ii. 4).

In Rom. xv. 13 we have all three Cases in one verse. "Now the God of hope (*i.e.*, 'who GIVES hope.' Gen. of Origin) fill you (Acc.. Case) of all joy (*i.e.*, ' WITH all joy.' Gen. Case) and peace, in (*i.e.*, 'BY or THROUGH') believing." (Dative Case).

So we have "Filled of wrath," *i.e.*, WITH wrath (Luke iv. 28).

"Filled of fear" (Luke v. 26).

"Filled of madness" (Luke vi. 11).

"Filled of wonder" (Acts iii. 10).

"Filled of joy" (Acts xiii. 52).

But not "filled of the spirit" in Eph. v. 18. For here it is the Dative Case and means " be filled BY wine . . . but be "filled BY the Spirit" with His own precious gifts, which the context shows to be the gift of speaking.[1]

(h) The Genitive of Partition.

Separation, or Ablation, where it denotes to be in or among, or *have part in; e.g.*:

"To obtain of that world" a PART, SHARE, or PLACE IN that world (Luke xx. 35).

"The least of the Apostles:" *i.e.*, the least AMONG the apostles (1 Cor. xv. 9).

"Sojourners of the dispersion," *i.e.*, sojourners being SOME OF the Dispersion (Greek, the *Diaspora*, or belonging to the "Scattered Nation").

(i) Two Genitives depending on one another.

These have both to be distinguished, and are often quite different, the one from the other.

"This is of (Partition) the anointing of Aaron (*Possession*, Aaron's anointing), and of the anointing (*Partition*) of his sons " (*Possession*) (Lev. vii. 35).

---

[1] See further under this head; *Things to Come*, Vol. X., pp. 88, etc; or, *Word Studies on the Holy Spirit*, republished by Kregel Publications.

"The Sea of Galilee (*Relation*) of Tiberias" (*Apposition*), and means "the sea PERTAINING TO Galilee, THAT IS TO SAY, Tiberias" (John vi. 1).

"We are witnesses of him (*Possession*, His witnesses) of these things" (*Relation* with respect to these things, Acts v. 32).

"The gospel of the grace (*Relation*) of God" (*Origin* or *Possession*, Acts xx. 24. 1 Thess. ii. 9).

"The earthly house of us (*Possession*, our) of the tabernacle" (*Apposition*, that is to say, our tabernacle, 2 Cor. v. 1).

The above passages are given only as examples of each class of Genitive: and they are sufficient to show how the door is open to a vast field of profitable study, if we see the importance of accuracy in our study of God's word.

It is wonderful to think how there can be so much to think of, and think out, in connection with this smallest of words, "of."

CANON 9

Figures of Speech

Here again we must refer our readers to our larger work on this great subject.[1]

When we say that most of the errors which cause our unhappy divisions to-day, arise from either taking literally that which is Figurative, or from taking Figuratively that which is literal, the importance of this branch of study cannot be overrated.

And yet it is practically neglected.

Only a few writers, who may all be counted on one hand, have ever bestowed any attention to the subject. And yet it lies at the very root of all translation; and it is the key to true interpretation.

John Vilant Macbeth, Professor of Rhetoric, etc., in the University of West Virginia, has said:[2] "There is no even tolerably good treatise on Figures existing at present in our language. Is there in any other tongue? There is no consecutive discussion of them of more than a few pages; the examples brought forward by all others being trivial in the extreme, and threadbare; while the main conception of what constitutes the chief class of Figures is altogether narrow, erroneous, and unphilosophical. Writers generally, even the ablest, are wholly in the dark as to the precise distinction between a *Trope* and a *Metonymy;* and very few even of literary men have so much as heard of *Hypocatastasis.*"

This witness is true. Journalism to-day has no idea of the subject. It never rises beyond a *Metaphor;* and it talks glibly of "Mixed Metaphors" as though there was no other Figure of Speech, and as though all Figures were "Metaphors."

The late Dean Alford often sneered at the Figure *Hendiadys;* and hardly a commentator gives any heed to Figures of Speech except John Albert Bengel. And since his *Commentary* was published (1687—1752) no commentator has taken up the subject or applied it to the elucidation of Scripture, as Bengel did.

---

[1] *Figures of Speech used in the Bible*, by the same author. Consisting of 1,104 pages (large 8vo), five Appendices, and seven Indexes.

[2] *The Might and Mirth of Literature.*

No one invented Figures of Speech. Everyone uses them, unknowingly. They arise of necessity in the use of language.

A Figure relates to *form*. When we speak of a person being "a Figure" we mean that he or she is dressed out of the usual or common fashion, as to colour or cut or material.

So, a Figure is a word used out of its ordinary sense; or put out of its usual order in a sentence; or it is a sentence thrown into a peculiar form, or expressing a thing in an unusual manner.

A Figure is a departure from the natural and fixed laws of grammar; a legitimate departure from law: not arising from ignorance or accident, but from design.

This departure is made with the set purpose of calling attention to what is said, in order to emphasize it.

Hence, the Figures, when used in connection with the "words which the Holy Ghost teacheth," give us the Holy Spirit's own *marking*, so to speak, of our Bible. We hear of a "marked Testament," but the marking is made by human beings according to the marker's own idea of what is important. How much more wonderful and important it must be to have the Holy Spirit's own marking; calling our attention to what He desires us to notice for our learning, as being emphatic, and conveying His own special teaching.

A Figure may not be true to fact, but it is true to *feeling*, and truer to truth.

We may say "the ground needs rain": that is a plain, cold statement of fact. But if we say "the ground is thirsty," we at once use a Figure, not so true to fact, but truer to reality, and to feeling; full of warmth and life.

Hence we say "the crops suffer," "a hard heart," "an iron will." Or when we say "the kettle boils" we do not mean the kettle, literally, but the water; nor do we state a fact. What we mean is that the water in the kettle boils.

So when we say "the glass is rising" we mean the mercury, not the glass, or barometer.

When we say "light the fire" we do not mean this literally, for fire is already alight; but what we mean is, put it to what we call the firing.

All these are Figures, and they all have names. These names were mostly given by the Greeks, centuries before Christ; and their number runs into hundreds, many of them having several varieties.

In our own work of over 1,000 pages we have classified 217 Figures; and have given some 8,000 passages of Scripture illustrated by them. When we state that these are only given by way of example, it will be seen that another vast field of study lies open before the Bible student.

It will also be seen that it is impossible here to do more than thus call attention to it; otherwise we should like to give a few examples of *Ellipsis, Metonymy, Metalepsis, Asyndeton, Polysyndeton, Hypocatastasis,* and *Metaphor,* which last is a special Figure by itself and not a general name for any Figure, as modern writers seem to think.

We said that errors are built up on ignorance of Figures.

These errors are therefore to be refuted not by argument merely, but by Scientific, Literary, and Grammatical facts. Thus:

"This is my body" can be proved to be *Metaphor,* meaning "this represents my body" (Matt. xxvi. 26).

"We have an altar" can be proved to be *Metonymy,* meaning "we have a sacrifice" (Heb. xiii. 10).

"The caperberry shall fail" (Eccles. xii. 5, R.V.) can be proved to be *Metalepsis,* meaning, as beautifully rendered by the A.V., "desire shall fail."

And so with many passages which have created confusion to readers, difficulties to commentators, and divisions among brethren.

We earnestly commend, therefore, close attention to "Figures of Speech," without which no study of the Bible can be complete.

CANON 10

Interpretation and Application

It is of the utmost importance that we should clearly and constantly discriminate between these two.

The Interpretation of a passage is one thing, but the Application of that passage is quite a different thing.

The Interpretation of a passage belongs to the occasion when, and the persons to whom, or of whom, the words were originally intended. When that has been settled, then it is open to us to make an application of those words to ourselves or others, so far as we can do so without coming into conflict with any other passages.

We have already seen[1] something of this, and of its importance in connection with Dispensational Truth and Teaching; but the principle extends far beyond this, and affects all kinds of Truth.

It is this that makes the precept to rightly divide the Word of truth so weighty and so indispensable.

It may even be, when the application is made in full accord with Scripture teaching given elsewhere, that it is not only true, but may have a far deeper and more real meaning than the interpretation itself; and may convey truths and lessons far beyond it.

This is very different from the common practice called spiritualizing. This too often ignores or denies all that may be learnt from the interpretation of a passage, and robs those to whom it belongs of a precious treasure; while it appropriates to itself or other parties the property which has thus been stolen.

Such a practice cannot be too strongly deprecated; not only because of the injury done to the Word itself, and the mistakes involved, but because it is so wholly unnecessary.

All the sweetness, all the blessing, all the truth can be obtained by a wise *application*, without in the slightest degree impairing the true *interpretation*. This may be left and preserved in all its integrity, and yet something really spiritual may be appropriated by *application;* all, in fact, that can be desired, without doing any violence

---

[1] Part I., Sect. IV., pp. 155—157, above; and in several other parts of this work.

to the Divine Word, as is done when its interpretation
is not only ignored, but often when the application is
actually substituted for the interpretation.

This Canon is very far-reaching as governing our study
of the Word and the words of God. Its importance cannot be over-estimated, if we would not only understand
but really enjoy our Bible studies.

It will come into operation on nearly every page of
Scripture; and on this account it is impossible to give
more than examples.

We content ourselves with a few as a guide to the
way in which other passages may be treated.

Take, for instance:

1. *The Account of Creation* (Gen. i.).—Instead of trou-
bling our heads with Babylonian "creation-tablets," which
were the incoherent babblings of people who had for-
gotten and corrupted, or knew little of, primitive truth,
we turn to the inspired record and endorse the Divine
assertion, "The beginning of Thy word is true" (Ps. cxix.
160, marg.).

We have already dealt with this interpretation of
Gen. i.,[1] and shown how the first chapter of Genesis, when
compared with other Scriptures, is far in advance of the
inferences drawn from the ever-shifting and changing
hypotheses of Geologists, which are foisted upon us under
the name of "science falsely so-called" (1 Tim. vi. 20).

"*In the beginning God created the heavens and the
earth.*"—This is "the world that then was" of 2 Pet. iii. 6.

And the earth became tohū and bohū.—The verb
"was" means, and is translated "became" in Gen. ii. 7;
iv. 14; ix. 15; xix. 26, etc.

It became תֹּהוּ (*tohū*). Whatever may be the meaning
of the word rendered "without form," it is distinctly
stated in Isa. xliv. 18 that God "created it not *tohū*." It
must therefore have "become" so, as stated in Gen. i. 2.

The combination of the two words *tohū* and *bohū*
occurs in Isa. xlv. 19; xxxiv. 11, and Jer. iv. 23, where
it may be seen that it denotes *ruin, emptiness, waste,
desolation.*

---

[1] See above, under Canon VIII., p. 351.

This was the end of "the world that then was" (2 Pet. iii. 5, 6).

The chapter next goes on to describe the creation of "the heavens and the earth which are now" (2 Pet. iii. 7); and in 2 Pet. iii. 13 we are informed that these will be followed hereafter by "a new heavens and new earth."

If we *interpret* the chapter on these lines, and do not make Moses or the Holy Spirit responsible for the mistakes of translators and commentators, we have a surer foundation for any *application* we make.

In doing this we destroy the miserable imagination of a criticism which regards it as either an "allegory" or as a "myth."

The interpretation tells us that at some time in the eternal ages past, "God created the heavens and the earth."

And then, that at some time, in some manner, and for some reason (which are not revealed) it became a ruin, empty, waste, desolate, and overwhelmed with water.

This is the *interpretation*.

Now, the *application* of this to the creation and the new creation of man rests on this sure foundation; and reveals truth and teaching of infinite importance.

(1) The earth was created *perfect*. This is implied in the word rendered "create," and is embodied in the word "cosmos."[1] So was man. "God made man upright" (Eccles. vii. 29).

(2) But the earth became a ruin, and so did man. We are not told *why* or *when* man thus fell: but in this case we are told *how* in Gen. iii. Man's natural condition is described as "dead" (Eph. ii. 1), "darkened" (Eph. iv. 18), and destitute of any good thing (Rom. vii. 18).

(3) While the old creation was in this ruined condition, the first act and movement was on the part of God: "the Spirit of God moved" (Gen. i. 2). Thus it is in the case of man. He must be "born of the Spirit" (John iii. 5, 6).

(4) The next act was also of God, "And God said" (Gen. i. 3). God spake: The Word of God came. So with

---

[1] It is rendered *ornament* in Exod. xxxiii. 4, 5, 6. Isa. xlix. 18; iii. 18. Jer. iv. 30. Ezek. vii. 20. And *adorning* in 1 Pet. iii. 3.

man. He must be "begotten by the Word of God" as
well as by the Spirit (1 Pet. i. 23—25).

(5) The next creative act was the creation of light.[1]
And this is true in the experience of the saved sinner:
"The entrance of thy words giveth light" (Ps. cxix. 130).
This is precisely the application made in 2 Cor. iv. 6:
"God who commanded the light to shine out of darkness,
hath shined in our hearts, to give us the light of the
knowledge of the glory of God in the face of Jesus
Christ."

(6) In the Old Creation the light shines on the ruin;
and so it is in the New Creation. Here it is that *we* first
come in. Here is where we begin. Here is where we
first experience and come to a knowledge of all that has
already been going on. A vast deal of work has been
wrought by God before we are cognizant of anything
except the misery through which we have passed. But
when we learn the true spiritual application of the
interpretation, then, in spite of all the evil which the
light has revealed, we look up, and thank God for the light,
and we say, as God said when He saw the light, that "it
was good."

We must not pursue the *application* which may be
made throughout the whole chapter,[2] but we commend
the above as an example of our Canon X.

Another example may be seen in

2. *The Rejection of Messiah* (Isa. liii.).—The *interpretation* belongs to those who were specially addressed by the
prophet Isaiah, who spake of and to "Judah and Jerusalem"; and that chapter must take its place in the
context in which God Himself has set it.

---

[1] Whatever that was. Scientists once thought they knew; but recent
discoveries of the X-rays and N-rays and Radium, etc., are so wonderful and
far-reaching that no scientist would now venture to frame a definition. One
thing we know, that whether they call it "luminiferous ether" or anything
else, it is not the same as the word rendered "lights" in Gen. i. 14, 16. The
sun and moon were called מָאוֹר (*māōr*), *light-holders*, or *candlesticks*. Thus,
we are taught in Gen. i. that which science is only just getting to know:
viz., that what God called "light" exists independently of the sun.

[2] This is done in the pamphlet entitled *The New Creation and the Old*, by
the same author.

Leaving its interpretation there we lose none of its precious truths for ourselves when we *apply* it as we may, and do, in accordance with our own Church Epistles. Its great and solemn lesson is even stronger and deeper in its *application* than in its interpretation.

It must be admitted by all that Israel will be able to use those words in a sense which we can never do.

The Lord Jesus did grow up in their midst (*v.* 2) as He has not in ours.

When He did so, there was a literal sense in which His People to whom He came did not see any form or comeliness in Him, or any beauty that they should desire Him (*v.* 2), which was not equally true of us, as Gentiles, though it can be truly *applied* to us.

There was a sense in which they "hid their faces from Him and esteemed Him not" (*v.* 3), which is not so literally true of us; though our application of the words finds a real counterpart.

We were not God's "sheep" and "people" as Israel was, and it could not be said of us as of them, "All we like sheep have gone astray" (*v.* 6). We were far more than "lost sheep" (Matt. x. 6): we are "dead in trespasses and sins," but of Israel it was specially said that they were "the sheep of His pasture" (Ps. xcv. 7; c. 3, etc.).

It was for Isaiah's people that Messiah was specially stricken (*v.* 8); but, as afterwards revealed, we may apply the words in a very true sense of ourselves.

3. *The mourning of Israel* (Rev. i. 7).—In like manner there is a very special sense in which the interpretation of the words in Rev. i. 7 will be true of Israel—"they which pierced him . . . shall mourn over him." There can be only a somewhat strained *application* to ourselves; certainly not an interpretation of us.

4. *The Potter's house* (Jer. xviii.).—This chapter affords an instructive example of this Canon. The prophet is told to go down to the Potter's house and note what he sees.

He sees the Potter make a vessel on the wheels, and the vessel was marred in his hands.

Then he made it again another vessel as it pleased the Potter to make it (*vv.* 1—4).

In the verses that follow, the *interpretation* is given by God Himself; and He interprets it of Israel.

But there are several *applications* which we may make, all equally true; and to us, more vitally important than the *interpretation* itself.

When Jehovah sent Jeremiah to the Potter's house, it was to teach him a great eternal principle, that *He would never mend that which man had marred*, but would make an end of it and put a new thing altogether in its place.

Jehovah's own *interpretation* of what Jeremiah saw, was that Israel, like that clay, had become marred. He, the great Potter, would not mend the nation; but would make a new nation, a new Israel in whom He could put a new spirit, and write His law in their hearts (Jer. xviii., xxxi. 31—37). This new nation is the interpretation of the Lord Jesus also, in Matt. xxi. 43, when He said to and of the nation, in His day, "Therefore say I unto you, The Kingdom of God shall be taken from you, and given to a nation bringing forth the fruits thereof."

That nation will not be the vessel that was marred. It will be the same clay, but re-made "another vessel as seemed good to the potter to make it."

This is God's own *interpretation,* and we may not ignore it; or rob Israel of the blessed hope which is revealed in it, and is yet in store for that nation.

But, leaving Israel in full and sure possession of this promise we are at liberty to make as many *applications* of the lesson in the Potter's house as may be consistent with the other teaching of the Word of God.

(1) We may apply it to "the heavens and earth which are now." This earth came under the curse, and is *marred:* marred, so that "the whole creation groaneth and travaileth in pain together until now" (Rom. viii. 22). God will not mend this earth; but will make "a new heaven and a new earth" (2 Pet. iii. 13); as may "seem good to the Potter to make it"; and of which this present earth will have a foretaste in millennial blessings (Rev. xxi., xxii.). Those who are labouring to mend this marred creation have not yet learned the lesson of this *application* of the Potter's house.

(2) We may apply it to man. Man was marred, and at the Fall became alienated from the life of God (Rom. v.

12--21. Eph. ii. 1—3; iv. 17—19, etc.). God will not mend or reform the natural man; but He makes "a new man" "a new creation, in Christ" (2 Cor. v. 17. Eph. ii. 10), and bestows a new nature, and gives a new spirit; "as it pleases the Potter to make it."[1]

(3) We may apply it to the Covenant which God made with Israel, "which my covenant they brake," He says. That Covenant is marred. But God will not mend it. He will "make a new Covenant." That is His own *application*, and we find it in Hebrews viii. 7—13; x. 16. (Compare Jer. xxxi. 33, 34.)

(4) We may apply it to the Sacrifices as ordained by God. But these were marred in the making. They, like the Covenant itself, "were not faultless;" "for it is not possible that the blood of bulls and of goats should take away sins." They were marred, and will not be mended. A new and living way has been made and opened by the sacrifice of Jesus Christ—once for all. "Lo, I come to do Thy will, O God. He taketh away the first that He may establish the second." The second is the new vessel "as it pleased the Potter to make it" (Heb. x. 1—23).

(5) We may apply it to the institution of Kings, and the setting up of the throne of David. The Kings failed (as the Priests also failed). The throne was marred. But, it is not in God's counsels to mend it. The confusion must go on, while all the nations of the earth are seeking, striving, and struggling to attain a better government by human remedies, reforms, or revolutions. This will go on—For in His own application of this, He has said. "I will overturn, overturn, overturn" until He comes whose right it is to reign (Ezek. xxi. 27. Isa. xxxii. 1). And, while kings fail and set themselves against Jehovah and His anointed, and thrones totter and fall, and dynasties change and pass away, yet, looking forward to that coming day when He will of this clay make another vessel, as it seemeth good for Him to make it, His counsel is declared even now, in the midst of the ruin: "Yet have I set my king upon my holy hill of Zion" (Ps. ii. 6).

(6) We may apply this great eternal principle of the Potter's house to our mortal bodies. Made in the image

---
[1] See *The Two Natures*, by the same author.

of Elohim, capable of living for ever through the virtues of the " tree of life," these human bodies became mortal ; marred through the Fall, and made subject to death through sin. Man may use his means, improve his arts ; and may mend by his medicines ; he may delay, but he cannot stay the appointment of God for man : "It is appointed unto men once to die " (Heb. ix. 27. Gen. iii. 19. Eccles. iii. 20).

God will not mend these marred bodies of our humiliation, but He has prepared for His people "another" body. A "house not made with hands," a "house from heaven," re-made, in resurrection, like Christ's own body of glory (2 Cor. iv. 14—v. 2).

Now, while in "our earthly house of this tabernacle" we are "absent from the Lord." Therefore it is that we are earnestly longing for that resurrection day when we shall be "clothed upon with our house[1] which is from heaven," when we shall be absent, out of, or away from these vile bodies, and present with the Lord, in bodies made like the glorious body of Christ (Phil. iii. 20, 21). Then, and only then, will "mortality be swallowed up of life" (2 Cor. v. 4).

If any ask, "How are the dead raised up ? And with what body do they come? " Then the answer is that which comes to us as the echo from the lesson in the Potter's house : "God giveth it a body AS IT HATH PLEASED HIM " (1 Cor. xv. 35, 38). Then, and then only, "shall be brought to pass the saying," "Death is swallowed up in victory" (1 Cor. xv. 54).

We could not give a better illustration of this important Canon than that of the Potter's house, which shows us how, after we have settled and distinguished the *interpretation* of a passage, we may make one or more *applications* of it, so long as they are in harmony with the general teaching of the whole Word of truth.

One more example, and that from the New Testament, must suffice.

5. *The parable of the Ten Virgins* (Matt. xxv.)—In no Scripture is this great principle less observed than in

---

[1] 2 Cor. v. 2. Greek, οἰκητήριον (oikētērion), *a spiritual body*, similar to that of the angels. See Jude 6.

the general treatment of this parable. For not only is the *interpretation* evaded and avoided, but it is ignored altogether; and the *application* is put in its place: indeed, it is actually substituted for it, and itself made the interpretation.

The application thus made is self-contradictory; for while the "kingdom of heaven" is supposed to be the Church, the Bride also is held to be the Church, "the Virgins her companions" are also taken as representing the Church; and we are constantly and universally exhorted to be "wise" and have our lamps trimmed and "oil in our vessels"; the oil being the Holy Spirit, which we refuse to give to the unwise, but bid them go and buy for themselves!

This farrago of Arminian theology is supposed to be what the Lord was then teaching to His disciples, and which we are to suppose them to have understood.

But there is a true *interpretation;* and there is also a true *application.* The latter cannot be made until the former is obtained; for the *interpretation* is the foundation on which the *application* is built. There can be no building till the foundation is laid.

The interpretation is clearly indicated by the first word with which it commences: "THEN."[1]

That is to say, at this stage of the Lord's last great prophetic address, and at this point in the succession of events which He was unfolding: "THEN shall the kingdom of heaven be likened unto ten virgins," etc.

When the interpretation of this prophecy shall be fulfilled those who are waiting for the Bridegroom will go forth to meet Him.

> "It shall be said in that day,
>   Lo, this is our God; we have waited for him,
>   And he will save us:
>   This is Jehovah, we have waited for him,
>   We will be glad and rejoice in his salvation."
>
> (Isa. xxv. 9.)

Having thus settled the *interpretation;* it is now open to us to make such *application* as we may be able;

---

[1] As we have seen above, p. 359.

and one lies on the surface: *viz.*, the general exhortation to *watchfulness;* which is none the less solemn and none the less powerful, weighty, and effective because the true interpretation has been made. For if they have need to watch who have and are to have "Signs" given to them, how much more watchful should we be who have no such signs, but are "waiting for God's Son from heaven," who may come at any moment to meet His risen and changed ones in the air and receive them up into glory.

CANON 11

The Limits of Inspiration

Though there is not much to be said on this subject, yet the importance of this Canon is very great.

Not only is the Spirit of God often held responsible for the mistakes and errors of translators and commentators, but other things are put down to Him when they are really the statements of others, for which the speakers alone are responsible.

The Scriptures contain records of conversations, and statements made by Satan, by demons, by the human enemies of God, and by His mistaken and erring servants. We have an *inspired record* of all that was said and done; but it does not follow that all that was said and done was *inspired!*

To Job and his friends, God categorically said, "Ye have not spoken of me the thing that is right" (Job xlii. 7, 8. Compare ch. xxxiii. 12). "Job hath spoken without knowledge, and his words without wisdom" (ch. xxxiv. 35), and he "multiplieth words without knowledge" (ch. xxxv. 16). "Who is this (God asked Job) that darkeneth counsel by words without knowledge" (ch. xxxviii. 2). Are we then to quote such words as inspired? Surely not, unless we are distinctly told that God "put them into the mouths" of the speakers as He did into Balaam's mouth (Num. xxiii. 5, 16).

Surely we have to be careful in all our quotations of God's Word, to see that they are the words of God, and that we are not making Him responsible for the words of fallen, erring, and ignorant human beings.

It is a question whether the song of Deborah (Judg. v.) was inspired: though we have an inspired record of the words of her song. We do not say it is not; but, if any do think so, they need not be at too great pains to reconcile her statements or her ethics with the attributes of Jehovah: though, as we have shown (Part I, iv. 2, pp. 108, etc.), they are perfectly in accord with the Dispensation in which we find them.

In many cases grave difficulties are created by not observing this Canon of interpretation; and hopeless

efforts are made to get out of the entanglements of our
own assumptions.

If exceptions prove the rule, then the truth of the
Inspired record is enhanced by the one or two exceptions
which are distinctly stated to be such by the Apostle
Paul himself. He thereby sets his seal to the fact that
all his other statements have Divine authority.

The same principle must be applied to actions of God's
servants.

David was "a man after God's own heart," as to his
being chosen as God's king : but it does not follow,
nor does it say, that all David's acts were according to
God's choice or even approval ; for we know how he was
judged by God for his sins and infirmities.   The word
"heart" in the above quotation has to do with *God's call*
and not with *David's walk.*

The same is the case with Paul's last journey to Jerusalem. It was commenced in disobedience ; characterized
by dissembling ; and concluded in disaster (personally).

Peter also at Antioch manifested the same weakness
of human nature.

God's servants were men of like passions with ourselves,
neither more nor less. And we have an inspired record
of their actions and their words, which have to be
distinguished and rightly divided from the "words which
the Holy Ghost teacheth"; and those acts which were
done by direct Inspiration.

See what mischief has been made of the words of
Mary in Luke ii. 48, "Thy father and I have sought thee
sorrowing." These words have been quoted and used as
supporting the denial of the Virgin birth of the Lord
Jesus. Various arguments have been used to explain
Mary's words.   In *The Record* of Feb. 1, 1907, a corre-
spondent labours to upset the Received Text, which, here,
is unquestioned, by setting above it some old Latin
Versions. But there is no need for all this if we remember
that this is not the only occasion when Mary "erred
with her lips." That she did so err is shown by the next
verse, where the Lord's correction is very pointed and
emphatic. She said "Thy father and I have sought
thee" (*v.* 48). He replies, "Wist ye not that I must be
about MY Father's business?" (*v.* 49). "They understood

not the saying which He spake unto them" (*v.* 50). But those who do not observe this Canon of interpretation do not "understand the saying"; and not only misunderstand it, but misuse it for the support of error. (See pp. 318 and 385.)

The need of observing it is clear enough in such cases as the words Satan, and evil spirits, and the enemies of God, such as Pharaoh, Rabshakeh, Herod, the Scribes and Pharisees who opposed the Lord Jesus.

When we consider the havoc wrought by the first two lies of the Old Serpent, we may see the importance of this Canon. Not only is the Old Theology permeated with these two lies, but they are the two pillars on which the "New Theology" is based:

> "Ye shall be as God" (Gen. iii. 5).
> "Ye shall not surely die" (Gen. iii. 4).

These two lies led to the Fall of man; and they are still the two great signs of his fallen condition, for fallen man prefers them to the truth of God. (Compare pp. 315, etc.)

When it comes to the words of others there is danger lest we put them on the same level with the "words which the Holy Ghost teacheth." The words and utterances of men have all to be judged by the words of God; hence the need of careful attention to this Canon of interpretation.

CANON 12

The Place of Various Readings

In speaking on or of the "words" of God, references are sometimes made to variations in the Original Text of the Old and New Testaments.

It may be well, therefore, to put the general reader, who has not time to devote to this subject, in possession of a few elementary facts in connection with it.[1]

The Word of God has come down to us in manuscript form; and not until the invention of printing was it possible to have it in any other form.[2]

These manuscripts are written by different hands at different times, and existing copies date from the fourth century.

Translations of them made *before the fourth century* are also in existence, though the MSS. of these versions (still in existence) are, of course, not so old.

There are also many quotations from these MSS. preserved in the writings of those who lived before the fourth century, though the MSS. of their works are not so old.

These transcriptions all bear the marks of human frailties and infirmities, notwithstanding the great care in copying them. In spite of all the safeguards invented and provided for insuring accuracy, there are many variations.

The human element in the transmission of the Divine Word is neither more nor less than in the transmission of ordinary literature.

Variations in reading are the normal characteristics of all manuscripts, and it has ever been a copyist's or

---

[1] Those who wish to go more deeply into it must study Dr. Ginsburg's *Introduction to the Hebrew Bible* (published by the Trinitarian Bible Society, 7, Bury Street, Bloomsbury, London); or a small pamphlet by the author on *The Massorah* (Eyre & Spottiswoode (Bible Warehouse), Ltd., 33, Paternoster Row, London, price 1s.). For the New Testament Dr. Tregelles' work on *The History of the Printed Text of the Greek New Testament* should be studied.

[2] This (in England) was in 1455, but as early as 1475 there are two dated books. These are in Hebrew. The first printed books of the Bible were the Hebrew Psalter, 1477, and the Hebrew Pentateuch, 1482 (Bologna).

editor's aim to spare no pains in securing a good copy and a sound text.

The mere mechanical act of copying, extending as it did for many hours a day, and often for many months and even years, not to speak of drowsy intelligences and numbed fingers in a draughty scriptorium, will easily account for deviations from an authentic text.

The many editions of Shakespeare, carried out by numerous editors, show a remarkable tendency to a progressive deterioration in textual accuracy.[1]

The original texts of the Bible have had a singularly happy exemption from the treatment of the texts of modern writers.

Emendations are confined for the most part to the pages of commentators, while the vast majority of textual variations are trivial in the extreme, very many being only a difference in spelling. Those which are really vital and which affect doctrine or teaching may be counted on one's fingers, if not on those of one hand.

There are many, of course, which are full of interest, and are of more or less importance. We speak first of

THE HEBREW MSS. (THE OLD TESTAMENT).

There were two great schools, or recensions of MSS., where they were transcribed between the sixth and tenth centuries. One at Babylon in the East, and the other at Tiberias in the West.

The variations are neither numerous[2] nor important, being confined to the vowel-points with a few exceptions.

There are five great standard Codices from which all subsequent copies have been made.

1. *The Codex of Hillel,* which Rabbi Kimchi (cent. xii.) says he saw at Toledo.

2. *The Codex of Ben Asher,* President of the School at Tiberias in the early part of the eleventh century, known as the Jerusalem Codex.

---

[1] Especially in the four well-known folio editions between 1623 and 1685. Milton, Pope, Gray, Keats, Shelley, Cowper, and Wordsworth have all suffered at the hands of their editors. Dr. Bentley's outrages, in 1732, on the text of *Paradise Lost* are inexcusable.

[2] They are estimated at 864 for the whole of the Old Testament.

3. *The Codex of Ben Naphtali*, President at Babylon, and hence known as the Babylonian Codex.

4. *The Pentateuch of Jericho*, which was held by Elias Levita to be the most perfect and correct.

5. *The Codex of Sinai*, also of the Pentateuch, and differing from that of Jericho only in some of the accents.

Besides these there are various readings noted in the Massorah, *i.e.*, the writing in small characters which is seen at the head, foot, and in the margins of all the ancient Hebrew MSS. No one MS. contains the whole of this Massorah, and no one man had set himself to collect the whole from vast numbers of MSS. until Dr. Christian D. Ginsburg devoted his life to it. His edition of the Hebrew Bible is the only one which exhibits these Various Readings[1]; and his *Introduction to the Hebrew Bible* is the only one which contains a complete history of the Hebrew written and printed text.

Unfortunately, the work was so long neglected by scholars, that we do not yet possess an *Apparatus Criticus* or recognized list of MSS. The scholars of various nations have not yet agreed on a universal or standard list by which the MSS. may be referred to or known by letters, numerals, or symbols, as is the case with the New Testament. This is a great work which is still needed to be done.

THE NEW TESTAMENT.

The Greek MSS. of the New Testament (in whole or in part) are over five hundred in number.

They are divided into two great classes, known as *Uncial* (*i.e.*, written in capital letters), or *Cursive* (*i.e.*, written in running-hand). The former are mostly earlier than the eighth century, the latter date from the tenth.

---

[1] It was published, in 1894, by the Trinitarian Bible Society of London (7, Bury Street, Bloomsbury), at the price of one guinea. A reprint of the edition was published in 1907.

There is a further classification, according to certain characteristics, into *Recensions* (which in the case of printed books, we speak of as *Editions*).

1. The Alexandrine or Egyptian.
2. The Western or Occidental.
3. The Oriental or Byzantine.

But the collators and editors of these MSS. are not all agreed, and their reckonings often overlap. There are other *Recensions* than these recognized and named by other scholars and critics.

The chief MSS. of the New Testament are known and referred to as follows :—

" A " is the recognized symbol of the *Codex Alexandrinus*. The MS is so called because it was brought from Alexandria by Cyrillus Lucaris, a native of Crete and patriarch of Constantinople, who sent it by Sir Thomas Rowe, the British Ambassador, to King Charles I. The proprietor of the MS., before it came into the hands of Cyrillus Lucaris, had written a subscription in Arabic, stating that it was written by Thecla, a Christian martyr, about 1300 years before. This would make the date of the MS. about the end of the fourth century. It could not be earlier, as it contains a letter of Athanasius. It is preserved in the British Museum.

" B " is the *Codex Vaticanus*. This MS. is so called because it is preserved in the Vatican Library at Rome.

It is generally supposed to belong to the fourth or fifth century.

" C " is the *Codex Ephræmi*. It is so called because the MS. contains, in the first part, several Greek writings of Ephrem the Syrian. It is generally believed to have been written in Egypt in the fifth or sixth century. It is preserved in the National Library at Paris.

"D (1)" is the *Codex Bezæ*. It is known also as the *Codex Cantabrigensis*, because it was presented, in 1581, by Theodore Beza to the library of the University of Cambridge, where it is still preserved. It is believed to belong to the fifth century. It contains only the Gospels and Acts.

"D (2)" is another MS. found by Beza at Clermont, and called the *Codex Claromontanus.* It contains the Pauline Epistles and Hebrews; and is in the National Library at Paris.

"א" denotes the *Codex Sinaiticus,* which is regarded by some as the most ancient and important of any of the MSS. at present known. It is so called from the fact that it was discovered by Tischendorf so recently as 1844 and 1859 at the Convent of St. Catherine on Mount Sinai. Its date may be fixed about the middle of the fourth century, and its authority is very great.

It will be noted that, from the dates assigned to the discovery of these several MSS., they were for the most part unknown to the translators of the Authorized Version; so that due allowance must be made for the weight (or the reverse) of their authority when we have to consider any particular passage.

The above are the principal Uncial MSS. There are many more; and it is quite possible that some of the later *Cursive* MSS. may be *transcripts of MSS. still older than any of the existing Uncial MSS.* So that no one critic can speak with absolute authority.

THE ANCIENT VERSIONS

have also to be taken into account. Passing over the Jewish (Hebrew) Targums or Commentaries,

1. The oldest is the Greek Version of the Old Testament, made about B.C. 277,[1] for the Jews dwelling in Egypt. It is known as THE SEPTUAGINT, from the traditional belief that it was made by seventy or seventy-two translators. Hence it is referred to by the abbreviation LXX. or by the Greek letter (sigma) for this number, σ.

2. *The Peschito, or Old Syriac Version,* was one of several versions made by Christians in the earliest period of the Christian Era. It is called "Peschito," which means *literal,* and it was so named because it was a literal translation from the Hebrew. It was made at the close of the first century or the early part of the second century.

---

[1] It could not be earlier than this date because in Prov. viii. 18 γαισος, a word of Gallic origin, is used for a short javelin, first known in Greece by an invasion of Gauls in B.C. 278.

There is a *later Syriac Version*, made in A.D. 488—518. It is known as the "Philoxenian," or "*Syro-Philoxenian*" *Version*, from the name of Philoxenus, Bishop of Hierapolis, in Syria, who employed Polycarp to make it.

3. *The Coptic* (or Memphitic) *Version* was made from the Septuagint in the third century, but not printed till 1716, at Oxford.

4. *The Ethiopic* (or Abyssinian) *Version* was made certainly in the second century.

5. *The Armenian Version*, made also from the Septuagint towards the close of Cent. IV, or early in Cent. V.

6. *The Vulgate Version* dates from the fourth century. As Latin gradually displaced the Greek as the common language of the people, so there soon sprang up a number of versions in that language. These were translated, part by one translator and part by another, until one complete copy was made by combining the several parts. This was known by the name of *Itala*, or *the Italic Version*, called by Jerome sometimes the *Vulgate* (or Common) Version, and sometimes *the Old*. Both Old and New Testaments were translated from the Greek.

This was revised by Jerome, who re-translated the Old Testament from the Hebrew. The work occupied him from A.D. 385—405, and by the year 604 had superseded all others, being known as *the Vulgate Version*. Since the seventh century it has been adopted by the Church of Rome, and in the sixteenth century it was declared by the Council of Trent to be the "Authentic" Version.

With the multiplication of copies came, inevitably, the multiplication of errors. An attempt at correcting these was ordered by Charlemagne in the eighth century. A further revision was attempted by Lanfranc, Archbishop of Canterbury, in the eleventh century, and by other scholars during the twelfth and thirteenth centuries.

It was first printed by Robert Stephens in 1528, and a revision of this was printed by Pope Sixtus V. at a printing office set up in the Vatican in 1590. So many corrections were introduced by Sixtus V. that another edition was prepared and printed by Pope Clement VIII. in 1592, which contained even more and greater divergencies, which gave Protestants like Thomas James[1] the opportunity of exposing the numerous additions, omissions, and alterations between these two Editions.

In spite of all this, the Vulgate has its place in the consideration of the subject of Various Readings.

THE PRINTED TEXT OF THE GREEK TESTAMENT.

The manuscripts mentioned above have been collated at various times by many who have, from this, been termed "Textual Critics."

These are quite different from the more modern generation of the so-called "Higher" Critics.

The former base their conclusions on documentary evidence which they see before them; while the latter base theirs on hypotheses which are the productions of their own imagination.

Some of the Textual Critics have published from time to time Greek Testaments which they have compiled from the manuscripts to which they have had access, and to which they have attached the greatest weight.

The most important are as follows:—

The Complutensian Polyglot . .	1514
Erasmus (1st Edition)	1516
Stephens	1546—9
Beza[2]	1624
Elzivir	1624
Griesbach	1774—5
Scholz	1830—6
Lachmann	1831—50
Tischendorf	1841—72
Tregelles	1856—72
Alford	1862—71
Wordsworth	1870
Revisers' Text	1881
Westcott and Hort . . .	1881—1903
Scrivener	1886
Weymouth	1886
Nestle	1904

---

[1] In his *Bullum Papale.* London, 1600.

[2] This, with the Elzivir, forms the Text used by the A.V. translators, and is known as the *Textus Receptus,* or Received Text.

All these have based their respective Texts on a careful consideration of the value they put upon the various MSS., Versions, etc.

We have put Dr. Scrivener's Text among these ; but it differs from them all in one important particular which makes it the very best Text for general use.

It gives the *Textus Receptus*, but prints every word which is the subject of a Various Reading in thicker type, quoting at the foot of the page the initial letter of the names of the above Editors, according as they are in favour of or reject the Reading in question.

All that now remains to be done is for us to give an idea of the principles on which they base their respective Texts, so that our readers may, as the net result of our own labours, be able to estimate, each one for himself, the value of the authority for or against any particular Reading.

GRIESBACH (G.) based his Text on the theory of Three Recensions of the Greek manuscripts (referred to above, p. 409), regarding the collective witness of each Recension as one ; so that a Reading having the authority of all three was regarded by him as genuine. It is only a theory, but it has a foundation of truth, and will always retain a value peculiarly its own.

LACHMANN (L.), disregarding these Recensions, professed to give the Text based only on the evidence of witnesses up to the end of the fourth century. All were taken into account up to that date; and all were discarded after it, whether Uncial MSS., or Cursives, or other documentary evidence. He even adopted Readings which were palpably errors, on the simple ground that it was the best attested Reading up to the fourth century.

TISCHENDORF (T.) followed more or less the principles laid down by Lachmann, but not to the neglect of other evidence as furnished by Ancient Versions and Fathers. In his eighth edition, however, he approaches nearer to Lachmann's principles.

TREGELLES (Tr.) produced his Text on principles which were substantially the same as Lachmann, but he admits

the evidence of uncial manuscripts down to the seventh
century, and includes a careful testing of a wide circle
of other authorities.

The chief value of his Text lies not only in this, but
in its scrupulous fidelity and accuracy ; and is probably
the best and most exact presentation of the Original Text
of the Old Testament ever published.

ALFORD (A.) constructed his Text, he says, "by following, in all ordinary cases, the united or preponderating
evidence of the most ancient authorities."

When these disagree he takes later evidence into
account, and to a very large extent.

Where this evidence is divided he endeavours to discover the cause of the variation, and gives great weight
to *internal probability;* and, in some cases, relies on his
own independent judgment.

He says, "that Reading has been adopted which, on
the whole, seemed most likely to have stood in the Text.
Such judgments are, of course, open to be questioned."

Consequently, he sometimes is found adopting a Reading contrary to all the ancient manuscripts. A word is
retained because it is "more usual" ; or, it is omitted
because it appears to be a " grammatical correction " of
some transcriber ; or, it is rejected because it seems to
have been inserted "carelessly from memory"; or, is a
"mechanical repetition."

All this necessarily deprives his Text of much of its
weight, especially where he differs from the other Editors;
and places it far below them in critical value; though,
where it is in agreement with them, it adds to the weight
of the evidence as a whole.

It follows, from the above, that, for the general reader,
who has not had the opportunity of becoming expert in
the value of the evidence of Ancient Manuscripts and
Versions, it is better to be guided by a consensus of the
above Textual Editors.

When Tregelles is supported by any (one or more) of
the others, his Readings may be relied upon as being the
best attested and most worthy of being regarded as the
original and inspired Text of the Greek New Testament.

We have already said that the best Greek Testament to use is that of Dr. Scrivener, not merely because it is not a new Text of his own, but because it gives the Received Text which the Authorized Version practically follows, while every word which is the subject of a Various Reading is, as we have said, printed in different type. The student, therefore, is able to see at a glance every such word; and at the foot of the page may learn which of the above Critical Editors favours or rejects the variation.

On the other hand, if he uses any of the other Texts, he has, after all, to refer to the *Textus Receptus* to see in what the variation consists.

In this, and in all our other works, we have adopted the plan of using the initials of the Various Critics, putting the word " All" where they are all in agreement as to the omission or the retention of any Various Reading.

If the Bible student desires to go further, then, without the necessity of consulting either the MSS. or all the Printed Texts referred to above, he will find all that he needs in a little book entitled *Textual Criticism of the New Testament for English Bible Students*, by C. E. Stuart.

CONCLUSION

There remain, now, only three things to be said by way of conclusion.

1. The first, indeed, is hardly necessary, for it is antecedent to all else in connection with this great subject.

It is assumed, from the first word to the last, that the readers have passed from death unto life, and have the Divine gift of a spiritual " understanding," apart from which all that has been said will be useless.

We must be able to say : "We know that the Son of God hath come, and hath given us an understanding, that we may get to know HIM that is true, and we are in Him that is true, even in His Son Jesus Christ" (1 John v. 20).

We have not written to convince unbelievers, though God may over-rule our work to that end.

We have not written in defence of the Bible, for not only does it not need any defence of ours, but it is our own "shield" (Ps. xci. 4) and "sword" (Eph. vi. 17), without which we are defenceless indeed.

We have written only for those who have "peace with God" (Rom. v. 1), and enjoy "the peace of God" (Phil. iv. 7), and know "the God of Peace" (Rom. xv. 33).

Only such have leisure to be occupied with God.

Only such can "sit at the Lord's feet and hear His Word" (Luke x. 39, R.V.).

All others must be "cumbered about much serving." They must needs be occupied with themselves: either as sinners taken up with their sins, or as penitents with their repentance, or as believers with their faith, or as saints with their holiness.

Unless and until we know our completeness in Christ (Col. ii. 10), and "believe God" when He declares that "He hath made us to be partakers of the inheritance of the saints in light" (Col. i. 12), we shall be in such a condition of conscience, and heart, and life as will not leave us any time for occupation with God.

Instead of going on our way "giving thanks to God" for what He has done, we shall be giving way to mourning for what we have not done. We shall be like David when he "sat in his house" and was occupied with what he would do for the Lord. For, not until we learn what the Lord has done and purposed to do for us, shall we be ready, with David, to go in and *sit before the Lord* (2 Sam. vii. 1, 18).

In the former case David's thought was, " *Who I am*"; in the latter he was exclaiming, " *Who am I*, O Lord God?"

2. The second thing, which follows on this, is, that this Word of God is the food of the new nature. Nothing else can sustain it.

Just as it is with our physical life; it cannot sustain itself, and its support must come from without; so it is with our spiritual life. Its food must come from without also.

As we cannot live on ourselves in the natural sphere, even so we cannot feed on ourselves in the spiritual sphere. We cannot live on our own feelings, nor on our experiences, nor upon the sweetest words which come from man. These may excite, or warn, or interest us, but they cannot *feed* us, nor support us, nor sustain our true spiritual life.

It was a solemn truth that the Lord Jesus asserted, when He compared Himself to food, saying : "As the living Father hath sent Me, and I live by the Father: so he that eateth Me, even he shall live by Me" (John vi. 57). For, as food must be eaten for one's self, and digested, and assimilated, so that it becomes part of us, and enters into our life, and gives us our strength, so is it with "the bread of life."

This brings us to our third and last point.

3. All Bible study must in the end be individual.

As with ordinary bodily food : others may prepare the food and serve it up in various forms : they may cook it in more senses than one : they may present it in "made dishes": they may carve it, and cut it up, and even put it in the mouth, as with babes; but, after all, there is no more that they can do. They cannot eat it or digest it for us; they cannot assimilate it for us; even so it is with the spiritual food of the Word of God.

Notwithstanding all that has been said in the foregoing pages, the great necessity remains : the work of Bible study must be, to the end, intensely personal and individual.

Each one must look out the references for himself. He must trace the words through all their occurrences where these are given; he must consider their usages; he must read the contexts; he must make his lists and tables, and do his countings for himself: for so only can he feed upon the Word and the words, and be nourished, and be strengthened himself, and grow thereby : so only will he be able to say with Jeremiah:

" Thy words were found, and I did eat them;
And thy word was unto me the joy and rejoicing of my heart."

INDEX OF SUBJECTS

INDEX OF TEXTS EXPLAINED

INDEX OF GREEK WORDS

INDEX OF HEBREW WORDS